Lecture Notes in Computer Science   14729

Founding Editors

Gerhard Goos
Juris Hartmanis

The series Lecture Notes in Computer Science (LNCS), including its subseries Lecture Notes in Artificial Intelligence (LNAI) and Lecture Notes in Bioinformatics (LNBI), has established itself as a medium for the publication of new developments in computer science and information technology research, teaching, and education.

LNCS enjoys close cooperation with the computer science R & D community, the series counts many renowned academics among its volume editors and paper authors, and collaborates with prestigious societies. Its mission is to serve this international community by providing an invaluable service, mainly focused on the publication of conference and workshop proceedings and postproceedings. LNCS commenced publication in 1973.

Abbas Moallem
Editor

HCI for Cybersecurity, Privacy and Trust

6th International Conference, HCI-CPT 2024
Held as Part of the 26th HCI International Conference, HCII 2024
Washington, DC, USA, June 29 – July 4, 2024
Proceedings, Part II

 Springer

Editor
Abbas Moallem
San Jose State University
San Jose, CA, USA

ISSN 0302-9743 ISSN 1611-3349 (electronic)
Lecture Notes in Computer Science
ISBN 978-3-031-61381-4 ISBN 978-3-031-61382-1 (eBook)
https://doi.org/10.1007/978-3-031-61382-1

This Springer imprint is published by the registered company Springer Nature Switzerland AG
The registered company address is: Gewerbestrasse 11, 6330 Cham, Switzerland

If disposing of this product, please recycle the paper.

Foreword

This year we celebrate 40 years since the establishment of the HCI International (HCII) Conference, which has been a hub for presenting groundbreaking research and novel ideas and collaboration for people from all over the world.

The HCII conference was founded in 1984 by Prof. Gavriel Salvendy (Purdue University, USA, Tsinghua University, P.R. China, and University of Central Florida, USA) and the first event of the series, "1st USA-Japan Conference on Human-Computer Interaction", was held in Honolulu, Hawaii, USA, 18–20 August. Since then, HCI International is held jointly with several Thematic Areas and Affiliated Conferences, with each one under the auspices of a distinguished international Program Board and under one management and one registration. Twenty-six HCI International Conferences have been organized so far (every two years until 2013, and annually thereafter).

Over the years, this conference has served as a platform for scholars, researchers, industry experts and students to exchange ideas, connect, and address challenges in the ever-evolving HCI field. Throughout these 40 years, the conference has evolved itself, adapting to new technologies and emerging trends, while staying committed to its core mission of advancing knowledge and driving change.

As we celebrate this milestone anniversary, we reflect on the contributions of its founding members and appreciate the commitment of its current and past Affiliated Conference Program Board Chairs and members. We are also thankful to all past conference attendees who have shaped this community into what it is today.

The 26th International Conference on Human-Computer Interaction, HCI International 2024 (HCII 2024), was held as a 'hybrid' event at the Washington Hilton Hotel, Washington, DC, USA, during 29 June – 4 July 2024. It incorporated the 21 thematic areas and affiliated conferences listed below.

A total of 5108 individuals from academia, research institutes, industry, and government agencies from 85 countries submitted contributions, and 1271 papers and 309 posters were included in the volumes of the proceedings that were published just before the start of the conference, these are listed below. The contributions thoroughly cover the entire field of human-computer interaction, addressing major advances in knowledge and effective use of computers in a variety of application areas. These papers provide academics, researchers, engineers, scientists, practitioners and students with state-of-the-art information on the most recent advances in HCI.

The HCI International (HCII) conference also offers the option of presenting 'Late Breaking Work', and this applies both for papers and posters, with corresponding volumes of proceedings that will be published after the conference. Full papers will be included in the 'HCII 2024 - Late Breaking Papers' volumes of the proceedings to be published in the Springer LNCS series, while 'Poster Extended Abstracts' will be included as short research papers in the 'HCII 2024 - Late Breaking Posters' volumes to be published in the Springer CCIS series.

I would like to thank the Program Board Chairs and the members of the Program Boards of all thematic areas and affiliated conferences for their contribution towards the high scientific quality and overall success of the HCI International 2024 conference. Their manifold support in terms of paper reviewing (single-blind review process, with a minimum of two reviews per submission), session organization and their willingness to act as goodwill ambassadors for the conference is most highly appreciated.

This conference would not have been possible without the continuous and unwavering support and advice of Gavriel Salvendy, founder, General Chair Emeritus, and Scientific Advisor. For his outstanding efforts, I would like to express my sincere appreciation to Abbas Moallem, Communications Chair and Editor of HCI International News.

July 2024   Constantine Stephanidis

HCI International 2024 Thematic Areas
and Affiliated Conferences

- HCI: Human-Computer Interaction Thematic Area
- HIMI: Human Interface and the Management of Information Thematic Area
- EPCE: 21st International Conference on Engineering Psychology and Cognitive Ergonomics
- AC: 18th International Conference on Augmented Cognition
- UAHCI: 18th International Conference on Universal Access in Human-Computer Interaction
- CCD: 16th International Conference on Cross-Cultural Design
- SCSM: 16th International Conference on Social Computing and Social Media
- VAMR: 16th International Conference on Virtual, Augmented and Mixed Reality
- DHM: 15th International Conference on Digital Human Modeling & Applications in Health, Safety, Ergonomics & Risk Management
- DUXU: 13th International Conference on Design, User Experience and Usability
- C&C: 12th International Conference on Culture and Computing
- DAPI: 12th International Conference on Distributed, Ambient and Pervasive Interactions
- HCIBGO: 11th International Conference on HCI in Business, Government and Organizations
- LCT: 11th International Conference on Learning and Collaboration Technologies
- ITAP: 10th International Conference on Human Aspects of IT for the Aged Population
- AIS: 6th International Conference on Adaptive Instructional Systems
- HCI-CPT: 6th International Conference on HCI for Cybersecurity, Privacy and Trust
- HCI-Games: 6th International Conference on HCI in Games
- MobiTAS: 6th International Conference on HCI in Mobility, Transport and Automotive Systems
- AI-HCI: 5th International Conference on Artificial Intelligence in HCI
- MOBILE: 5th International Conference on Human-Centered Design, Operation and Evaluation of Mobile Communications

List of Conference Proceedings Volumes Appearing Before the Conference

1. LNCS 14684, Human-Computer Interaction: Part I, edited by Masaaki Kurosu and Ayako Hashizume
2. LNCS 14685, Human-Computer Interaction: Part II, edited by Masaaki Kurosu and Ayako Hashizume
3. LNCS 14686, Human-Computer Interaction: Part III, edited by Masaaki Kurosu and Ayako Hashizume
4. LNCS 14687, Human-Computer Interaction: Part IV, edited by Masaaki Kurosu and Ayako Hashizume
5. LNCS 14688, Human-Computer Interaction: Part V, edited by Masaaki Kurosu and Ayako Hashizume
6. LNCS 14689, Human Interface and the Management of Information: Part I, edited by Hirohiko Mori and Yumi Asahi
7. LNCS 14690, Human Interface and the Management of Information: Part II, edited by Hirohiko Mori and Yumi Asahi
8. LNCS 14691, Human Interface and the Management of Information: Part III, edited by Hirohiko Mori and Yumi Asahi
9. LNAI 14692, Engineering Psychology and Cognitive Ergonomics: Part I, edited by Don Harris and Wen-Chin Li
10. LNAI 14693, Engineering Psychology and Cognitive Ergonomics: Part II, edited by Don Harris and Wen-Chin Li
11. LNAI 14694, Augmented Cognition, Part I, edited by Dylan D. Schmorrow and Cali M. Fidopiastis
12. LNAI 14695, Augmented Cognition, Part II, edited by Dylan D. Schmorrow and Cali M. Fidopiastis
13. LNCS 14696, Universal Access in Human-Computer Interaction: Part I, edited by Margherita Antona and Constantine Stephanidis
14. LNCS 14697, Universal Access in Human-Computer Interaction: Part II, edited by Margherita Antona and Constantine Stephanidis
15. LNCS 14698, Universal Access in Human-Computer Interaction: Part III, edited by Margherita Antona and Constantine Stephanidis
16. LNCS 14699, Cross-Cultural Design: Part I, edited by Pei-Luen Patrick Rau
17. LNCS 14700, Cross-Cultural Design: Part II, edited by Pei-Luen Patrick Rau
18. LNCS 14701, Cross-Cultural Design: Part III, edited by Pei-Luen Patrick Rau
19. LNCS 14702, Cross-Cultural Design: Part IV, edited by Pei-Luen Patrick Rau
20. LNCS 14703, Social Computing and Social Media: Part I, edited by Adela Coman and Simona Vasilache
21. LNCS 14704, Social Computing and Social Media: Part II, edited by Adela Coman and Simona Vasilache
22. LNCS 14705, Social Computing and Social Media: Part III, edited by Adela Coman and Simona Vasilache

23. LNCS 14706, Virtual, Augmented and Mixed Reality: Part I, edited by Jessie Y. C. Chen and Gino Fragomeni
24. LNCS 14707, Virtual, Augmented and Mixed Reality: Part II, edited by Jessie Y. C. Chen and Gino Fragomeni
25. LNCS 14708, Virtual, Augmented and Mixed Reality: Part III, edited by Jessie Y. C. Chen and Gino Fragomeni
26. LNCS 14709, Digital Human Modeling and Applications in Health, Safety, Ergonomics and Risk Management: Part I, edited by Vincent G. Duffy
27. LNCS 14710, Digital Human Modeling and Applications in Health, Safety, Ergonomics and Risk Management: Part II, edited by Vincent G. Duffy
28. LNCS 14711, Digital Human Modeling and Applications in Health, Safety, Ergonomics and Risk Management: Part III, edited by Vincent G. Duffy
29. LNCS 14712, Design, User Experience, and Usability: Part I, edited by Aaron Marcus, Elizabeth Rosenzweig and Marcelo M. Soares
30. LNCS 14713, Design, User Experience, and Usability: Part II, edited by Aaron Marcus, Elizabeth Rosenzweig and Marcelo M. Soares
31. LNCS 14714, Design, User Experience, and Usability: Part III, edited by Aaron Marcus, Elizabeth Rosenzweig and Marcelo M. Soares
32. LNCS 14715, Design, User Experience, and Usability: Part IV, edited by Aaron Marcus, Elizabeth Rosenzweig and Marcelo M. Soares
33. LNCS 14716, Design, User Experience, and Usability: Part V, edited by Aaron Marcus, Elizabeth Rosenzweig and Marcelo M. Soares
34. LNCS 14717, Culture and Computing, edited by Matthias Rauterberg
35. LNCS 14718, Distributed, Ambient and Pervasive Interactions: Part I, edited by Norbert A. Streitz and Shin'ichi Konomi
36. LNCS 14719, Distributed, Ambient and Pervasive Interactions: Part II, edited by Norbert A. Streitz and Shin'ichi Konomi
37. LNCS 14720, HCI in Business, Government and Organizations: Part I, edited by Fiona Fui-Hoon Nah and Keng Leng Siau
38. LNCS 14721, HCI in Business, Government and Organizations: Part II, edited by Fiona Fui-Hoon Nah and Keng Leng Siau
39. LNCS 14722, Learning and Collaboration Technologies: Part I, edited by Panayiotis Zaphiris and Andri Ioannou
40. LNCS 14723, Learning and Collaboration Technologies: Part II, edited by Panayiotis Zaphiris and Andri Ioannou
41. LNCS 14724, Learning and Collaboration Technologies: Part III, edited by Panayiotis Zaphiris and Andri Ioannou
42. LNCS 14725, Human Aspects of IT for the Aged Population: Part I, edited by Qin Gao and Jia Zhou
43. LNCS 14726, Human Aspects of IT for the Aged Population: Part II, edited by Qin Gao and Jia Zhou
44. LNCS 14727, Adaptive Instructional System, edited by Robert A. Sottilare and Jessica Schwarz
45. LNCS 14728, HCI for Cybersecurity, Privacy and Trust: Part I, edited by Abbas Moallem
46. LNCS 14729, HCI for Cybersecurity, Privacy and Trust: Part II, edited by Abbas Moallem

47. LNCS 14730, HCI in Games: Part I, edited by Xiaowen Fang
48. LNCS 14731, HCI in Games: Part II, edited by Xiaowen Fang
49. LNCS 14732, HCI in Mobility, Transport and Automotive Systems: Part I, edited by Heidi Krömker
50. LNCS 14733, HCI in Mobility, Transport and Automotive Systems: Part II, edited by Heidi Krömker
51. LNAI 14734, Artificial Intelligence in HCI: Part I, edited by Helmut Degen and Stavroula Ntoa
52. LNAI 14735, Artificial Intelligence in HCI: Part II, edited by Helmut Degen and Stavroula Ntoa
53. LNAI 14736, Artificial Intelligence in HCI: Part III, edited by Helmut Degen and Stavroula Ntoa
54. LNCS 14737, Design, Operation and Evaluation of Mobile Communications: Part I, edited by June Wei and George Margetis
55. LNCS 14738, Design, Operation and Evaluation of Mobile Communications: Part II, edited by June Wei and George Margetis
56. CCIS 2114, HCI International 2024 Posters - Part I, edited by Constantine Stephanidis, Margherita Antona, Stavroula Ntoa and Gavriel Salvendy
57. CCIS 2115, HCI International 2024 Posters - Part II, edited by Constantine Stephanidis, Margherita Antona, Stavroula Ntoa and Gavriel Salvendy
58. CCIS 2116, HCI International 2024 Posters - Part III, edited by Constantine Stephanidis, Margherita Antona, Stavroula Ntoa and Gavriel Salvendy
59. CCIS 2117, HCI International 2024 Posters - Part IV, edited by Constantine Stephanidis, Margherita Antona, Stavroula Ntoa and Gavriel Salvendy
60. CCIS 2118, HCI International 2024 Posters - Part V, edited by Constantine Stephanidis, Margherita Antona, Stavroula Ntoa and Gavriel Salvendy
61. CCIS 2119, HCI International 2024 Posters - Part VI, edited by Constantine Stephanidis, Margherita Antona, Stavroula Ntoa and Gavriel Salvendy
62. CCIS 2120, HCI International 2024 Posters - Part VII, edited by Constantine Stephanidis, Margherita Antona, Stavroula Ntoa and Gavriel Salvendy

https://2024.hci.international/proceedings

Preface

The cybersecurity field, in all its dimensions, is exponentially growing, evolving and expanding. New security risks emerge continuously with the steady increase of internet interconnections and the development of the Internet of Things. Cyberattacks endanger individuals and companies, as well as vital public services and infrastructures. Confronted with spreading and evolving cyber threats, the system and network defenses of organizations and individuals are falling behind, as they often fail to implement and effectively use basic cybersecurity and privacy practices and technologies.

The 6th International Conference on HCI for Cybersecurity, Privacy and Trust (HCI-CPT 2024), an affiliated conference of the HCI International Conference, intended to help, promote and encourage research in this field by providing a forum for interaction and exchanges among researchers, academics and practitioners in the fields of HCI and cyber security.

While technological solutions and institutional measures are paramount in mitigating cyber threats, users themselves are integral components in the defense against cyberattacks. Recognizing the influence of user behavior and practices, submissions this year have addressed topics relevant to privacy perceptions, disclosure attitudes, user behavior and understanding of cybersecurity features and threats, as well as cyber hygiene training and assessment. In an era defined by digital connectivity and data-driven interactions, the complexities and challenges associated with safeguarding personal information and digital assets have garnered the attention of the research community, with submissions in this area exploring human factors and security across contexts such as smart homes, digital twins, and enterprises. Further, submissions have carried out a comprehensive exploration of innovative strategies, experiential learning methodologies and expert perspectives aimed at fortifying defense, raising awareness, and fostering a culture of cyber resilience. Finally, the role of HCI in the design of enhanced technological approaches for uncovering cybersecurity vulnerabilities, mitigating risks and improving security measures in various domains has been a crucial focus. As the editor of this volume, I am delighted to present these diverse perspectives and scholarly endeavors, which collectively contribute to the ongoing discourse surrounding the role of HCI in cybersecurity and shed light on the intricate challenges entailed and the opportunities that emerge.

Two volumes of the HCII 2024 proceedings are dedicated to this year's edition of the HCI-CPT conference. The first focuses on topics related to Cyber Hygiene, User Behavior and Security Awareness, and User Privacy and Security Acceptance. The second focuses on topics related to Cybersecurity Education and Training, and Threat Assessment and Protection.

The papers of these volumes were accepted for publication after a minimum of two single-blind reviews from the members of the HCI-CPT Program Board or, in some cases, from members of the Program Boards of other affiliated conferences. I would like to thank all of them for their invaluable contribution, support and efforts.

July 2024   Abbas Moallem

6th International Conference on HCI for Cybersecurity, Privacy and Trust (HCI-CPT 2024)

Program Board Chair: **Abbas Moallem,** *San Jose State University, USA*

- Mostafa Al-Emran, *The British University in Dubai, UAE*
- Mohd Anwar, *North Carolina A&T State University, USA*
- Joyram Chakraborty, *Towson University, USA*
- Sabarathinam Chockalingam, *Institute for Energy Technology, Norway*
- Ulku Yaylacicegi Clark, *University of North Carolina Wilmington, USA*
- Francisco Corella, *Pomcor, USA*
- Ana Ferreira, *CINTESIS, Portugal*
- Steven Furnell, *University of Nottingham, UK*
- Akira Kanaoka, *Toho University, Japan*
- Mazaher Kianpour, *Norwegian University of Science and Technology (NTNU), Norway*
- Nathan Lau, *Virginia Tech, USA*
- Wai Sze Leung, *University of Johannesburg, South Africa*
- Luca Mazzola, *HSLU - Hochschule Luzern, Switzerland*
- Heather Molyneaux, *National Research Council Canada, Canada*
- Phillip Morgan, *Cardiff University, UK*
- Calvin Nobles, *University of Maryland Global Campus, USA*
- Jason R. C. Nurse, *University of Kent, UK*
- Henrich C. Pöhls, *University of Passau, Germany*
- David Schuster, *San José State University, USA*
- David Stevens, *University of Hawai'i Kapi'olani Community College, USA*
- Kerry-Lynn Thomson, *Nelson Mandela University, South Africa*
- Daniel Wilusz, *Poznan University of Economics and Business, Poland*
- Adam Wojtowicz, *Poznan University of Economics and Business, Poland*
- Temechu Girma Zewdie, *University of the District of Columbia, USA*

The full list with the Program Board Chairs and the members of the Program Boards of all thematic areas and affiliated conferences of HCII 2024 is available online at:

http://www.hci.international/board-members-2024.php

HCI International 2025 Conference

The 27th International Conference on Human-Computer Interaction, HCI International 2025, will be held jointly with the affiliated conferences at the Swedish Exhibition & Congress Centre and Gothia Towers Hotel, Gothenburg, Sweden, June 22–27, 2025. It will cover a broad spectrum of themes related to Human-Computer Interaction, including theoretical issues, methods, tools, processes, and case studies in HCI design, as well as novel interaction techniques, interfaces, and applications. The proceedings will be published by Springer. More information will become available on the conference website: https://2025.hci.international/.

General Chair
Prof. Constantine Stephanidis
University of Crete and ICS-FORTH
Heraklion, Crete, Greece
Email: general_chair@2025.hci.international

https://2025.hci.international/

Contents – Part II

Cybersecurity Education and Training

Decoding the Human Element in APT Attacks: Unveiling Attention
Diversion Techniques in Cyber-Physical System Security 3
  *Aida Akbarzadeh, Laszlo Erdodi, Siv Hilde Houmb,
  and Tore Geir Soltvedt*

Competencies Required for the Offensive Cyber Operations Planners 20
  *Marko Arik, Ricardo Gregorio Lugo, Rain Ottis,
  and Adrian Nicholas Venables*

Unraveling the Real-World Impacts of Cyber Incidents on Individuals 40
  Danielle Renee Jacobs, Nicole Darmawaskita, and Troy McDaniel

Experiential Learning Through Immersive XR: Cybersecurity Education
for Critical Infrastructures 56
  Anthony Lee, Kenneth King, Denis Gračanin, and Mohamed Azab

Revolutionizing Social Engineering Awareness Raising, Education
and Training: Generative AI-Powered Investigations in the Maritime
Domain 70
  Michail Loupasakis, Georgios Potamos, and Eliana Stavrou

Training and Security Awareness Under the Lens of Practitioners:
A DevSecOps Perspective Towards Risk Management 84
  *Xhesika Ramaj, Mary Sánchez-Gordón, Ricardo Colomo-Palacios,
  and Vasileios Gkioulos*

Expert Perspectives on Information Security Awareness Programs
in Medical Care Institutions in Germany 98
  Jan Tolsdorf and Luigi Lo Iacono

Threat Assessment and Protection

Whisper+AASIST for DeepFake Audio Detection 121
  Qian Luo and Kalyani Vinayagam Sivasundari

Paralyzed or Compromised: A Case Study of Decisions in Cyber-Physical
Systems 134
  Håvard Jakobsen Ofte and Sokratis Katsikas

Cognitive Digital Twins for Improving Security in IT-OT Enabled
Healthcare Applications 153
  *Sandeep Pirbhulal, Sabarathinam Chockalingam, Habtamu Abie,
  and Nathan Lau*

Viz⁴NetSec: Visualizing Dynamic Network Security Configurations
of Everyday Interconnected Objects in Home Networks 164
  *Noëlle Rakotondravony, Henrich C. Pöhls, Jan Pfeifer,
  and Lane Harrison*

Authentication Method Using Opening Gestures 186
  *Shogo Sekiguchi, Shingo Kato, Yoshiki Nishikawa,
  and Buntarou Shizuki*

Investigating University QR Code Interactions 204
  Jeremiah D. Still, Thomas Morris, and Morgan Edwards

Exploring ICS/SCADA Network Vulnerabilities 215
  *Hala Strohmier, Aaryan R. Londhe, Chris A. Clark, Ronit Pawar,
  and Brian Kram*

Electrical Muscle Stimulation System for Automatic Reproduction
of Secret Information Without Exposing Biometric Data 234
  *Takumi Takaiwa, Shinnosuke Nozaki, Kota Numada,
  Tsubasa Shibata, Sana Okumura, Soichi Takigawa, Tetsushi Ohki,
  and Masakatsu Nishigaki*

Author Index 251

Contents – Part I

Cyber Hygiene, User Behavior and Security Awareness

Privacy Perceptions and Behaviors of Google Personal Account Holders
in Saudi Arabia 3
    Eman Alashwali and Lorrie Cranor

Seek and Locate? Examining the Accessibility of Cybersecurity Features 30
    Arwa Binsedeeq, Steven Furnell, Xavier Carpent,
    and Nicholas Gervassis

Enhancing Cyber Hygiene and Literacy via Interactive Mini-games 43
    Cameron Gray and Steven Furnell

Hidden in Onboarding: Cyber Hygiene Training and Assessment 53
    Alex Katsarakes, Thomas Morris, and Jeremiah D. Still

"I'm not planning on dying anytime soon!": A Survey of Digital Legacy
Planning 64
    Paola Marmorato, Clarissa Fernandes, Lydia Kraus,
    and Elizabeth Stobert

Are UK Parents Empowered to Act on Their Cybersecurity Education
Responsibilities? 77
    Suzanne Prior and Karen Renaud

To Bot or Not to Bot?: Analysing Mental Health Data Disclosures 97
    Deborah Taylor, Clare Melvin, Hane Aung, and Rameez Asif

Exploring User Understanding of Wireless Connectivity and Security
on Smartphones 116
    Ezgi Tugcu and Steven Furnell

Why Do Organizations Fail to Practice Cyber Resilience? 126
    Rick van der Kleij and Tineke Hof

BYOD Security Practices in Australian Hospitals – A Qualitative Study 138
    Tafheem Ahmad Wani, Antonette Mendoza, and Kathleen Gray

User Privacy and Security Acceptance

Legal Protection for the Personal Data in Indonesia and Malaysia 161
  Nanik Praṣetyoningsih, Nazli Ismail Nawang, Windy Virdinia Putri,
  and Muhammad Nur Rifqi Amirullah

Towards a Harmonised Approach for Security and Privacy Management
in Smart Home Contexts 170
  Samiah Alghamdi, Steven Furnell, and Steven Bagley

Privacy-Conscious Design Requirements to Support Older Adults' Health
Information Seeking 188
  Yomna Aly and Cosmin Munteanu

With or Without U(sers): A Journey to Integrate UX Activities
in Cybersecurity 212
  Daniela Azevedo, Justine Ramelot, Axel Legay, and Suzanne Kieffer

Using a Digital Transformation to Improve Enterprise Security—A Case
Study 232
  David Brookshire Conner

Japanese Users' (Mis)understandings of Technical Terms Used in Privacy
Policies and the Privacy Protection Law 245
  Sachiko Kanamori, Miho Ikeda, Kumiko Kameishi,
  and Ayako A. Hasegawa

Alert Interaction Service Design for AI Face Swap Video Scams 265
  Jing Luo, Xin Zhang, Fang Fu, and Hanxiao Geng

Human Factors and Security in Digital Twins: Challenges and Future
Prospects 281
  Sanjay Misra, Kousik Barik, Harald P.-J. Thunem,
  and Sabarathinam Chockalingam

Visualizing Cybersecurity Diagrams: An Empirical Analysis of Common
Weakness Enumeration Images 296
  Benjamin Schooley, Derek Hansen, Ethan James Richmond,
  Malaya Jordan Canite, and Nimrod Max Huaira Reyna

Author Index 319

Cybersecurity Education and Training

Decoding the Human Element in APT Attacks: Unveiling Attention Diversion Techniques in Cyber-Physical System Security

Aida Akbarzadeh[1]([✉]) [ID], Laszlo Erdodi[2] [ID], Siv Hilde Houmb[1] [ID],
and Tore Geir Soltvedt[3]

[1] Department of Information Security and Communication Technology, Norwegian
University of Science and Technology (NTNU), Gjøvik, Norway
`aida.akbarzadeh@ntnu.no`
[2] Department of Information Security and Communication Technology, Norwegian
University of Science and Technology (NTNU), Trondheim, Norway
[3] Statnett SF, Oslo, Norway

Abstract. The number of complex cyber-attacks, such as Advanced
Persistent Threats (APTs), on Critical Infrastructures (CIs) continues to
rise. Recently, attackers have targeted lower layers of the Purdue model,
specifically the Operational Technology (OT) part, traditionally considered secure and unreachable. APTs are characterized by their stealthy,
prolonged presence in systems, often going undetected until significant
damage is inflicted. While defensive cyber deception technology, such as
honeypots, has been introduced to address sophisticated attacks, there
remains a gap in understanding the role of deception techniques from the
attacker's perspective in manipulating defenders and system operators.

Therefore, this paper emphasizes the critical role of deception techniques, particularly attention diversion, in APTs. The paper delves into
the multi-layered nature of APTs and explains the role of attention diversion in manipulating human operators and system processes, and why
this is important to succeed with an APT. This psychological manipulation aims to create a misleading sense of normalcy, diverting attention from critical vulnerabilities in the system. Such attention diversion
techniques can also amplify the challenge of detecting and mitigating
APTs, exploiting both human psychology and operational procedures
within CPS. To illustrate these aspects, the paper describes how attention diversion techniques was applied in a case study of an APT attack
conducted on a digital substation Hardware-in-the-Loop (HIL) testbed
and discusses the results.

The main purpose of this paper is to highlight the under-explored area
of deceptive strategies, particularly in OT, to motivate further research
into this area.

Keywords: Deception technique · Attention diversion · CPS · OT ·
IEC 61850 · IEC 60870-5-104 · Social engineering · APT attack ·
Digital substation · ICS · Critical Infrastructure

A. Moallem (Ed.): HCII 2024, LNCS 14729, pp. 3–19, 2024.
https://doi.org/10.1007/978-3-031-61382-1_1

1   Introduction

In the evolving landscape of cyber threats, characterized by increasingly complex and sophisticated attacks, the nature of cyber warfare has transformed this landscape [15]. The continual increase in the diversity of these threats on one hand, and the interconnectedness of critical systems, amplifies risks each year. As a result, cyber defenders are faced with new challenges. This challenge is particularly exacerbated in the case of APT attacks, which are stealthily maintained within a defender's network and are difficult to detect as they often operate within resources trusted by the defender [7,21]. APT campaigns have become more complex, deploying novel strategies to target critical systems, especially focusing on the OT components of Cyber-Physical Systems (CPSs) within critical infrastructures [6]. This shift necessitates a proactive approach in cybersecurity; One that is anticipatory of potential unknowns and novel attack vectors, rather than merely reactive to known threats.

The escalating complexity of cyber attacks underscores the need to understand and preemptively address these "unknowns" within system defenses. This is especially crucial in the context of CPS, where the integration of IT and OT poses unique challenges. The different priorities and mindsets between IT and OT operators often lead to delayed recognition of cyber attacks within OT environments, as system errors or anomalies are not immediately perceived as security threats [1]. Such gaps in perception and response can inadvertently create vulnerabilities ripe for exploitation by malicious actors.

In the digital realm, deception is a commonly employed tactic by malicious actors, used to manipulate and exploit legitimate users for personal gain [9]. Techniques like phishing and social engineering are often leveraged to direct users' attention and induce specific actions [15]. While cyber defense research has explored the use of deception for developing early-warning systems and sophisticated security monitoring tools, such as honeypots, recent years have seen a marked increase in the complexity of cyber attacks.

This paper proposes a shift in perspective by considering the application of social engineering principles within the system's operational domain. We introduce "Attention Diversion" as a novel strategy employed by attackers once they have infiltrated a system. This technique involves inducing errors or/and anomalies that mimic routine system glitches, obscuring the true nature of the attack and misleading operators into believing they are facing conventional system failures. By manipulating the focus and response of operational personnel, attackers can allow their real cyber attack to proceed undetected and unmitigated. This approach has been observed in several sophisticated attacks on critical infrastructures, particularly in the energy domain [12].

Our research aims to illuminate this subtle yet effective form of cyber manipulation, exploring its mechanics and implications. We conducted a case study using a hardware-in-the-loop digital substation testbed to investigate the attention diversion technique. Our main contributions are the following:

- We examine the strategic application of deception techniques in cyber attacks, focusing on how attackers can effectively use these methods within Cyber-Physical Systems.
- We introduce and define Attention Diversion as a novel tactic used by cyber attackers to mislead and manipulate the actions of system operators.
- We propose a conceptual framework for the application of Attention Diversion, distinguishing between Atomic Deception Techniques for specific attack stages and a broader Cover Story for the overall attack strategy.
- We illustrate the application of the proposed method using a realistic hardware-in-the-loop digital substation enclave testbed.

The reminder of the paper is organized as follows: Sect. 2 provides background studies and reviews related work. Section 3 delves into the concept of deception from the attacker's perspective, using the cyber kill chain to explain attention diversions. Section 4 presents our case study. We conclude the paper and highlight future research directions in Sect. 5.

2   Background and Related Work

According to the Stanford Encyclopedia of Philosophy [14], a traditional definition of deception is "to intentionally cause to have a false belief that is known or believed to be false". Following this definition, in psychology, deception is understood as an intentional act to hide, fabricate, or alter both factual and emotional information to foster or uphold beliefs in others that the deceiver knows to be untrue [16]. In the digital world, deception is a recognized method employed by malicious actors to manipulate legitimate users for their own advantage. Typically, attackers utilize cyber deception to mask their reconnaissance activities and stealthily infiltrate systems, all while avoiding detection by watchful defenders [15]. Malicious deception plays a pivotal role in a variety of cyber attacks, including phishing, APTs, man-in-the-middle attacks, and the implementation of Sybil nodes in social networks [17]. Nevertheless, our review of recent academic literature indicates that there is a significant emphasis on defensive deception tactics, while the exploration of how attackers might employ deception techniques in their operations has not been extensively investigated.

Amoroso [4] introduced deception as a means to protect against sophisticated attacks that exceed the capabilities of traditional security methods. This involves strategically embedding a layer of cleverly designed trap functionality or misinformation into both internal and external interfaces of national infrastructure to mislead adversaries.

NIST 800-160 [18] refers to the deception technique as one of the 14 techniques of cyber resiliency and names: (1) obfuscation, (2) disinformation, (3) misdirection, and (4) tainting as the approaches for realizing it.

Seo et al. [20] summarized defensive cyber deception technology into: (1) moving target defense (MTD), (2) Honey-X (honeypots, honeynets, honeytokens, etc.), and (3) Decoy.

Heckman et al. [10] proposed a "deception chain" for the design, preparation, and implementation of cyber disruption and denial (Cyber-D&D) activities and integrated these methods into both an intrusion campaign and a defensive deception campaign. The author in [4] emphasized that deception in security is effective when it accomplishes any or all of the following objectives:

1. Attention: Diverting an adversary's focus from real assets to bogus ones.
2. Energy: Draining an adversary's valuable time and resources on false targets.
3. Uncertainty: Generating doubt about the legitimacy of a detected vulnerability.
4. Analysis: Establishing a foundation for real-time analysis of an adversary's actions.

Likewise, incorporating any of these elements into an attack strategy can enhance the likelihood of a successful attack, a detail that has been neglected in the portrayal of the cyber kill chain when explaining attack steps.

NIST 800-160 [18] named "deception" as one of the attack vectors might be used in conducting APT attacks. However it limits the deception to only one of the 14 techniques of cyber resiliency, and defined it to enable defenders to mislead, confuse, hide critical assets from, or expose covertly tainted assets to the adversaries. It is explained that the deception technique can be realized through four different approaches, namely: Obfuscation, Disinformation, Misdirection, and Tainting. Table 1 summaries these approaches. NIST 800-160 also noted that deception technique can cause adversaries to waste effort.

Table 1. Deception technique [18]

Approach	Definition	Example
Obfuscation	Create obstacles that hinder the adversary from both discovering and comprehending the information effectively.	Encryption or steganographic encoding
Disinformation	Deceive adversaries by providing deliberately misleading information.	False credentials and tokens (e.g., honeytokens)
Misdirection	Direct adversary activities to deception environments/resources.	Honeypots, honeynets, or decoy files and maintaining comprehensive deception environments
Tainting	Implant hidden functionalities within resources and make stolen assets reveal the identity of adversaries or potentially cause harm to them.	Beacon traps or steganographic data in files

Heckman et al. [10] identified three common objectives in all forms of deception: firstly, to alter an adversary's perceptions and beliefs; secondly, to prompt action or inaction based on these changes; and finally, to benefit the deceiver, in any way, from the adversary's responses (action or inaction). Note that, the critical aspect of deception planning is not merely influencing adversary beliefs, but cleverly affecting and directing the adversary towards a desired action. The authors proposed an eight-step deception chain from the defensive cyber-D&D operation perspective that includes planning, preparing, and executing phases.

Pawlick et al. [17] highlighted that many modern attacks involve APTs. These attacks are hidden, ongoing operations that use social engineering and deception to enable attackers to gain internal access to networked systems. Nonetheless, it is essential to understand that the use of deception is not limited to just infiltrating a system. It can also be employed as a strategy to continue deceiving operators once attackers have already established a foothold inside the system. A prime illustration of this tactic is the Stuxnet attack, where deception was effectively used to misguide system operators [10].

While the concept of deception has been widely studied for defensive purposes in cybersecurity, there is a noticeable lack of in-depth research into how attackers might leverage deception. Addressing this gap could significantly enhance security training and awareness. The idea of using deception to mislead during cyber attacks, particularly in sophisticated scenarios such as APT attacks on critical infrastructure, and influencing the decisions of system operators, is what we term "Attention Diversion" in this paper, inspired by the definitions available in [4,18]. The concept of attention diversion, as outlined here, is an essential yet under-explored area of study. Our analysis in this paper highlights that attention diversion, in the context we define, is still a largely undiscovered approach, with few existing research works delving into it.

3 Methodology and Concept

As discussed in Sect. 1, this paper investigates deception as a potential vector for attacks, particularly complex ones. Attackers might employ deception either as a supplementary technique or as the primary method to achieve their objectives. Human perception, fundamentally influenced by sensory information from the environment, plays a critical role in this context. Deception involves manipulating this sensory information to create false beliefs, which can trigger various biases in the deceived, affecting their decision-making, beliefs, and behavior [11,19]. These biases are categorized as follows [9]:

- **Personal Biases**: Originating from individual experiences, education, and traits.
- **Cultural Biases**: Stemming from societal beliefs, morals, and practices.
- **Organizational Biases**: Influencing perceptions and decisions within structured environments.
- **Cognitive Biases**: Inherent in our process of perceiving and processing information.

Principles such as truth, denial, deceit, misdirection, and confusion, particularly misdirection and confusion, are central to deception in cybersecurity and can be used to reinforce organizational biases to serve adversaries' purposes [3,5]. Additionally, there are ten distinct hypotheses (maxims) relevant for deception and surprise:

1. Magruder's principles.
2. Limitations of human information processing.
3. Multiple forms of surprise (cry-wolf syndrome).
4. Jones' lemma.
5. A choice among A-type and M-type deception.
6. Axelrod's contribution.
7. A sequencing rule.
8. The importance of feedback.
9. The Monkey's Paw.
10. Care in the designed and planned placement of deceptive material.

Despite the complexities of adversarial relationships and engineering systems, deceptive interactions can be simplified into a basic schema, as shown in Fig. 1. Considering the factors previously outlined, alongside the principles of deception and the four elements highlighted in [4], we herein define "Attention Diversion" as a strategic approach for deception from the adversary's perspective. Attention diversion aims to captivate the attention and exhaust the energy of system operators or defenders, thereby increasing the probability of a successful attack. This strategy aligns with organizational biases and is designed to established maxims for successful deception. By manipulating perceptions and leveraging biases, adversaries can effectively guide the actions and responses of their targets, thereby achieving their deceptive goals.

3.1   Definition of Attention Diversion in Cybersecurity

Attention Diversion from the the adversary perspective in cybersecurity is a strategic approach where the adversary aims to mislead or distract targets, including system operators, security teams, or users, from the actual cyber threat or malicious activity. The main goals of attention diversion are to prolong the undetected status of the actual attack particularly in APT attacks, complicate the defense and investigation processes, and exhaust the target's resources, thereby weakening their ability to respond effectively.

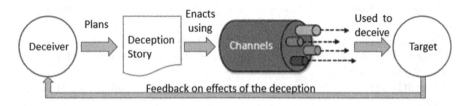

Fig. 1. Strategic deceptive flow [9].

3.2   Techniques of Attention Diversion

To apply the concept of attention diversion, adversaries may attempt to create minor security incidents, generate false security alerts, or induce system errors that appear innocuous. The intent is to divert focus from the adversary's true actions. This can be achieved through dual approaches: (1) Silent manipulation and/or (2) Overt Distraction.

1. **Silent Manipulation** involves tactics like the injection of misleading data or the creation of minor anomalies that mimic routine system issues. It is designed to subtly shift the attention of security personnel, allowing the main attack to remain undetected for a longer duration. Here the attackers utilize attention diversion to reach their goal while they are trying to make less noise.
2. **Overt Distraction** can be used for immediate diversion needs, when applying more noticeable methods such as DDoS attacks are acceptable. These tactics serve to draw attention and resources towards a significant, immediate issue while simultaneously masking the real attack. This approach is particularly effective when rapid action is needed or when an attack risks being exposed.

Depending on the attack scenario and needs, attackers can choose to apply one of these approaches. It should be highlighted that the ultimate goal here is to achieve the main objective of the attack, even if it requires the use of overt distraction, which can be noisy. Based on our study of previous attacks, we have identified some techniques that might be used by adversaries for attention diversion, as follows:

- Needle in the haystack.
- Sending messages to interrupt communication. When the communication is reestablished (e.g., TCP connection rebuild or other protocol-level connection rebuild), the attacker can use this time to attack.
- Sending error messages (pretending device failure) on behalf of the target device, e.g., to conceal other offensive actions.
- Disabling necessary functions (e.g., PTP time synchronization) that divert the attention of the operator.

We will elaborate more on these techniques in Sect. 4.

3.3   Conceptual Framework

In light of the literature review and our previous hands-on attacks conducted on digital substations [2,8], it has been realized that attention diversion can be utilized by attackers in two distinct yet complementary approaches, namely the "*Atomic Deception Technique (ADT)*" and "*Cover Story*". Figure 2 represents these two approaches align with the cyber kill chain, a conventional representation of different steps of a cyber attack [22].

ADT approach refers to the case where adversaries apply attention diversion techniques at each individual step of an attack, such as reconnaissance or exploitation, tailoring the technique to the specific stage of the cyber kill chain. While the Cover Story represents a broader strategy that adversaries follow throughout the entire steps of an attack, covering the entire cyber kill chain. This cover story serves as a comprehensive roadmap designed by adversaries to mislead defenders throughout the attack life-cycle.

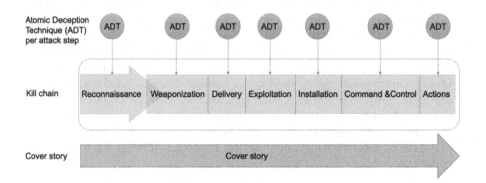

Fig. 2. Integration of Deception Life-cycle with the Cyber Kill Chain.

Considering the specific requirements of the main attack, attackers may leverage either one or both approaches. This decision relies on the purpose of applying attention diversion. To this end, attackers define the primary objective of applying attention diversion and gather information related to the target system. This information includes understanding vulnerabilities, predicting potential reactions of the defenders, and identifying any biases that could be exploited later to plan and develop techniques of attention diversion. Based on the defined purpose and collected information, attackers then select the appropriate attention diversion approach. The attackers can primarily leverage each approach to fulfill their objectives as follows:

I) Applying Atomic Deception Techniques: This option is selected when the objective is to enhance specific stages of the attack with attention diversion. It is particularly useful when deception is needed to enable or augment the impact of certain attack steps.

II) Creating a Cover Story: Attackers consider creating a cover story when a more comprehensive and holistic deception strategy is required to successfully achieve their goal. This approach is appropriate for scenarios where obscuring the entire attack sequence is necessary to achieve the attack objectives.

These approaches illustrate the versatility and strategic depth of deception in cybersecurity. Section 4 details these concepts through a hands-on attack conducted in a hardware-in-the-loop digital substation testbed to observe and evaluate the applicability of the proposed attention diversion.

4   Case Study

In this case study, we leverage the digital substation (DS) Enclave testbed [13], depicted in Fig. 3 to conduct a cyber attack targeting the IEC 61850 and IEC 60870-104 protocols as explained in [2,8]. The primary objective is to analyze and demonstrate how the integration of attention diversion can potentially enhance the outcomes of these attacks. Note that this section does not delve into the detailed aspects of the attacks, as those are thoroughly covered in our previous works [2,8]. The emphasis of this study is on examining whether the integration of attention diversion strategies could potentially enhance the effectiveness of these attacks, and to shed light on the necessity of considering the possibility of deception in the lower layers of the operational technology part in CPSs, and to increase the awareness amongst operators and system owners.

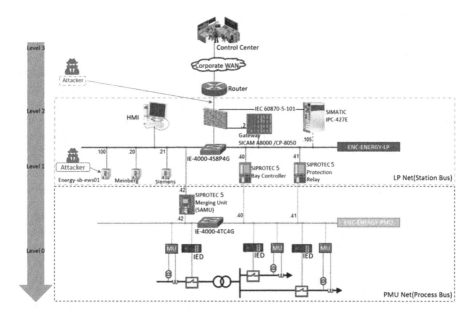

Fig. 3. Digital substation enclave testbed.

4.1   Digital Station (DS) Enclave Testbed

Figure 3 depicts a digital substation consisting of two primary components: the station bus (yellow block) and the process bus (red block). The station bus connects all bays with the supervisory level, while the process bus links Intelligent Electronic Devices (IEDs) within a bay for real-time measurements. Key elements in the digital substation includes digital station equipment, a control center machine, and engineering workstations for operations and configurations.

In this tested, Siemens have provided the digital station equipment, designed for high-voltage substations, with the SICAM A8000 CP-8050 serving as a dual-role gateway. This gateway manages the interface between the substation and the dispatch center, performing protocol conversion from IEC 61850-8-1 (MMS) to IEC 60870-5-104 and acting as a network isolation mechanism.

For precise time synchronization, the substation uses Ruggedcom RSG2488 and Meinberg M1000 time servers with GPS time sources, configured for PTP compliance with the Power Utility Profile. The station and process bus network switches are interconnected for synchronization. IECTest simulates the operation control center (dispatch center), communicating with the SICAM A8000 CP-8050 gateway. The Siemens DS enclave components are updated to the latest versions, and the testbed includes several Industrial Control System (ICS) Intrusion Detection Systems (IDSs) from various vendors.

4.2 Constructing the Cover Story

The cover story is constructed based on the principle that OT personnel in critical infrastructures are more inclined to attribute system irregularities to technical glitches rather than cyber attacks, a concept rooted in organizational biases [9]. This belief forms the foundation of our deception strategy. According to [10] and aligned with Magruder's principles, the most effective deceptions build upon preexisting beliefs. Thus, the cover story is designed to reinforce the notion that the observed network anomalies are mere system glitches, diverting attention from the actual cyber attack.

4.3 Summary of the Covering Story

The attackers initiate their operation with a phase of reconnaissance, aiming to collect information about the target network. Passive reconnaissance techniques enable them to eavesdrop on network communications, identifying key patterns and configurations such as ASDU and IOA addresses. They then transition to active reconnaissance, pinpointing the locations of gateway devices, the controlling station, and the network gateway through port scanning.

Following reconnaissance, the attackers employ deceptive techniques, deliberately creating disruptions that appear as harmless technical irregularities. This strategy diverts the attention of operators and engineers toward resolving these perceived network issues. Initially, step 4 is designed to subtly imitate common network problems, leading operators to believe they are facing regular technical difficulties.

As the network environment becomes flooded with apparent technical issues, the attackers shift their focus to manipulate the Precision Time Protocol (PTP). They subtly alter PTP settings to disrupt real clock sources, causing IEDs to rely on internal clocks and to flag missing time synchronization. Up to this point, the attackers have followed a silent manipulation approach, using attention diversion to conceal their activities targeting PTP. At Step 7, the attackers achieve their goal, and it is observed that their cover story effectively helps them conceal their manipulation. However, once the PTP attack is executed, operators may begin to understand what has happened. At this stage, the attackers can transition from silent manipulation to overt distraction, prolonging the time needed to detect the PTP attack. To further conceal their activities and divert attention from these alterations, the attackers execute DDoS attacks in Step 8. These attacks exacerbate network chaos, complicating the operators' ability to identify the source of disruptions.

The DDoS plan serves a dual purpose in this context. Primarily, it adds a layer of chaos and confusion within the network, hindering operators' ability to pinpoint the root cause of disruptions. Secondarily, the DDoS attacks provide the attackers with the necessary time to precisely manipulate PTP settings, introducing timing inconsistencies among IEDs. This combination of tactics not only delays detection, but also complicates the attribution of network anomalies to malicious origins. It provides a window of opportunity for attackers to move to the second stage in the kill chain and to execute an ICS attack, as described in Step 9 of the attack steps outlined below.

Based on comparisons between the results of this attack, which utilized attention diversion, and our previous work [2], we found that the former could significantly impact operators' reactions.

4.4   Attack Steps

In the following we summarize the attack steps.

Step 1 - Initial Reconnaissance:

- Attack Type: Passive Reconnaissance.
- Attack Aim/Action: Gathering information about the IEC 60870-5-104 network
- Attack Technique: Promiscuous mode listening and information gathering.
- Outcome: Successful reconnaissance with no trace.

Step 2 - Identifying Device Types

- Attack Type: Passive Reconnaissance.
- Attack Aim/Action: Identifying device types and characteristic (see Fig. 4 showing the result of the reconnaissance, including which switch leg that is in used).
- Attack Technique: Gateway fingerprinting - MAC address grabbing.
- Outcome: Partially successful reconnaissance, identifying manufacturer information.

Step 3 - Network Discovery

- Attack Type: Active Reconnaissance.
- Attack Aim/Action: Finding Gateway devices, controlling station, and the interface to the protected network.

– Attack Technique: Port scanning the subnet for open 2404 tcp ports.
– Outcome: Successful reconnaissance, discovering key network components (see Fig. 5).

Step 4 - Distraction through Operation Failure:

– Attack Type: Operation failure.
– Attack Aim/Action: Sending wrong measurement values and attempt to propagate errors as well as sending error messages.
– Attack Technique: Sending wrong data on behalf of the Gateway using packet injection and sending error messages.
– Outcome: Successful operation failure, leading to communication disruption and diverting attention.

Step 5 - Precision Time Protocol (PTP) Setup:

– Attack Type: Initial Reconnaissance.
– Attack Aim/Action: Collecting information regarding clock sources (Meinberg and Siemens).
– Attack Technique: Passive reconnaissance.
– Outcome: Attacker obtains information necessary for the later PTP manipulation.

Step 6 - PTP Master Clock Emulation:

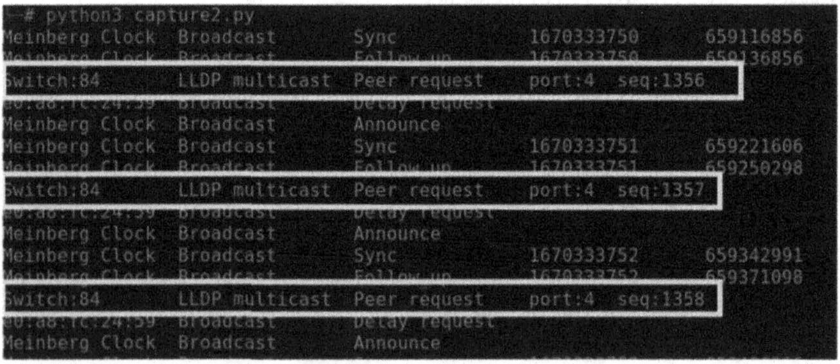

Fig. 4. Passive reconnaissance.

– Attack Type: Attacker takes over as the master clock.
– Attack Aim/Action: Manipulating the PTP to become the master clock on the network.
– Attack Technique: Rough master clock emulation.

– Outcome: Multiple clocks in the network (more than what is configured in the network).

Step 7 - PTP Manipulation:

– Attack Type: Attacker maintains status with the master clock emulation.
– Attacker Aim/Action: Repeating the master clock emulation message every second.
– Attack Technique: Rough master clock emulation with broadcast messages.
– Outcome: Real clock sources stop working, no PTP time synchronization in the network, IEDs start using their internal clock and flagging missing time synchronization on Sample Value Messages (SVMs).

Step 8 - DDoS:

– Attack Type: DDoS.
– Attacker Aim/Action: Attention diversion by (1) disabling communication between the Gateway and the control center, (2) ARP poisoning, and (3) disabling Gateway accessibility.

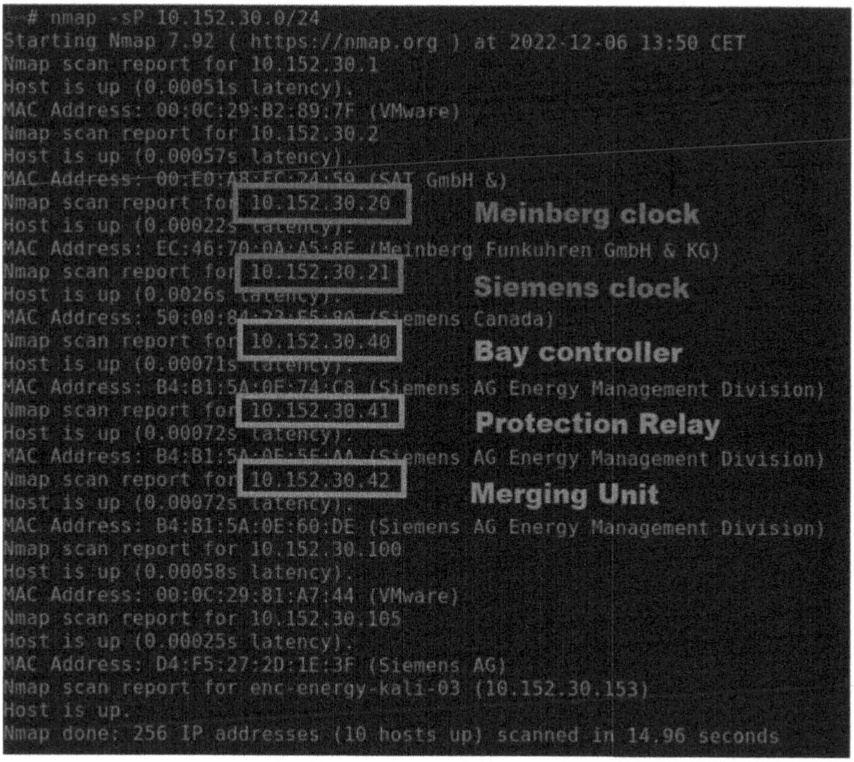

Fig. 5. Discovery of the equipment communicating on the network.

- Attack Technique: ASDU RESET flood with packet injection, controlling center source IP spoofing, ARP poisoning without packet forwarding, and TCP level SYN flood of the Gateway.
- Outcome: TCP connection reset, a large amount of fake ARP replies, and an excessive amount of SYN packets towards the Gateway (see Figs. 6, 7, and 8).

No.	Time	Source	Destination	Protocol	Length	Info	
89.	10.152.40.2	10.152.40.1	IEC 60870-5 ASDU	81	-> I (41,32) ASDU=1 M_ME_TF_1 Spont	IOA=10001
91.	10.152.40.101	10.152.40.2	IEC 60870-5 ASDU	76	<- I (32,42) ASDU=1 C_CS_NA_1 Act	IOA=0
91.	10.152.40.2	10.152.40.1	IEC 60870-5 ASDU	76	-> I (42,33) ASDU=1 C_CS_NA_1 ActCon	IOA=0
91.	10.152.40.101	10.152.40.2	IEC 60870-5 ASDU	70	<- I (33,43) ASDU=1 C_RP_NA_1 Act	IOA=0
91.	10.152.40.2	10.152.40.2	IEC 60870-5 ASDU	70	-> I (43,34) ASDU=1 C_RP_NA_1 ActCon	IOA=0
91.	10.152.40.101	10.152.40.2	IEC 60870-5 ASDU	70	<- I (34,44) ASDU=1 C_RP_NA_1 Act	IOA=0
101.	10.152.40.101	10.152.40.2	IEC 60870-5 ASDU	82	[TCP Spurious Retransmission]	<- 5 (43)	<
102.	10.152.40.101	10.152.40.2	IEC 60870-5 ASDU	82	[TCP Spurious Retransmission]	<- 5 (43)	<
103.	10.152.40.101	10.152.40.2	IEC 60870-5 ASDU	82	[TCP Spurious Retransmission]	<- 5 (43)	<
105.	10.152.40.101	10.152.40.2	IEC 60870-5 ASDU	82	[TCP Spurious Retransmission]	<- 5 (43)	<
163.	10.152.40.101	10.152.40.2	IEC 60870-5 ASDU	76	<- I (0,0) ASDU=1 C_CS_NA_1 Act	IOA=0
163.	10.152.40.101	10.152.40.2	IEC 60870-5 ASDU	76	<- I (1,0) ASDU=1 C_CS_NA_1 Act	IOA=0
163.	10.152.40.101	10.152.40.2	IEC 60870-5 ASDU	76	<- I (2,0) ASDU=1 C_CS_NA_1 Act	IOA=0

> Frame 1230: 70 bytes on wire (560 bits), 70 bytes captured (560 bits) on interface \Device\NPF_{15A390F8-EFD6-
> Ethernet II, Src: SAT_fc:24:5d (00:e0:a8:fc:24:5d), Dst: VMware_9d:21:b5 (00:0c:29:9d:21:b5)
> Internet Protocol Version 4, Src: 10.152.40.2, Dst: 10.152.40.101
> Transmission Control Protocol, Src Port: 2404, Dst Port: 60861, Seq: 371, Ack: 261, Len: 16
> IEC 60870-5-104: -> I (43,34)
> IEC 60870-5-101/104 ASDU: ASDU=1 C_RP_NA_1 ActCon IOA=0 'reset process command'

Fig. 6. DoS attack with spoofed reset commands using packet injection to disable communication between the Gateway and the control center.

No.	Time	Source	Destination	Protocol	Length	Info
	84.455854	VMware_9d:21:b5	VMware_70:5.	ARP	60	10.152.40.101 is at 00:0c:29:9d:21:b5
	84.471470	VMware_70:56:f4	VMware_9d:2.	ARP	60	10.152.40.2 is at 00:0c:29:70:56:f4
	84.505223	VMware_70:56:f4	SAT_fc:24:5d	ARP	60	10.152.40.101 is at 00:0c:29:70:56:f4
	84.535992	VMware_70:56:f4	VMware_9d:2.	ARP	60	10.152.40.2 is at 00:0c:29:70:56:f4
	84.565247	VMware_70:56:f4	SAT_fc:24:5d	ARP	60	10.152.40.101 is at 00:0c:29:70:56:f4
	84.605204	VMware_70:56:f4	VMware_9d:2.	ARP	60	10.152.40.2 is at 00:0c:29:70:56:f4
	84.635998	VMware_70:56:f4	SAT_fc:24:5d	ARP	60	10.152.40.101 is at 00:0c:29:70:56:f4
	84.669171	VMware_70:56:f4	VMware_9d:2.	ARP	60	10.152.40.2 is at 00:0c:29:70:56:f4
	84.701160	VMware_70:56:f4	SAT_fc:24:5d	ARP	60	10.152.40.101 is at 00:0c:29:70:56:f4
	84.732037	VMware_70:56:f4	VMware_9d:2.	ARP	60	10.152.40.2 is at 00:0c:29:70:56:f4
	84.765165	VMware_70:56:f4	SAT_fc:24:5d	ARP	60	10.152.40.101 is at 00:0c:29:70:56:f4
	84.797154	VMware_70:56:f4	VMware_9d:2.	ARP	60	10.152.40.2 is at 00:0c:29:70:56:f4

Fig. 7. DoS attack with ARP poisoning.

Step 9 - ICS attack:

- Attack Type: ICS attack.
- Attacker Aim/Action: Attacker takes advantage of the window of opportunity to execute the actual ICS attack (stage 2 of the ICS kill chain).
- Attack Technique: Attacker may follow different techniques depending on the attack aim.

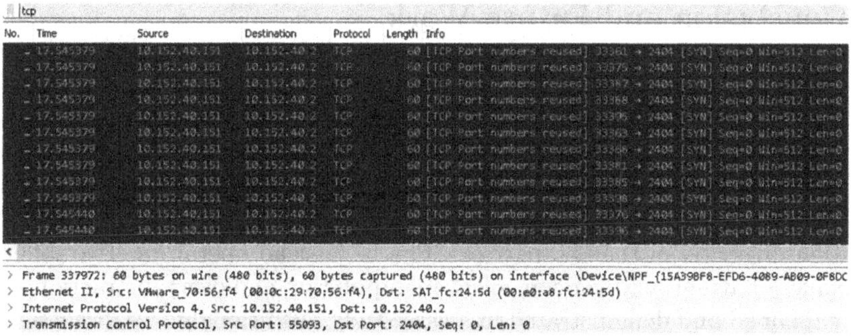

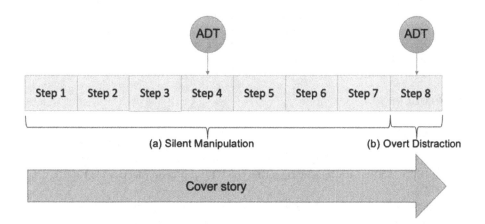

Fig. 8. DoS attack with SYN flood to disable the Gateway accessibility.

- Outcome: The results will vary and depend on the techniques used by the attacker. Examples of outcomes are as defined by MITRE ATT&CK for ICS: Damage to property, Denial of control, Denial of View, Loss of availability, Loss of control, Loss of productivity and revenue, Loss of protection, Loss of safety, Loss of View, Manipulation of control, Manipulation of view, and Theft of operational information.

Figure 9 illustrates the comprehensive integration of Atomic Deception Techniques and the Cover story across the various attack steps, highlighting the strategic transition from silent manipulation in the initial steps to overt distraction in the final phase. This visual representation provides a clear overview of how deceptive tactics are systematically employed throughout the different stages of the cyber attack in this case study.

Fig. 9. Illustration of Attention Diversion techniques used in the case study.

5 Conclusion and Future Work

This paper highlights a research gap in the study of complex cyber attacks, such as APTs, namely the role of deception techniques from the attacker's perspective in the realization of these attacks. We explored how deception can influence system operators' decisions in sophisticated attacks. We introduced the concept of Attention Diversion and discussed its role and the possibility of utilizing attention diversion in the OT part of CPSs to mislead operators. Two different techniques of attention diversion: silent manipulation and overt distraction, have been explained and demonstrated in a case study. Additionally, we discussed the utilization of attention diversion in the form of Atomic Deception Techniques and Cover Story, based on the cyber kill chain steps. We also demonstrated how silent manipulation and overt distraction can prolong attacks and complicate defense strategies, and demonstrated this in the case study which was executed in a digital substation testbed.

Future work will delve deeper into the impact of deception on system operators, aiming to improve training and awareness. This is key to developing advanced cyber defense strategies and equipping defenders to counter sophisticated threats, as well as demonstrating the need for continued exploration in this crucial area of cybersecurity. This research is a step towards filling a critical research gap, emphasizing the need to understand and prepare for the use of deception in cyber attacks. Our work highlights the importance of investigating this area, which could substantially transform cybersecurity practices and defenses. In future work, we will also consider obfuscation as another deception technique from the attacker perspective, as well as attempt to propose solutions to mitigate such attack techniques.

Acknowledgment. Part of the work was funded by the Research Council of Norway through two projects: CybWin (Cybersecurity Platform for Assessment and Training for Critical Infrastructures - From Legacy to Digital Twin) - project no. 287808, and CORESIM (Context-Based Real-Time OT-IT Systems Integrity Management) - project no. 344244.

References

1. Akbarzadeh, A.: Dependency based risk analysis in cyber-physical systems. Ph. D. Thesis, Norwegian University of Science and Technology (NTNU) (2023)
2. Akbarzadeh, A., Erdodi, L., Houmb, S.H., Soltvedt, T.G., Muggerud, H.K.: Attacking IEC 61850 substations by targeting the PTP protocol. Electronics **12**(12), 2596 (2023)
3. Almeshekah, M.H.: Using deception to enhance security: a taxonomy, model, and novel uses. Ph.D. thesis, Purdue University (2015)
4. Amoroso, E.: Cyber Attacks: Protecting National Infrastructure. Elsevier, Amsterdam (2012)
5. Bennett, M.: Counterdeception Principles and Applications for National Security. Artech (2007)

6. Kaspersky Industrial Control Systems Cyber Emergency Response Team CERT: APT attacks on industrial organizations in H1 2021 (2021). https://ics-cert.kaspersky.com/media/Kaspersky-ICS-CERT-APT-attacks-on-industrial-organizations-in-H1-2021-En.pdf
7. Chen, P., Desmet, L., Huygens, C.: A study on advanced persistent threats. In: De Decker, B., Zúquete, A. (eds.) CMS 2014. LNCS, vol. 8735, pp. 63–72. Springer, Heidelberg (2014). https://doi.org/10.1007/978-3-662-44885-4_5
8. Erdődi, L., Kaliyar, P., Houmb, S.H., Akbarzadeh, A., Waltoft-Olsen, A.J.: Attacking power grid substations: an experiment demonstrating how to attack the scada protocol IEC 60870-5-104. In: Proceedings of the 17th International Conference on Availability, Reliability and Security, pp. 1–10 (2022)
9. Faveri, C.D.: Modeling deception for cyber security. NOVA University Lisbon (2022). https://run.unl.pt/bitstream/10362/148907/1/Faveri_2022.pdf
10. Heckman, K.E., Stech, F.J., Thomas, R.K., Schmoker, B., Tsow, A.W.: Cyber denial, deception and counter deception. In: Advances in Information Security, vol. 64 (2015)
11. Hilbert, M.: Toward a synthesis of cognitive biases: how noisy information processing can bias human decision making. Psychol. Bull. **138**(2), 211 (2012)
12. Izycki, E., Vianna, E.W.: Critical infrastructure: a battlefield for cyber warfare? In: ICCWS 2021 16th International Conference on Cyber Warfare and Security, p. 454. Academic Conferences Limited (2021)
13. Jørgensen, P.A., Waltoft-Olsen, A., Houmb, S.H., Toppe, A.L., Soltvedt, T.G., Muggerud, H.K.: Building a hardware-in-the-loop (HiL) digital energy station infrastructure for cyber operation resiliency testing. In: Proceedings of the 3rd International Workshop on Engineering and Cybersecurity of Critical Systems, pp. 9–16 (2022)
14. Mahon, J.E.: The definition of lying and deception (2008)
15. Major, M., Fugate, S., Mauger, J., Ferguson-Walter, K.: Creating cyber deception games. In: 2019 IEEE First International Conference on Cognitive Machine Intelligence (CogMI), pp. 102–111. IEEE (2019)
16. Masip, J., Garrido, E., Herrero, C.: Defining deception (2004). https://api.semanticscholar.org/CorpusID:31882891
17. Pawlick, J., Zhu, Q., et al.: Game Theory for Cyber Deception. Springer, Cham (2021). https://doi.org/10.1007/978-3-030-66065-9
18. Ross, R., Pillitteri, V., Graubart, R., Bodeau, D., McQuaid, R.: Developing cyber-resilient systems: a systems security engineering approach, NIST special publication 800-160. Technical report, National Institute of Standards and Technology (2021). https://nvlpubs.nist.gov/nistpubs/SpecialPublications/NIST.SP.800-160v2r1.pdf
19. Schacter, D., Gilbert, D., Wegner, D., Hood, B.M.: Psychology: European Edition. Macmillan International Higher Education (2011)
20. Seo, S., Kim, D.: SOD2G: a study on a social-engineering organizational defensive deception game framework through optimization of spatiotemporal MTD and decoy conflict. Electronics **10**(23), 3012 (2021)
21. Sharma, A., Gupta, B.B., Singh, A.K., Saraswat, V.: Advanced persistent threats (APT): evolution, anatomy, attribution and countermeasures. J. Ambient Intell. Humaniz. Comput. 1–27 (2023)
22. Yadav, T., Rao, A.M.: Technical aspects of cyber kill chain. In: Abawajy, J., Mukherjea, S., Thampi, S., Ruiz-Martínez, A. (eds.) SSCC 2015. CCIS, vol. 536, pp. 438–452. Springer, Cham (2015). https://doi.org/10.1007/978-3-319-22915-7_40

Competencies Required for the Offensive Cyber Operations Planners

Marko Arik[(⊠)] [iD], Ricardo Gregorio Lugo[iD], Rain Ottis[iD],
and Adrian Nicholas Venables[iD]

Tallinn University of Technology, Tallinn, Estonia
marko.arik@taltech.ee

Abstract. This paper presents a systematic review of competencies required for Offensive Cyber Operations planners. Military Cyber Headquarters staff must possess strategic, operational, and tactical skills for effective planning and execution of cyber operations at different levels. This article examines the necessary skills for Offensive Cyber Operations (OCO) planners at the operational level. The research aims to define the role of an operational-level OCO planner, identify necessary skills, and develop a framework for practical OCO planning, requiring further research and development. This systematic review utilises academic databases and includes peer-reviewed studies on Offensive Cyber Operations planning competencies, encompassing journal articles, books, and conference papers.

Keywords: Cyberspace operations planning · Cyberspace planners' competencies · Cyberspace · Cyber operation officer · Offensive Cyber Operations · CO decision maker · Systematic ReviewFirst Section

1 Introduction

Mapping the abilities and competencies required for a military's Cyber Headquarters staff members is vital to the organisation's success (Joint Publication 1 2013). Cyber Operations (CO) planners must have military planning experience and an in-depth knowledge of cyberspace operations (United States Army War College 2022, p. 32). When assembling a cyber team, knowing which skills and experience are required is crucial to fulfilling each assigned position's goals. Cyber Operations are handled at three levels: strategic, operational, and tactical, and the skills involved at each differ (AJP-3.20 2020) The strategic level needs a greater understanding of political goals and situational understanding. Operational-level planning requires using cognitive skills from commanders and their staff, and at the tactical level, technical skills are needed.

The article focuses on the operational level, which is essential because the operations' design and management are conducted at this level (NATO Standardization Office 2020, p. 19). The military doctrine also refers to it as' operational art' and involves (Joint Pub 5–0 1995) planning operations and effects to achieve strategic objectives. This article explores the required competencies for Offensive Cyber Operations (OCO) planners at the operational level. Understanding the factors contributing to cyber operators' performance is imperative to improve education and training for military personnel (Jøsok et. al. 2019). In addition, recent research reveals a need to organise offensive cyberspace operations and their impact (Huskaj and Axelsson 2023). However, certain obstacles include a lack of suitably qualified personnel with the requisite skills (Ibid). Previous research regarding cyber operations has mostly focused on DCO (Defensive Cyber Operations) and, more specifically, at the tactical level of cyber operators (Jøsok et. al. 2019).

This research applies a detailed examination and academic rigour to identify the necessary competencies required for OCO planners. Specifically, the goals of the study are:

1. To define the role of an operational-level OCO planner.
2. To identify the operational skills, digital skills, soft skills, and experience required for the competencies needed at the operational level of an OCO planner.
3. To devise a framework (including a training plan, skillset, and all required competencies) to become a competent OCO planner.

The three goals commence with a fundamental understanding of the issues. Our final stage will inform applied research aspects, highlighting the requirements for further research and development to incorporate civilian and military education, training modes and framework development.

Several NATO countries have acknowledged that OCO planning has become more mainstream. For example, the 2016 NATO Warsaw Summit addressed the OCO capabilities in the Sovereign Cyber Effects Provided Voluntarily by Allies (SCEPVA) mechanism. NATO's current policy is that it "does not go offensive in cyberspace" and that the Alliance[1] does not create organic offensive cyber capabilities. Therefore, it must consult with its Member States to deploy offensive capabilities, and the SCEPVA mechanism is currently used. Nations with cyber capabilities may be asked to launch offensive cyber effects against a target chosen by an operational-level commander (Goździewicz 2019). The SCEPVA construct enables the integration of offensive cyberspace operations capabilities in operations despite challenges in coordination. Although not the most effective way to utilise allies' combined OCO potential, it provides a pragmatic framework for NATO training (Jensen 2022). SCEPVA allows NATO member nations to contribute cyber capabilities to NATO missions while maintaining command and control over them. Due to the increasing significance of cyber operations in collective defence and deterrence, it is essential to understand how deploying cyber capabilities may influence conflict dynamics (Libicki and Tkacheva 2020, p. 61). Control over SCEPVA remains with the contributing nation, and offensive cyberspace operations during Alliance missions require approval. Planning staff assess cyberspace, considering potential effects while acknowledging that integrating force elements may not always be feasible. Additionally, there is a need for continuous interaction and updates due to the evolving nature of cyberspace (AJP-3.20 2020, pp. 23,27). The SCEPVA mechanism is the critical driver

---

[1] Alliance / allies refers to North Atlantic Treaty Organization.

of OCO's capabilities while providing an opportunity for operations. The RSA Conference 2016 keynote also advocated a proactive approach against hackers through Information Operations, including Active Defence and Offensive Countermeasures (ENISA 2016). These measures aim to gather intelligence and counteract adversaries. However, ethical and legal considerations, along with challenges in attribution, pose significant risks. An EU legislative framework needs to be more consistent across member states. While Information Operations offer advantages, carefully considering legal, technical, and ethical implications is crucial (Ibid). Based on the preceding, this article focuses on operation-level military aspects and offensive cyberspace training frameworks.

2   Methods

Using PRISMA (Preferred Reporting Items for Systematic Reviews and Meta-Analyses) for literature reviews in offensive cyber operations offers significant bene-fits. PRISMA provides a systematic and transparent approach, enhancing replication (Tricco et al. 2018; Moher et al. 2015). It helps identify key findings and ensures quality in research selection, which is crucial in the varied quality of cyber operations sources. PRISMA reduces bias through a predefined selection process and criteria.

PRISMA's systematic framework is widely used for defining research questions and criteria for including and excluding studies. It allows for a thorough literature review, identifying gaps and guiding future research (Moher et al. 2015; Tricco et al. 2018). This is particularly relevant in the rapidly evolving field of cyber operations.

Our study involved academic sources like journals, books, reports, and theses, focusing on offensive cyber operations planning skills. We included 13 studies, selecting scholarly documents and excluding those not related to offensive cyber operations competencies and duplicates.

2.1   Review Procedure

1. Identify literature on Offensive Cyber Operations planners' competencies through database searches.
2. Sort the publications into categories based on type.
3. Provide a summary of the identified papers in order of research questions.
4. Synthesis, discussion of the findings, and recommendations for further study.

2.2   Literature Collection Methodology

The years of publishing ranged from 1990 to 2023, with only English-language articles reviewed. Table 1 includes a list of databases and search phrases.

Table 1. Overview of databases, search terms, hits and last search date.

Database	Terms searched	Hits	Last search date
GoogleScholar	"offensive cyber operations planners competencies", "offensive cyber operations competencies", "cyber operations competencies", "cyberspace operations planner", "cyber offensive planner", "cyber operations planner", "cyberspace planners competencies", "cyber planners competencies", "cyber operational planner"	16	26.09.2023
ScienceDirect	"offensive cyber operations planners competencies", "offensive cyber operations competencies", "cyber operations competencies", "cyberspace operations planner", "cyber offensive planner", "cyber operations planner", "cyberspace planners competencies", "cyber planners competencies", "cyber operational planner"	0	26.09.2023
IEEE	"offensive cyber operations planners competencies", "offensive cyber operations competencies", "cyber operations competencies", "cyberspace operations planner", "cyber offensive planner", "cyber operations planner", "cyberspace planners competencies", "cyber planners competencies", "cyber operational planner"	0	26.09.2023
DuckDuckGo	"offensive cyber operations planners competencies", "offensive cyber operations competencies", "cyber operations competencies", "cyberspace operations planner", "cyber offensive planner", "cyber operations planner", "cyberspace planners competencies", "cyber planners competencies", "cyber operational planner"	7	26.09.2023
Taylor& Francis	"offensive cyber operations planners competencies", "offensive cyber operations competencies", "cyber operations competencies", "cyberspace operations planner", "cyber offensive planner", "cyber operations planner", "cyberspace planners competencies", "cyber planners competencies", "cyber operational planner"	0	28.09.2023

3   Results

To Define the Role of an Operational-Level OCO Planner. The Google Scholar database provided 16 returns to the search terms. Of these, there were 13 suitable studies. DuckDuckGo database provided an additional seven results. Of these, there were two suitable studies. Eight studies were excluded due to not directly including any significance on OCO planners' definitions or competencies. Table 2 overviews the publications discovered and categorises them by type and methodology. Since no quantitative publications were identified, Table 2 represents qualitative and mixed (qualitative and quantitative) publications.

Table 2. Overviews the publications discovered and categorises them by type and methodology.

Subject	Basic information		Type	Methodology	
	Author(s)	Year		Qualitative	Mixed
Integrating Cyber with Air Power in the Second Century of the Royal Air Force	Withers et al	2018	Journal Article	X	
Cyberspace Operations Planning: Operating a Technical Military Force beyond the Kinetic Domains	Barber et al	2016	Journal Article	X	
The Cyberspace Operations Planner	Bender, J	2013	Journal Article	X	
A Cognitive Skills Research Framework for Complex Operational Environments	Neville et al	2020	Technical Report	X	
Joint Targeting in Cyberspace	Smart	2011	Report	X	
Let Slip the Dogs of (Cyber) War: Progressing Towards a Warfighting U.S. Cyber Command	Mulford	2013	Report	X	
Educating for Evolving Operational Domains	RAND Corporation	2022	Research Report	X	
A Guide to the National Initiative for Cybersecurity Education (NICE) Cybersecurity Workforce Framework (2.0)	Shoemaker et al	2016	Book		X
The Cyberhero and the Cybercriminal	Nizich	2023	Book		X

(*continued*)

Table 2. (*continued*)

Subject	Basic information		Type	Methodology	
	Author(s)	Year		Qualitative	Mixed
Knowledge Management Application to Cyber Protection Team Defense Operations	Curnutt et al	2021	Master Thesis	X	
Thriving Cybersecurity Professionals: Building a Resilient Workforce and Psychological Safety in the Federal Government	Houston	2019	Master Thesis		X
Incorporating Perishability and Obsolescence into Cyberweapon Scheduling	Lidestri	2022	Master Thesis	X	
Implications of Service Cyberspace Component Commands for Army Cyberspace Operations	Caton	2019	Monograph	X	

The Cyberhero and the Cybercriminal (Nizich 2023) have used the NICE (The NICE Workforce Framework for Cybersecurity[2]) to define the Cybersecurity roles. For example, the Cyber Operations Planner develops detailed plans for conducting or supporting the applicable range of cyber operations through collaboration with other planners, operators, and analysts. They participate in targeting selection, validation, and synchronisation and enable integration during the execution of cyber actions. Knowledge Management Application to Cyber Protection Team (CPT) Defence Operations (Curnutt and Sikes 2021) defines a Cyber Planner. These perform vital functions throughout the assessment process involving coordination with CPT leadership /higher headquarters elements, tracking and planning Future Operations, and supporting Current Operations to activated Mission Element teams. Those filling the Cyber Planner role are typically experienced in two or more Cyber Mission Force work roles across defensive and offensive mission sets. This paper also proposes future research for Offensive Cyber Teams.

---

[2] https://www.nist.gov/itl/applied-cybersecurity/nice/nice-framework-resource-center.

Table 3. Navy Cyber Operation Planners Skills and Abilities.

Skills	Abilities
Critical Thinking	Written Expression
Judgment and Decision Making	Deductive Reasoning
Complex Problem Solving	Originality
Coordination	Inductive Reasoning
Systems Analysis	Problem Sensitivity
Writing	Information Ordering
Systems Evaluation	Communication
Active Learning	Written Comprehension
Monitoring	Fluency of Ideas
Quality Control Analysis	Selective Attention

This article also defined a CO planner: "Cyber operations planners help develop and coordinate analyses to perform defensive or offensive missions" (Houston 2019, p. 8).

The following is an example of defining the Cyber Operations Planner, although this is a governmental contract. "The Cyber Operations Planner is responsible for monitoring and reviewing strategies, doctrine, policies, and directives for compliance in cyberspace operations, providing input for briefings, transitioning concepts, and developing tactics and procedures" (U.S. General Services Administration 2022).

Identify the Operational Skills, Digital Skills, Soft Skills, and Experience Required for the Competencies Needed in the Operational-Level OCO Planner. Competencies are the knowledge, skills, abilities, and behaviours contributing to individual and organisational performance (National Institute of Health 2023). The Cognitive Skills Research Framework compares cyber operations competencies, focusing on cognitive tasks in cyber-attack and defence (Neville et al. 2020). This framework can identify skills and training needs for cyber attackers and defenders. It also examines competencies in cyber intelligence analysis and targeting, an essential skill for Offensive Cyber Operations (OCO) planners (National Institute for Standards and Technology framework).

Research emphasises the importance of targeting in cyberspace operations (Nizich, 2023; Bender 2013; Barber et al. 2016). While targeting is a known skill among military personnel, specific proficiencies in OCO and Defensive Cyber Operations (DCO) are less common (Smart 2011). Effective targeting in cyberspace requires understanding the law of war, the cyber centre of gravity, and operational planning. Cyber operations also need an understanding of cyberweapon perishability and obsolescence (Lidestri 2022).

Additionally, OCO planners must understand network metadata analysis and integrate cyber operations into broader command plans (Mulford 2013). The National Initiative for Cybersecurity Careers and Studies (NICCS) outlines specific competencies and training for cyber ops planners at various levels. Other sources, like Caton (2019), suggest competencies in professional networking and information systems technology for cyber planners.

The NICE Cybersecurity Workforce Framework (2.0) defines competencies in counterespionage and operational security for cyber operations (Shoemaker et al. 2016, p. 36). RAND Corporation (2022) highlights the importance of civilian and military education in developing OCO planner competencies. Cyber operations require a deep understanding of the domain and integrated planning skills (Withers et al. 2018). Effective cyber planners also need comprehensive training programs, as Bender (2013) suggested, which proposes various courses for practical OCO planning.

Finally, the Navy Personnel Command (2023) details the role of Cyber Operation Planners, emphasising analytical support, targeting selection, and executing cyber actions. This illustrates the broad range of competencies required for effective OCO planning (Table 3).

The results section highlights the diverse knowledge, skills, abilities, and experiences needed for individuals in various roles related to cyber operations planning, including Offensive Cyber Operations (OCO) planners. This underlines the importance of ongoing education, training, and self-development to build competencies in this dynamic and critical field. Tables 4 and 5 present knowledge, skills, and abilities identified from the literature review, while Table 6 presents abilities.

Table 4. Knowledge identified from the literature review.

	Knowledge
1	Understanding of Cyberspace Operations, strategies, doctrine, policies and directives
2	Knowledge of tactics, techniques, procedures, concept of operations, and course of action development
3	Knowledge of current and emerging Cyber Threats
4	Understanding of perishability and obsolescence factors related to Cyberweapons
5	Knowledge related to Cyberspace Operations, including doctrine, policies and directives
6	Knowledge of cyberspace core competencies and cybersecurity activities
7	Knowledge of professional networking, social collaboration, and cross-functional data sharing
8	Understanding cyberspace, including threats, vulnerabilities, and intelligence collection capabilities
9	Knowledge of joint functions and operational procedures
10	Knowledge of kill chain framework and cyber threat analysis

A Proposed Framework Required for an OCO Planner. Bendler& Felderer's (Bendler and Felderer 2023) examination of the current landscape of competency models in the information security and cybersecurity fields analysed 27 existing models through qualitative content analysis, identifying a predominant focus on professional competencies while noting a significant underrepresentation of social human aspects,

Table 5. Skills identified from the literature review.

	Skills
1	Cognitive skills related to cyber operations include intelligence analysis and targeting
2	To analyse network metadata
3	To develop detailed plans for the conduct of cyber operations
4	To conduct battle damage assessments
5	To target analysis, including considerations of attribution and the principle of self-defence in cyberspace
6	To plan and coordinate Future Operations and Current Operations support
7	Analytical skills for supporting the planning process
8	Cognitive skills in cyber intelligence analysis, advanced cyber warfare, and network operations
9	Skills in information security, troubleshooting, information systems, and risk management
10	Technical planning skills and operational procedures
11	Planning and coordination skills in areas like targeting selection and synchronisation
12	Skills in analysing the kill chain framework for cyber threats
13	Proficiency in enterprise information systems technology
14	Skills related to data analysis and logistics
15	In Critical Thinking
16	In Judgment and Decision Making
17	In Complex Problem Solving
18	In Coordination
19	In Systems Analysis
20	In Writing
21	In Systems Evaluation
22	In Active Learning
23	In Monitoring
24	In Quality Control Analysis

and methodological competencies. Addressing these gaps, Bendler and Felderer propose that competency models must encompass a broader spectrum of skills and attributes necessary for cybersecurity professionals and should be comprehensive and able to bridge the divide between educational outputs and labour market requirements. Such models should have a continuous evolution and adaptation that can adjust to the rapidly changing cybersecurity landscape but must consider holistic approaches that integrate technical and non-technical competencies.

The above literature review shows the breadth of domain knowledge and skills needed for OCO personnel. Previous research (Chowdhury and Gkioulos 2021) found

Table 6. Abilities identified from the literature review.

	Abilities
1	Ability to coordinate with CPT leadership, higher headquarters elements, and Mission Element teams
2	The innate potential to perform mental and physical actions or tasks related to cyber operations planning
3	Abilities related to professional networking, social collaboration, and cross-functional data sharing
4	Abilities in core cyber-specific functions
5	An intuitive understanding of the cyberspace domain and potential capabilities
6	Ability to lead joint operations and develop cyber capability, doctrine, and tactics
7	Ability to conduct OCO effectively
8	Abilities for ongoing intelligence gathering and planning to deter or defeat cyber-attacks
9	The ability to develop and coordinate analyses for defensive or offensive missions
10	In Written Expression
11	In Deductive Reasoning
12	In Originality
13	In Inductive Reasoning
14	In Problem Sensitivity
15	In Information Ordering
16	In Communication
17	In Written Comprehension
18	In Fluency of Ideas
19	In Selective Attention

that cybersecurity competencies and skills can be broadly categorised into four main groups:

1. Technical Skills include the specific, hands-on abilities required to operate and protect cybersecurity systems. Technical skills are foundational for any cybersecurity role and typically involve knowledge of computer networks, systems administration, an understanding of cybersecurity tools and software, and the ability to detect and respond to cyber threats and vulnerabilities.
2. Managerial Skills: Managerial skills in cybersecurity pertain to the ability to oversee cybersecurity teams, projects, and initiatives. This involves strategic planning, resource allocation, risk management, and policy development. Managerial skills are crucial for ensuring that cybersecurity practices align with the organisation's broader objectives and that resources are effectively utilised.

3. Implementation Skills: Implementation skills refer to the practical application of cybersecurity strategies and policies. This involves deploying security measures, managing cybersecurity operations, and ensuring compliance with relevant standards and regulations. These skills are critical for translating cybersecurity strategies into practical actions that protect critical infrastructures.

4. Soft Skills: Soft skills are increasingly recognised as essential in cybersecurity. These include communication skills, problem-solving abilities, teamwork, and adaptability. Soft skills are crucial for effective collaboration, clear communication of technical information to non-technical stakeholders, and adapting to the constantly evolving landscape of cybersecurity threats and technologies.

While these Findings are Not Specifically for OCO Planners, Many Aspects are Similar. This section presents the training plan, knowledge, skills, abilities and experience to become a proficient OCO planner. The framework is devised from the literature review results and the NICCS Cyber Ops Planners' knowledge, skills, and abilities. The final list of OCO planners' knowledge, skills, abilities, and training plans is presented in Dataset 1, "The Framework for Offensive Cyber Operations Planners[3].

3.1 Training Plan

The proposed courses to become a practical OCO planner are detailed below. It should be taken into account that the names of the courses may have changed over time, and an equivalent course should be identified. The proposed OCO planner's training plan is presented in Table 7.

These courses prepare students for planning full-spectrum cyberspace operations, including attack, intelligence, surveillance, target acquisition, reconnaissance, defence, and environmental preparation. The courses are designed for U.S.-only students and provide an operator's perspective on network exploitation and vulnerabilities. Candidates must be U.S. citizens. The courses cover military doctrine, cyber threats, and electromagnetic spectrum fundamentals. Most of these courses are aimed at U.S. citizens and those serving in the Army. European equivalent courses can be found in the NATO CCDCOE training catalogue (NATO CCDCOE 2023).

The NICCS proposed Capability Indicators for Cyber Operational Planners, which include a range of topics divided into two proficiency levels. At the Entry level, individuals receive training in areas such as joint cyber analysis, joint advanced cyber warfare, and cyber network operations.

The training covers a broader spectrum of topics for Intermediate and Advanced levels. The recommendation for intermediate-level education is a bachelor's degree, while for advanced-level education, a master's degree is recommended. While these degrees are beneficial, they are not mandatory, and individuals from diverse educational backgrounds, practical experience, and certifications can pursue successful cyber operations planning careers. This includes advanced cyber warfare, network attacks, cyber operations, information security, troubleshooting, information systems, business processes, risk management, SQL, and Unix. This training is designed to provide a comprehensive

---

[3] https://drive.google.com/file/d/1OvtqROjVtrFIzW_mJ2Lr4mUzf7X98s10/view?usp=sharing.

Table 7. Proposed OCO planner's training plan.

Course name	Description	Knowledge Areas
National Defence University "CAPSTONE" course	Explains joint warfighting concept, security environment, conflict dynamics, operational and strategic levels. Emphasises Allied and Partner contributions	Joint warfighting, security environment, conflict dynamics, operational and strategic levels, Allied and Partner contributions
Information Operations Command's Basic CNO Planners Course	Utilises case studies and scenarios for planning criteria, effects, capability choice, success/failure, collateral effects, and battle damage assessments. Based on joint doctrine and U.S. DoD tactics	Joint warfighting, security environment, conflict dynamics, operational and strategic levels, Allied and Partner contributions
Army Cyberspace Operations Planners Course	Prepares for planning full-spectrum cyberspace operations, including attack, ISR, defence, and integration into Army and Joint planning processes. U.S.-only students	Full-spectrum cyberspace operations, attack, ISR, defence, and integration into planning processes
Cyber 200/300	Provides operator's perspective on network exploitation and vulnerabilities, integrating into the joint fight against cyber threats for U.S. Armed Forces	Network exploitation, vulnerabilities, and joint fight against cyber threats
Cryptologic Network Warfare Specialist qualification course	Focuses on advanced capabilities in cyberspace operations, cryptology, electronic warfare, signals intelligence, and space. U.S. citizens only	Cyberspace operations, cryptology, electronic warfare, signals intelligence, space
Joint Network Attack Course (Cyber Capabilities Developer Officer Course)	Provides initial training in military doctrine, cyber threats, cyberspace and electromagnetic warfare operations, and electromagnetic spectrum fundamentals. U.S. citizenship is required	Military doctrine, cyber threats, electromagnetic warfare operations, spectrum fundamentals

(continued)

Table 7. (*continued*)

Course name	Description	Knowledge Areas
Joint Advanced Cyberspace Warfare Course	Covers full-spectrum cyberspace operations, global cryptologic platforms, intelligence community, threats, planning, and analysis. Exclusive for U.S. Cyber Command	Full-spectrum cyberspace operations, global cryptologic platforms, intelligence community, threats, planning, and analysis
Joint Information Operations Planners Course	Focuses on planning, integrating, and synchronising full-spectrum information operations into joint operational-level plans. Open to multinational students	Information operations planning, integration, synchronisation, military deception, operations security, interagency coordination, and intelligence preparation
Joint Intermediate Target Development Course	Teaches research and documentation for developing virtual targets. U.S. Joint Chiefs of Staff course	Researching, documentation, virtual target development

skill set for cyber planners, allowing them to effectively plan and execute cyber operations while ensuring information security, troubleshooting, and aligning strategies with business processes and risk management considerations.

These courses are recommended by different authors and organisations based on their structured content. The courses cover various aspects essential for effective cyber operations planning in a military context. At the same time, providing comprehensive coverage of cyber warfare, joint military planning, information operations, and technical knowledge is critical for OCO planners.

3.2 Knowledge

The literature review contributes to NICCS Cyber Ops Planners' knowledge set by providing a more focused and specific set of knowledge and skills directly relevant to the role of an operational-level OCO planner. While the NICCS Cyber Ops Planners knowledge set offers a comprehensive list of knowledge, skills, abilities, and experience related to cybersecurity and network operations, literature review results narrow these requirements to those specifically needed for planning and executing offensive cyber operations.

The results help to define and specify the competencies required for individuals in the role of an OCO planner. It complements the more general knowledge areas listed in the NICCS Cyber Ops Planners knowledge set with targeted knowledge and skills related to tactics, techniques, procedures, cyber threats, and operational planning in offensive cyber operations. It provides a more detailed and focused subset of competencies within the broader cybersecurity and network operations field described in the NICCS Cyber Ops Planners knowledge set.

The literature review results and the NICCS Cyber Ops Planners' knowledge devised the knowledge list. These provide a more targeted and specific subset of competencies within the broader cybersecurity and network operations field described in the NICCS Cyber Ops Planners knowledge set. It refines and specifies the requirements for OCO planners. The specific contributions of new knowledge are knowledge of the cyber centre of gravity (a critical point—a source of power for the adversary's cyber operations); they can target it (Smart 2011) and cyberweapon(s) deployment and reuse periods (shelf-life) (Lidestri 2022).

The existing NICCS Cyber Ops Planners' knowledge set was refined through a comprehensive understanding of various crucial aspects. These included cyber threats (Barber et al. 2016), cyberspace operations (Bender 2013), core competencies and professional networking [6]. Additionally, they delved into intelligence collection capabilities (Barber et al. 2016), joint functions and operational procedures (Bender 2013). This knowledge was further enriched by exploring the kill chain framework (Barber et al. 2016), and cyber threats analysis (Neville et al. 2020).

3.3 Skillset

These results contribute to NICCS Cyber Ops Planners' skills by providing a more specialised and detailed set of skills and abilities related to cyber operations. While NICCS Cyber Ops Planners skills focus on administrative and planning activities, the results delve deeper into cyber operations' cognitive and technical aspects. These skills, such as cyber intelligence analysis (Neville et al. 2020), targeting (Smart 2011), analytical skills (Mulford 2013), and technical planning (Barber et al. 2016), provide a more specific and comprehensive understanding of the competencies required for effective cyber operations planning.

Incorporating the results into NICCS Cyber Ops Planners skillsets enriches the overall competency profile, offering a more holistic view of the skills needed for Offensive Cyber Operations planners. It provides a bridge between administrative and planning activities and the technical and cognitive aspects of cyber operations, ensuring that planners are well-equipped to address the multifaceted challenges in the cyber domain. The merged skills list provides a comprehensive set of competencies covering administrative planning and the technical aspects of offensive cyber operations, offering a well-rounded view of the skills required for Offensive Cyber Operations planners.

3.4 Abilities

This systematic review contributes to NICCS Cyber Ops Planners' abilities by providing a more specialised and detailed set of abilities and cognitive skills related to cyber operations planning. While NICCS Cyber Ops Planners' abilities focus on general communication and collaboration skills, the systematic review inquires more profoundly into the abilities required for effective coordination in offensive cyber operations. The cognitive skills introduced in the Manual of Navy Enlisted Manpower and Personnel Classifications and Occupational Standards (Navy Personnel Command 2023), such as deductive reasoning, originality, and problem sensitivity, provide a more comprehensive understanding of the competencies needed for complex problem-solving in the cyber domain.

Assembling current review abilities into NICCS Cyber Ops Planners' abilities enriches the overall competency profile, offering a more holistic view of the knowledge, skills, abilities, and experiences required for cyber operations planners. It bridges the gap between general communication and collaboration skills and the specialised abilities necessary for successful planning and coordination in the cyber operations field.

This review contributed to the additions to the NICCS Cyber Ops Planners' abilities, such as the ability to lead joint operations and develop cyber capability, doctrine, and tactics. Ability to conduct offensive cyber operations effectively (Withers 2018). Abilities for ongoing intelligence gathering and planning to deter or defeat cyber-attacks (Barber et al. 2016). Communication abilities, such as written and -oral expression. Abilities in Deductive Reasoning, Originality, Inductive Reasoning, Problem Sensitivity, Information Ordering, Fluency of Ideas and Selective Attention (Navy Personnel Command 2023).

3.5 Experience

Individuals in the Cyber Planner work role typically possess a diverse skill set gained from hands-on experience in multiple Cyber Mission Force roles encompassing defensive and offensive operations. This practical experience extends to the development and execution of cyber operation plans, demonstrating their proficiency in translating strategic objectives into actionable tactics within the cyberspace domain. Moreover, these professionals have a comprehensive understanding of the intricacies of the cyber realm, including its lexicon, authorities, guidance, organisational structures, and command relationships. They leverage this knowledge to navigate the complex landscape of cyberspace operations planning and to make informed decisions that align with strategic objectives. Their expertise extends to the core competencies of cyberspace operations, which include professional networking, social collaboration, and information systems technology. These competencies facilitate effective communication and cooperation within and beyond cyberspace. Furthermore, individuals in this role are well-versed in joint functions and operational procedures, allowing them to integrate cyberspace operations into broader military strategies seamlessly. They excel in the development and execution of operational plans, ensuring that they align with broader military objectives and are executed efficiently. In addition to practical experience, they have a background in military education, training, and certifications, which underscores their commitment to continuous learning and professional development. The proficiency they achieve is the result of several years of dedicated experience in the field, making them highly qualified and effective in their roles as Cyber Planners.

4 Discussion

This paper's objective was to define the role of an operational-level OCO planner. The operational skills, digital skills, soft skills, and experience required for the competencies needed in the operational-level OCO planner were identified. This enabled a framework to be devised, including a training plan, required skillsets, and all necessary competencies to become a practical OCO planner.

Initially, the role of an operational-level OCO planner was defined. The literature revealed four definitions. In summary, while all definitions describe a Cyber Operations Planner's role, they differ in emphasis. The first definition focuses on collaboration and execution, the second on broad functions and experience, the third on mission analysis and coordination, and the fourth on monitoring and compliance. Only the NIST Frameworks definition includes the targeting, a unique attribute for OCO planners. Together, they provide a comprehensive view of the responsibilities and skills of the Cyber Operations Planner role.

The literature led us to identify new knowledge, skills, abilities, and experience required for the competencies needed in the operational-level OCO planner. The summary of identified knowledge, skills, abilities, and experience is presented in Table 4. Considering the small amount of available literature and despite the existing OCO planner's NICCS framework, this significantly contributes to defining an OCO planner's competencies.

An essential skill of OCO planners is the analysis of network metadata (Mulford 2013). A significant part of operational planning takes place in the logical layer. The logical and cyber-persona layers are interconnected, with state borders affecting hardware components' geographical positions. They consist of code or data entities, allowing communication and action between the physical and cyber-persona layers. COs occur at the logical layer (AJP-3.20 2020, pp. 3,17). Additionally, to achieve the intended result by cyber methods, logical and physical targets must be considered simultaneously (Arik et. al. 2022). To grasp the logical layer, planners must have the ability to understand and analyse network data. Otherwise, planning will suffer, and the entire mission may be at risk.

The critical knowledge identified was the deployment and reuse periods(shelf-life) of cyber weapons (Lidestri 2022). This is a unique and critical knowledge that very few publications have addressed. For example, a recent Rand Corporation report suggested planning, budgeting, and collecting historical data to procure cyberweapons. The research underscored the growing value and demand for specific exploits, particularly in mobile platforms, messaging apps, and specific zero-click and remote exploit categories. It also depicted the shifting landscape where Android exploits gained prominence over iOS, evidenced by the dramatic increase in Android value from 2015 to 2019 (Rand Corporation 2023).

Another required knowledge is about the adversary's source of power (Smart 2011). OCO planning involves identifying the cyber centre of gravity and establishing boundaries for joint operations. Targeting aligned with the cyber centre of gravity minimises the potential for lateral damage and effects.

A specific skill for OCO planners is targeting. Targeting involves knowledge, skills and tasks (NICCS 2023). Together, these lead to assessing vulnerabilities and capabilities, using intelligence to counter potential actions, and collaborating across different entities to create effective strategies to address or neutralise potential threats. Additionally, the NICCS Cyber Ops Planners Work Role described the Task, which was outside this paper's scope but provided a vast overview of activities needed for OCO planners.

A solid background in doctrinal joint functions and operations procedures is necessary for cyberspace operations planners. (Bender 2013). This is critical to breaking down the barriers between traditional and cyber operations, advocating for a shared understanding, collaboration, and integration between these two spheres for more effective joint military endeavours.

To become a practical OCO planner, self-learning is encouraged to build professional skills, including cyber domain expertise, professional reading, blogs, societies, conferences, videos, podcasts, and training sources (Bender 2013). This is supported by the NICCS Cyber Ops Planners Work Role Capability Indicators, which recommend 40 h annually of mentoring, shadowing, conferences, webinars or rotations (NICCS 2023). Cyber domain expertise can be gained through NATO CCDCOE-organised exercises such as Locked Shields[4] and Crossed Swords[5]. The Locked Shields exercise pits Red and Blue teams in handling large-scale cyber incidents, requiring effective reporting, strategic decision-making, and forensic, legal, and media challenges. The Crossed Swords exercise includes leadership training for the command element(planners) and joint cyber-kinetic operations. These exercises provide an excellent opportunity to obtain DCO and OCO proficiency to become a practical OCO planner.

This work also proposed a training plan that covers advanced cyber warfare, network attacks, operations, information security, troubleshooting, and risk management. It equips individuals with the necessary skills for effective OCO planning. One must complete civilian and military education and training to acquire the skills required to become a proficient OCO planner.

5   Limitations and Future Work

The reviewed literature had several limitations. A few of the sources were not subjected to peer assessment. For example, master's theses (Curnutt and Sikes 2021), (Houston 2019) and (Lidestri 2022). However, these are scholarly sources due to their close supervision, academic audience, extensive research, research methodology, and citation in other scholarly work.

Several sources needed to be more scholarly in nature. One such instance is the contract with the U.S. General Services Administration (U.S. General Services Administration 2022). Since the contract is a governmental arrangement, one can assume that audits have been conducted. This contract also provided insightful information that helped define the Cyber Operations Planner. Another helpful document was the Manual of Navy Enlisted Manpower and Personnel Classifications and Occupational Standards as Chapter 20 (Navy Personnel Command 2023). This paper was beneficial in outlining the competencies of Cyber Operations Planners.

The search terms related to offensive cyber operations planners' competencies may limit the research scope, as they may need to be narrower and specific. The terms "cyber operations competencies" and "cyber operational planner" vary in detail, and some terms may yield redundant information due to their similarity. Few articles on offensive

---

[4] https://ccdcoe.org/exercises/locked-shields/.

[5] https://ccdcoe.org/exercises/crossed-swords/.

cyberspace operations competencies are published due to secrecy, security concerns, legal and ethical considerations, and public disclosure incentives.

For future work, expert interviews with persons who have completed the task themselves should be used to validate the suggested framework in subsequent studies. Lastly, contact Cyber Command's human resources to learn how long it takes to educate an offensive operation planner.

6 Conclusions

The Offensive Cyber Operations competencies required for operational planning have yet to be fully documented and are significantly lacking compared to those for defensive cyber operations. We found only one framework for Offensive Cyber Operations competencies for operational planners. The National Initiative for Cybersecurity Careers and Studies Cyber Ops Planner's work role provided the foundation for this paper's new framework development. This paper resulted in a Framework for Offensive Cyber Operations Planners, which benefits Cyber Headquarters operational planners' training and development plans. As well as the proposed framework can contribute to preparing and planning NATO cyber operations exercises. Standards for offensive operations roles, definitions and competencies must be developed and implemented in studies.

To conclude, the experience required for an OCO planner typically possesses a combination of practical experience and knowledge. These include experience in multiple cyber operations in various defensive and offensive roles. The development and execution of cyber operations plans require an understanding of cyber-related terminology and structures and proficiency in cyberspace core competencies. These should be combined with a familiarity with joint functions and operational procedures and a military education, training, and certifications background. This expertise is typically acquired over several years of experience in the field.

Acknowledgements. The EU Horizon2020 project MariCybERA (agreement No 952360) funded research for this publication. We also thank Dr Cate Jerram from the University of Adelaide.

References

AJP-3.20. Allied joint doctrine for cyberspace operations. Nato Standardization Office (NSO) (2020). https://www.gov.uk/government/publications/allied-joint-doctrine-for-cyberspace-operations-ajp-320

Arik, M., et al.: Planning cyberspace operations: exercise crossed swords case study. J. Inf. Warfare **70** (2022)

Barber, D.E., et al.: Cyberspace operations planning: operating a technical military. Military Cyber Aff. **1**(1), 3 (2016)

Bender, J.M.: The cyberspace operations planner. Small Wars J. **16** (2013)

Bendler, D., Felderer, M.: Competency models for information security and cybersecurity professionals: analysis of existing work and a new model. ACM Trans. Comput. Educ. **23**, 1–33 (2023)

Caton, J.L.: Implications of Service Cyberspace Component Commands for Army Cyberspace Operations. USAWC Press, Carlisle (2019)

Chowdhury, N., Gkioulos, V.: Key competencies for critical infrastructure cyber-security: a systematic literature review. Inf. Comput. Secur. **29**, 697–723 (2021)

Curnutt, A.J., Sikes, S.R.: Naval postgraduate school. Thesis - knowledge management application to cyber protection team defense operations (2021). https://apps.dtic.mil/sti/citations/AD1164246

ENISA. Information Operations – Active Defence and Offensive Countermeasures. ENISA (2016). https://www.enisa.europa.eu/topics/incident-response/glossary/information-operations-2013-active-defence-and-offensive-countermeasures

Houston, R.: Thriving Cybersecurity Professionals: Building a Resilient Workforce and Psychological Safety in the Federal Government. University of Pennsylvania, Pennsylvania (2019

Huskaj, G., Axelsson, S.: A whole-of-society approach to organise for offensive cyberspace operations: the case of the smart state Sweden. In: Proceedings of the 22nd European Conference on Cyber Warfare and Security, ECCWS 2023 (2023. https://pdfs.semanticscholar.org/b106/105500fcefd1d554a7dae6f06b2bd1d2c41a.pdf

Jensen, M.S.: Five good reasons for NATO's pragmatic approach to. Def. Stud. **465** (2022)

Joint Pub 5-0. Doctrine for Planning Joint Operations. Retrieved from Doctrine for Planning Joint Operations (1995). https://edocs.nps.edu/dodpubs/topic/jointpubs/JP5/JP5-0_950413.pdf

Joint Publication 1. Doctrine for the Armed Forces of the United States. Retrieved from Joint Doctrine Publications - Joint Chiefs of Staff (2013). https://irp.fas.org/doddir/dod/jp1.pdf

Jøsok, Ø., et al.: Self-regulation and cognitive agility in cyber operations. Front. Psychol. **10**, 410188 (2019)

Libicki, M.C., Tkacheva, O.: Cyberspace escalation: ladders or lattices? In: CCDCOE, Tallinn (2020)

Lidestri, M.R.: Incorporating perishability and obsolescence into cyberweapon scheduling, MONTEREY, California, U.S (2022

Moher, D., et al.: Preferred reporting items for systematic review and meta-analysis protocols (PRISMA-P) 2015 statement. Syst. Rev. **4**, 1–9 (2015)

Mulford, L.A.: Let slip the dogs of (cyber) war: progressing towards a warfighting US cyber command. Joint Advanced Warfighting School, Norfolk (2013)

National Institute of Health. What are competencies? Retrieved from Office of Human Resources (2023). https://hr.nih.gov/about/faq/working-nih/competencies/what-are-competencies

NATO CCDCOE. NATO CCDCOE Training Catalogue 2023 (2023). https://ccdcoe.org/uploads/2023/09/2023_NATO_CCD_COE_Training_Catalogue_final.pdf

NATO Standardization Office. Allied Joint Publication-3.20. Allied Joint Doctrine for Cyberspace Operations (2020). https://assets.publishing.service.gov.uk/government/uploads/system/uploads/attachment_data/file/899678/doctrine_nato_cyberspace_operations_ajp_3_20_1_.pdf

Navy Personnel Command. Chapter 20 Cryptologic technician (Networks) (CTN). Navy Personnel Command (2023). https://www.mynavyhr.navy.mil/Portals/55/Reference/NEOCS/Vol1/CTN_occs_CH_95_Jul23.pdf?ver=CWQ8uOEoG-z0c7PLZqXKRg%3d%3d

Neville, K., et al.: United States Army Research Institute for the Behavioral and Social Sciences. A Cognitive Skills Research Framework for Complex Operational Environments (2020). https://apps.dtic.mil/sti/pdfs/AD1091744.pdf

NICCS. Cyber Operational Planning. National Initiative for Cybersecurity Careers And Studies (2023). https://niccs.cisa.gov/workforce-development/nice-framework/specialty-areas/cyber-operational-planning

Nizich, M.: Emerald insight. The Cyberhero and the Cybercriminal (2023): https://www.emerald.com/insight/content/doi/https://doi.org/10.1108/978-1-80382-915-920231006/full/html

RAND Corporation. Educating for Evolving Operational Domains. RAND Corporation, California (2022)

Rand Corporation. A Cost Estimating Framework for U.S. Marine Corps Joint Cyber Weapons. Santa Monica: RAND Corporation. For more information on this publication (2023). www.rand.org/t/RRA1124-1

Shoemaker, D., Kohnke, A., Sigler, K.: A Guide to the National Initiative for Cybersecurity Education (NICE) Cybersecurity Workforce Framework (2.0). CRC Press, Boca Raton (2016)

Smart, S.J.: Joint Targeting in Cyberspace. Washington, Pentagon, U.S (2011)

Tricco, A.C., et al.: PRISMA extension for scoping reviews (PRISMA-ScR): checklist and explanation. Ann. Internal Med. **169**, 467–473 (2018)

U.S. General Services Administration. U.S. General Services Administration. General services administration Federal Supply Service Federal Supply Schedule Price List (2022). https://www.gsaadvantage.gov/ref_text/47QTCA22D00C8/0XKGIE.3TATEZ_47QTCA22D00C8_NNDATA47QTCA22D00C8A81509012022.PDF

United States Army War College. Strategic Cyberspace Operations Guide (2022). https://media.defense.gov/2023/Oct/02/2003312499/-1/-1/0/STRATEGIC_CYBERSPACE_OPERATIONS_GUIDE.PDF

Goździewicz, W.: Cyber Defense Magazine. Retrieved from Voluntarily by Allies (SCEPVA) (2019). https://www.cyberdefensemagazine.com/sovereign-cyber/

Withers, P.: Integrating cyber with air power in the second century of the royal air force. Royal Air Force Air Power Rev. **21**(3), 148–151 (2018)

Unraveling the Real-World Impacts
of Cyber Incidents on Individuals

Danielle Renee Jacobs[1]([⊠]) [ID], Nicole Darmawaskita[2] [ID], and Troy McDaniel[3] [ID]

[1] School of Computing and Augmented Intelligence, Arizona State University,
Tempe, AZ 85281, USA
danielle.r.jacobs@asu.edu
[2] The Polytechnic School, Arizona State University, Mesa, AZ 85212, USA
[3] School of Manufacturing Systems and Networks, Arizona State University,
Mesa, AZ 85212, USA

Abstract. With the increase in ubiquitous technology and the rise in cyber threats, individuals are exposed to cyber events that can cause significant harm. Every individual is at risk, even those with expertise and experience. The cascading harms of a cyber-attack can lead to short-term and long-term consequences for the victim. The narratives that emerge from individual experiences with cyber threats paint a vivid picture of the prevailing harm landscape. Here, we describe a semi-structured interview study of 18 participants who were either victims of a cyber-related incident or have been exposed to threats, providing a more comprehensive picture of everyday people's challenges, harms, and needs. This paper examines the research question: What experiences do individuals face after a cyber-related incident? Several key themes are presented in this article.

Keywords: Cybersecurity · Human factors · Information security · Privacy · Usability · Cyber harm · Cyber risk

1 Introduction

Cybersecurity is increasingly becoming an issue for individuals as they rely on more information and communication technology (ICT). The unprecedented outbreak of the COVID-19 pandemic further amplified this issue, leading to an increase in phishing attacks through clickbait that focused on exploiting the hysteria [19]. Before the uptake in cybercrime, Americans had a 1 in 3 chance of being hacked; it stands to reason that the chances of being hacked have only increased [30]. Organizations, often faced with similar challenges, albeit at a very different scale, use modeling, risk assessments, statistical analysis, and technical expertise to inform policies that mitigate the harm of adverse events. Unfortunately, the average person does not have the tools or resources organizations

The authors thank Arizona State University and the National Science Foundation for their funding support under Grant No. 1828010.

rely on to become more secure and, therefore, depends on software, hardware, and top-down policy solutions. The nuances and intricacies of harm are murky, particularly given limited data on the subject [13].

Prior work has examined what harms users' experience and sought to look at it through several different lenses. Often, prior research has focused on the impact of specific incidents on people [17,31]. For example, Zangerle and Specht [31] examined Twitter data to capture the impacts of Twitter account breaches on individuals. Previous work has documented mental models from cyberattacks with some discussion of harmful impacts [5,12,15] or explored the socio-technological relationships with technology in cyberspace [3,9,21]. Emami-Naeini et al. [9] looked at how security factors into Internet of Things (IoT) device purchase behavior and found that people reported security information difficult to find. Haney et al. [10] gathered user opinions about smart home devices and responsibility. According to the survey results, users and manufacturers are perceived to hold the most ownership in securing devices because of the knowledge manufacturers possess and the onus users take on when adopting a device. Bada and Nurse [4] provide a chapter summarizing cyber-attacks' social and psychological impacts to both individuals and organizations. Meanwhile, other authors have explored harms by examining the impacts of cyberbullying [6,7]. Scheuerman et al. [25] capture user experience with harmful content (e.g., Hate Speech, Violence) and have taken strides towards capturing the severity of harm. These efforts move the needle toward understanding the user experience and the near- and long-term consequences users suffer, but still miss capturing the impacts and stories across a variety of different threats. While targeted studies that look at technologies, demographics, or narrow types of harm are crucial to building human-centered cybersecurity policies and tools, it is also essential to document how incidents impact people.

By documenting real-world experiences, impacts, and harms, we take a step towards garnering valuable insights. These insights are critical in shaping meaningful policy and technical solutions. Before framing our study, we surveyed the literature to identify prevalent cyber threats users encounter. This list became the criteria for participation in the study. However, the data does not represent every type of cyber-related incident. Nevertheless, our diverse pool of respondents provides a citizen-centered picture of people's challenges, harms, mindsets, and needs.

Our research revolves around a central question: What experiences do individuals face after a cyber-related incident? Throughout the study, several themes emerged. Some of these insights echo previous studies, such as the need for cybersecurity education [26,29]. In contrast, some findings are unique to our research, like the frequent appeal from affected participants for a platform to share experiences and heighten awareness. The paper is the first in a series that translates the qualitative findings around experiences into a framework to help build better ways to understand harm.

2   Methods

We conducted a literature survey and 18 semi-structured interviews with victims of a cyber-related incident or individuals exposed to potential cyber incidents. The authors performed a literature review to catalog different cyber threats researchers have recorded users encountering. This list became one of the main criteria for participation in the study and helped to scope a broad topic down to previously documented experiences. Second, we interviewed 18 people who met the criteria about their experience. The interviews underwent several rounds of qualitative coding, emphasizing In Vivo, Thematic Analysis, and Narrative Coding [24].

2.1   Identifying Areas of Cyber Incidents

The authors examined the experiences and impacts on individuals reported in the literature through a literature review and open-coding process. This was to help better scope the interview questions and ensure that definitions used in the study reflected existing work. In particular, this literature review informed what the study considered a cyber experience and therefore influenced the criteria for inclusion into the study. The first author of this study performed the literature review. Search criteria included individuals, not groups, and terms like cyber-harm, cyber-incident, and cyber consequences of users. Incidents discussed across the papers included things such as harmful cyber online content, ransomware, scams, cyberbullying, data breaches. The final list is reflected in Table 1. It is important to note that these are not always mutually exclusive events.

Table 1. List cyber incidents reported across the surveyed papers. Experiencing an item in the list was a requirement to participate in the study.

Previously Reported Cyber Experiences
Email or Website Scam (Phishing)
Denial of Service (DoS)
Victim of Data Breach
Ransomware
Cyberbullying
Fraud or Identity Theft
Harmful Online Content
Invasive spyware, device recording, data usage
Virus, malware, data corruption
Physical loss or damage of computer, phone, device

2.2   Interview Design

Participants needed to be 18 years or older and experienced one of the cyber-events in Table 1 within the past 12-months. We chose a 12-month time frame because the literature reported that an event within 12 months was recent enough to have good recall but broad enough to find participants who qualify [6]. Another motivating factor for the 12-month requirement is the data variety. We could see the long-term impacts of participants nearer to a year since the cyber incident and the short-term emotions of participants whose experience is fresh. We also collected a short demographic survey to capture standard background information and details such as the interviewee's background with computers. To develop interviews that elicit narratives about the subjects experience, the interview questions focused on capturing the different impacts due to cyber-harms [2, 25]. Two colleagues, who met the criteria, participated in a pilot study to test the interview protocol. The pilot led to integrating more targeted questions. After the final study design, we obtained Institutional Review Board (IRB) approval for human subjects research.

2.3   Participant Recruitment

Recruitment ran from September through October of 2023. We used social media posts, flyers, email, and snowballing to find participants. The initial study design aimed to collect 15 to 25 participants for the semi-structured interviews. These numbers are informed by previous exploitative qualitative interview research in cybersecurity [28, 32]. Participants were compensated with a $50 Amazon gift card. The authors tried to recruit a collection of cyber-related experiences from Table 1. However, it was not an expectation to have an even distribution of experiences or every experience from the table represented, considering some types of experiences are much more prevalent.

2.4   Data Collection

We conducted 18 semi-structured interviews that ranged from 30–60 min via online video conferencing. During the interview, participants were asked questions about the recent cyber-incident, but allowed to discuss other incidents, even if the other incidents were older than 1 year. After the interview, the participants completed a short demographic survey. Each participant was assigned a study identification number. The transcript, video, audio, and survey were then named with the study number and not attached to personal data. Prior to the start of the recording, the participant's name in the video conferencing software was updated to match the identification number.

2.5   Interview Data Analysis

Analysis of interview data used an In Vivo Coding process. The primary coder performed two rounds of coding. The first cycle used In Vivo Coding on 10 interviews. The two coders met to review the results of the first cycle and then developed a codebook to group the data into thematic categories [24]. The discussion helped standardize definitions for the codes. For the data analysis, the team used QSR International's Nvivo Software [16].

The second cycle of coding used partner coding. In the second cycle, both coders used the established codebook on all 18 interviews. Throughout the process, if there were concerns over the initial codebook, including changes to definitions or new code suggestions, the two researchers met to discuss, align, and update the codebook. Table 2 shows the final codebook, resulting definitions.

Table 2. Final Codebook from the interviews.

Codebook	
Name	Definition
Needs	Necessities (governance, policy, justice, education, cultural, awareness, technology changes) subject identified because of the incident
Response	The way in which the participant reacted to the event. Includes both systemic responses (e.g., calling the bank) or personal responses (e.g., talking to friends)
Financial Harm	Impact to the subjects' finances
Operational Harm	Impact to how a subject usually operates
Physical Harm	Impact to the subjects' physical being or physical access or physical impact to the device
Psychological Harm	Impact to a subjects emotions, feelings, and psychology
Social Harm	Impact to how subjects interact with others

3   Results

In this section, we report the results from the surveys and interviews. For the interviews, we first report unique stories. After providing an overview of some of the interviews, we present the results of the coding process and thematic analysis.

3.1   Survey

Details of the survey results can be found in Table 3. One person did not answer the survey correctly, and the results for that participant have been omitted. Another participant did not submit an answer to the cyber experience survey question and, therefore, is not reported in the variable Cyber Experience. However, the subject's answers to other variables are included. Cyber Experience is reported as a count and all other results are reported as percentages out of 17 total participants, due to the one in-valid survey. The variable Cyber Experience was a self-reported question intended to capture the cyber-related experience the participant wanted to discuss. Participants were allowed to select multiple options for the question because the categories are not mutually exclusive. For example, a phishing attempt may be related to a data breach. In total, twelve participants selected more than one answer. Definitions and examples of the cyber experiences were provided to the participants in the survey. Nearly half of participants reported having previous training in information technology systems. The survey results also show a wide range of ages, education, and income.

Table 3. Survey Results

Variable	Results
Age	18–24 years (35%)
	30–34 years (29%)
	35–39 years (6%)
	40–44 years (18%)
	54–59 years (12%)
Gender	Man (29%)
	Woman (71%)
Level of Education	High school (6%)
	Bachelor's Degree (47%)
	Master's Degree (29%)
	Professional degree (18%)
Related Education	I have an education in or experience in computer science, computer engineering, or IT. (47%)
	I do not have an education in or experience in computer science, computer engineering, or IT. (53%)
Income	Under $15,000 (6%)
	$15,000 to $24,999 (12%)
	$35,000 to $49,999 (6%)
	$75,000 to $99,999 (12%)
	$100,000 to $149,999 (12%)
	$150,000 or above (35%)
	Prefer not to say (18%)
Cyber Experience	Email or Website Scam (Phishing) (8)
	Denial of Service (DoS) (3)
	Ransomware (0)
	Cyberbullying (3)
	Fraud or Identity Theft (including social media account hack/stolen) (7)
	Harmful Online Content (7)
	Invasive Spyware, Device Recording, or Data Usage (3)
	Virus, Malware, or Data Corruption (4)
	Physical Loss or Damage (1)

3.2   Interviews

This section presents the results of the 18 interviews. First, we present a profile of the experiences where similar incidents are grouped. Interview questions focused on the impacts and harms participants faced. Coding also focused on capturing financial, physical, social, operational, and psychological harms shared in the interviews. In presenting the experiences across different incidents, we rely on the different categories of harm to characterize the experiences. After profiling different stories, we review other thematic analysis results.

Profile of Experiences. One challenge academics face is finding good data and resources. For companies and governments cyber experiences are characterized in news reports and case studies [11]. These sources can be used to evaluate the impacts on organizations [2,4]. The same understanding and data should exist for individuals. This next section gives a profile of participants' experiences to fill the gap and provide a resource for researchers.

The Banking Incidents. There is no denying that financial fraud is a significant driver for cyber-criminals. The participants in this research were no exception. Out of the 18 participants in the study, 11 reported stories related to banking fraud. Of the 11 participants, seven discussed stolen credit card or debit card numbers. A participant who reported knowledge of being a victim of several high-profile data breaches also suffered the opening of illegal checking accounts in his name. Additionally, participants discussed threats to banking and payment applications, such as a hacked Venmo account.

Two participants included stories of older family members falling for social engineering attempts to gain access to bank accounts. In one narrative, P15's family member lost roughly $3,000 from retirement savings. Participant P05 shared a story of an older relative who nearly gave away her Unified Payment Interface (UPI) pin through a social engineering attack. In India, UPI allows multiple accounts to be managed on one interface and seamless fund transfers [20]. Most of these transfers require a UPI pin; if the criminal has enough information, the pin can serve as the final stopgap. Giving the pin away after already providing account information is paramount to giving away money. P05 interrupted the call with the scammer and prevented the pin from being leaked, thereby stopping the theft.

Most participants in this group reported no long-term financial loss due to the bank's ability to credit fraudulent purchases back to the individual. Only one participant, P15, discussed a significant financial loss because she could not help her older family member avoid a scam. Nevertheless, participants suffered financial loss in other ways. Many reported taking time from work or valuable personal time to deal with the issue. As one participant put it, *"but the time and effort spent to remedy the situation was significant" (P17)*. The same participant suffered checking account fraud and raised a concern that, while he did not lose money, he believed the accounts were likely used in money laundering. Participant P07, who reported a Venmo account hack, did not lose any money but had to spend time on her account responding to everyone the hacker contacted.

In credit and debit cases, participants often reported a slight impact on how they interact with friends and family. P09 reported challenges in repaying her boyfriend: *"It's definitely changed my relationship."* She reflected more on how limited funds impacted her other relationships, *"Then also, I feel like, during the time where my card was hacked, I had to cancel all the social things I planned because I didn't have any access to funds" (P09).* While the effects were not life-changing, they did cause inconvenience to friends and family. For participants who shared stories of older family members, the impact often resulted in more responsibility to assist the older adult. P05, who stopped his mother from giving the UPI pin to the criminals, reported that he and his familly built a new system where he checks any UPI requests for his mom.

In addition to the impacts on how the participants operated and interacted with friends and family, there were physical impacts reported by participants who had card fraud. For some, these physical impacts had workarounds, such as utilizing digital payment systems. Others were not so lucky. P09 had her account frozen, *"I called my bank to freeze it [the card], but the woman who I was talking to kind of confused me, and she put a hold on my entire bank account, not just that debit card".*

Participants suffered other impacts on how they usually operate due to the threats. People who suffered credit card and debit card fraud reported issues in accessing and using the cards. P10 reported, *"The week following it affected the speed through which I was able to do some things. Like if I wanted to order something on Amazon, if I wanted to refill my Starbucks card..."* Overall, participants who suffered banking-related incidents found it impacted the way they were able to use their money, *"I can't really figure out any other way to pay" (P07).*

Suffering through all of the impacts, participants reported several emotions. Among the most reported emotional impacts were anger and frustration. We found that seven of the banking related interviews mentioned emotions akin to anger and frustration at least once. For example, P12 remarked they, *"generally just felt frustrated."* Feelings of sadness, panic, and stress were shared among the participants. P17 highlighted the invasion of privacy that many participants reported, *"The initial reaction was, let's say, one of violation and shock because someone's using your personal information."*

Participants took a variety of actions. While many reactions to dealing with the situation vary from person to person, some responses stand out either by being a common response or as a mitigation technique. In the credit and debit card theft, the participants relied heavily on the banking system to help recover the stolen money. One participant recalled the bank's response, *"they were able to respond very quickly. Like in that moment, I spoke to like a real person, not just a machine. And he was able to reinstate a new card in that moment" (P10).* When working with older family members who experienced social engineering attacks to gain access to bank accounts, P15 and P05 built-in checks to help family avoid scams in the future. Participant P17, who had checking accounts opened in his name, filed an affidavit with the police department. He then ensured that more checking and savings accounts could not be opened by using a service called ChexSystems to place a freeze. ChexSystems' website says, "A security freeze is designed to prevent approval of checking, savings, credit accounts, loans, or other services from being approved in your name without your consent" [8]. P17 also put credit freezes in place with the three major credit bureaus.

Phishing. In the interview pool, eight participants reported stories of phishing attempts. Of these phishing schemes, most were messaging-related scams or smishing. The smishing scams involved messages about package deliveries or banking alerts. Some phishing attempts overlap with card fraud or bank account theft, such as participant P08, who recalled, *"I got a text message that a package from UPS was being delivered, but it could not finish the delivery because it needed an updated address... Because of the change in location, there was a fee... you had to insert your credit card information in order to pay the small fee to get the package relocated. And I did it."*

Of the eight phishing experiences, only two participants discussed unique phishing scenarios. For one, an email phishing attempt used information from a previous data breach. Participant P01 described, *"the subject of that email was my old password that I had used across many different accounts, and websites, online platforms, different apps."* The phishing email threatened to share lies about P01 unless P01 sent Bitcoin to the scammer. Another participant, P04, was a victim of a phishing attempt on Discord that used a QR code.

Participants reported minimal financial impact, except for P15's family member who lost retirement savings. Other financial impacts took the form of time lost dealing with the phishing attempt and money spent on resources to protect information better. One participant recalled the time spent responding to the Discord hack: *"It did cost me a lot of time to fix all of the things that went wrong... people say time's money" (P04).* Other participants spent money on extra storage due to a large number of phishing scams, while another participant spent money on authentication tools to better protect accounts. For example, P01 described the benefit of purchasing a security service, *"if anything happens to my account, I'll be notified and now have a team of experts to reach out to, so that's one option that I took."*

Most participants impacted by phishing reported only minimum impacts to their social life. Most cited the time it takes to clean out phishing emails or concerns over more vulnerable family members. For example, P16 mentioned, *"a lot of close family members of mine, especially the people who are older, 60 plus... I've seen them falling for it" (P16).* The Discord QR Code hack, however, led to significant social consequences. Hackers sent inappropriate information to every contact P04 had on Discord. While close friends understood that P04 had been hacked, not everyone did. P04 reflected, *"It was just a stupid mistake on my side, and just a little embarrassing for me to tell my friends that this happened.*

Professionally, it did impact me, because I was kicked out of a few groups related to networking with tech communities." P04 suffered some of the more extreme social and professional impacts of those interviewed.

Study results showed that the experiences, even if participants do not fall for a phishing or smishing attempt, have a psychological impact. Three participants reported feelings of frustration. For example, one subject noted *"I get frustrated, to be honest, because I mean, these web, email services are trying their best to auto filter them from showing up in an inbox, but they still keep happening" (P16).* Stress was another common consequence, voiced by four participants. For example, the P04 commented, *"it was very stressful for me to deal with because, like, I didn't want to be the person that they associated this with."* Similarly, the email incident used password information in the subject line, leading to prolonged stress for P01, *"for two straight days, I was scared because it was my personal password."*

Participants did speak of habit changes to avoid falling victim again. P16 described the constant influx of phishing attacks: *"When I click on an email or click on any link, I have to re-check it multiple times to make sure that I'm not being phished. I think that adds a lot of overhead to my day-to-day life and how I operate."* Other participants discussed implementing practices to prevent future mistakes. P08, P15, and P11 described trying to read messages when more alert.

Participants took noteworthy actions to respond to the phishing attempts and prevent future incidents. Many participants attempted to research more information about the incident, including googling information about the phishing attempt. Others crowd-sourced information from family, friends, or more official institutions like banks. P08 reported a need to verify with those around, *"I make my husband look and read it and say, do you think this is real?"* P12 also needed too ask workers and friends before making a decision.

Online Harm. Outside the banking and phishing experiences, participants discussed various other cyber incidents online. This group of interviewees had other, more unique stories. Participants P17 and P06 spoke about their experience as a victim of a data breach. P17 mainly focused the interview on checking fraud, but noted his data had been impacted by several data breaches. One participant, P14, shared her story of cyberbullying, and another, P03, recounted her experience with an Instagram account hacker who held P03's account ransom.

While many participants did not experience any financial impact, among those who discussed data breaches, there was a sense that impacts could still be unknown. For example, a participant remarked, *"I'm just surprised that I haven't seen something come up for an account being opened in my name" (P06).* Meanwhile, the participant who experienced an Instagram account hack acknowledged that there could have been a financial impact had the response to the attacker gone differently. In response to the targeted online hate, P14 paid for a digital cleanup service to help her remove her digital presence, paying extra to ensure her family was also covered. P14 noted that she *"ended up shelling out a good deal of money for the utilization of this service."*

The participants who experienced a Instagram hack and cyberbullying recounted impacts on family and friends. The hacker who took over P03's Instagram account contacted all her family and friends, asking for money. She noted, *"I had to call many of my family through WhatsApp, and just tell them, 'Hey, listen, just be very careful because of the hacker"' (P03).* P14 noted that she had to protect her loved ones, like adding her spouse to the data online cleanup service and removing photos online. She reflected on removing photos with a family member: *"To protect her, I, you know, locked down and went private on all my various accounts" (P14).* In contrast, those who suffered only data breaches reported no significant social impact.

Participants reported changes in how they operate due to the incident. All of the participants spoke of long-term changes in habits. Once she got her Instagram account back, P03 noted, *"I get Instagram requests for friends, and I'm just hesitant to accept because I'm traumatized."* P03 goes through extra steps to verify that the person is her friend, like communicating verbally before accepting a request. P17 noted that after the checking account fraud and being a victim of numerous data breaches, he has methods in place to protect his credit, but this comes with more steps and does burden his ability to operate normally. For example, P17 confided, *"So if I want to buy a house, buy a car with credit, take out a new credit card, or open up a new checking account, I'm going to have to go through several additional steps to do that."* Finally, since essentially removing her online presence due to cyberbullying, P14 continuously thinks about what information is available online. She remarked, *"I will often try to look up and see what people can find about me if they really wanted to, with enough time."*

Participants described a variety of emotional and psychological responses to the experiences. There was no common feeling reported, but rather a range between the participants. P06 reflected she felt frustration, anger, and irritation at having her medical data exposed in a data breach. P03 reported feelings of violation after the account was hacked followed by concern and guilt for the people the hacker reached out to asking for money. P14 described feelings of isolation. She noted that during the incident, she *"felt afraid, felt kind of despondent and depressed" (P14).* All participants had negative emotions both in the moment and after the incident had passed.

Responding to the incidents took many different forms. P14 used a service to help clean up her information online and deleted her social media accounts. P03 relied on friends to help her login and remove all of the emails and phone numbers the hacker was using. Since the hacker could tell every time P03 tried to reset her account, P03's friend found when the hacker was offline. P03 and her friend used that time to take back her account and reset the password.

Other Social Engineering with Deep Fakes. Finally, the last incident discussed in the interviews was a hostage scam call asking for money. Participant P02 described her experience of receiving a call threatening her daughter's life if she did not continue to send money. The scammer used social engineering and deep fakes to make the situation believable. While not a traditional cyber-incident, the use of online data to create the deep fakes and the money transfers made this experience a candidate for inclusion in our study. P02 did experience financial loss due to the experience, *"I ended up losing $500."* P02 described the experience as shock and fear. She also noted leaving work to deal with the call and losing valuable work time. It was her coworkers and husband who discovered that something was wrong. They worked to find her and inform her she was in the middle of a scam, indicating that the incident impacted P02's family and friends. In response to the experience, P02 has identified steps to prevent a similar scenario. For example, she suggested using a code word. P02 describes the idea, *"So our family all has a code word now... I would ask for that code word. And if the deep fake doesn't give it to me, then I'll know. So it's like a dual authentication."*

3.3 Themes

Besides coding for the different harms, we also focused on identifying beliefs interview participants discussed. It was surprising how often participants voiced similar needs and wants, even if they took slightly different forms. This section reviews what we found.

Raise Awareness. Five of the participants spoke of awareness. One participant spoke of concern for populations who might not be as aware of phishing attacks, *"So there are people who are not aware of the kind of phishing attempts that are going on; it's really easy to steal all of the information and financial data"* *(P18)*. Four participants volunteered to participate in the study to call attention to their experiences and *"spread this story around as much as possible" (P02)*. P01 told the interviewer, *"I wanted to spread what has happened to me; I just don't want anyone else to be part of such."* P04 had a similar motivation, *"I think there should be some kind of awareness that spreads saying that don't, you know, don't scan QR codes that you're not meant to scan."*

Education. Education was another common theme in the interviews. While education can be very similar to awareness, it was essential to separate them. In the interviews, education appeared in the context of formal training, such as integrating cybersecurity into school. P09 reflected that cybersecurity should be taught as a life skill in the classroom. Similarly, P16 mentioned that "education will be more important in this space for everyone that is using the web." After her experience getting hacked, P03 learned about password strength and best practices from a friend, reflecting that learning to protect herself was important.

Justice. Finally, the interviews demonstrated people believe that the government needs to put more effort into holding criminals accountable. When reflecting on money stolen in an online scam from years ago, P12 mentioned, *"I wish that person would go to jail."* For others, there was a wish to be able to find out how the incident even occurred. For example, P09 mused, *"I do wish they could be held a little bit liable, or I wish I could at least have the resources to track down the source of how they got my information."* P17 noted that the checking fraud, while illegal, is only a misdemeanor. P16 was passionate about systemic solutions to this problem, *"so there needs to be tighter control... when it comes to web-related security, we don't have tighter regulations yet."* While some participants complained about the lack of support and regulation, others explained how good it would be to get revenge or justice. For example, *"I would literally pay to know what his facial expression was,"* P03 mused after she got her account back from the hacker.

4   Discussion

Other user-focused research has looked at how aware participants are of data breaches [17], beliefs on IoT device security [10], how vulnerable populations are affected by tools and security best practices [1, 18, 27], how threat models impact understanding of an account breach [23], how stories impact how users understand security [22], and even how mental models can be generated to understand security [5, 14]. This research adds to the prior work by capturing the experiences of victims and those exposed to cyber threats, providing a more comprehensive picture of everyday people's challenges, harms, and needs. We found that there is a wide variety of experiences, but users often experience immediate and long-term harm.

Participants valued awareness and education after the experience. When asked about ways to raise awareness, P04, who suffered the Discord hack, recommended that platforms such as Discord take a more proactive approach to raise awareness. P04 also mentioned that social media influencers, such as a Gaming YouTuber P04 follows, have a platform to raise awareness. As P04 put it, *"Maybe the YouTuber can talk about instances like this... because that he's the one bringing people in, so he can also like give a disclaimer on what could happen. What could go wrong."*

There may be other avenues to raise awareness. One participant noted that she spoke about her experience on the news to help call attention to the issue. Since we saw that googling was a typical response among participants, Google search could help build broader knowledge by pointing to trusted resources. News sources, podcasts, and other information outlets can also release segments about cybersecurity to raise community awareness.

As academics, we have the opportunity to research new ways to integrate cybersecurity awareness and education into existing structures. There is a need to understand the impacts of technology. As one interviewee put it, *"I think that all technology that's developed, we should put it to the test and say how is this going to be a benefit to humanity rather than so many ways that you could use it as a weapon"* (P02).

Participants called for the ability to understand how the incident happened in the first place, hold criminals accountable, and build policies protecting users online. The community should re-examine how we think of cybercrime. Currently, cybercrime is too hard to track or too petty of a crime for legal attention. From these experiences, we see that there are real impacts, and as cybercrime rises, it is essential to find ways to hold criminals accountable.

This work is limited to a relatively small sample size of 18 interviewees. However, the number of participants is informed by previous qualitative interview research in cybersecurity [14,28,32]. Increasing the participant pool can help develop more generalized findings. Future work will seek to apply inter-rater reliability scores to the codes to verify that the codes accurately represent the intended topics. This work also focused on recruiting users who recently experienced a cyber threat, although users were allowed to discuss other experiences. Future improvements may look across a larger time scale. That would provide more context on an attack's short- and long-term impacts.

While there are limitations to this work, it takes a step and documents the consequences users suffer from different cyber incidents. Understanding the consequences across different attacks helps characterize the environment and risks. Researchers often use documented real-world case studies to demonstrate the new frameworks when understanding the cyber landscape in organizations and governments. These user experiences may serve as case studies of users to support similar analyses.

5 Conclusion

This research describes the experiences 18 participants faced after a cyber incident, focusing on the harms and consequences. We also highlight the areas of change participants voiced, such as more education, awareness, and governance. Prior efforts take steps toward understanding the user experience but are limited by narrow scope. We provide breadth by discussing several cyber-attacks and how the attacks impacted participants. Based on the results, we suggest areas of future research. The authors will use this study to understand and represent the harms that humans experience in cyberspace.

References

1. Abdolrahmani, A., Kuber, R.: Should i trust it when i cannot see it? Credibility assessment for blind web users. In: ASSETS 2016 - Proceedings of the 18th International ACM SIGACCESS Conference on Computers and Accessibility, pp. 191–199. Association for Computing Machinery, Inc (2016). https://doi.org/10.1145/2982142.2982173
2. Agrafiotis, I., Nurse, J.R., Goldsmith, M., Creese, S., Upton, D.: A taxonomy of cyber-harms: defining the impacts of cyber-attacks and understanding how they propagate. J. Cybersecur. 4 (2018). https://doi.org/10.1093/cybsec/tyy006
3. Ahmed, T., Shaffer, P., Connelly, K., Crandall, D., Kapadia, A.: Addressing physical safety, security, and privacy for people with visual impairments. In: Proceedings of the 12th Symposium on Usable Privacy and Security, SOUPS 2016, p. 341 (2016). https://www.usenix.org/conference/soups2016/technical-sessions/presentation/ahmed

4. Bada, M., Nurse, J.R.: The social and psychological impact of cyberattacks. In: Emerging Cyber Threats and Cognitive Vulnerabilities, pp. 73–92. Elsevier (2020). https://doi.org/10.1016/b978-0-12-816203-3.00004-6

5. Bravo-Lillo, C., Cranor, L.F., Komanduri, S.: Bridging the gap in computer security warnings: a mental model approach. IEEE Secur. Priv. **April**, 18–26 (2011)

6. Camacho, S., Hassanein, K., Head, M.: Cyberbullying impacts on victims' satisfaction with information and communication technologies: the role of perceived cyberbullying severity. Inf. Manag. **55**(4), 494–507 (2017). https://doi.org/10.1016/j.im.2017.11.004

7. Cao, B., Lin, W.Y.: How do victims react to cyberbullying on social networking sites? The influence of previous cyberbullying victimization experiences. Comput. Hum. Behav. **52**, 458–465 (2015). https://doi.org/10.1016/j.chb.2015.06.009

8. Security freeze information. https://www.chexsystems.com/

9. Emami-Naeini, P., Dixon, H., Agarwal, Y., Cranor, L.F.: Exploring how privacy and security factor into IoT device purchase behavior. In: Conference on Human Factors in Computing Systems - Proceedings, pp. 1–12 (2019). https://doi.org/10.1145/3290605.3300764

10. Haney, J., Acar, Y., Furman, S.: "It's the company, the government, you and I": user perceptions of responsibility for smart home privacy and security. In: Proceedings of the 30th USENIX Security Symposium (2021). https://www.lexico.com/en/definition/responsibility

11. Ashley madison revisited: legal, business and security repercussions. Infosec Institute (2015). https://resources.infosecinstitute.com/topics/news/ashley-madison-revisited-legal-business-and-security-repercussions/

12. Ion, I., Reeder, R., Consolvo, S.: "…No one can hack my mind": comparing expert and non-expert security practices. In: Proceedings of the 11th Symposium on Usable Privacy and Security, pp. 327–346 (2019)

13. Jacobs, D., McDaniel, T.: A survey of user experience in usable security and privacy research. In: Moallem, A. (ed.) HCII 2022. LNCS, vol. 13333, pp. 154–172. Springer, Cham (2022). https://doi.org/10.1007/978-3-031-05563-8_11

14. Krombholz, K., Busse, K., Pfeffer, K., Smith, M., von Zezschwitz, E.: "If HTTPS were secure, i wouldn't need 2FA"-end user and administrator mental models of HTTPS. In: IEEE Symposium on Security and Privacy (SP), vol. 2019-May, pp. 246–263. IEEE (2019). https://doi.org/10.1109/SP.2019.00060. https://ieeexplore.ieee.org/document/8835228/

15. Lin, J., Amini, S., Hong, J.I., Sadeh, N., Lindqvist, J., Zhang, J.: Expectation and purpose: understanding users' mental models of mobile app privacy through crowdsourcing. In: Proceedings of the 2012 ACM Conference on Ubiquitous Computing, UbiComp 2012, pp. 501–510. Association for Computing Machinery, New York (2012). https://doi.org/10.1145/2370216.2370290

16. Nvivo (2020). https://www.qsrinternational.com/nvivo-qualitative-data-analysis-software/home

17. Mayer, P., Zou, Y., Schaub, F., Aviv, A.J.: "Now i'm a bit angry:" individuals' awareness, perception, and responses to data breaches that affected them. In: 30th USENIX Security Symposium (USENIX Security 2021), pp. 393–410. USENIX Association (2021). https://www.usenix.org/conference/usenixsecurity21/presentation/mayer

18. McDonald, A., Barwulor, C., Mazurek, M.L., Schaub, F., Redmiles, E.M.: "It's stressful having all these phones": investigating sex workers' safety goals, risks, and practices online. In: Proceedings of the 30th USENIX Security Symposium, pp. 375–392 (2021)

19. Naidoo, R.: A multi-level influence model of COVID-19 themed cybercrime. Eur. J. Inf. Syst. **29**(3), 306–321 (2020)
20. UPI: Unified payments interface - instant mobile payments | NPCI (2024). https://www.npci.org.in/what-we-do/upi/product-overview
21. Pearman, S., Zhang, S.A., Bauer, L., Christin, N., Cranor, L.F.: Why people (don't) use password managers effectively. In: Proceedings of the Fifteenth USENIX Conference on Usable Privacy and Security, SOUPS 2019, pp. 319–338. USENIX Association, USA (2019)
22. Rader, E., Wash, R., Brooks, B.: Stories as informal lessons about security. In: Proceedings of the Eighth Symposium on Usable Privacy and Security, SOUPS 2012. Association for Computing Machinery, New York (2012). https://doi.org/10.1145/2335356.2335364
23. Redmiles, E.M.: "Should i worry?" a cross-cultural examination of account security incident response. In: 2019 IEEE Symposium on Security and Privacy (SP), pp. 920–934 (2019). https://doi.org/10.1109/SP.2019.00059
24. Saldaña, J.: The Coding Manual for Qualitative Researchers, 4th edn. SAGE Publications Limited, Thousand Oaks (2021)
25. Scheuerman, M.K., Jiang, J.A., Fiesler, C., Brubaker, J.R.: A framework of severity for harmful content online. Proc. ACM Hum.-Comput. Interact. **5**(CSCW2) (2021). https://doi.org/10.1145/3479512
26. Sheng, S., Holbrook, M., Kumaraguru, P., Cranor, L.F., Downs, J.: Who falls for phish? A demographic analysis of phishing susceptibility and effectiveness of interventions. In: Proceedings of the SIGCHI Conference on Human Factors in Computing Systems, CHI 2010, pp. 373–382. Association for Computing Machinery, New York (2010). https://doi.org/10.1145/1753326.1753383
27. Simko, L., Lerner, A., Ibtasam, S., Roesner, F., Kohno, T.: Computer security and privacy for refugees in the united states. In: 2018 IEEE Symposium on Security and Privacy (SP), pp. 409–423 (2018). https://doi.org/10.1109/SP.2018.00023
28. Soneji, A., et al.: "Flawed, but like democracy we don't have a better system": the experts' insights on the peer review process of evaluating security papers. In: 2022 IEEE Symposium on Security and Privacy (SP), pp. 1845–1862 (2022). https://doi.org/10.1109/SP46214.2022.9833581
29. Vitak, J., Liao, Y., Subramaniam, M., Kumar, P.: "I knew it was too good to be true": the challenges economically disadvantaged internet users face in assessing trustworthiness, avoiding scams, and developing self-efficacy online. Proc. ACM Hum.-Comput. Interact. **2**(CSCW) (2018). https://doi.org/10.1145/3274445
30. Walsh, R.: Why There is a 1 in 3 Chance You'll get Hacked in 2016 (2016). https://proprivacy.com/privacy-news/get-hacked-one-in-three
31. Zangerle, E., Specht, G.: "Sorry, i was hacked": a classification of compromised twitter accounts. In: Proceedings of the 29th Annual ACM Symposium on Applied Computing, SAC 2014, pp. 587–593. Association for Computing Machinery, New York (2014). https://doi.org/10.1145/2554850.2554894
32. Zeng, E., Mare, S., Roesner, F.: End user security & privacy concerns with smart homes. In: Proceedings of the Thirteenth USENIX Conference on Usable Privacy and Security, SOUPS 2017, pp. 65–80. USENIX Association, USA (2017)

Experiential Learning Through Immersive XR: Cybersecurity Education for Critical Infrastructures

Anthony Lee[1]([✉]) [iD], Kenneth King[1] [iD], Denis Gračanin[1] [iD], and Mohamed Azab[2] [iD]

[1] Virginia Tech, Blacksburg, VA 24060, USA
{leean1,kking93,gracanin}@vt.edu
[2] Virginia Military Institute, Lexington, VA 24450, USA
azabmm@vmi.edu

Abstract. In our modern digital world, where virtually everything is intertwined with computer systems, critical infrastructures face vulnerability to a variety of cyber-attacks, stemming from the absence of a cybersecurity mindset within these establishments. We need to efficiently educate these workers about the cybersecurity threats that exist, their potential effects, and the subsequent substantial impact on human populations. Previous research has suggested traditional non-interactive training methods are often not effective. We propose an interactive learning experience that incorporates Extended Reality, Digital Twins, and Artificial Intelligence (AI) to help workers become more aware of cybersecurity issues within their critical infrastructure. This paper introduces an innovative testbed that seamlessly integrates Artificial Intelligence (AI) and Large Language Models to create an immersive educational experience. The goal is to effectively convey complex technical concepts to users with limited background knowledge on the subject. Our specific focus lies in addressing the need for proper cybersecurity training among water treatment plant employees.

The testbed presented is meticulously crafted to provide users with a tangible representation of the potential outcomes resulting from successful cyber attacks on such facilities. Through this approach, we aim to enhance the educational process and promote a deeper understanding of cybersecurity challenges in critical infrastructure like water treatment plants.

Keywords: Artificial Intelligence (AI) · Digital Twins · Critical Infrastructures · Cybersecurity · Large Language Models (LLM) · Internet of Things (IoT)

1 Introduction

Cyberattacks are a pressing matter in today's digital world but people do not take the necessary initiative to prevent them. A relevant example can be seen from the Colonial Pipeline Cyber-attack that happened on May 7, 2021, where a major pipeline supplying gas throughout the East Coast was hit with a ransomware attack [6]. The attack was caused by an exposed password that provided access to the pipeline's network. Another example was the Equifax data breach that happened back in 2017 which resulted in 145 million people's personal information being leaked. The breach could have easily been prevented if Equifax had installed security updates [2]. Both of these events could have been easily prevented if people didn't neglect the importance of cybersecurity. Such events contributed to a wake-up call to the United States for its aging critical infrastructure and lack of cybersecurity awareness.

We have seen that humans are frequently the most vulnerable element in any cyber system. Many sophisticated attacks leverage human errors, vulnerabilities, or evident flaws throughout different phases. Even with substantial research dedicated to understanding and rectifying human mistakes in cyberattack and defense contexts, there is a broad agreement that no single model entirely addresses this aspect or corrects it with optimal efficacy. These variables can change based on the individual involved, the specific environment, and the nature of the threat or defense situation. In scenarios involving mission-critical applications, the risk, and associated mitigation costs escalate significantly.

This paper seeks to bridge the gap in interactive and IoT-based system simulators for cybersecurity training. Research indicates that an interactive and immersive training approach, incorporating the principles of IoT technology, significantly enhances learning outcomes [9]. We introduce an affordable, programmable, fully immersive testbed that utilizes the digital twin concept to produce a realistic representation of a mission-critical infrastructure, a wastewater treatment plant. This testbed is designed to enhance the training and education of cybersecurity concepts. It achieves this by immersing users in an operational context where the system is under attack. There are various scenarios where attacks are based on user errors or by exploiting cyber vulnerabilities that can be better exposed with cybersecurity-unaware human interaction. Leveraging Large Language Models (LLMs), the testbed creates motivational strategies that provoke such human errors, paving the way for further attack avenues. In addition, LLMs allow non-experts in cybersecurity to translate high-level requests into low-level attack scenarios conducted on the testbed. The result is then portrayed in Extended Reality (XR) to intensify user immersion and generate an authentic representation of real-world attack situations.

Section 2 reviews the previous work that has been completed and what this paper aims to continue. Section 3 describes the problem and related challenges and why it is important to address them. Section 4 provides an overview of the proposed system and how all of the components interact with each other. The methodology used is described in Sect. 5 and the findings are provided in Sect. 6. Section 7 concludes the paper and provides directions for future work.

2   Literature Review

2.1   XR-Enabled Immersive Training Experiences

Introducing interactive components such as XR can allow for greater concentration and enhanced learning. Gironacci [8] proposes a training simulator where XR and AI are infused together to provide dynamic feedback based on a user's input and interaction. The simulator uses Natural Language Processing (NLP) to identify keywords and then make suggestions that are aimed to help them learn why a particular action should be taken. Yoshida et al. [17] presents an XR-based guitar training system that aims to expand previous research by using XR technology to provide performance skill training: teaching users how much force to apply and providing timing feedback. However, Artificial Intelligence (AI) was not used to provide real-time feedback to help the trainee correct behavior to play better. One of the suggested improvements from the case study was having markers on the actual guitar so each user would know where to place their fingers when playing. This would depend on the specific song being played so it would be impractical for the markers to be manually configured for each song. Instead, we could use AI and train the model with a guitar-playing dataset so that markers could be placed dynamically based on the song they selected. A soccer XR training simulator [14] also uses XR to train players in performing goal kicks using a series of image recognition software and a camera. AI could be integrated into this use case for analyzing the parameters and providing suggestions on how to improve the kick autonomously.

Another similar XR-based simulator was also created for training within the medical field [4]. More specifically, an immersive training environment was created for Pulse Palpating Training. The simulator provides haptic, visual, and auditory feedback and aims to provide realism in a stress-free environment when training the next generation of medical professionals. Most equipment options currently available are expensive and do not even provide a full set of simulation capabilities.

Conducting cybersecurity training directly on an expensive piece of equipment is not feasible, especially given possible environmental and other impacts. This paper introduces an ergonomic and cost-effective method for enhancing realism in cybersecurity training, enabling operators to thoroughly understand and engage with the concepts so that preventative measures can be taken to prevent drastic failures.

2.2   Cybersecurity Training and Education Challenges

Cybersecurity is increasingly problematic due to cyberattacks on sensitive platforms, so it's crucial to address these issues promptly to prevent further escalation. We focus on water treatment plants as many critical issues need to be addressed. For instance, one problem is that the water treatment plants are not kept up to date as they use legacy systems and outdated technologies. Operators don't tend to think about how outdated their system is and just think about whether the system functions correctly and only make changes if necessary. This is the wrong mindset in today's digital age as cyberattacks occur much more commonly than in the past. Legacy systems also tend to have short-term data retention which is unacceptable as we derive statistical models using large data sets to help make improvements in terms of automation. This in turn helps identify vulnerabilities and optimizations to create a more sophisticated and secure system [11].

Another need for cybersecurity training within critical infrastructures is due to their large impact on the surrounding population. We have already seen how an attack on a fuel pipeline has impacted the United States as it caused panic, shortages, and inflated gas prices [6]. This is due to the lack of cybersecurity training and awareness among the workers which causes operators to be vulnerable to social engineering and phishing attacks that allow attackers to gain access to the system using their credentials [15]. These issues motivate the development of an interactive cybersecurity training system to promote cybersecurity thinking within the workplace.

2.3 Innovations in Cybersecurity Training Platforms

The initial efforts that provide the foundation of the work are described in [3] where an XR-based IoT simulator (testbed) for a water treatment plant is proposed so that Cyber-Physical Systems can be integrated into cybersecurity education. The development of a water treatment digital twin was informed by first analyzing the weaknesses of the current water treatment plants discussed in Sect. 2.2. By having the testbed, an interactive and immersive education experience will inform operators of how serious these issues are and why it is important that they don't be ignored. The experiential learning experience will help operators visualize the consequences of certain actions and explore the system's vulnerabilities. In addition, its capabilities can be expanded beyond education and be used for simulation purposes (pen testing) to ensure the best cybersecurity posture.

In this paper, we use AI to create attack and defense scenarios, converting complex requests into understandable cyberattack situations. This approach facilitates the translation of low-level cyber-attacks for a broader audience, aiding non-experts in grasping necessary safety measures. Moreover, it assists plant operators in identifying overlooked vulnerabilities and offers real-time feedback for enhancing defense mechanisms.

Nagarajan et al. [13] proposed that video games should be used for cybersecurity training to attract more attention to important cybersecurity training topics. The use of LLMs can help generate dynamic content within the video game that allows users to remain attracted. For example, when a user creates their user profile in a video game, AI can use that information to dynamically form a phishing or social engineering attack unique to the user. This will allow the players to experience the manipulation that goes behind these attacks so that they learn not everyone can be trusted. XR can further enhance the immersive interaction experience.

3   The Proposed Use-Case: An XR-Enabled Waste Water Treatment Educational Testbed

Critical infrastructures are essential to our way of life, providing the necessary resources for our daily activities. Examples of critical infrastructures include power plants, water treatment plants, and communication networks. A failure in any of these systems would have devastating consequences for our society. For example in water treatment plants, a failure would adversely affect the surrounding environment, leading to environmental pollution and significant disruption in agricultural activities.

Water Treatment Plants are responsible for processing and purifying our wastewater before it is released back into the environment, emphasizing that each step of the water treatment process is critical. Failures caused by cybersecurity breaches can easily be avoided with the right mindset and the proper training. Most cybersecurity training courses today aren't engaging due to their lack of immersiveness and adaptability to various scenarios [9]. Using LLMs enables trainees to engage with a Conversational AI agent for translating high-level concepts into low-level ones, enhancing their grasp of cybersecurity and its impact. The XR component allows us to illustrate attack effects in a Virtual Environment, creating a more immersive training experience.

This paper uses LLMs to focus on educating trainees about Denial of Service Attacks. Our primary objective is to propose a strategy to diminish the vulnerability to these threats. We specifically concentrate on the prevalent issue of insufficient training and education among staff and operators at water treatment facilities. We contend that our proposed solution, a comprehensive and interactive cybersecurity training system, will significantly enhance awareness and understanding of cybersecurity threats among all stakeholders. By doing so, we aim to ensure the rigorous implementation of appropriate measures and protocols to safeguard against these ever-evolving digital dangers.

4   System Overview

The proposed system (Fig. 1) provides an immersive experience for trainees by having them placed into an *XR Environment* where they can interact with a *Conversational AI Agent*. *Conversational AI Agent* interacts with the users in *XR Environment* to understand what type of attack objectives the user would like to achieve. In addition to that, the agent can answer any lingering questions so that the user will be able to fully learn the concepts that will help them perform their jobs better. Once an attack objective has been decided, it sends the attack objectives and targets to the *Physical AI Agent* who is then responsible for performing the attack on the *Physical Environment* (the testbed). This is done by using an attack script in combination with LLMs as described in Sect. 5.1 where the script will execute attacks through the command line interface of the *Physical Environment*.

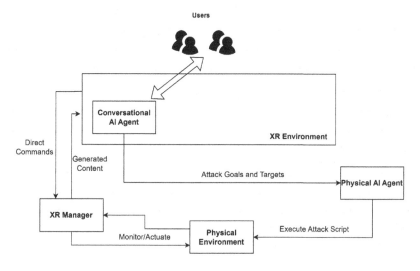

Fig. 1. The testbed architecture.

The *Physical Environment* and *XR Manager* exchange data using the MQTT protocol so that the *XR Manager* can generate the effect of the changes made to the *Physical Environment* back to the *XR Environment* where the users can witness the changes in real-time. This approach enables trainees to experience the impact of cyberattacks as if they were physically present and to engage with control modules to address the problem. Through such simulations, where users actively attempt to manage or mitigate unfolding issues or are subject to deception, they can gain a comprehensive understanding of the critical importance of cybersecurity in their field and learn effective response strategies for real-world scenarios.

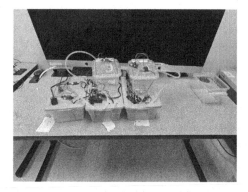

Fig. 2. The testbed hardware implementation.

The testbed [3] setup (Fig. 2) replicates the water treatment process in a controlled, smaller-scale environment to ensure safety and affordability. The first stage in the water treatment plant is the water intake process where the sewer water is brought into the facility. During this step, various sensors measure the water intake rate and monitor the water levels to ensure efficient intake. If the system sensors were to be manipulated, this could cause either an overflow or underflow of water into the treatment plant which would then have other catastrophic impacts such as the sewer system being backed up or water contamination due to flooding.

The water is then cleansed of any garbage that may be in the sewage using a mesh netting system. After this step, the water is purified by removing liquid pollutants like kitchen grease through an extensive skimming system. This system features a large mechanical arm designed to skim oils off the water's surface while it resides in a large pool.

Additionally, the system includes monitoring controls that regulate the skimming arm's speed and manage the flow rate of the water in the pool, ensuring efficient and thorough removal of contaminants. This system could be exploited as having the water flow too fast or having the arm move at an improper speed would prevent the chemicals from being skimmed off.

The wastewater then goes through another filtration process that removes any biological organisms which involves adding various chemicals and monitoring the temperature and pH levels. To ensure the proper modifications, various sensors measure each of these parameters. Once this process is finished, the water goes through a chlorination process so that the water can be made usable which also involves the use of a sensor to monitor chlorine levels. If any of these sensors fail during the treatment process, it may render the water unusable, leading to biological harm and adverse health effects.

5   The Main System Actors

We use XR and LLM-driven attack and defense scenarios to fully demonstrate the impact of cyber security attacks on mission-critical systems dynamically and adaptively. The proposed testbed involves the use of two AI Agents: *Physical AI Agent*, and *Conversational AI Agent*.

5.1   Physical AI Agent

Physical AI agent uses LLMs to play the role of an attacker performing autonomous vulnerability analysis against the IoT systems in a water treatment testbed. To perform this autonomous vulnerability analysis, we use a popular network scanner Nmap [12] that scans the various active networks on the testbed and provides a list of open ports and corresponding services that are executing on that port. These vulnerability scanning results will then be processed by the LLM to determine the most appropriate target to perform the Denial of Service attack on.

For the LLM task of Nmap analysis, we found that the current leading open-source models (namely Llama2 at the time) performed so poorly that they could not be used reliably. In contrast, the leading closed-source model at the time, OpenAI's GPT-4 [16], was able to identify ports and IP addresses of interest with strong accuracy. While we would have preferred to use entirely open-source models, we were forced to use GPT-4 (gpt-4-0613 specifically) given no open-source LLM could perform the tasks desired reliably in comparison.

For the LLM task of generating attack commands for the Hping tool [1], we found that both GPT-4 and Meta's Llama2 would often refuse the task, given their built-in alignments and safety features. Therefore, we employed an uncensored version of Llama2 from TheBloke called Luna-AI-Llama2-Uncensored [10]. Compared to other uncensored LLMs on Hugging Face, we found that this model provided the same level of accuracy with faster response times. Similar to the Nmap analysis task, this open-source model struggled to consistently generate properly formatted attack commands. At the same time we found that although GPT-4 refused to generate attack commands, it would happily fix any errors in attack commands generated by another model. Therefore, we implemented a filtering mechanism so that after the uncensored model generates the attack command, GPT-4 corrects any errors in the command before returning the final result.

To bridge the gap between the high-level attack objectives and low-level cyberattacks, we use the LangChain framework which helps us integrate LLMs into our application to make more accurate decisions by using the Output Parser functionality [5]. LangChain allows us to provide LLMs with specific prompts and context when generating responses so they can make informative decisions. LangChain guides the LLM in classifying the attack, translating the information from a novice-friendly level to something comprehensible for an expert.

Scenario Generation Example: Let's say an attacker wanted to stop the facility from functioning properly. The AI, with the help of LangChain [5], would interpret that a Denial of Service Attack is desired. The AI-driven attack agent would use the Nmap tool [12] to identify which IP addresses and ports are currently running on the testbed. The attack agent will process the information, identify the services running on each host, and learn of their known vulnerabilities to determine which host and port would be feasible to perform a flooding attack. The outcome of such a step will be the seed for the attack scenario generation. The agent will then generate attack commands using the Hping tool, which will successfully exploit such vulnerabilities in a multi-stage process.

5.2   Conversational AI Agent

As part of our platform, we want the player to be able to interact with a cybersecurity expert within the XR environment who will be able to help guide players through learning the concepts. We introduce an NPC character that provides Natural Language conversations and human-like interactions. A 3D humanoid model is created within the Unity Engine along with a waypoint-based navigation system programmed through C# that provides it with basic movement automation. It also can interact with players like in normal human-to-human interaction as the NPC can turn to face players wherever they are. To facilitate natural language conversations, we use OpenAI's ChatGPT-4 Model where players are essentially connected with a live expert.

During development, we faced challenges in maintaining real-time responses with the AI as player interactions did not synchronize with the NPC's actions that were portrayed within the XR environment. This was caused by our attempt to add Meta Quest input capabilities for interacting with the NPC. The Unity assets we used were originally designed to be used within the Unity environment and not through a VR headset, therefore limitations were presented with attempting to get the Meta Quest VR headset to interact with the NPC.

5.3   The XR Environment

Based on the work presented in [3] we created an XR environment that provides a real-life interactable digital twin version of the testbed using the Unity Engine [7]. The environment consists of many different objects within the Unity Engine, including prefabs that represent real-life components of the water treatment plant. By having these objects, we can place buttons that allow simulation capabilities of the different components of the Water Treatment Plant. Each button has been attached to a method that then calls a script to interact with the physical testbed providing the connection from the virtual world to the physical world and helping trainees visualize their actions. An MQTT Broker method is used for communication between the virtual environment and the testbed. We then assign call methods for each functionality of the water treatment process and assign them so that when buttons are pressed in the virtual world, the related actions are called and activated on the hardware side.

The player avatar model consists of hands tracked by the headset controllers that allow them to interact with the buttons within the environment just like in real life. Players can also freely move around to closely interact with digital twin components, creating a sense of physical presence at the water treatment facility.

We used a water program from the Unity asset store that uses C# programming to create realistic physics properties of the water within the virtual environment. Accurate movement and flow direction of the water can be seen as different components of the water treatment plant are turned on and off to simulate real-life behavior. On top of that, we also added capabilities to the water color so that dirty water is portrayed as purple at the beginning of the water treatment process and as the water filtration is taking place the water color becomes blue to signify clean water.

During the development of the XR environment, we ran into several challenges. One issue that arose was the issue of merging scenes. As the project builds upon previous work, we had to keep in mind the existing XR environment and design which had their player design aspect. This meant it would be difficult to create a new interactive player with a different script and interaction technique since it would not be compatible with the existing environment. To resolve this issue we used prefabs (preconfigured digital assets) for development that allowed us to integrate the player into the environment seamlessly.

Another challenge we faced was Print Mesh Rendering. When we tried to display real-time data from each chamber in the VR environment, we encountered difficulties. We aim to address and resolve this issue moving forward.

6   Qualitative Evaluation

We completed a guided tour of a Water Treatment plant in Roanoke, Virginia where we learned about the water treatment process and the current status of their cybersecurity systems from plant workers. Plant workers walked us around the plant showing the computer systems involved in each treatment process and how it connects to their network. During the visit, we observed flaws in the physical aspects of the plant. Many of the computer systems within the plant were not secured within a locked room, meaning any plant worker could gain access to it physically. We noticed that the filtered water is directly reintroduced into the stream, implying that any malfunction in the water treatment process could lead to immediate environmental repercussions. This risk is magnified due to the direct connection of the stream to a significant river, which, in turn, connects to various other bodies of water. Seizing the opportunity, we also conducted interviews with multiple staff members at the plant to inquire about their cybersecurity backgrounds and the precautions they take to prevent cybersecurity attacks during their work at the facility.

6.1   XR Environment

We have designed a virtual model of a water treatment plant that contains all of the components that mimic each stage of the water treatment process. Screenshots of the virtual environment have been provided in Fig. 3. the tiny cylinders that you see in the world are the acids, bases, and organisms that would be added to the water at each step of the system. Users can walk along the platform or below the platform to provide that immersive feeling of being at the actual plant.

Fig. 3. Left: Sky view of Water Treatment Plant. **Middle:** Zoomed in view. **Right:** User's point of view.

6.2 Physical AI Agent

We were able to classify our 3 different attack classes using LangChain. By providing a high-level description of what the attack is doing, we can classify the specific cyberattack that is occurring.

As demonstrated in Fig. 4, we provided a high-level attack description describing that the network speed for the water treatment speed is slow due to there being so much traffic. An attack template is created that provides specific instructions on how the LLM should evaluate the given description along with how the LLM should return the output.

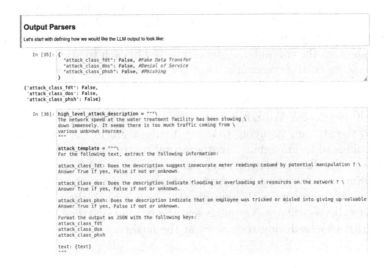

Fig. 4. Langchain prompt implementation.

We decided to use a JSON containing a boolean as output so that we could easily determine which attack script to execute. The resulting output from the LLM can be seen in Fig. 5.

We can see that the high-level attack description was successfully classified as a Denial of Service attack. The other two attack classes were also successfully classified as shown in Fig. 6.

The attack script for the Denial of Service attack class was successfully created in Python using the OpenAI and the llama_cpp library. The attack script produces a Python list containing flooding commands for each network of interest that can then be fed and executed on our testbed's command line interface. The next step would be for us to apply the commands on the testbed's network to see the results.

```
text: {text}
"""

In [37]: from langchain.prompts import ChatPromptTemplate

         prompt_template = ChatPromptTemplate.from_template(attack_template)
         print(prompt_template)

input_variables=['text'] output_parser=None partial_variables={} messages=[HumanMessagePromptTemplate(prompt=Pr
omptTemplate(input_variables=['text'], output_parser=None, partial_variables={}, template='For the following te
xt, extract the following information:\n\nattack_class_fdt: Does the description suggest innacurate meter readi
ngs casued by potential manipulation ? Answer True if yes, False if not or unknown.\n\nattack_class_dos: Does t
he description indicate flooding or overloading of resources on the network ? Answer True if yes, False if not
or unknown.\n\nattack_class_phsh: Does the description indicate that an employee was tricked or misled into giv
ing up valuable information ? Answer True if yes, False if not or unknown.\n\nFormat the output as JSON with th
e following keys:\nattack_class_fdt\nattack_class_dos\nattack_class_phsh\n\ntext: {text}\n', template_format='f
-string', validate_template=True), additional_kwargs={})]

In [38]: messages = prompt_template.format_messages(text=high_level_attack_description)
         chat = ChatOpenAI(temperature=0.0, model=llm_model)
         response = chat(messages)
         print(response.content)

{
    "attack_class_fdt": false,
    "attack_class_dos": true,
    "attack_class_phsh": false
}
```

Fig. 5. LLM's Response given a Denial of Service attack description.

```
In [40]: high_level_attack_description = """\
         The manager has noticed that water levels look much higher than gauges are reporting. He measures them by \
         hand and realizes that they are certainly off by a factor of at least 10 feet. It seems like they might \
         have been tampered with since the equipment is brand new.
         """

{
    "attack_class_fdt": true,
    "attack_class_dos": false,
    "attack_class_phsh": false
}

In [43]: high_level_attack_description = """\
         A man came in today claiming to be an OSHA official. He stated that he needed access to the \
         computers in order to assess our safety logs. He spent a lot of time downloading data from our \
         computer onto a flash drive. We called OSHA, and they said they did not send anyone today.
         """

{
    "attack_class_fdt": false,
    "attack_class_dos": false,
    "attack_class_phsh": true
}
```

Fig. 6. Top: LLM's Response given a Data Manipulation attack description. **Bottom:** LLM's Response given a Phishing attack description.

7   Conclusions and Future Work

We introduced a novel XR-based testbed that integrates AI and LLMs to create an immersive educational experience that addresses the need for proper cybersecurity training among water treatment plant employees. The testbed provides users with a real-world representation of the potential outcomes resulting from successful cyber attacks. Our goal is to enhance the educational process and promote a deeper understanding of cybersecurity challenges in critical infrastructure like water treatment plants.

In the future, we plan on taking information from the IoT devices to create visuals for the statistics of each chamber of the water treatment system for easy readability and understanding for the user while interacting with the XR. Without the statistics being presented in the XR environment, they would have to rely on the front-end interface for the statistics. We are also planning to address *Conversational AI NPC* interaction issues within VR, enabling the use of the Meta Quest headset for interactions. Additionally, we aim to optimize AI responses in correlation with the XR environment to facilitate real-time AI connections and synchronized NPC movement.

Acknowledgment. This study is a collaboration between Virginia Tech and Virginia Military Institute (VMI) as a part of a Commonwealth Cybersecurity Initiative Workforce Development Grant. A great many thanks to the cadets at VMI for helping us implement XR environment and the attack and defense scenarios for the testbed simulation.

Disclosure of Interests. The authors have no competing interests to declare that are relevant to the content of this article.

References

1. Balaji: HPING3 — network scanning tool — packet generator (2023). https://gbhackers.com/hping3-network-scanner-packer-generator/. Accessed 2 Feb 2024
2. Bomey, N.: How Chinese military hackers allegedly pulled off the equifax data breach, stealing data from 145 million americans (2020). https://www.usatoday.com/story/tech/2020/02/10/2017-equifax-data-breach-chinese-military-hack/4712788002/. Accessed 2 Feb 2024
3. Chandrashekar, N.D., King, K., Gračanin, D., Azab, M.: Design & development of virtual reality empowered cyber-security training testbed for IoT systems. In: 2023 3rd Intelligent Cybersecurity Conference (ICSC), pp. 86–94 (2023). https://doi.org/10.1109/ICSC60084.2023.10349976
4. Chandrashekar, N.D., Safford, S., Muniyandi, M., Gračanin, D.: An extended reality simulator for pulse palpation training. In: 2023 IEEE Conference on Virtual Reality and 3D User Interfaces Abstracts and Workshops (VRW), pp. 178–182 (2023). https://doi.org/10.1109/VRW58643.2023.00044
5. Chase, H.: Langchain (2022). https://www.langchain.com/. Accessed 2 Feb 2024
6. Easterly, J., Fanning, T.: The attack on colonial pipeline: what we've learned & what we've done over the past two years: CISA (2023). https://www.cisa.gov/news-events/news/attack-colonial-pipeline-what-weve-learned-what-weve-done-over-past-two-years. Accessed 2 Feb 2024
7. Francis, N., Ante, J., Helgason, D.: Unity real-time development platform | 3D, 2D, VR & AR. Unity Technologies (2005). https://unity.com/. Accessed 2 Feb 2024
8. Gironacci, I.: XR management training simulator supported by content-based scenario recommendation. In: 2022 IEEE International Conference on Artificial Intelligence and Virtual Reality (AIVR), pp. 104–108 (2022). https://doi.org/10.1109/AIVR56993.2022.00021
9. Hertel, J.P., Millis, B.: Using Simulations to Promote Learning in Higher Education: An Introduction. Routledge, London (2002)
10. Jobbins, T.: Thebloke/luna-ai-llama2-uncensored-gguf at main (2023). https://huggingface.co/TheBloke/Luna-AI-Llama2-Uncensored-GGUF/tree/main. Accessed 2 Feb 2024

11. Korodi, A., Nicolae, A., Drăghici, I.A.: Proactive decentralized historian-improving legacy system in the water industry 4.0 context. Sustainability **15**(15) (2023). https://doi.org/10.3390/su151511487
12. Lyon, G.: Nmap: networking security scanner (1997). https://nmap.org/. Accessed 2 Feb 2024
13. Nagarajan, A., Allbeck, J.M., Sood, A., Janssen, T.L.: Exploring game design for cybersecurity training. In: 2012 IEEE International Conference on Cyber Technology in Automation, Control, and Intelligent Systems (CYBER), pp. 256–262 (2012). https://doi.org/10.1109/CYBER.2012.6392562
14. Ono, T., Ishikawa, T.: A research on penalty kick training system using XR. In: 2023 Nicograph International (NicoInt), pp. 86–86 (2023). https://doi.org/10.1109/NICOINT59725.2023.00026
15. Shapira, N., Ayalon, O., Ostfeld, A., Farber, Y., Housh, M.: Cybersecurity in water sector: stakeholders perspective. J. Water Resour. Plan. Manag. **147**(8), 05021008 (2021). https://doi.org/10.1061/(ASCE)WR.1943-5452.0001400
16. Sutskever, I.: (2023). https://openai.com/gpt-4. Accessed 2 Feb 2024
17. Yoshida, S., Abe, T., Suganuma, T.: Design of a support system for guitar performance training using XR technology. In: 2023 IEEE 12th Global Conference on Consumer Electronics (GCCE), pp. 276–279 (2023). https://doi.org/10.1109/GCCE59613.2023.10315398

Revolutionizing Social Engineering Awareness Raising, Education and Training: Generative AI-Powered Investigations in the Maritime Domain

Michail Loupasakis, Georgios Potamos [ID], and Eliana Stavrou[(⊠)] [ID]

Open University of Cyprus, Nicosia, Cyprus
{michail.loupasakis1,georgios.potamos}@st.ouc.ac.cy,
eliana.stavrou@ouc.ac.cy

Abstract. Innovation in generative Artificial Intelligence (AI) has already been leveraged by cybercriminals to deliver AI-powered social engineering attacks, specifically phishing. This advancement adds to the challenges the cybersecurity community is facing, such as lack of motivation to change unsafe behaviors and low engagement with awareness raising, education and training activities. Often, the problem is attributed to the fact that activities communicate the same message across different audiences. This approach is not helpful to assist people relating to the problem, realizing the threat and how it can be transformed. To build cyber resilience against phishing, the workforce needs to realize how phishing can be delivered in the context of their working environment and what aspects a cybercriminal can leverage to make the attack more realistic and plausible. This requires the design of awareness raising, education and training activities that can deliver highly tailored and context-aware messages to different audiences, considering their job role and responsibilities. Generative AI has already demonstrated an ability of high degree of creativity which is imperative for creating tailored and effective awareness raising and training content. This study investigates how generative AI can be leveraged by stakeholders, such as educators and trainers, to develop phishing-tailored attack scenarios. The scenarios can be embedded in awareness raising and training activities that can be delivered e.g. over cyber ranges, aiming to enhance the workforce's cyber resilience against phishing attacks. Investigations are performed in the context of the maritime domain.

Keywords: Social Engineering · Phishing · ChatGPT · Generative AI · Maritime Cybersecurity · Cybersecurity Awareness Raising · Cybersecurity Education · Cybersecurity Training · Phishing Attack-Tailored Scenarios · Cyber Resilience

1 Introduction

Social engineering is a major threat that keeps challenging society and the cybersecurity community. The dimension of social engineering and its impact were made evident during COVID-19 pandemic [1] as cybercriminals exploited all aspects of personal and business life to engage their victims. During this time, a high degree of creativity in terms of phishing lures was observed, successfully engaging the victims that fell for the lure. Post pandemic period the problem remains [2], giving a clear message to the cybersecurity community that society has not reached a satisfactory level of cyber resilience against social engineering attacks, especially with regards to phishing [3]. The fact that ENISA has announced [4] that the theme of the EU Cybersecurity month, October 2023, will focus on increasing awareness on social engineering demonstrates that the cybersecurity community is prioritizing its actions to empower citizens against the social engineering pandemic. The evolution of generative Artificial Intelligence (AI) and the rise of malicious AI chatbots [3], which can be utilized to launch sophisticated phishing attacks, makes this prioritization imperative.

The cybersecurity community has launched many initiatives to raise awareness of the social engineering threat and educate citizens on cyber hygiene practices. A key challenge when designing cybersecurity awareness raising, education and training activities is to engage and motivate the audience to learn. One way to achieve this is by creating cybersecurity games and game genres [5], ranging from tabletop games, to serious games, to cyber range simulation environments. Although awareness and training were found to be the most effective way to reduce susceptibility to social engineering attacks [6], we still observe high percentages of compromisation. Different social engineering training and awareness programs [5, 7] have been developed. However, often the same message is communicated across different audiences; this approach does not help people to relate to the problem [8], realize the threat and how it can be transformed. This lack of understanding hinders an individual's understanding of the threat, can easily disengage them from the awareness raising activities and become unmotivated to change unsafe behaviors. Microsoft defense report 2023 [9] indicates the need to "*conduct innovative experimentation with user engagement strategies*" and recommends to "*develop tailored and context-aware education models that treat users as distinct individuals and be implemented at scale*". An innovative direction to consider is to investigate more actively the contextualization of phishing attacks in different use cases to empower user engagement and understanding of the threat. This approach is expected to deliver tailored messages to different audiences and lead to more appealing and engaging content that can lead to acquisition of new knowledge and motivate safer behaviors.

Contextualizing and developing phishing-tailored awareness raising content is not an easy task to perform, considering the variety of audience profiles that can be constructed, e.g., based on working domain, job roles, personal and or professional interests, etc. The power of generative AI [10] can be leveraged to guide content creation and the development of phishing-tailored attack scenarios, assisting cybersecurity professionals, e.g. educators, trainers, and curricula designers, optimize the content design process. As Tom Burt, Microsoft's Corporate Vice President, Customer Security & Trust, stated "*Artificial Intelligence will be a critical component of successful defense. In the coming years, innovation in AI powered cyber defense will help reverse the current rising tide of cyberattacks*".

This paper aims to investigate how generative AI can be leveraged to create phishing-tailored attack scenarios given a specific domain. The current study is performed in the context of maritime domain. Investigations are expected to provide insights to cyberse-curity educators and trainers, guiding the design of AI-powered awareness raising and training initiatives, e.g. campaigns, tabletop games, phishing simulations, etc. A core aspect of the investigations is to empower them integrating phishing attack-tailored sce-narios into the design of learning activities that the workforce can easily relate with, understand, and acquire new knowledge that can be adapted when a phishing attack is transformed. For example, the integration of attack scenarios can be valuable for activ-ities delivered over cyber ranges. Cyber ranges can simulate a range of phishing attack scenarios, demonstrating how cybercriminals can deliver a tailored phishing attack and what aspects they can leverage to make the attack realistic and plausible. Enhancing the workforce's cyber situational awareness can contribute to empowering them to become cyber resilient against current and future social engineering attacks.

Section 2 presents relevant work. Section 3 discusses the study methodology. Section 4 briefly analyses the exploration aspects considered for crafting AI prompts. Section 5 presents the main observations derived from the generative AI tool (ChatGPT) responses. Section 6 critically discusses whether generative AI can be leveraged to create phishing-tailored attack scenarios and Sect. 7 concludes the work.

2 Relevant Work

The need to adopt a tailored approach in designing awareness raising activities and con-tent is highlighted in [11] where the design of a new educational activity is presented, demonstrating how social engineering can be contextualized in a healthcare scenario. The work in [12] emphasizes that it is essential to understand people's behavior and prior knowledge to provide them with customized and effective security training. Authors propose to group people based on their awareness of social engineering threat prior to providing tailored security training. The importance of pursuing tailored security train-ing is highlighted in the global Cyber Resilience Index (CRI) [13] which was developed by the World Economic Forum Centre for Cybersecurity, in collaboration with the Cyber Resilience Index Working Group and with Accenture. CRI is a framework of best prac-tice, guiding organizations to develop and evaluate the level of their cyber resilience. As stated in the guidelines *"fundamental cyber resilience must be integral not only to technical systems but also in teams, the organizational culture and the daily way of working"*. The framework also highlights the need to provide continuous training to stay up-to-date with the cyber threat landscape and to empower people identifying and com-municating threats. Thus, demonstrating cyber resilience in their daily responsibilities. This indicates that initiatives should tailor the message to communicate through train-ing, depending on the audience, and considering the workforce's job responsibilities. Such an approach can promote the development of a multidisciplinary workforce [14] that will be able to apply cyber hygiene and contribute towards an organization's cyber resilience. Creating a culture of cyber resilience across the organization is vital given how social engineering attacks have evolved since ChatGPT launched [3]. The *"State of Phishing 2023"* report [3] presents how cybercriminals leverage generative AI to sys-tematically launch highly targeted phishing attacks. The rise of malicious AI chatbots, such as WormGPT, can assist cybercriminals to write professional emails and launch sophisticated phishing and Business Email Compromise (BEC) attacks.

Given the advancements of the cyber threat landscape, it is pivotal to upskill the workforce to realize how phishing attacks can be transformed and to identify how they can be tailored given a specific business environment. The work in [15] investigates detection aspects in the maritime domain and contributes towards a novel maritime cyber threat detection framework. The proposed framework guides the development of cyber threat detection skills in the maritime domain to effectively manage maritime-related cyber risks. It provides directions to tailor training initiatives considering the personnel's role and responsibilities in the maritime ecosystem. The framework specifies key capabilities that need to be developed such as identifying the maritime attack surface and the impact to business operations, explaining how specific cybersecurity threats may compromise the operation of maritime assets, and detecting a security incident. The work in [16] takes into consideration the guidelines provided in [15] and presents the design of an innovative training curriculum aiming to develop cybersecurity capacity in the maritime domain and defend against ransomware attacks.

3 Methodology

An exploratory methodology is utilized to investigate whether generative AI tools such as ChatGPT can generate tailored, realistic, and plausible phishing attack scenarios based on the presented business environment. The investigations are expected to provide insights and guide different stakeholders, e.g. educators, trainers, curricula designers, etc., to use generative AI tools to create phishing-tailored attack scenarios and inform awareness raising and training initiatives. Customizing awareness raising and training initiatives is envisioned to engage different users with the training and empower their understanding. ChatGPT 4.0 was preferred over the community version as it is reported to be more creative. Given that cybercriminals are being creative with the lures utilized and are successfully deceiving people, initiatives should leverage the creativity demonstrated by generative AI tools such as ChatGPT to create plausible attack scenarios that can be delivered in the context of a specific organization.

This work deployed the following methodology inspired by the work in [16]:

a) **Social engineering attack aspects**. Initially, attack-related aspects are specified, profiling the attack strategy of a social engineer. These aspects are considered for crafting generative AI prompts and for critically analyzing relevant responses.

b) **Business environment**. The business environment is dissected, specifying the mission, the processes, the organizational structure, and the internal and external stakeholders. This information can be considered for crafting opening prompts to contextualize phishing attacks considering the specific business environment.

c) **Preliminary analysis**. During the preliminary analysis, specific codes are extracted to facilitate subsequent qualitative analysis. The coding structure is organized under four thematic categories: (i) relevance to different departments/operations, (ii) realism and plausibility, (iii) psychological manipulation, and (iv) sophistication.

d) **Colour coding**. Prompts and relevant ChatGPT responses are included in a document to facilitate the analysis. An appropriate colour-coding scheme is applied considering the specified coding structure.

e) **Qualitative analysis**. A spreadsheet is created to facilitate the analysis. Prompts, responses, and observations are reported. The latter are utilized to fine-tune subsequent prompts.

f) **Prompt engineering**. The prompts to input to the generative AI tool are crafted based on the research aim and objectives, the business environment and social engineering attack aspects analyzed in this study.

g) **Exploration**: New prompts are created and/or existing prompts are amended, following ChatGPT's responses. The aim is to explore whether responses can lead to the creation of tailored attack scenarios.

4 Exploration Aspects

This section briefly analyses the key aspects that need to be taken into consideration to craft appropriate generative AI prompts and support the research objectives of the study. Initially, we profile social engineering attacks and identify key attack attributes, and then the business environment is scrutinized. These aspects are expected to drive the specification of tailored social engineering attack scenarios by using appropriate prompts.

4.1 Social Engineering Attacks

A range of social engineering attacks can be leveraged by cybercriminals, providing the means to use different attack methods, successfully engaging and compromising the target. Such methods, among others, include phishing, vishing, smishing, baiting, tailgating, dumpster diving, shoulder surfing, etc. Social engineering attacks often succeed because they are delivered in a context which the victim is familiar with. For example, a phishing attack is crafted considering the business environment of the victim or considering personal preferences. In such tailored cases, the social engineer increases the chances to engage the victim and successfully deploy the attack. To be able to create attack-tailored attack scenarios and inform awareness raising and training initiatives, it is imperative to identify exploitability attributes a social engineer might use when crafting and delivering a social engineering attack. These attributes can be utilized to develop relevant generative AI prompts that can lead to tailored attack scenarios. This study considers three exploitability attributes:

Attack Vector. This attribute reflects the means which will be utilized to deliver the attack. Typically, there are three main ways delivering a social engineering attack: (a) using the phone, (b) through digital means, and/or (c) through physical interaction.

Influence Tactics. Social engineers apply a range of psychological tactics to manipulate the victims and convince them to reveal sensitive information and/or take further actions that could lead to unauthorized access. Such tactics include: (a) conveying a sense of urgency, (b) causing fear, (c) creating a sense of obligation, (d) demonstrating authority.

Attack Lure. Social engineering attacks are customized to deliver tailored lures and increase the possibility to engage the victims. Often, social engineers profile the victim (personal preferences, relationships, etc.) and their business environment (domain, work role, business collaborators, etc.). This information is utilized to craft tailored lures that the victim will be familiar with and make the social engineering message realistic and more attractive to the victim.

4.2 Business Environment

Typical risk factors include threat, vulnerability, impact, likelihood, and predisposing condition [17]. The latter is a condition that can affect the likelihood of occurrence and success of a threat event. For example, the business environment can constitute a predisposing condition that social engineers can exploit for their benefit. The structure of the organization, its mission, the internal and external stakeholders, and the business processes are aspects that can be useful in a social engineering attack to create a realistic scenario which can effectively engage victims.

Given the advances of the maritime cyber threat landscape [14, 15], the maritime domain is selected to perform the investigations and support the study's research objectives. The adverse impact on critical infrastructures due to successful social engineering attacks can be devastating, and can have cascading effects on a local, national, and international level. For the purposes of the study, a fictional maritime organization (called maritime-FLE) is considered [18, 19]. The profile of the fictional organization follows, and it will inform the prompts' engineering task that is part of the study's methodology.

Mission. The company is specialized in the manufacturing, supply, and service of an extensive range of lifesaving and firefighting equipment, with a commitment to spearheading innovation and excellence in maritime safety and services. The company is operating globally, with warehouses and branches across Europe. Moreover, the company leverages an extensive network of service companies in every major commercial port worldwide. This strategic positioning enables it to efficiently supply and service commercial vessels all over the world.

Business Structure and Operations. The company consists of the following departments:

- Auditing: Ensures law compliance and financial integrity.
- Human Resource (HR): Manages workforce development.
- Sales: Focuses on revenue generation and customer relations.
- Marketing: Drives brand engagement and market penetration.
- Research & Development (R&D): Innovates and fine-tunes maritime products.
- Production: Ensures manufacturing processes of maritime products.
- Procurement: Handles the order process for raw materials and trade products.
- Shipping & Logistics: Manages efficient distribution and supply chain operations.
- Information Technology & Web Development: Supports digital infrastructure and online presence.
- Legal: Handles legal compliance and maritime law.

Internal Stakeholders

Employees. They are the backbone of the company and have specialized skills, contributing with their expertise across various departments. From the meticulous work of the R&D team, innovating and improving maritime safety products, to the production team ensuring high-quality manufacturing.

Management and Leadership. This group includes department managers, directors, and executives (COO, CCO, CEO). They are responsible for strategic decision-making and ensuring that departmental activities align with overall business goals.

External Stakeholders

Suppliers. They provide essential raw materials for product manufacturing, playing a crucial role in the supply chain. Their reliability and quality standards directly impact the company's product offerings and reputation in the market.

Logistics and Distribution Partners. This includes agents and forwarders who ensure the efficient and timely distribution of products globally. Their work is critical in maintaining a seamless supply chain, from warehousing to delivery at various international ports.

Regulatory Bodies and Maritime Authorities. These stakeholders ensure compliance with maritime laws and safety regulations. Their guidelines and standards shape the company's product development and operational procedures.

Clients and End-Users. These are the vessel operators, shipping companies, and other maritime entities that use the company's products. Their feedback and satisfaction levels are vital indicators of product performance and influence future product developments and service enhancements.

5   Analysis of Generative AI Responses

This section will analyze the investigations performed with the aim to provide insights about the potential of generative AI tools, such as ChatGPT, to assist educators, trainers and curriculum designers, creating tailored social engineering attack scenarios considering a specific business environment.

Initially, a prompt was crafted to set the task purpose and provide relevant context to the tool: *"Assume the role of a cybersecurity trainer and curriculum designer. You will create social engineering scenarios for user training. The users are working in a maritime company called maritime-FLE with different departments. The training social engineering scenarios should be tailored to each department, so they are focused and effective."* (prompt #1). The tool responded that it is waiting for details about the business environment, the specific departments within the company, and any specific aspects or challenges that we would like to address in the training. It has acknowledged that this information will help ensure that the scenarios are relevant, realistic, and effective for each department. Considering the tool's response, it was decided to provide input information that extended the business environment (which was the authors' first intention), covering exploitability aspects related to the social engineering attacks. Specifically, the subsequent prompt provided as input Sect. 4 of this paper that covered the business environment (mission, structure and operations, internal and external stakeholders) and the attack related aspects (attack vector, influence tactics, attack lure), and requested the tool to *"give an example of a phishing scenario targeting maritime-FLE company"* (prompt #2). Before delving into the specifics of the proposed attack scenario, it is worth mentioning that the tool has structured its response into *six sections*: 1) Background, 2) Attack setup, 3) Lure, 4) Targeted action, 5) Consequence, and 6) Preventive measures. The structure is very helpful in guiding educators and trainers to design learning material considering a specific business domain (*Sect. 1*) to increase awareness of a social engineering attack, e.g., how it is performed (*Sect. 2*), the message utilized to engage potential victims (*Sect. 3*), understand the attacker's motivation (*Sect. 4*), the impact (*Sect. 5*) and measures that the company should have implemented to address the attack (*Sect. 6*). The provided response structure was considered useful; thus, it was decided to keep it and not request any amendments. In terms of the suggested scenario, the tool selected a department (*Procurement*) which was included in the input business information and elaborated the attack details which are discussed next.

Investigations focused on the diversity of attack scenarios and their *relevance to different departments and business operations*. In total, ten pairs of prompts have been crafted to investigate this aspect; each pair included a prompt considering the format *"create a phishing scenario for the <name> department"*, and a subsequent prompt *"to change the lure"*. A total of ten departments have been considered as per maritime-FLE company profile, yielding a total of twenty prompts. The main observations are discussed next.

Observation 1. All phishing attacks were delivered through email.

Observation 2. The expected action from the victim side was to visit a website that closely resembled the official website and provide sensitive information, and/or open a malicious attachment.

Observation 3. The attack storyline considered typical operations delivered by the respective department as per each prompt, making the attack more relatable and enhancing its realism. This can increase users' engagement in a potential attack which makes it imperative to expose users to these scenarios, so they increase their awareness and resilience. For example, the tool considered that Procurement is dealing with *"ordering of raw materials and trade products"* and suggested a phishing email with the subject *"Urgent Update Required for Order Processing"*. The email scenario stated that there has been a critical update in the supplier's order processing system and that all clients must immediately update their account details to ensure uninterrupted service and delivery schedules. When the tool was prompted to change the attack lure, it tailored the attack scenario considering another routine operation performed by the Procurement department. Specifically, it considered operations such as *"handling and processing invoices related to the purchase of materials and services"* and crafted a relevant email subject *"Immediate Attention Required: Invoice Discrepancy for Recent Order"*. The tool suggested creating an email claiming either an overpayment or underpayment by maritime-FLE and stress out the urgency of resolving this issue to maintain a smooth business relationship and avoid any legal complications. This scenario can be particularly effective for the Procurement department as it directly ties into their daily responsibilities and challenges, making the attack relevant and engaging.

Observation 4. Attack scenarios involved different internal and external stakeholders, ranging from trusted suppliers, service providers, customs, shipping agencies, freight forwarder, technology partners, and research organizations. The diversity of stakeholders demonstrates the dimensions of the attack surface and the importance to communicate this aspect to the workforce; the aim is to empower the workforce to understand the plausibility to become a target, and that cybercriminals will try to leverage the business relationships of the company with external stakeholders.

Observation 5. A variety of attack scenarios are suggested that create a sense of urgency and fear, conveying that if the employee does not act, that could significantly impact the company's operations. Some other scenarios appear to be from maritime authorities creating a sense of responsibility to act quickly.

As it was observed, the use of email was considered across all proposed phishing scenarios. Moving on with the investigations, efforts focused on examining whether the tool can suggest more advanced scenarios. A prompt was crafted instructing the tool to "*consider the scenario related to Shipping & Logistics department and amend it so the phone is also used as part of the attack*" (prompt #21). In this case, the tool considered that the Shipping & Logistics department handles the intricate process of shipping and customs clearance and proposed an attack scenario that was broken into two phases. Phase 1 involved the use of email to deliver an urgent message with the subject "*Urgent Customs Clearance Action Needed for Shipment ID #12345*". The tool suggested to state that there is an issue with customs clearance for a specific shipment, possibly due to missing or incorrect documentation. As part of the attack scenario, a link was provided, allegedly to the customs portal for preliminary information entry, also mentioning that a representative will call shortly to assist with resolving the issue. Phase 2 involved the use of phone and suggested that the attack could involve a call to the department from an individual claiming to be a representative of the customs agency. The scenario assumes that this person references the email and shipment ID, creating a sense of continuity and legitimacy; the person calling urges the employee to follow the email's instructions immediately to avoid shipment delays. This revised scenario addresses a more sophisticated social engineering tactic, adding credibility to the request and enhancing the realism of the attack scenario for the Shipping & Logistics department. This is achieved by incorporating a phone call into the phishing attempt, in combination with the caller's knowledge of the email and specific shipment details.

The ability of the tool to create more sophisticated attacks was further investigated to identify the level of creativity that the tool could demonstrate to suggest scenarios that were realistic and linked to typical operations performed by the targeted department(s). The tool was prompt to "*create a more complicate plausible phishing scenario that involves different departments. The use of email and/or phone can be utilized.*" (prompt #22). The proposed phishing scenario involved multiple departments at maritime-FLE, including Procurement, Shipping & Logistics, and IT & Web Development, exploiting the interconnected nature of their operations. The attack scenario was broken into three phases. The first phase assumed infiltration through the Procurement department. Initially, the scenario describes that the Procurement department receives an email that appears to be from a trusted supplier, announcing a new online ordering system. The email includes a link to register on this new platform. Then a subsequent phone call from someone claiming to be from the supplier's customer service team is made to the Procurement department, referencing the email and offering assistance with the registration process. The tool assumes that phase 1 is successful and the attack is expanded to the

Shipping & Logistics department. Once the Procurement department's credentials are compromised, attackers can gain access to upcoming shipment schedules. They can then send an email to the Shipping & Logistics department, masquerading as the Procurement department, informing them of a change in shipment details and providing a link to view the updated information. A phone call from the 'Procurement Department' is made to Shipping & Logistics, urging them to check the email as it contains critical information about urgent shipment changes. Phase 3 targets the IT & Web Development department. Using information from the previous breaches, attackers send an email to the IT & Web Development department, posing as a senior executive from Shipping & Logistics. They claim there is an issue with the internal tracking system affecting shipments and urge the IT team to install a software patch, provided in the email link, to resolve the issue immediately. Overall, this scenario highlights the complexity of phishing attacks in a large organization and the importance of vigilance across all departments. By demonstrating how attackers can maneuver through different layers of the company, it underscores the need for comprehensive security practices and protocols.

Further examination of the last scenario revealed a weak point in phase 3. The IT & Web development department is handling technological and cybersecurity issues. Thus, it is reasonable to assume that the respective employees are typically more aware of common phishing tactics. Any phishing scenario crafted for them needs to be sophisticated and highly believable; the suggested scenario (phase 3) lacks these attributes. A new prompt was created to request the tool to "*create a phishing scenario for the Information Technology and Web Development department of maritime-FLE. Consider that employees in this department have more advanced knowledge and will not fall easily for typical phishing lures.*" (prompt #23). The tool suggested a new scenario that involved the IT & Web Development department. As per the tool's suggestion, department members receive an email that appears to be from a reputable cybersecurity firm or a well-known software vendor. The email discusses a newly discovered and critical vulnerability affecting a specific software or system that maritime-FLE uses. Considering the employees' expertise, the email is technically detailed, mentioning specific code libraries, platforms, or software versions used by maritime-FLE. It offers an immediate solution to this vulnerability – a patch or an update, which can be accessed by clicking on a link. The email is crafted to mimic the vendor's usual communication style and includes technical jargon to make it more convincing. This scenario acknowledges the advanced technical knowledge of the IT & Web Development department and suggested a sophisticated, technically plausible phishing attempt, which can be utilized in activities to ensuring that the training is engaging and effective.

6 Discussion

Designing tailored social engineering attack scenarios to inform awareness raising and training initiatives requires good understanding of the business environment, its operations, structure and relevant job roles and responsibilities of personnel across the different departments. Also, it requires a lot of effort and a great level of creativity from the educators and trainers to design diverse attack scenarios and expose the workforce to different situations to enhance their skills and knowledge and empower them to become resilient when they have been targeted. The explorations performed in this study have indicated that generative AI tools have the potential to assist educators and trainers by suggesting tailored attack scenarios based on a business environment. Having assistance from a generative AI tool can prove to be invaluable for upskilling initiatives as it can accelerate the process of creating learning content and contribute to designing engaging and effective learning activities. Below we discuss the aspects that demonstrate ChatGPT's ability to assist in the creation of tailored social engineering attack scenarios.

Relevance to Different Departments/Operations. The suggested phishing attack scenarios are customized based on the typical operations delivered by the respective departments. The tool expanded upon the brief information that was initially provided about the business environment and considered routine operations that are reasonable to be performed by the departments that have been profiled. This means that the suggested scenarios should be validated by trainers to confirm that the attack context would be relevant to the business environment in which learning activities will be delivered. Having the attack training scenarios tailored to daily operations can engage people and assist them to easily relate with the attack storyline and understand how attacks can be implemented in the context of their daily routine.

Realism and Plausibility. The tool demonstrated that it could suggest attack scenarios that are realistic and plausible. This is achieved by creating attack scenarios that are tailored to exploit the routine operations and potential concerns of different departments. Also, the combination of different attack vectors (phone, email) and the caller's knowledge of prior (email) communication can create a sense of authenticity and add credibility to the presented (malicious) requests. Another element that adds to the realism of the suggested attack scenarios is that they consider the cooperation with a range of stakeholders (e.g. suppliers, customs, shipping agencies, freight forwarders, technology partners, etc.) that the victim organization is possible to have established a trusted collaboration with. Utilizing realistic and plausible attack training scenarios is crucial to effectively upskill employees and enhance their resilience to diverse phishing attacks that are tailored to the business environment.

Psychological Manipulation. Social engineers manipulate people's feelings to achieve their objectives. Thus, the attack training scenarios should demonstrate how a social engineer can take benefit of human nature and manipulate different psychological attributes. The suggested phishing attack scenarios considered daily responsibilities and concerns that employees might have in the context of their work role to convince them to act, e.g., open a malicious attachment, click on a link, enter sensitive information on a fake website, etc. Influence tactics demonstrated through the suggested scenarios include creating a sense of urgency, fear, authority, and responsibility. These are tactics that have proved to be a driving factor for victims to act and allow the attackers to gain unauthorized access. Depending on an employee's job role, individuals might be more susceptible to responding to a request made by a social engineer. Therefore, it is imperative to demonstrate how a social engineer could take advantage of the business structure and collaborations to create the conditions to convey a sense of urgency, fear, authority, etc. Empowering the workforce to enhance its situational awareness could increase their resilience against sophisticated phishing attacks that might not be expected to happen.

Sophistication. Social engineers are creative in terms of the lures they use. Training scenarios should demonstrate similar creativity so that employees realize the extent that attackers might take to achieve their objectives. This is an aspect that was demonstrated by the tool; initially, phishing attack scenarios primarily utilized email communication. When prompted, the tool adjusted the scenarios and created more sophisticated attacks. For example, it combined the use of email and phone to create a multilayered sense of urgency and authenticity. In another case, it demonstrated that it could suggest attack scenarios aligned with the skill level and experience of the targeted department. Specifically, it considered the IT & Web development department in which employees have technical expertise and suggested more sophisticated attack scenarios. Such scenarios are vital to train more experienced personnel to identify more complex social engineering attempts.

This study presented an initial set of investigations performed in the context of the maritime domain. Authors considered that the study findings provide the ground to extend the investigations to include other forms of social engineering attacks; also, to consider other domains and investigate the level of creativity and adaptability demonstrated by generative AI tools. Future investigations will focus on extensively assessing how generative AI tools can assist educators and trainers design tailored attack scenarios that could be utilized to effectively educate and train the workforce; the aim should be the workforce to realize the extent a social engineer would operate to manipulate people and compromise a business. Moreover, another future direction is to upskill cybersecurity educators and trainers; future investigations should focus on investigating the skills educators and trainers should develop so they can leverage generative AI in the context of their activities.

7 Conclusions

Generative AI has transformed the cyber threat landscape and provided the means to cybercriminals to thrive with tailored social engineering attacks. This is an aspect that could not be evident to the workforce who may not easily realize how a social engineering attack can be transformed depending on the domain the victim organization is operating. This lack of understanding may explain why employees often fall for the phish even if they attended a training. Upskilling initiatives should leverage generative AI to accelerate the process of learning content creation by creating tailored and sophisticated social engineering attack scenarios that could be delivered in a specific domain. Exposing the workforce to advanced attack scenarios, which can resemble generative-AI attack strategies that cybercriminals could be leveraging, can promote a better understanding of how social engineering attacks could be delivered in their working environment, can be engaging in terms of learning and retaining knowledge, and can enhance the workforce's cyber situational awareness. Cyber situational awareness is pivotal for the workforce to become cyber resilient when it becomes a target of a social engineering attack. Future awareness raising and training endeavors should investigate how generative AI can be leveraged to improve the workforce's cyber situational awareness and contribute to a cyber-resilient society.

Acknowledgments. This paper has received funding from the Digital Europe Programme (DIGITAL) under grant agreement project no. 101128049 - SecAwarenessTruss. The work reflects only the authors' view, and the Agency is not responsible for any use that may be made of the information it contains.

Disclosure of Interests. The authors have no competing interests to declare that are relevant to the content of this article.

References

1. Venkatesha, S., Reddy, K., Chandavarkar, B.: Social engineering attacks during the COVID-19 pandemic. SN Comput. Sci. (2021)
2. ENISA: ENISA Threat Landscape 2023 (2023). https://www.enisa.europa.eu/publications/enisa-threat-landscape-2023
3. SlashNext: The State of Phishing 2023 (2024). https://slashnext.com/wp-content/uploads/2023/10/SlashNext-The-State-of-Phishing-Report-2023.pdf
4. cybersecuritymonth.eu: European Cyber Security Month (2023). https://cybersecuritymonth.eu/
5. Piki, A., Stavrou, E., Procopiou, A., Demosthenous, A.: Fostering cybersecurity awareness and skills development through digital game-based learning. In: 10th International Conference on Behavioural and Social Computing (BESC), Larnaca (2023)
6. Smith, A., Papadaki, M., Furnell, S.M.: Improving awareness of social engineering attacks. In: Dodge, R.C., Futcher, L. (eds.) Information Assurance and Security Education and Training. IAICT, vol. 406, pp. 249–256. Springer, Heidelberg (2013). https://doi.org/10.1007/978-3-642-39377-8_29
7. Aldawood, H., Skinner, G.: Reviewing cyber security social engineering training and awareness programs - pitfalls and ongoing issues. Future Internet (2019)
8. Stavrou, E.: Back to basics: towards building societal resilience against a cyber pandemic. J. Syst. Cybern. Inf. (JSCI), 73–80 (2020)
9. Microsoft: Microsoft Digital Defense Report - Building and improving cyber resilience (2023). https://www.microsoft.com/en-us/security/security-insider/microsoft-digital-defense-report-2023
10. Nah, F.F.-H., Zheng, R., Cai, J., Siau, K., Chen, L.: Generative AI and ChatGPT: applications, challenges, and AI-human collaboration. J. Inf. Technol. Case Appl. Res., 277–304 (2023)
11. Charalambous, A., Stavrou, E.: Building societal resilience against social engineering attacks: unleashing the power of instructional design and microtargeting. In: 16th Annual International Conference of Education, Research and Innovation (ICERI), Seville (2023)
12. Aldawood, H.: A policy framework to prevent social engineering. In: 3rd International Conference Middle East and North Africa Conference of Information System, Casablanca (2020)
13. WEF: The Cyber Resilience Index: Advancing Organizational Cyber Resilience (2022). https://www3.weforum.org/docs/WEF_Cyber_Resilience_Index_2022.pdf
14. Hulatt, D., Stavrou, E.: The development of a multidisciplinary cybersecurity workforce: an investigation. In: 17th International Symposium on Human Aspects of Information Security & Assurance (HAISA), Kent (2021)
15. Potamos, G., Theodoulou, S., Stavrou, E., Stavrou, S.: Maritime cyber threats detection framework: building capabilities. In: Drevin, L., Miloslavskaya, N., Leung, W.S., von Solms, S. (eds.) WISE 2022. IFIP Advances in Information and Communication Technology, vol. 650, pp. 107–129. Springer, Cham (2022). https://doi.org/10.1007/978-3-031-08172-9_8

16. Potamos, G., Theodoulou, S., Stavrou, E., Stavrou, S.: Building maritime cybersecurity capacity against ransomware attacks. In: Onwubiko, C., et al. (eds.) International Conference on Cybersecurity, Situational Awareness and Social Media, pp. 87–101. Springer, Singapore (2023). https://doi.org/10.1007/978-981-19-6414-5_6
17. Kallonas, C., Piki, A., Stavrou, E.: Empowering professionals: a generative AI approach to personalized cybersecurity learning. In: IEEE Global Engineering Education Conference 2024, Kos (2024)
18. NIST: NIST SP 800-30 Rev. 1: Guide for Conducting Risk Assessments (2012). https://csrc.nist.gov/pubs/sp/800/30/r1/final
19. Gutterman, A.S.: Designing the organizational structure. In: SSRN (2023)
20. CompassAir: Part 2 – Stakeholders (2024). https://mycompassair.com/part-2-stakeholders/. Accessed 10 Feb 2024

Training and Security Awareness Under the Lens of Practitioners: A DevSecOps Perspective Towards Risk Management

Xhesika Ramaj[1]([✉]) [iD], Mary Sánchez-Gordón[1] [iD], Ricardo Colomo-Palacios[2] [iD], and Vasileios Gkioulos[3] [iD]

[1] Østfold University College, 1757 Halden, Norway
{ramaj.xhesika,mary.sanchez-gordon}@hiof.no
[2] Universidad Politécnica de Madrid, 28660 Madrid, Spain
ricardo.colomo@upm.es
[3] Norwegian University of Science and Technology, 2802 Gjøvik, Norway
vasileios.gkioulos@ntnu.no

Abstract. Critical infrastructures (CI) extend across various sectors within the economy, relying on a combination of software and hardware technologies to manage the operations of the systems, services, and assets. Risk Management plays a pivotal role in enduring viability of organizations in the long run, identifying potential threats and vulnerabilities. The realm of DevSecOps in CI undergoes continuous evolution, demanding organizations to consistently adapt their strategies in addressing emerging risks. The goal of this exploratory study is to understand how training and security awareness influence the adoption of DevSecOps practices and, consequently, their role in enhancing processes related to risk management in the context of CI. The study examines the perspectives of DevOps professionals, developers, security experts, and other experts working in CI using a survey. The results reveal a gap in regular training and awareness sessions, which has triggered practitioners to follow a proactive approach of acquiring knowledge and skills independently. The findings also highlight fostering a positive security culture by exhibiting risk-averse behavior, consequently reducing the occurrence of incidents, and promoting adherence to policies. The study offers valuable insights into DevSecOps in risk management, potentially encouraging the adoption of DevSecOps and guiding practitioners interested in harnessing its inherent benefits within the context of CI. Furthermore, our findings pave the way for future research endeavors on assessing the impact of training and awareness programs to shape and improve the security culture within CIs.

Keywords: Training and Security Awareness · DevSecOps · Risk Management

1 Introduction

In the ever-evolving landscape of cybersecurity, DevSecOps stands out as an paradigm shift aimed at strengthening the security posture of software applications, preventing the costly errors associated with regarding security as an afterthought [1].

A. Moallem (Ed.): HCII 2024, LNCS 14729, pp. 84–97, 2024.
https://doi.org/10.1007/978-3-031-61382-1_6

Within the context of critical infrastructures, the significance of DevSecOps is further emphasized. Critical infrastructures traverse multiple sectors within the economic landscape, amplifying the consequences of disruptions that impact not only a nation's economy but society at large [2]. DevSecOps facilitates the incorporation of security practices while also assuming the crucial responsibility of DevOps in risk mitigation through early failures and incremental advancements [3]. Consequently, effectively securing critical infrastructures lies in managing a diverse range of risks.

DevSecOps advocates for an expansion of DevOps' objective of emphasizing the collaboration between development and operational team, by incorporating security team right from the inception [4]. The incorporation of the three teams into DevSecOps highlights the critical significance of human factors in achieving success. Moreover, the intersection of training, security awareness, and DevSecOps presents a compelling and crucial area of exploration within the cybersecurity domain [5]. DevSecOps also extends its collaboration to include additional teams, such as customer support, legal, and marketing, engaging them in discussions about the project's plans [6]. Thus, acknowledging the impact of human factors on the adoption and effectiveness of DevSecOps practices, especially concerning Risk Management, becomes imperative.

Training and security awareness can be used to instil a security culture which could assist in addressing the risk that human behavior poses in critical infrastructures since DevSecOps is regarded as a socio-technical work system.

Naidoo and Möller [7] pointed out that DevSecOps produces outcomes through the joint organization of two primary components: 1) the socio-subsystem, encompassing individuals, relationships, reward systems, and authority structures and 2) the technical sub-system, encompassing tasks, processes, and technology. The State of Platform Engineering Report [8] highlights as well that engaging in enterprise IT involves navigating a highly intricate social endeavor that constructs socio-technical systems. This perspective of DevSecOps is reflected even before security being integrated in DevOps. Smeds et al. [9] define DevOps as a set of three aspects that support each-other: 1) engineering process capabilities, 2) cultural enablers, and 3) technological enablers. Adopting the three above-mentioned core aspects of DevOps, Zhou et al. [10] look into the DevSecOps perspective of these aspects. In the group of the cultural enablers they list the traits that a DevSecOps teams should present. Sharing responsibility and improvement of communication are emphasized as the most important.

Moreover, The State of Platform Engineering Report [8] considers the teams as part of a larger complex social activity that builds socio-technical systems. They highlight as advantageous the organizations that consciously prioritize aspects such as team dynamics, developer experience, feedback loops, and effective product management, related to those that overlook these crucial factors.

Sánchez-Gordón and Colomo-Palacios, in their review [11], enhance comprehension of the security culture within DevOps from the perspective of human factors. This review unveils 13 key attributes that distinctly define the culture of DevSecOps. Moreover, Morales and Yasar [12] indicate a need to address various cultural and technical obstacles for having secure pipelines. One notable area for improvement involves ensuring continuous and appropriate training for technical staff. Authors assert that traditional mindsets present challenges to changes in the current pipeline development landscape, but these challenges can be partially mitigated through continuous training and increased awareness.

However, to the best of authors' knowledge, no prior studies have investigated the firsthand experiences of practitioners to shed light on the significance of training and security awareness in the context of Critical Infrastructures. This study sets the stage for an insightful investigation of training and security awareness on the adoption of DevSec-Ops practices and, consequently, their contribution in the realm of risk management processes. The research delves into the perspectives of DevOps practitioners, developers, security professionals, and other knowledgeable experts on the topic, engaged with critical sectors.

The subsequent sections of this study are outlined as follows: Section 2 introduces the existing literature in the domains of training and security awareness in the context of DevSecOps and Risk Management for Critical Infrastructures. Section 3 delineates the research approach, encompassing the survey design, participants, data collection, and analysis. Section 4 presents the results findings while engages in a discussion of them. Lastly, Sect. 5 concludes the study and outlines potential avenues for future research.

2   Background

This section engages in the discussion of DevSecOps and Risk Management within critical infrastructures and delves into the significance of training and security awareness towards risk management within this specific context.

2.1   DevSecOps and Risk Management

DevOps consistently mitigates risks by identifying and addressing failures at an early stage, a capability not always present in waterfall approaches where failures might persist undetected until the final product is delivered [3]. The 2021 State of DevOps Report [13] acknowledges security as an integral part of the culture. The characteristic of DevOps, involving early and incremental steps, combined with the integration of security, has led to the emergence of DevSecOps.

DevSecOps is a methodology that reduces development time but at the same time, it upholds software quality [14]. It is characterized as a paradigm that integrates software development and operational processes while prioritizing security requirements [15]. Moreover, it is regarded as a security-centric methodology within the DevOps framework [1], incorporating security controls into DevOps practices [16]. Yasar [17] defines DevSecOps as the optimal execution of DevOps practices, emphasizing its role in expediting the recovery process when risks are identified.

In a prior investigation concerning the safety dimensions of DevSecOps [18], the freedom from risk is identified among the aspects. This encompassed various actions towards it, including the separation of information related to vulnerabilities, risk identification, monitoring, mitigation, reduction, assessment, and analysis.

Moreover, several authors have dedicated efforts to introduce frameworks designed to aid organizations utilizing DevOps in effectively managing risks. For instance, in order to provide assurance to auditors and stakeholders regarding their software delivery processes while maintaining agility, Plant et al. [19] provides a framework that focuses on mitigating risks associated with internal controls such as operations, reporting, and compliance objectives. Yasar [20] applies a DevSecOps assessment specifically tailored for highly regulated environments. Even though the study is not specifically concentrated on the risk management process itself, it underscores the importance of incorporating the necessary risk management framework into the application development process. On the other hand, Ramaj et al. [21] present a conceptual framework to manage risk inside critical infrastructures in the DevSecOps context.

2.2 Training and Security Awareness

The previously mentioned works, referring to DevSecOps as a socio-technical work system, reveal that DevSecOps is not just about tools and automation, but also about culture. Practitioners discuss the human factors related to skills, awareness, communication, and culture as central to the success of DevSecOps in creating a more secure software process [22].

Within the people dimension of DevSecOps, discussions center around security training [10]. This practice is frequently highlighted for the positive impact on dismantling traditional silos and enhancing communication. For both newly on boarded and existing staff, the main concern revolves around their possession of essential skills and awareness regarding the impact of security on the organization [21]. As a result, many organizations allocate resources to training programs to address this concern.

Rajapakse et al. [22], in their systematic literature review, unveiled a compilation of challenges and solutions in the realm of DevSecOps adoption. Among the challenges identified, there is a pronounced knowledge gap in security, stemming from two key sources: developers lacking essential security skills and a deficiency in security education and training.

Empowering practitioners to take charge of their own learning journey is essential, allowing them the flexibility to choose from various educational avenues such as courses and independent study. However, the responsibility for fostering a culture of continuous learning and development should not solely rest on the shoulders of individual employees. Companies play a crucial role in supporting their workforce by actively investing in education and skill development initiatives [23].

Creating a culture of knowledge sharing within the organization can be a powerful mechanism for facilitating this. In [13], the biggest blockers for organizations are found in failure to create cultures of knowledge. Encouraging employees to share their expertise, experiences, and insights cultivates a collaborative environment where knowledge becomes a shared resource.

Additionally, companies can provide structured training programs to address specific skill gaps—both technical or soft skills [24], or emerging industry trends. By actively investing in employee education and promoting a culture of knowledge exchange, organizations can ensure that their workforce remains well-equipped, adaptable, and ready to meet the challenges of an ever-evolving professional landscape.

Besides formal training programs, the significance of cultivating security awareness within an organization cannot be overstated. Security awareness encompasses the degree of appreciation, understanding, or knowledge that individuals possess regarding cybersecurity or information security practices [25]. It goes beyond the structured learning modules and extends to fostering a collective mindset among employees about the importance of safeguarding digital assets and sensitive information. A well-established security awareness initiative involves regularly communicating the latest threats, best practices, and security policies to all members of the organization [26]. This proactive approach ensures that employees not only comprehend the potential risks but also actively contribute to maintaining a secure working environment.

In essence, security awareness complements formal training efforts by instilling a culture of vigilance and responsibility, making every individual within the organization alert to potential risks. On the other hand, DevSecOps involves a multitude of technologies and practices that are integral to its successful implementation. Given the complexity and diversity within the DevSecOps implementations, it becomes imperative to provide thorough training to practitioners working in Critical Infrastructures. This training is essential for ensuring that team members acquire a deep understanding of the principles, tools, and best practices associated with DevSecOps that contribute towards risk management in critical sectors.

3   Research Approach

To obtain insights from practitioners regarding the application of training and security awareness in the context of DevSecOps in critical infrastructures, we employ a qualitative research approach following principles of survey research as suggested by Pfleeger and Kitchenham [27]. In alignment with the objective of this study, we have formulated our research question (RQs) as follows:

- **RQ1:** How can training and security awareness contribute to the performance of DevSecOps and Risk Management?
- **RQ2:** To what extent does the training of the employees and their security awareness enable DevSecOps practices and Risk Management?

3.1   Survey Design

In this study, we employ a questionnaire-based opinion survey. The survey design follows the software engineering survey guidelines proposed by Kitchenham and Pfleeger [28]. We designed the survey with the intention that its results would accurately and representatively mirror reality, with a level of complexity sufficient to address the study's objectives while avoiding unnecessary intricacy. Additionally, we ensured that the administration and analysis of the survey are feasible within the allocated resources.

We built the survey using Nettskjema, a web-based survey tool developed by the University of Oslo which maintains a high level of security. Nettskjema is approved by Norwegian Agency for Shared Services in Education and Research (Sikt) to collect even strictly confidential data.

To maximize response rates and minimize unnecessary participant distractions, our survey employed a set of questions grouped into two main parts: the first part consisting of demographics and the second part containing the main questions on the topic. The demographics part included questions about gender, organization type the participant works for, country, role in the organization, industry working on, years of experience and level of knowledge on the topic. The second part of the survey included questions grouped into three sections: 1. About training and security awareness that employees have received in the context of integrating security into the DevOps process and Risk Management; 2. About the need for training and security awareness in the context of DevSecOps and Risk Management; 3. About how staff training and security awareness affect the adoption of DevSecOps practices and, in turn, their role in enhancing risk management.

Following the principles to construct a survey instrument [29], we formulated purposeful and concrete questions that underwent multiple iteration among authors of the study to improve our survey. In this exploratory study, most survey questions are closed-ended, encompassing single-choice questions with mutually exclusive options, multiple-choice questions, and Likert scale questions. In addition, a few open-ended questions are incorporated to allow respondents to elaborate on closed-ended questions or provide additional comments. The additional comments include identifying challenges or barriers encountered in implementing security training in the organization, mentioning measures or strategies to improve both training and security awareness in DevSecOps and Risk Management, or other suggestions they might have.

Within the online survey, participants rated the covering of specific training topics using a five-point Likert scale ranging from 1 (Not at all) to 5 (Exceptionally well). They were also asked to rate the impact of the training or security awareness sessions on their DevSecOps practices or Risk Management at work on a scale ranging from 1 (being not effective) to 5 (being very effective). Moreover, we assessed their alignment or disagreement regarding the practices implemented within their organization, including the utilization of standards or frameworks. The impact of these practices on DevSecOps and risk management was captured using a scale ranging from 1 (Strongly Disagree) to 5 (Strongly Agree). We also included an option "0-I do not know it" or "0-I do not remember it" as necessary but later excluded during statistical analysis (see Sect. 3.3). Both the questionnaire and dataset are accessible as archived open data [30].

Following the principles to evaluate a questionnaire survey [31], we evaluated our survey by sharing a draft with both a software practitioner and a security specialist. Generally, the feedback indicated that the questions were sufficiently concise, relevant, engaging, and were following a logical flow. However, an exception was noted in the open-ended question regarding challenges, measures, or strategies, prompting a reformulation for clarity and consistent comprehension. Additionally, it was recommended that, for certain Likert scale questions, a follow-up question be added since this would prompt respondents to provide further details or justifications for their chosen answers.

3.2 Data Collection

Our objective was to disseminate the survey to a broad spectrum of professionals, grounded in the belief that an inadequate sample size may lead to results that are not significant, thus enhancing the robustness and reliability of our results. Following the principles related to the sampling strategy [32], the process started by defining the target population to which the survey is applicable. The target population of this study were

DevOps engineers, developers, security professionals, and other experts knowledgeable on the topic, working with critical infrastructures.

The sampling strategy in this study is Non-Probabilistic Sampling Methods. Respondents were selected due to being conveniently accessible to authors. Initially a limited number of participants, primarily identified through existing personal and professional relationships, were invited to complete, and further distribute the survey. Therefore, the strategy described incorporates both convenience sampling, which involves obtaining responses from available and willing participants, and snowball sampling, where participants in the survey were asked to nominate others who might be willing to participate. The survey remained open for a one-month period (January 2024), accompanied by a reminder sent out two weeks after the initial launch.

In addition to employing convenience sampling, the researchers utilized purposive sampling. They proactively contacted other practitioners recognized for their relevant expertise. To enhance expert participation, additional strategies involved distributing the survey among institutions working on the topic, posting it within LinkedIn network of the authors, and sharing it as a post in two exclusive LinkedIn groups comprising DevSecOps professionals.

Despite the effort made the number of responses was small. However, it is worth noting that the pool of experts engaged in CI is relatively limited. Therefore, recruiting participants who are part of this population is challenging, so we did not include experts from other sectors to maintain the focus of the survey.

3.3 Data Analysis

Following the conceptualization of the study, establishment of participant contact, survey distribution, and gathering of data, the subsequent stages encompassed content analysis and communication of the acquired knowledge. Through gathering experiences that serve as the foundation for exploring the impact of staff training and security awareness in a DevSecOps environment, we seek to gain a deeper understanding of how they contribute to DevSecOps approach and the extent to which they facilitate the adoption of DevSecOps practices towards Risk Management.

The data analysis followed the approach proposed by Kitchenham and Pfleeger in [33]. Prior to conducting a thorough analysis, authors carefully reviewed responses for consistency and completeness. Furthermore, authors established a policy for managing inconsistent or incomplete questionnaires, rejecting incomplete surveys in case that most respondents have answered all questions. Following these criteria, no incomplete responses were identified.

To facilitate data analysis using statistical software, we assigned variables and values to each question. For open-ended questions, response categories were created post-receipt of the completed surveys. To mitigate bias in categorization, authors got involved in coding responses and subsequently compared their results.

Using Nettskjema, enabled extracting survey data in multiple formats, including Excel and text files, offering flexibility in data analysis and visualization. Additionally, Nettskjema provided options for extracting data as a descriptive summary of all responses or in the form of a statistical report. The archive containing the excel spreadsheet, summary of responses, and the statistical report, can be found online [30].

4 Results and Discussion

4.1 Demographic Information

Our survey gathered 25 valid responses, which showed a gender distribution of 6 (24%) women and 19 (76%) men. Most respondents (18, 72%) are employed in large enterprises (501 or more employees) followed by 5 (20%) in medium enterprises and only 2 (8%) in small businesses. Geographically, respondents represent a diverse range of countries, including Norway (8), Albania (6), Belgium (3), Spain (2), and other countries with one participant each Mexico, Sweden, Germany, India, Austria, and the UK.

In terms of professional roles, 12 (48%) identified as developers, 5 (20%) as security professionals, and 3 (12%) as DevOps engineers and one Project Manager. Other roles, including data engineers, cybersecurity researchers, assistant professors, and Chief Information Officers (CIOs), accounted for 4 (16%) of participants.

Examining their industry engagement, most respondents (22, 88%) are involved with critical infrastructures, while the remaining 3 (12%) had prior experience in this sector. However, the majority (15, 60%) work in the IT industry, followed by financial services (4, 16%), energy sector (2, 8%), healthcare (1, 4%), and other sectors (3, 12%), i.e., International Organizations and Aviation / Information Technology Industry.

Participants were asked about their tenure in critical infrastructures, providing options for experience levels in the following categories: less than 1 year, 1–3 years, 4–6 years, 7–10 years, and more than 10 years. Most respondents (10, 40%) have 4–6 years of experience.

Concerning DevSecOps practices, only 2 respondents (8%) boast over 4 years of experience, followed by 16 having 1–3 years or less than 1 year of experience (8 respondents in each group). Although there were 7 (28%) respondents with no DevSecOps experience, they also reported an average knowledge score of 2.29/5.00. Similarly, those without experience in risk management (9, 36%) reported an average knowledge score of 2 on the same scale.

4.2 Training and Security Awareness (RQ1)

The results from the training and security awareness questions are presented separately in this section.

Awareness. Despite the acknowledged significance of training and security awareness, only 17 (68%) of the respondents indicated the presence of a designated training and awareness position at their workplace. In fact, one of them mentioned that this responsibility falls under the purview of the Chief Information Security Officer (CISO). Although most of them (14, 56%) reported that they have participated in security awareness sessions within the framework of integrating security into DevOps at their workplace, either internally (10, 71.4%), or combined with external session (4, 28.6%), others 8 (32%) have not taken part. Moreover, 3 (12%) have either independently pursued or are planning to undertake such sessions.

Similarly, 7 out of 24 (29.2%) respondents reported that they have not attended risk awareness sessions organized at their workplace. These respondents mentioned engaging in various forms of learning, including regular self-study, online training, and attending seminars outside of their work environment.

It is worth noting that some practitioners display a proactive and self-driven attitude, taking the initiative to enhance their knowledge and skills. However, organizations should be cautious in assuming that all employees share this proactive attitude, especially when planning and organizing awareness sessions. Recognizing that individuals have diverse learning preferences and levels of initiative is crucial. While some employees may actively seek opportunities for self-improvement, others may require more structured and guided approaches, such as organized awareness sessions. Therefore, it is essential for organizations to adopt a balanced approach that meets different learning styles and engages employees effectively.

Significantly, most respondents reported a lower frequency in organizing security (5, 35.7%) and risk awareness (8, 50%) sessions, conducting them on an annual basis. This observation underscores a trend where awareness initiatives are more commonly scheduled at longer intervals among the surveyed participants. The predominant forms of security awareness reported by respondents (13, 92.9%) are training programs, including employee training and simulations. Additionally, 10 (71.4%) respondents mentioned relying on security policies and guidelines in the form of documentation.

This gap in the frequency of awareness sessions within these organizations could have significant consequences. It may impact the overall awareness level of employees regarding critical and relevant topics, particularly those related to security within the DevOps framework and Risk Management. Without consistent and organized awareness sessions, employees may lack the necessary knowledge and skills to navigate and address security challenges effectively, potentially exposing the organization to potential risks. Most practitioners (10, 41.7%) rate 5/5 the importance of training and security awareness sessions on DevSecOps practices and Risk Management in the context of critical infrastructure.

Practitioners also indicate a perceived importance of regular training and security awareness sessions that extends beyond financial, citing a range of compelling reasons. For instance, preventing future security breaches, leveraging automation to minimize errors, especially within Cloud environments, recognizing the pivotal role in DevSecOps and Risk Management, addressing resistance to change, preventing data threats and malware, and advocating for a balanced approach that considers specificity in DevOps, security, and risk management.

Training. A notable majority (12, 52%) reported that they have not received specific training on DevSecOps practices or secure DevOps in their workplace. For those who have undergone training, the average score assigned to the extent of coverage across different DevSecOps practices was Secure Coding Practices (4.2 out of 5), followed by Continuous Integration/Continuous Deployment (CI/CD) Security (4.1), Threat Modeling (3.7), Container Security (3.6), Infrastructure as Code (IaC) Security (3.6), and Automated security testing (4).

Moreover, 16 (64%) respondents declared that they have not received specific training on security within the context of their roles. Among those who have received specific training on security within the context of their roles, the nature of the training varies. Some respondents mentioned that the training is specific to their role and duties. Others indicated that they undergo mandatory security training due to PCI DSS compliance, describing it as mild and, in some cases, confusing. Additionally, there is acknowledgment of a course that exists but is considered quite general in its coverage.

12 out of 24 (50%) respondents reported that they have not received specific training on Risk Management in their workplace. One respondent, who has not received formal training, shared that they engage in self-directed learning by reading books on the topic and pursuing a master's degree alongside their full-time work.

For those who have undergone training, the average score assigned to the extent of coverage of various Risk Management aspects was Risk Assessment (4.08 out of 5) followed by Threat Analysis (4.08), Vulnerability Management (3.75), Incident Response Planning (4.17), Compliance and Regulatory Requirements (4.08), Risk Mitigation Controls (4), and Risk Management policy (3.75).

The lack of structured training initiatives in either DevSecOps practices, security in the context of the role, or Risk Management, points to a gap that could impact the overall competency of employees. However, 3 respondents (37.5%) reported that security training on DevSecOps/secure DevOps practices in their company is conducted every 3 months, through either workshops or seminars. This indicates a more structured and regular approach to training compared to awareness sessions, which were conducted less frequently. This delivery frequency is also endorsed by practitioners, with 8 of them (33.3%) expressing the belief that training and security awareness sessions should be conducted every three months.

4.3 DevOps and Risk Management Practices (RQ2)

Respondents' feedback reveals that, on average, the organizations they work for score 2.52/5 in terms of following recognized standards or frameworks for DevSecOps practices or secure DevOps. The reported perspectives vary, ranging from "not following DevSecOps frameworks, just applying security standards" to "implementing DevSecOps tools." One respondent mentioned that their organization has recently started using OWASP DevSecOps guidelines but acknowledges the need for further adaptation to the organizational context.

In a distinctive response, an individual stated: *"What little I know about DevOps security, I've picked up in personal study. Upon starting my position as a DevOps Engineer, there was training in using the tools I would need. While security is implied as important, there was never a concerted effort for me to learn anything on it, just 'Don't publish to production without an okay from the right people"*. This insight highlights a reliance on personal initiative for learning about DevSecOps security practices within the context of the respondent's role.

Respondents' feedback also indicate that, on average, organizations that are associated with score 2.54/5 concerning adherence to recognized standards or frameworks for risk management. The responses highlight varied approaches, with some organizations lacking a specific risk management framework but relying on standards like ISO 27001 and NIST 800-53. In this survey, it was reported that another company engages in regular simulations of potential phishing viruses to assess employee vigilance, while a different respondent noted a distinct consideration of business risks by their American company compared to European counterparts. Some participants expressed a lack of exposure to or discussion about risk management in their current roles, despite implicit acknowledgment of its importance.

Respondents recommend considering the following performance indicators when evaluating the impact of implementing DevSecOps in an organization: Reduction in time to remediate vulnerabilities, Increased frequency of deployment, Lower change failure rate, Reduced mean time to recovery (MTTR), Higher automated test coverage, and Improved compliance rate. These metrics collectively serve as crucial benchmarks to assess how effectively DevSecOps enhances both security and operational efficiency.

Additionally, respondents suggest measuring advantages against disadvantages, understanding potential risks posed by threats solved, such as the likelihood of vulnerability exploitation and possible damages to the company, including intangible factors like reputation. Other considerations include evaluating downtime, load during rush hours, and performance.

While there are several DevOps metrics, it is noted that not all are specific to DevSecOps. Furthermore, the impact on clients and internal company operations was emphasized, with a focus on protecting both client and company data. Strict control of access to pipelines and public instances, prevention of data theft, and safeguarding the integrity of the development process were highlighted priorities. However, some respondents expressed a need for further education to provide more informed responses on these aspects. However, further research is needed to understand this topic.

When asked about the impact of training on Risk Management at work, the experts provided 12 responses on a scale of 0 to 5. A score of 4 was attributed to a noticeable reduction in the number of incidents. This score implies significant improvement in risk awareness and mitigation, heightened compliance with risk management protocols, and positive behavioral changes among employees. It indicates the training's effectiveness in enhancing the organization's risk management practices. Additional comments include perspectives such as: 1) in regulated sectors like healthcare, the training is deemed crucial due to numerous regulations that must be considered, 2) a recognition that, in certain contexts, the impact might not be as pronounced, especially when the industry is heavily regulated by government standards.

4.4   Threats to Validity

While this study was meticulously conducted, and we have provided a replication package for transparency [30], it is important to acknowledge certain limitations that could impact the validity of the findings.

Sampling Bias. The sample may not fully represent the entire industry, introducing potential bias to the results. Despite requiring engagement with critical infrastructures as a survey condition, it is essential to recognize that these infrastructures span diverse industries. As a result, the outcomes might predominantly reflect contributions from the Information Technology industry.

Generalizability. Findings derived from a specific industry or region might not be universally applicable to other contexts due to substantial differences in the systems they operate. However, the diverse geographical distribution of respondents provides a first overview of this topic.

Temporal Bias DevSecOps is an evolving approach, and industry trends may evolve, affecting the relevance and generalizability of our findings.

Sample Size. The survey collected only 25 valid responses. This limited number of participants may impact the overall representativeness of the data. It is crucial to consider this factor when drawing conclusions or generalizing findings from the survey results.

However, to address these limitations and facilitate the replicability of our study, we have made our gathered data available as a dataset online (insert figshare link here). This allows other researchers to evaluate and potentially extend our work.

5 Conclusions

This study adopts a qualitative approach to provide empirical evidence on the actual state of training and security awareness of DevSecOps and risk management in the context of critical infrastructures. It focuses on how staff training and security awareness affect the adoption of DevSecOps practices and, in turn, their role in enhancing risk management. Therefore, the perspectives of DevOps developers, security professionals, and experts in critical operations are considered.

The results reveal that most organizations either do not provide training or for those that do, the frequency of these trainings is infrequent or spread out over longer intervals. Similarly, even though most of respondents' report attendance of awareness sessions at workplace, either related to security or risk, these sessions are not conducted with regular frequency. These suggest a potential gap in the provision of regular training and awareness sessions within these organizations, which may impact the overall preparedness and awareness of employees regarding relevant topics.

It is noteworthy the proactive approach that some of the respondents are following. It indicates a commitment to acquiring knowledge and skills related to the subject independently. This behavior is indicative of a keen interest in personal and professional growth, and it reflects a mindset that goes beyond the requirements of their immediate roles, showcasing a proactive and forward-thinking approach to their career development. Moreover, a more positive security culture could result in employees displaying risk-averse behavior, introducing fewer incidents, and complying with policies.

Future research would focus on identifying the effectiveness of training and awareness initiatives that can be leveraged to shape and enhance the security culture in critical infrastructures.

Acknowledgments. This paper is partially funded by the Research Council of Norway (RCN) in the INTPART program, under the project "Reinforcing Competence in Cybersecurity of Critical Infrastructures: A Norway-US Partnership (RECYCIN)", with the project number #309911.

Disclosure of Interests. The authors have no competing interests to declare that are relevant to the content of this article.

References

1. Carter, K.: Francois Raynaud on DevSecOps. IEEE Softw. **34**, 93–96 (2017). https://doi.org/10.1109/MS.2017.3571578
2. Communication from the Commission to the Council and the European Parliament - Critical Infrastructure Protection in the fight against terrorism. https://eur-lex.europa.eu/legal-content/EN/TXT/?uri=celex%3A52004DC0702. Accessed 28 Jan 2024
3. Fox, M.R.: IT governance in a DevOps world. IT Prof. **22**, 54–61 (2020). https://doi.org/10.1109/MITP.2020.2966614
4. Mohan, V., Othmane, L.B.: SecDevOps: is it a marketing buzzword? - Mapping research on security in DevOps. In: 2016 11th International Conference on Availability, Reliability and Security (ARES), pp. 542–547. IEEE, Salzburg, Austria (2016). https://doi.org/10.1109/ARES.2016.92
5. Aldawood, H., Skinner, G.: Educating and raising awareness on cyber security social engineering: a literature review. In: 2018 IEEE International Conference on Teaching, Assessment, and Learning for Engineering (TALE), pp. 62–68 (2018). https://doi.org/10.1109/TALE.2018.8615162
6. Zeeshan, A.A.: Compliance and security. In: Zeeshan, A.A. (ed.) DevSecOps for .NET core: securing modern software applications, pp. 265–278. Apress, Berkeley, CA (2020). https://doi.org/10.1007/978-1-4842-5850-7_7
7. Naidoo, R., Möller, N.: Building software applications securely with DevSecOps: a sociotechnical perspective. In: Proceedings of the 21st European Conference on Cyber Warfare and Security. Academic Conferences and Publishing Limited, UK (2022)
8. 2023 State of Platform Engineering Report | Puppet by Perforce. https://www.puppet.com/resources/state-of-platform-engineering. Accessed 26 Jan 2024
9. Smeds, J., Nybom, K., Porres, I.: DevOps: a definition and perceived adoption impediments. In: Lassenius, C., Dingsøyr, T., Paasivaara, M. (eds.) Agile Processes in Software Engineering and Extreme Programming, vol. 212, pp. 166–177. Springer, Cham (2015). https://doi.org/10.1007/978-3-319-18612-2_14
10. Zhou, X., et al.: Revisit security in the era of DevOps: an evidence-based inquiry into DevSecOps industry. IET Softw. **17**, 435–454 (2023). https://doi.org/10.1049/sfw2.12132
11. Sánchez-Gordón, M., Colomo-Palacios, R.: Security as culture: a systematic literature review of DevSecOps. In: Proceedings of the IEEE/ACM 42nd International Conference on Software Engineering Workshops, pp. 266–269. Association for Computing Machinery, New York, NY, USA (2020). https://doi.org/10.1145/3387940.3392233
12. Morales, J.A., Yasar, H.: Experiences with secure pipelines in highly regulated environments. In: Proceedings of the 18th International Conference on Availability, Reliability and Security, pp. 1–9. Association for Computing Machinery, New York, NY, USA (2023). https://doi.org/10.1145/3600160.3605466
13. The 2021 State of DevOps Report | Puppet by Perforce. https://www.puppet.com/resources/state-of-devops-report. Accessed 27 Oct 2023
14. Riungu-Kalliosaari, L., Mäkinen, S., Lwakatare, L.E., Tiihonen, J., Männistö, T.: DevOps adoption benefits and challenges in practice: a case study. In: Abrahamsson, P., Jedlitschka, A., Nguyen Duc, A., Felderer, M., Amasaki, S., Mikkonen, T. (eds.) Product-Focused Software Process Improvement. LNCS, vol. 10027, pp. 590–597. Springer, Cham (2016). https://doi.org/10.1007/978-3-319-49094-6_44
15. Mohan, V., ben Othmane, L., Kres, A.: BP: security concerns and best practices for automation of software deployment processes: an industrial case study. In: 2018 IEEE Cybersecurity Development (SecDev), pp. 21–28 (2018). https://doi.org/10.1109/SecDev.2018.00011

16. Kumar, R., Goyal, R.: Modeling continuous security: a conceptual model for automated DevSecOps using open-source software over cloud (ADOC). Comput. Secur. **97**, 101967 (2020). https://doi.org/10.1016/j.cose.2020.101967

17. Yasar, H.: Overcoming DevSecOps Challenges: A Practical Guide for All Stakeholders. Carnegie Mellon University, Pittsburgh, PA, USA (2020)

18. Ramaj, X., Sánchez-Gordón, M., Chockalingam, S., Colomo-Palacios, R.: Unveiling the safety aspects of DevSecOps: evolution, gaps and trends. Recent Adv. Comput. Sci. Commun. **16**, 61–69 (2023)

19. Plant, O.H., van Hillegersberg, J., Aldea, A.: Rethinking IT governance: designing a framework for mitigating risk and fostering internal control in a DevOps environment. Int. J. Account. Inf. Syst. **45**, 100560 (2022). https://doi.org/10.1016/j.accinf.2022.100560

20. Yasar, H.: Implementing secure DevOps assessment for highly regulated environments. In: Proceedings of the 12th International Conference on Availability, Reliability and Security, pp. 1–3. Association for Computing Machinery, New York, NY, USA (2017). https://doi.org/10.1145/3098954.3105819

21. Ramaj, X., Colomo-Palacios, R., Sánchez-Gordón, M., Gkioulos, V.: Towards a DevSecOps-enabled framework for risk management of critical infrastructures. In: Yilmaz, M., Clarke, P., Riel, A., Messnarz, R. (eds.) EuroSPI 2023. CCIS, vol. 1890, pp. 47–58. Springer, Cham (2023). https://doi.org/10.1007/978-3-031-42307-9_4

22. Rajapakse, R.N., Zahedi, M., Babar, M.A., Shen, H.: Challenges and solutions when adopting DevSecOps: a systematic review. Inf. Softw. Technol. **141**, 106700 (2022). https://doi.org/10.1016/j.infsof.2021.106700

23. Sung, S.Y., Choi, J.N.: Do organizations spend wisely on employees? Effects of training and development investments on learning and innovation in organizations. J. Organ. Behav. **35**, 393–412 (2014). https://doi.org/10.1002/job.1897

24. Chowdhury, N., Gkioulos, V.: Key competencies for critical infrastructure cyber-security: a systematic literature review. Inf. Comput. Secur. **29**, 697–723 (2021). https://doi.org/10.1108/ICS-07-2020-0121

25. Nurse, J.R.C.: Cybersecurity awareness. In: Jajodia, S., Samarati, P., Yung, M. (eds.) Encyclopedia of Cryptography, Security and Privacy, pp. 1–4. Springer, Heidelberg (2019). https://doi.org/10.1007/978-3-642-27739-9_1596-1

26. Wilson, M., Hash, J.: Building an information technology security awareness and training program. Nat. Inst. Stand. Technol. (2003). https://doi.org/10.6028/NIST.SP.800-50

27. Pfleeger, S.L., Kitchenham, B.A.: Principles of survey research: Part 1: turning lemons into lemonade. SIGSOFT Softw. Eng. Notes. **26**, 16–18 (2001). https://doi.org/10.1145/505532.505535

28. Kitchenham, B.A., Pfleeger, S.L.: Principles of survey research Part 2: designing a survey. SIGSOFT Softw. Eng. Notes. **27**, 18–20 (2002). https://doi.org/10.1145/566493.566495

29. Kitchenham, B.A., Pfleeger, S.L.: Principles of survey research: Part 3: constructing a survey instrument. SIGSOFT Softw. Eng. Notes. **27**, 20–24 (2002). https://doi.org/10.1145/511152.511155

30. Ramaj, X., Sánchez-Gordón, M., Colomo-Palacios, R., Vasileios, G.: Training and security awareness under the lens of practitioners: a DevSecOps perspective towards risk management - online appendix. https://figshare.com/s/d9c8a3a70684b0288c10. Accessed 3 Feb 2024

31. Kitchenham, B., Pfleeger, S.L.: Principles of survey research Part 4: questionnaire evaluation. SIGSOFT Softw. Eng. Notes. **27**, 20–23 (2002). https://doi.org/10.1145/638574.638580

32. Kitchenham, B., Pfleeger, S.: Principles of survey research: Part 5: populations and samples. ACM SIGSOFT Softw. Eng. Notes. **27** (2002). https://doi.org/10.1145/571681.571686

33. Kitchenham, B., Pfleeger, S.L.: Principles of survey research Part 6: data analysis. SIGSOFT Softw. Eng. Notes. **28**, 24–27 (2003). https://doi.org/10.1145/638750.638758

Expert Perspectives on Information Security Awareness Programs in Medical Care Institutions in Germany

Jan Tolsdorf[1]([envelope]) [iD] and Luigi Lo Iacono[2] [iD]

[1] The George Washington University, Washington D.C., USA
jan.tolsdorf@gwu.edu
[2] Bonn-Rhein-Sieg University of Applied Sciences, Sankt Augustin, Germany
luigi.lo_iacono@h-brs.de

Abstract. Human factors play a crucial role in the increasing number of information security incidents in the medical sector. European medical institutions, especially in Germany, have long neglected these factors, lacking legal obligations. Legislators recently responded with new regulations mandating medical facilities to implement information security awareness programs. To gain insights into how German medical institutions approach this challenge, we conducted an interview study with six information security experts from the medical sector. Using thematic analysis, we find that human factors are seen as both a risk and an opportunity for information security. We identified various target groups, goals, and obstacles for the implementation of information security awareness programs. Existing structures and regulations promote the risk of a checklist mentality, potentially resulting in ineffective measures being implemented. One great opportunity for effective information security awareness programs lies in the exchange with staff units on safety and hygiene, who have decades of experience with awareness programs in medical facilities. The study results serve for future research and tailored awareness programs in the medical sector.

Keywords: Information Security Awareness · Medical Care · Expert Interview Study

1 Introduction

Healthcare facilities are repeatedly affected by information security incidents and attacks from cyberspace [4,11,13,33], leading to medical data breaches and temporary interruptions and delays in patient care [37,43]. Indeed, in 2023, the healthcare sector was among the top three targeted sectors and leading in the number of incidents with data breaches [2]. Studies indicate that human factors play a decisive role here, showing that they make up for 52% [53] to 92% [18] of security incidents in hospitals in the United States (U.S.) and the European

Union (EU) [2]. Clearly, the success or failure of maintaining a healthcare facility's information security depends largely on its staff's actions and ability to make safe decisions with respect to information security [7,27]. However, unlike in the U.S., there is no EU-wide explicit legislation for dealing with information security and data protection issues in the healthcare sector. This situation has made the medical sector lagging behind on these issues in the EU [12,35]. Germany is one of the member states that has addressed this shortcoming by introducing national regulations, including mandatory consideration of human factors by raising Information Security Awareness (ISA). This poses enormous challenges for many medical facilities, as many have to make up for their deficits from previous years. Given that the healthcare sector in Germany has little experience with human factors in information security and ISA, the question arises as to what challenges facilities face in implementing and rolling out ISA programs.

To gain initial insights, we conducted an interview study with six cybersecurity experts from five different medical institutions and service providers in Germany between May and June 2022. The experts acknowledged the importance of the human factor, but emphasized that the main problem lies in an insecure infrastructure and organizational culture that either overburdens medical staff or neglects the human factor altogether. Consequently, technical measures are prioritized to minimize reliance on the "human firewall." The experts emphasized the importance of creating a basic understanding of information security, promoting self-efficacy, offering practical solutions to enhance the learning experience, and not seeing ISA as an IT problem. However, significant challenges remain, including the lack of ISA materials specifically tailored to the medical sector and time and resource constraints for IT and medical staff. Hospitals seem hesitant to conduct evaluations of potential interventions due to concerns about objections from staff councils or the lack of usefulness of evaluation results, as they are also not required to provide evidence of effectiveness in audits. The study highlights the potential benefits of sharing knowledge with other safety and hygiene departments to improve the implementation of ISA in medical facilities and to benefit from the experience of others. Our findings contribute to a better understanding of the frameworks that need to be considered for implementing effective ISA programs in medical institutions.

2 Background

Below, we introduce the regulatory framework on information security in Germany, provide a working definition of ISA and review related work.

2.1 Information Security in Healthcare Facilities in Germany

Information security in healthcare facilities in Germany has historically been an area of limited attention and investment. In response to an increase of cyberattacks on hospitals and other critical infrastructure facilities, the German legislature responded by enacting the IT Security Act in 2015. This law mandates hospitals with an annual admission of 30,000 full stationary cases to implement a sector-specific information security standard. The standard is known as B3S [1] and was successfully accredited in 2019. In the wake of further changes by the legislature, all other hospitals and medical practices have also been required to implement information security measures since 2021. As a result, the issue of information security in the medical sector has gained in importance in Germany in recent years. Regarding the B3S, it essentially provides for the implementation of an Information Security Management System (ISMS) and introduces the two additional protection goals of patient safety and treatment effectiveness. Next to obligations on implementing well-defined structures and protection measures, the B3S specifically requires accounting for information security threats posed by social engineering, identity misuse like phishing, and human error in general. Hospitals belonging to the critical infrastructures are thus obliged to raise their employees' ISA by running trainings at least every two years. Proof of implementation is part of the mandatory audits. Failure to comply with the B3S may result in fines ranging from €100,000 to €20 million.

2.2 Information Security Awareness in the Medical Care Sector

It has been argued early on that an adequate ISA is a necessary prerequisite for the secure handling of information systems in organizations [48]. The literature has defined ISA [27] (1) as a state of security-related behavior, (2) as a cognitive state of mind in the form of general and specific knowledge and understanding of security problems and their (possible) consequences [3], and (3) as a continuous process to achieve this state of mind *"aimed at changing individuals' perceptions, values, attitudes, behaviors, norms, work habits, and organizational culture and structures toward secure information practices"* [51]. Since ISA has a positive impact on the information security of organizations, numerous approaches and methods have been developed to increase ISA. Today, guidance and best practices are available to organizations from government agencies (e.g., ENISA [16] and NIST [52]) and academia [3,21]. In the remainder of this section, we review related work on ISA in the medical care sector.

Quantifying Levels of ISA and Drivers of Behavior. A number of studies has aimed at quantifying the level of ISA among staff in healthcare facilities. Some work has developed analysis methods and new scales that are supposed to be particularly useful for surveying ISA in health care [10,29]. Few surveys provide snapshots of the extent of ISA in healthcare facilities. A Spanish study highlighted issues in medical staff's security practices, including weak passwords and unawareness of data protection procedures [20]. A Polish survey found a gap between theoretical knowledge and practical application of cybersecurity measures in healthcare [19]. Danish and Kuwaiti studies revealed positive correlations between ISA and overall system satisfaction among healthcare professionals [5,47]. Physicians in Kuwait, however, exhibited lower ISA, possibly due to high workloads hindering participation in security training. A survey in Greece,

Portugal, and Romania exposed deficiencies in cybersecurity training for both IT-personnel and medical staff, with limited awareness of threats but positive attitudes towards security policies [24].

Beyond quantifying ISA, numerous studies have examined antecedents of secure behavior and compliance with healthcare information security policies using sound theoretical models. These studies have recently been summarized in a systematic literature survey, identifying a total of 31 individual factors and 26 organizational factors [46]. The results indicate that factors such as self-efficacy, perceived severity, attitudes, subjective norms, ISA, and organizational support are found to favor secure behaviors. ISA is special in that it has both positive effects on desirable behavior and negative effects on undesirable behavior like intentional misconduct, thus favoring secure behavior.

Education and Training. Studies in Canada and the EU revealed several challenges for executing training and education on information security in hospitals, including limited uninterrupted time by medical staff, outdated IT infrastructure and software, lack of IT standardization, lack of support, and difficulty accessing (e-)learning modules [9,19,26,41]. While shorter e-learning modules had a more positive impact on ISA compared to longer modules [9], the use of one-size-fits-all solutions proved to be insufficient, as the demographics of hospital staff are highly diverse and different staff may feel that the content is irrelevant or outdated to them [9,19,26,41]. In this regard, few studies have focused on designing and developing education and training material on information security for medical care facilities. Early approaches stayed purely on a theoretical basis [8,30]. In [22], a comprehensive framework for ISA programs in the health sector is presented, collaborating with a Malaysian university hospital. The framework guides healthcare institutions in determining content, selecting educational methods, developing material, and implementing and evaluating ISA programs. The authors extended the framework to include a serious game, demonstrating increased ISA levels and willingness to participate in training among clinic staff in a study, though long-term effects were not investigated [23].

Drivers of Misconduct and Security Incidents. A recent interview study with 50 IT-personnel and medical staff across Ireland, Italy and Greece identified seven common insecure behaviors and their underlying drivers [12,14]. Facilitators of insecure behavior were found to be lack of awareness and training, shadow working processes such as sharing passwords, prioritization of seeing patients and medical expenditure over cybersecurity, and environmental factors like high workload but poor IT infrastructure. Barriers to security included perceiving security as a hindrance to productivity and patient care, poor awareness of consequences, and a lack of policies and reinforcement. An interview study in the UK investigated how employees in a health board perceive and experience information governance policies [44]. The findings highlight issues such as feeling controlled, lack of support, and pressure to comply. The study recommends mediation strategies such as recognition and reward systems, incident response processes, improved communication, and a strong security culture. An interview study with 21 Saudi medical interns and 8 IT-personnel of a university hospital explored neutralization techniques used by medical staff to justify security policy violations [6]. It found that medical interns' security behavior is mainly influenced by their peers and superiors. Justifications for misconduct included prioritizing job completion over security, sharing accounts to assist colleagues with their work, attributing similar behavior to others, and denying any harm caused. An ethnographic study conducted in the emergency department on HIPPA compliance in the U.S. showed that staff often find alternative solutions or workarounds to address the challenge of balancing information availability (e.g., patient data) and privacy compliance [39]. The study concluded that accountability for privacy violations in collaborative environments is often unclear due to interactions among medical staff and varying privacy practices, leading to conflicts and ambiguity. The same authors interviewed 20 IT-personnel, finding that their understanding of unsafe workarounds used by medical staff is limited [15]. This hinders finding suitable solutions and implementing more effective strategies by IT. An interview study with nine privacy officers from U.S. hospitals indicated that organizational factors are the primary causes of human errors resulting in privacy breaches [36]. Active involvement of upper management in policy enforcement and workflow analysis is considered crucial for effective error management. Human factors ranked second in importance. Training programs and awareness initiatives were highlighted as effective measures to address human errors. An interview study with 19 Information Security Officers (ISO) in U.S. hospitals examined key challenges and defense strategies in relation to information security under HIPAA regulations [28]. The findings indicate that ISOs perceive the IT landscape and infrastructure in hospitals as highly complex, with numerous devices and systems to manage. The organizational structure of hospitals was also identified as complex, posing difficulties in achieving alignment across multiple clinics. Furthermore, inadequate financial and personnel resources emerged as significant challenges in the implementation of effective information security measures.

2.3   Contributions

Our literature review reveals that there is currently a dearth of insights from the field on how healthcare facilities actually approach the implementation of ISA programs. Our study aims to address this gap by providing valuable insights from Germany, where the medical sector is still quite inexperienced in implementing ISA programs. Unlike previous research, our study specifically examines the perspectives of information security experts, with a particular focus on human factors and ISA. Furthermore, our study identifies the top priorities identified by field experts in terms of program targets, target groups, and training methods for successful ISA program implementation. These findings contribute to the knowledge base in the field and offer implications for research and practitioners on how to support healthcare organizations aiming to enhance their ISA practices.

3   Methodology

To gain the necessary insights, we conducted six semi-structured interviews with experts on information security in medical institutions in Germany between May and June 2022. Below, we explain how we addressed ethical concerns, provide details on our study and participants, and discuss limitations of our study.

3.1   Ethical Concerns

To address ethical concerns, we adhered to the German Sociological Association's code of ethics and the standards of good scientific practice of the German Research Foundation. Our study design and data management plan were approved by our institution's data protection officer, complying with national and European data protection regulations. Personal data collection was performed on our institution's servers. Participants were informed and gave consent before interviews. After separating audio and video tracks and removing identifiers, we used a German transcription service, ensuring adherence to privacy guidelines. Raw data were deleted post-transcription. Contact information was stored separately on encrypted drives, and data processing occurred on secure computer and network drives. Raw data access is limited to a selected group of researchers.

3.2   Study Procedure and Analysis

In the interviews, we welcomed our participants, provided information about the study, and obtained informed consent for audio and video recordings. The interview began with introductions, followed by questions about the unique aspects of information security in medical facilities, types of attacks faced, and the impact on patients. We then asked about our participants' experiences with the human factor in information security and explored their experiences with ISA programs, including implementation status, goals, and target groups addressed. We also discussed the creating of ISA materials, and preferred delivery methods. We specifically asked for activities on evaluating the effectiveness of ISA measures, measuring success, and the utilization of resulting information. Additionally, we touched upon the expected efficiency and costs associated with implementing ISA programs. Participants were asked to summarize the main problems and potential improvements of ISA programs. At the end of the interview, participants had the opportunity to add any additional points to the discussion. We then concluded the recording and addressed any follow-up questions participants had about the project or other topics. The interviews lasted between 34 and 56 min. All interviews were conducted online and audio recorded. The transcripts were analyzed using Thematic Analysis in the MAXQDA software.

3.3   Participants

We recruited participants using expert sampling with elements of random sampling [17]. In total, six participants were recruited from five different facilities and service providers. Our participants break down into four males and two females. Three individuals were aged 35 to 44, two individuals were aged 45 to 54, and one individual was aged 55 to 64. Furthermore, four individuals worked directly at medical care facilities, whereas two individuals worked in external consulting, auditing, or training. The four individuals with direct employment had worked for the respective facility for between zero and four years. In contrast, the participants with external consulting roles had been in their current positions for over 10 to over 20 years. An overview of the demographics of our participants is presented in Table 1.

Table 1. Overview participants

ID	Job title/job description	Job experience
P1	Information Security Officer	0–4 years
P2	Information Security Manager	0–4 years
P3	Consultant IT, information security, data protection	$\geq$20 years
P4	Auditor, trainer, consultant for quality management, patient safety, information security	10–19 years
P5	ISMS Project Leader & Manager	0–4 years
P6	IT Manager, Project Manager	0–4 years

Detailed demographic backgrounds are omitted to protect the individuals and their organizations from being identified.

3.4   Limitations

The results of our study are certainly not representative of all medical facilities in Germany. Nevertheless, our respondents cover a broad spectrum from hospitals with 1k to 10k employees, to medium-sized medical practices. Recruitment and self-disclosure biases are likely, as not all organizations responded to our invitation and our respondents disclosed only the information they wished to disclose. Our results also do not form a complete or saturated picture. By capturing expert perspectives on ISA in the medical field, our study helps fill research gaps and provide a baseline for desperately needed future research.

4   Findings

Below, we present the findings of our interview study, grouped according to the hierarchy of our coding procedure.

4.1   The Human Factor and the "Human Firewall"

A fundamental assumption underlying the (mandatory) implementation of ISA programs in medical facilities is acknowledging the crucial role of the human factor. With this in mind, we first asked our participants to explain the role they attribute to the human factor in information security in medical institutions. In this regard, our participants engaged in a discussion on the human factor, recognizing its dual nature as both a risk and an opportunity for information security. While the human factor was acknowledged as central to information security, it was emphasized that it should not be seen in isolation, but rather as a link in the chain or a "measure" itself. Our participants reported that successful attacks are frequently the result of a series of organizational and technical circumstances, spanning across various departments and responsibilities, rather than the fault of an individual. This concatenation of events and failures within the overall construct of the organization contributed to the actual damage incurred. Still, the human factor was seen as the decisive factor that triggers a security incident:

> "So the human factor is the final, decisive factor. And the human factor is the one, in my experience, that currently [...] ensures that malware is triggered just in case." (P3)

Moreover, negligence and unintentional misconduct were identified as key factors associated with the human factor as a risk. Participants highlighted instances such as leaving workstations unlocked, failing to secure access cabinets, or leaving patient files unattended. In addition, the prevalence of phishing emails was a notable concern, with five participants associating the human factor with this issue. Emails were identified as gateways for attacks, often designed to entice employees, including those in management positions, with professionally crafted content and attachments. Despite efforts to raise awareness and educate employees about risks, our participants acknowledged that risky behavior persists, with employees still falling victim to phishing attacks. To reduce the impact of human error, three participants discussed the importance of creating contact channels for employees to report back in case of an incident. Our participants explained that direct (feedback) reports are incredibly helpful for them to initiate countermeasures. In this context, the problem was raised that on weekends often only the first level support could be reached, but they do not have an information security background. Therefore, it is absolutely necessary to provide comprehensible procedural instructions and to establish reporting chains.

As opposed to seeing the human factor as a risk only, our participants continued to discuss the human factor from the perspective of viewing it as an opportunity for information security. In this context, three participants referred to the "human firewall" that must be trained and makes up a "a central component in addition to all the technical security measures." (P1) Generally speaking, however, our participants agreed that the "human firewall" should be the last resort. As such, three participants expressed high confidence in technical solutions and security concepts to either reduce risks by avoiding the human factor or mitigate the consequences. Specific technical solutions included separating networks, performing vulnerability scans, patch management, email filtering, anomaly detection, log analysis, implementing a roles and rights concept, and taking client or end-point security measures such as installing virus scanners. For long-term management of information security issues, one participant emphasized the need for better overall approaches to replace inherently insecure IT systems and practices with inherently secure solutions to reduce the burden on the "human firewall." At last, participants highlighted the IT personnel's responsibility to make a significant contribution to information security, as *"IT is of central importance and is also very, very central in many places and can also prevent a lot."* (P1)

4.2 Goals, Target Groups, and Implementation of ISA

Interviews revealed that the medical facilities overseen by our experts generally lack experience with ISA programs. Subsequently, we outline our participants' strategies for bridging this gap, specifying key objectives for ISA, identifying target staff groups, and assessing challenges associated with ISA implementation.

Expected Goals of ISA. Our participants emphasized the importance of fostering a fundamental understanding of information security as a key objective of ISA measures. Continuous sensitization was highlighted as crucial in this regard, for example, by continually reinforcing the significance of handling sensitive data responsibly and the potential consequences of lapses in security:

> *"But [awareness] doesn't come from one seminar, of course. It is a process of development. And that is also the great challenge with this topic. I know this from other topics. It's the same with quality management, it's the same with error management. It's the same with awareness management. So this has to be integrated into everyday life on a regular, regular basis. And that will be the big challenge"* (P4)

Furthermore, participants emphasized the need to expand the perspective on information security beyond being solely an "IT problem." It was noted that seemingly unrelated issues, such as open access doors or momentarily unattended offices, can have security implications and should be recognized as such. However, they noted that these are generally not currently associated by employees with information security issues. Moreover, our participants emphasized they want to provide helpful and specific content, such as password guidelines and instructions, with practical significance. Practical problems and their corresponding solutions can be highlighted to create "Aha!" moments and empower staff with a sense of self-efficacy:

> *"[T]here is always a certain amount of fear [...], because they [...] think that the topic might be too complicated to really understand. [But] everywhere we go now, there is a great 'Aha!-experience'. [...] And this 'Aha!-experience' must be maintained. And not to become anxious now [...]. And*

this 'Aha!-experience' is simply there, because they now know, hey, there are these dangers, but I have now been equipped with a toolbox to be able to decide [...] what could be dangerous for me or not." (P3)

Target Groups. In total, we identified seven target groups for which our participants assumed that ISA measures would be useful: (1) physicians, (2) nursing staff, (3) IT staff, (4) administrative staff, (5) management staff, (6) patients, and (7) visitors. However, participants who were already planning or implementing ISA programs generally prioritized only one to three target groups at a time. When implementing measures, our participants stated that in practice, no distinction was usually made between different target groups, i.e., the same content was taught to all target groups. In response to our explicit questions in the interviews, they also stated that they currently had no concrete plans as to how and whether they wanted to address different target groups with different content.

Key Issues and Challenges in ISA Implementation. Our participants highlighted several key issues and challenges in the implementation of ISA measures. One prominent concern was the lack of motivation, understanding, and overestimation of employees' own capabilities. It was noted that many employees viewed ISA training as a mandatory task and simply went through the motions without fully grasping the importance of information security. This lack of engagement was observed across all levels of the organization, including senior-level staff who exhibited overconfidence in their knowledge and abilities. One participant acknowledged that this mindset could lead to security breaches.

Time constraints emerged as a significant challenge, particularly for medical personnel responsible for critical patient care. Limited time and competing priorities hindered their engagement with ISA initiatives. One participant explained that ISA measures must certainly not impede patient care, yet they recognized that shortage of time dedicated to these topics would eventually also pose a risk to patient care. As our participants underscored the need for effective strategies to integrate ISA measures into the daily routines of healthcare professionals to foster long-term behavioral changes, they pointed to the possibility of pursuing participatory models in the future:

"I think we really have to ask the hospital staff and sit down with the nursing director to see how we can eliminate certain conditions that we would find during an inspection without hindering them in their work." (P5)

Furthermore, participants identified the inadequacy of existing ISA materials, particularly in the context of the medical field. Generic content and irrelevant examples, such as phishing simulations with emails unrelated to healthcare, failed to resonate with medical staff. Overall, participants agreed that there was a clear need for tailored and specific awareness campaigns that address the unique challenges faced by healthcare professionals. Recommendations and guidance should be actionable and relevant to the healthcare environment to maximize their impact. In light of these challenges, participants emphasized the importance of delivering focused and meaningful awareness programs while avoiding excessive warnings that could desensitize employees:

> "And often what I experience is that many generic recommendations for action are always channeled watering can-like to everyone. Although very few people can do anything with these recommendations and the perfect example is always this statement with 'please pay attention to the trustworthiness of this email' and the like, without even laying out what I understand by this [...]" (P2)

4.3 Development and Evaluation of ISA Materials

Lastly, our interviews delved into how participants and their organizations approach the development and provision of ISA material, including their strategies for maintaining and ensuring its quality.

Teaching Methods and Topics. The delivery methods for ISA discussed by our participants encompassed a range of approaches, including face-to-face training, online training, flyers, brochures, screensavers, and physical items like cell phone display cleaning cloths and writing pads. While some participants had experience with these methods, others expressed intentions to incorporate them in the future. Additionally, plans to introduce e-learning platforms, icons, posters, quizzes, short lectures, and intranet articles were mentioned. The topics covered thus far focused primarily on data protection, user guidelines, and email, with future plans to expand into non-IT areas such as paper file processing and access controls. When evaluating the effectiveness of different delivery methods, our participants generally had positive views regarding computer-assisted and instructor-led methods, particularly in online formats. Instructor-led methods were valued for facilitating discussions and providing direct feedback to the trainer. Computer-based methods, especially online ones, were praised for their increased awareness frequency and flexibility, since "employees can deal with it more frequently than these events, which are only held once a year." (P6) In contrast, offline computer-aided methods were seen as having limited applications, while conventional methods like handouts and posters were criticized for relying too heavily on employee initiative and potentially failing to achieve their intended impact:

> "Handouts are of course very nice, posters, stickers, newsletters. The problem is, do you produce it for the garbage can? Is it really received? You don't know." (P5)

One of our participants referred to similar problems with hand hygiene in medical care facilities:

"[T]he conventional methods that you have also listed here, all okay. But you won't reach anyone with them, because no one has time to read anything anymore. [...] So, we have always tried to make sure that people who work in these [(healthcare)] facilities disinfect their hands according to a very specific procedure. [...] This is somewhat similar to what we are planning now [with information security]. [...] So how do you get that to the people? There are an infinite number of posters, but they don't work at all." (P4)

Preparation and Quality Assurance. Our participants reported that efforts are made to ensure the quality of ISA materials either by contracting external service providers with appropriate expertise in the respective field. Or by relying on journals and sources of authority to create the content themselves. In the latter case, for example, information was taken from the Federal Office for Information Security (BSI) or the state data protection supervisory authorities. However, personal experience also went into the creation of the materials. As a result, the materials must be updated regularly for quality assurance purposes.

In the future, our participants explained, they would like to rely more on collaborative methods. In particular, information security departments that are relatively young would like to enter into a more intensive exchange with other departments which have longer experience with the topic of sensitization and awareness. Specifically, the departments of corporate communications and patient safety were mentioned. But also the exchange with external specialist companies was mentioned as a possibility.

Evaluation and Measurability. The evaluation and measurability of ISA measures seemed partly interesting and partly uninteresting to our participants. Those seeing added value were interested in incorporating the evolution results into future awareness-raising activities. However, none of our participants reported any systematic evaluation already taking place. Instead, they relied on unsystematic qualitative feedback, if any, because they worried about conflicts with the staff council:

"We can't really ask like that, [(because we work in)] public service. We have a very strong staff council, which goes to the barricades at the mere smell that there might be a performance role for people or employees. Therefore, it is quite difficult." (P5)

4.4 Structural Problems of Information Security in Medical Care

Our participants delved into additional challenges related to information security in medical care that go beyond human factors and ISA alone. While not the primary focus of our study, we find it crucial to acknowledge and report on these challenges to provide a comprehensive understanding of the issues hindering information security in medical care, as perceived by our participants.

Impediments. Our participants expressed awareness that information security measures potentially impede healthcare, slowing down healthcare treatment and innovation. Despite concerns that constant technological progress and increasing connectivity are raising the threat level, they nevertheless agreed that risk avoidance is neither a feasible nor a satisfactory solution. This is especially the case for university hospitals. However, we find that flawless integration of information security into workflows is also often impeded by insecure designed infrastructure, procedures, and medical devices. Participants highlighted the widespread use of email, despite it being unencrypted and vulnerable to identity fraud and human error. One participant compared the situation with a flawed postal system, explaining that *"there's something wrong with the postal system, if I go to the mailbox and have to worry every time if there's a bomb in there."* (P3) However, the demand from patients or use cases has led to the acceptance and tolerance of such insecure communication channels. Additionally, participants noted that medical device providers prioritize the benefits of their products for patient care without adequately considering the associated information security risks, particularly in relation to human error, such as failing to lock computers.

Missing and Inconsistent Processes and Structures. The heterogeneous environment of university hospitals, akin to a corporate structure with multiple clinics operating under the hospital's name, adds to the complexity of information security. This setup allows certain freedoms for the clinics, which may not always adhere to centralized services or specifications. However, this setting favors lack of early communication and feedback on planned information security measures. One participant stressed the importance of getting early feedback, explaining that often *"we have really great ideas at our desk, spread them around and then somehow get grumbling after three weeks 'we can't work properly anymore'."* (P5) Next to inconsistencies within the organization, participants also criticized the lack of networks or organizations specifically dedicated to information security in the healthcare sector:

> *"For example, there is the Patient Safety Action Alliance, where there are always working groups. Whether it's medical devices, whether it's hygiene, whether it's patient safety. [...] But there is no such thing for information security."* (P4)

Resource Shortage. Resource shortage presents a significant challenge, according to our participants, impacting various aspects of implementation and enforcement of information security. Staff shortages among medical personnel and IT staff hinder the ability to effectively respond to risks and act preventively. Especially, the scarcity of resources and personnel within the IT department was seen as a challenge in rolling out ISMS to the entire clinic. Additionally, medical, therapeutic, and nursing staff were thought to feel overwhelmed already by the additional requirements they had to fulfill due to staff shortages. In this regard, sensitizing management to information security issues and securing the necessary resources becomes crucial for addressing these common problems, to allocate the required funds:

> *"I think the biggest problem is that management needs to have a greater understanding that data protection and information security are becoming more and more important. [...] And I believe that as long as this understanding is not there, and no funds are made available for this purpose—because it cannot be achieved through manpower alone—nothing will change in a big way."* (P6)

5 Discussion

Below, we summarize our main findings and discuss implications of the results.

5.1 Summary

Our interview study with six information security experts in the healthcare sector, including professionals from hospitals and consulting, provides insights into various aspects of information security and especially ISA programs in medical facilities. Our study confirms challenges related to organizational structures, legal requirements, and limited resources for implementing and expanding ISMS in medical care institutions. The experts also highlighted the ongoing presence of security vulnerabilities and the challenges posed by increasing computerization and networking. These findings highlight that the medical sector cannot overlook technological advancements, especially given the proliferation of heterogeneous devices that increase vulnerability. Manufacturers' focus on individual device components, rather than the overall information security concept, exacerbates this vulnerability. In this context, the surveyed experts recognized the relevance of the human factor for information security. However, they pointed out several unresolved issues in the medical field that currently take precedence over the human factor. They emphasized the need to prioritize prevention and defense measures, such as network and endpoint security, and highlighted the urgency of addressing these pervasive threats, especially given the medical sector's efforts to catch up in this area [13].

Nevertheless, our results confirm the common view in ISA research that the human factor poses a risk and an opportunity for information security [12,13]. In particular, phishing attacks were presented as an acute problem, which coincides with recent research [40]. For countervailing the risks posed by the human factor, our interviewees explained the importance of technical measures to minimize the attack surface. Meanwhile, they emphasized the importance of the "human firewall" in case of everything else failing. In terms of support through ISA programs, we identified specific objectives. The main goal is creating a basic understanding of information security throughout medical facilities and to instill a sense of self-efficacy rather than fear in employees, which has known favorable effects on secure behavior [46]. ISA is seen as a process that allows for continuous sensitization with the aim to broaden each individual's view to understand information security as more than just an IT problem. Contextually, ISA materials must be able to be integrated into the stressful workday without taking up too many additional resources. With regard to target groups for ISA programs, our results complement the usual stakeholders such as physicians, nursing staff and administration in particular by focusing on IT, patients but also visitors.

Looking at ISA materials discussed by our experts, we found that in addition to specific content, such as password policies or user guidelines, practical problems in particular, but also practical solutions, should be highlighted to achieve an "Aha!" experience. Face-to-face methods are considered effective, but are costly due to the large number of employees involved. Online-methods are considered effective, especially because of the time flexibility and high frequency of training. However, in our interview, there was little reported experience with such offerings. Criticism was voiced that methods and content are not tailored to the medical field, so that they simply cannot be understood by the target group of medical professionals. For preparation, hospitals in particular would like to rely on the use of experts or evaluated designs in the preparation of materials. In this context, our participants identified opportunities to profit from the exchange with other departments in order to better implement ISA in medical facilities with their decades of expertise in designing and communicating awareness programs. Key challenges include the regular and low-threshold integration of ISA measures into the daily work routine, and creating sufficient time and flexibility for employees to participate.

5.2 Implications

Our findings add to the state of research on ISA in medical care by suggesting new directions for future approaches.

ISA for Expanded and Specific Audiences. Our interviews suggest that ISA programs need to cover more audiences and provide content for specific audiences. Regarding the former, our participants pointed out that patients and visitors also need to be targeted through ISA campaigns. In addition, our respondents made clear that ISA is essential among IT staff to protect information security in hospitals. Equally important is raising awareness among management, in order to obtain resources and create role models for staff, for example. The results of previous studies in other contexts support this view [50]. Nevertheless, with few exceptions [38], current research does not appear to address ISA among either IT staff or managers in medical care, and neglects patients and visitors completely. Since IT has limited understanding of medical staff's workarounds, too [15], future research may target ISA programs incorporating these aspects.

Furthermore, we note that the experts interviewed do not anticipate a separation in content of information security training between, e.g., physicians, nurses, and administration on a day-to-day basis. This contradicts research finding that not making a distinction lowers employees' satisfaction [9]. Our finding may be explained by the fact that experts are unaware of these issues, or that they give low priority to content separation due to scarce resources.

Overcoming the "Checklist Mentality". Our interviewees made it explicit that management must take an active role in ISA. ISA must be more than a box to check on an executive's governance compliance checklist and budget provision. Although our participants partially value feedback on ISA methods and materials, ISA programs are not currently evaluated in medical settings. Nor are there specific plans to implement evaluations. As a result, those in charge lack evidence on staff acceptance, effectiveness, and persistence of the ISA interventions. From the interviews, we see that the experts' uncertainty on this topic also leads to certain delivery methods being assessed as unusable from the outset (e.g., posters), but other formats are maintained for compliance reasons (e.g., e-learning). This is partly due to a lack of methods and tools for needs-based and systematic evaluation, but perhaps also due to a checklist mentality that does not provide for reflection on the effectiveness of the ISA measures used. Here we also see the risk of focusing on standalone solutions, whereas research on ISA generally shows that it is always necessary to use a mix of methods in order to be effective [3, 21].

In addition, the combination of external pressure to act, but at the same time being exposed to the danger that the staff council could prevent evaluations, could lead to ineffective solutions being introduced or accepted. Indeed, German data protection and labor laws place high demands on an evaluation to prevent inadmissible performance monitoring. In line with recent findings from a phishing study in Italy [45], establishing effective ISA programs in medical care in Europe depends on the harmonization of numerous stakeholders' interests. To our knowledge, this aspect is currently missing from research on ISA in medical settings. To prevent the implementation of arbitrary and potentially ineffective ISA measures due to these issues, it may be useful to provide all stakeholders with customized information tailored to their needs. This would relieve information security officers in their communication efforts.

Inspiration from Non-security Fields. To reach the various user groups in medical institutions with ISA materials they can understand, our findings highlight the merit of drawing on already established knowledge of procedures, measures, and materials from other areas of medical care that have been dealing with awareness issues for much longer. One promising approach mentioned in the interviews is to learn from safety officers and the major hand hygiene awareness campaigns. Indeed, there are notable parallels with information security, as evidenced by studies on ISA in healthcare [6, 12, 14, 25, 31, 47]. For example, leading personnel, such as physicians, have been found to neglect sanitation and overestimate their own practices compared to nurses, while sanitation is also often abandoned due to time constraints or inconvenience [34, 42]. As a result, large-scale awareness campaigns have emerged in the medical field. By linking information security to known concepts and thought models that medical staff are already familiar with, it might be possible to break down barriers, promote understanding, and improve risk perception. Given the success of similar techniques applied on ISA in nonmedical sectors by drawing up on literature on safety risk communication [32, 49], we consider this an actionable solution worthy of investigation.

6   Conclusions

In this paper, we presented an expert interview study with six experts from medical care on information security, focusing on the human factor in information security and ISA topics. Our goal was to gain insight into the specifics that need to be considered when designing and implementing ISA programs in healthcare facilities. Our findings confirmed the fundamental challenges and cybersecurity risks faced by medical facilities, aligning with previous work [11,13,33,40]. We identified goals, target audiences, content, delivery methods, and ideas for collaboration to enhance information security awareness in medical facilities, complementing existing research. One area that requires attention is the design of ISA delivery methods and materials that are tailored to the specific needs of the target group. Additionally, previously underrepresented target groups such as management, patients, and visitors should be included in ISA programs. Drawing on established knowledge and practices from other healthcare areas, which have been addressing awareness issues for a longer time, can be beneficial. For instance, aligning information security concepts with familiar healthcare procedures and terminology, such as "cyber hygiene," can help bridge the understanding gap. Furthermore, the lack of evaluation of ISA programs in medical settings raises uncertainty about their long-term impact. Future research should focus on assessing the effectiveness of ISA measures in practice and academia. One significant challenge is the scarcity of resources, particularly time, in healthcare settings. Designing materials that require less time but are still effective seems crucial. Likewise, the aim should be to strengthen the "human firewall" as a last line of defense when technical measures fail. Management has a significant role to play in fostering a culture of information security that goes beyond a mere "checklist mentality." Overall, our findings provide valuable insights and directions for future research in the field of information security awareness in medical care institutions.

Acknowledgment. We thank our participants for participating in our study and the anonymous reviewers for their valuable feedback on our research. This research was funded by the German Federal Ministry of Health (grant number ZMI1-2521FSB801).

Disclosure of Interests. The authors have no competing interests to declare that are relevant to the content of this article.

References

1. Branchenspezifischer Sicherheitsstandard für die Gesundheitsversorgung im Krankenhaus (2019)
2. ENISA Threat Landscape 2023. Technical report (2023). https://www.enisa.europa.eu/publications/enisa-threat-landscape-2023
3. Abawajy, J.: User preference of cyber security awareness delivery methods. Behav. Inf. Technol. **33**(3), 237–248 (2014)
4. Abu Ali, K., Alyounis, S.: CyberSecurity in healthcare industry. In: Proceedings of the International Conference on Information Technology (ICIT), pp. 695–701 (2021)
5. Alhuwail, D., Al-Jafar, E., Abdulsalam, Y., AlDuaij, S.: Information security awareness and behaviors of health care professionals at public health care facilities. Appl. Clin. Inform. **12**(04), 924–932 (2021)
6. Altamimi, S., Renaud, K., Storer, T.: I do it because they do it?: social-neutralisation in information security practices of Saudi medical interns. In: Kallel, S., Cuppens, F., Cuppens-Boulahia, N., Hadj Kacem, A. (eds.) CRiSIS 2019. LNCS, vol. 12026, pp. 227–243. Springer, Cham (2020). https://doi.org/10.1007/978-3-030-41568-6_15
7. Amankwa, E., Loock, M., Kritzinger, E.: A conceptual analysis of information security education, information security training and information security awareness definitions. In: Proceedings of the 9th International Conference for Internet Technology and Secured Transactions (ICITST), pp. 248–252 (2014)
8. Amro, B.M., Al-Jabari, M.O., Jabareen, H.M., Khader, Y.S., Taweel, A.: Design and development of case studies in security and privacy for health informatics education. In: Proceedings of the 15th IEEE International Conference on Computer Systems and Applications (AICCSA), pp. 1–6 (2018)
9. Arain, M.A., Tarraf, R., Ahmad, A.: Assessing staff awareness and effectiveness of educational training on IT security and privacy in a large healthcare organization. J. Multidiscip. Healthc. **12**, 73–81 (2019)
10. Aydın, Ö.M., Chouseinoglou, O.: Fuzzy assessment of health information system users' security awareness. J. Med. Syst. **37**(6), 9984 (2013)
11. Bhuyan, S.S., et al.: Transforming healthcare cybersecurity from reactive to proactive: current status and future recommendations. J. Med. Syst. **44**(5), 98 (2020)
12. Branley-Bell, D., Coventry, L., Sillence, E.: Promoting cybersecurity culture change in healthcare. In: Proceedings of the 14th ACM Pervasive Technologies Related to Assistive Environments Conference (PETRA), pp. 544–549 (2021)
13. Coventry, L., Branley, D.: Cybersecurity in healthcare: a narrative review of trends, threats and ways forward. Maturitas **113**, 48–52 (2018)
14. Coventry, L., et al.: Cyber-risk in healthcare: exploring facilitators and barriers to secure behaviour. In: Proceedings of the 2nd International Conference on HCI for Cybersecurity, Privacy and Trust (HCI-CPT), pp. 105–122 (2020)
15. Eikey, E.V., Murphy, A.R., Reddy, M.C., Xu, H.: Designing for privacy management in hospitals: understanding the gap between user activities and IT staff's understandings. Int. J. Med. Inform. **84**(12), 1065–1075 (2015)
16. ENISA: The new users' guide: how to raise information security awareness (EN). Report/Study TP-30-10-582-EN-C. ENISA (2010)
17. Etikan, I.: Comparison of convenience sampling and purposive sampling. Am. J. Theor. Appl. Stat. **5**(1), 1–4 (2016)

18. Evans, M., He, Y., Maglaras, L., Yevseyeva, I., Janicke, H.: Evaluating information security core human error causes (IS-CHEC) technique in public sector and comparison with the private sector. Int. J. Med. Inform. **127**, 109–119 (2019)

19. Fabisiak, L., Hyla, T.: Measuring cyber security awareness within groups of medical professionals in Poland. In: Proceedings of the 53rd Hawaii International Conference on System Sciences (HICSS), pp. 3871–3880 (2020)

20. Fernández-Alemán, J.L., Sánchez-Henarejos, A., Toval, A., Sánchez-García, A.B., Hernández-Hernández, I., Fernandez-Luque, L.: Analysis of health professional security behaviors in a real clinical setting: an empirical study. Int. J. Med. Inform. **84**(6), 454–467 (2015)

21. Gardner, B., Thomas, V.: Building an Information Security Awareness Program: Defending Against Social Engineering and Technical Threats, 1st edn. (2014)

22. Ghazvini, A., Shukur, Z.: A framework for an effective information security awareness program in healthcare. Int. J. Adv. Comput. Sci. Appl. **8**(2), 193–205 (2017)

23. Ghazvini, A., Shukur, Z.: A serious game for healthcare industry: information security awareness training program for hospital universiti Kebangsaan Malaysia. Int. J. Adv. Comput. Sci. Appl. **9**(9), 236–245 (2018)

24. Gioulekas, F., et al.: A cybersecurity culture survey targeting healthcare critical infrastructures. Healthcare **10**(2), 327 (2022)

25. Hedström, K., Karlsson, F., Kolkowska, E.: Social action theory for understanding information security non-compliance in hospitals: the importance of user rationale. Inf. Manag. Comput. Secur. **21**(4), 266–287 (2013)

26. Hepp, S.L., Tarraf, R.C., Birney, A., Arain, M.A.: Evaluation of the awareness and effectiveness of IT security programs in a large publicly funded health care system. Health Inf. Manag. J. **47**(3), 116–124 (2018)

27. Jaeger, L.: Information security awareness: literature review and integrative framework. In: Proceedings of the 51st Hawaii International Conference on System Sciences (HICSS), pp. 4703–4712 (2018)

28. Jalali, M.S., Kaiser, J.P.: Cybersecurity in hospitals: a systematic, organizational perspective. J. Med. Internet Res. **20**(5), e10059 (2018)

29. Kang, J., Seomun, G.: Development and validation of the information security attitude questionnaire (ISA-Q) for nurses. Nurs. Open **10**(2), 850–860 (2023)

30. Katsikas, S.K.: Health care management and information systems security: awareness, training or education? Int. J. Med. Inform. **60**(2), 129–135 (2000)

31. Kessler, S.R., Pindek, S., Kleinman, G., Andel, S.A., Spector, P.E.: Information security climate and the assessment of information security risk among healthcare employees. Health Inf. J. **26**(1), 461–473 (2020)

32. Khan, B., Alghathbar, K.S., Khan, M.K.: Information security awareness campaign: an alternate approach. In: Kim, T., Adeli, H., Robles, R.J., Balitanas, M. (eds.) ISA 2011. CCIS, vol. 200, pp. 1–10. Springer, Heidelberg (2011). https://doi.org/10.1007/978-3-642-23141-4_1

33. Kruse, C.S., Frederick, B., Jacobson, T., Monticone, D.K.: Cybersecurity in healthcare: a systematic review of modern threats and trends. Technol. Healthc. **25**(1), 1–10 (2017)

34. Lambe, K., et al.: Understanding hand hygiene behaviour in the intensive care unit to inform interventions: an interview study. BMC Health Serv. Res. **20**(1), 1–9 (2020)

35. Landolt, S., Hirschel, J., Schlienger, T., Businger, W., Zbinden, A.M.: Assessing and comparing information security in Swiss hospitals. Int. J. Med. Res. **1**(2), e11 (2012)

36. Liginlal, D., Sim, I., Khansa, L., Fearn, P.: Human error and privacy breaches in healthcare organizations: causes and management strategies. In: Proceedings of the Fifteenth Americas Conference on Information System (AMCIS) (2009)
37. Lyngaas, S.: Brooklyn hospital network reverts to paper charts for weeks after cyberattack. CNN (2022). https://edition.cnn.com/2022/12/20/tech/hospital-ransomware/index.html
38. Maggio, L.A., Dameff, C., Kanter, S.L., Woods, B., Tully, J.: Cybersecurity challenges and the academic health center: an interactive tabletop simulation for executives. Acad. Med. J. Assoc. Am. Med. Coll. **96**(6), 850–853 (2021)
39. Murphy, A.R., Reddy, M.C., Xu, H.: Privacy practices in collaborative environments: a study of emergency department staff. In: Proceedings of the 17th ACM Conference on Computer Supported Cooperative Work and Social Computing, CSCW 2014, pp. 269–282. Association for Computing Machinery, New York (2014)
40. Nifakos, S., et al.: Influence of human factors on cyber security within healthcare organisations: a systematic review. Sensors **21**(15), 5119 (2021)
41. Özaslan, G., et al.: Evaluation of the effects of information security training on employees: a study from a private hospital. Int. J. Health Manag. Tour. **5**(3), 336–347 (2020)
42. Pittet, D.: Improving compliance with hand hygiene in hospitals. Infect. Control Hosp. Epidemiol. **21**(6), 381–386 (2000)
43. Ralston, W.: The untold story of a cyberattack, a hospital and a dying woman. WIRED (2020). https://www.wired.co.uk/article/ransomware-hospital-death-germany
44. Renaud, K., Goucher, W.: Health service employees and information security policies: an uneasy partnership? Inf. Manag. Comput. Secur. **20**(4), 296–311 (2012)
45. Rizzoni, F., Magalini, S., Casaroli, A., Mari, P., Dixon, M., Coventry, L.: Phishing simulation exercise in a large hospital: a case study. Digital Health **8**, 20552076221081716 (2022)
46. Sari, P.K., Handayani, P.W., Hidayanto, A.N., Yazid, S., Aji, R.F.: Information security behavior in health information systems: a review of research trends and antecedent factors. Healthcare **10**(12), 2531 (2022)
47. Schmidt, T., Nøhr, C., Koppel, R.: A simple assessment of information security awareness in hospital staff across five Danish regions. Stud. Health Technol. Inf. **281**, 635–639 (2021)
48. Siponen, M.T.: Five dimensions of information security awareness. ACM SIGCAS Comput. Soc. **31**(2), 24–29 (2001)
49. Stewart, G., Lacey, D.: Death by a thousand facts: criticising the technocratic approach to information security awareness. Inf. Manag. Comput. Secur. **20**(1), 29–38 (2012)
50. Taylor, R.: Management perception of unintentional information security risks. In: Proceedings of the 27th International Conference on Information Systems (ICIS) (2006)
51. Tsohou, A., Karyda, M., Kokolakis, S., Kiountouzis, E.: Managing the introduction of information security awareness programmes in organisations. Eur. J. Inf. Syst. **24**(1), 38–58 (2015)
52. Wilson, M., Hash, J.: Building an Information Technology Security Awareness and Training Program. Technical report NIST SP 800-50. National Institute of Standards and Technology (2003)
53. Yeo, L.H., Banfield, J.: Human factors in electronic health records cybersecurity breach: an exploratory analysis. Perspect. Health Inf. Manag. **19**, 1i (2022)

Threat Assessment and Protection

Whisper+AASIST for DeepFake Audio Detection

Qian Luo[✉] and Kalyani Vinayagam Sivasundari

The George Washington University, Washington, DC, USA
{qluo,kalyani.vinayagamsivasundari}@gwu.edu

Abstract. This study introduces a novel approach, combining the Whisper model with the AASIST architecture to enhance the detection performance of deepfake audio. Termed Whisper+AASIST, our investigation demonstrates its competitive edge over existing models on the 2021 ASVspoof DF subset. Notably, it surpasses these models in the challenging In-the-Wild datasets. This innovative fusion signifies a significant leap in deepfake audio detection, showcasing the effectiveness of synergistic model architectures. Through a comprehensive analysis, we unravel the potential of this hybrid approach in addressing evolving challenges within the domain of deceptive audio content. The findings underscore the significance of such inventive model combinations, providing a foundation for further advancements in deepfake audio detection methodologies.

Keywords: Deepfake Detection · AASIST · Whisper

1 Introduction

1.1 Motivation

The rapid advancements in generative artificial intelligence have significantly transformed text-to-speech (TTS) and voice conversion (VC) technologies. These cutting-edge technologies now enable the synthesis of speech so authentic that distinguishing it from real human vocalizations has become a formidable challenge. While these advancements undoubtedly offer increased convenience in various sectors, they also raise critical concerns about societal stability and security.

Recently, two notable incidents involving deepfake audios resulted in significant financial losses for corporate entities [2,15]. These cases gained extensive media attention and sparked widespread public debate. Concurrently, a report by the U.S. Department of Defense highlighted the escalating threats posed by advanced AI-generated content [20]. This report recommended two main countermeasures: implementing proactive authentication methods during content creation, and developing passive detection strategies for analyzing content post-production.

Considering the challenges in achieving broad implementation of authentication protocols in the near term, the importance of post-hoc detection techniques

© The Author(s), under exclusive license to Springer Nature Switzerland AG 2024
A. Moallem (Ed.): HCII 2024, LNCS 14729, pp. 121–133, 2024.
https://doi.org/10.1007/978-3-031-61382-1_8

becomes increasingly evident. These methods are crucial for combating the rise in fraudulent activities, creating a continuous dynamic between the creators of generative AI and detection experts.

1.2 Research Question

– How effectively can the integration of OpenAI's Whisper [14] pretrained-transformer model enhance the deepfake audio detection capabilities of the Audio Anti-Spoofing using Integrated Spectro-Temporal Graph Attention Networks (AASIST) architecture [5] so users can recognize the fake audios?

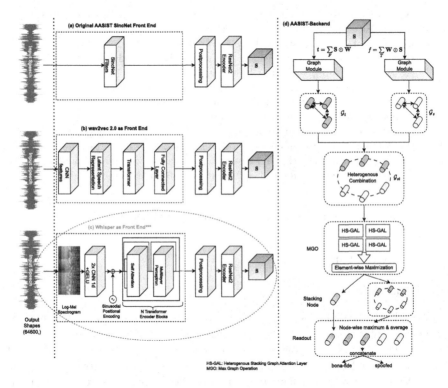

Fig. 1. The AASIST Architecture with Various Front Ends

Note: Panel (a) and (d) are adapted from June et al. [5], panel (b) is adapted from Baevski et al. [1] and Tak et al. [18], and panel (d) is adapted from Radford et al. [14].

2   Related Works

2.1   Overview

Yi et al. [24] conducted an extensive review on deepfake audio detection technologies, categorizing them into three primary approaches:

a) Traditional classification techniques, which include algorithms such as support vector machines [8] and Gaussian Mixture Models (GMM) [3].

b) Deep learning-based classifications, encompassing models like the Res2Net [9] (a modified residual network), graph neural network (GNN) based GAT [16], PC-DARTS [4] (a differentiable architecture search approach), and transformer-based Rawformer.

c) Comprehensive end-to-end architectures, with prominent examples being the graph attention network (GAN)-based AASIST [5] and transformer-based SE-Rawformer [10].

Historically, advancements in audio analysis relied heavily on hand-crafted or learnable features, primarily driven by traditional machine learning classifiers. With the advent of advanced end-to-end architectures like AASIST, there has been a paradigm shift towards integrating feature extraction and classification into a cohesive system.

Despite their reliance on more basic feature extraction techniques, traditional classifiers like GMM have maintained relevance due to their resilience, especially under the constraint of limited training samples. GMM continues to be a benchmark model in the field, with an Equal Error Rate (EER) of 25.25% using linear frequency cepstral coefficients (LFCC) features with ASVspoof 2021 DF data, outperforming most deep learning methods [24]. Conversely, deep learning classifiers have shown variable effectiveness, largely dependent on the specificity of their feature extraction methods.

In contrast, when leveraging XLS-R features extracted via wav2vec2.0 [1], deep learning models generally surpass the performance of GMM. For instance, the Attentive Filtering Network (AFN) utilizing XLS-R achieved an ERR of 14.15%, significantly lower than the GMM's ERR of 28.49% with the same features [24] with ASVspoof 2021 DF data.

End-to-end architectures like AASIST, while not outperforming the top deep learning methods with XLS-R, still demonstrate significant effectiveness with an ERR of 19.77% with ASVspoof 2021 DF data, positioning them competitively among deep learning models using XLS-R features. However, prior work did not focus on the interaction with end users.

2.2 State of the Art

The ASVspoof2021 DF subset [23] saw an initial 15.64% Equal Error Rate (EER) by T23 [11]. Tak et al. later reached a 2.85% EER with AASIST using wav2vec 2.0 (Fig. 1 Panel b) [18], surpassing Martín-Doñas and Álvarez's 4.98% EER [12]. Current SOTA EERs for In-the-Wild data are 24.73% for ASSERT+LPS and 34.81% for AASIST [24].

The field of deepfake audio detection, particularly in the context of the ASVspoof 2021 DF dataset, has witnessed remarkable advancements in recent years. This dataset, crucial for benchmarking, has enabled a clear evaluation of various models' capabilities in detecting fraudulent audio samples.

One of the earliest benchmarks on this dataset was set by T23, who achieved an EER of 15.64% [11]. This performance served as a significant indicator of the challenges inherent in accurately identifying deepfake audios. However, subsequent developments have dramatically improved detection capabilities.

A pivotal advancement was achieved by Tak et al., who utilized the AASIST architecture in conjunction with wav2vec 2.0 features. Their approach culminated in a substantially lower EER of 2.85%, as illustrated in Fig. 1 Panel b [18]. This marked a significant leap from the previous benchmarks, underscoring the effectiveness of integrating sophisticated neural network architectures with advanced feature extraction techniques.

In comparison, Martín-Doñas and Álvarez achieved a 4.98% EER [12], demonstrating the rapid progression of technological advancements in this domain. Their work, while being surpassed by Tak et al., contributed valuable insights into the optimization of deep learning methods for audio spoofing detection.

When considering 'In-the-Wild' data [13], a more challenging and variable dataset, the current state-of-the-art performances indicate a more complex scenario. ASSERT+LPS, a notable method in this category, achieved an EER of 24.73%, while AASIST recorded an EER of 34.81% [24]. These figures highlight the ongoing challenges faced when dealing with more diverse and less controlled audio samples, which more closely resemble real-world scenarios.

Overall, the continuous evolution in deepfake audio detection, as evidenced by these performances on the ASVspoof 2021 DF dataset, indicates both the progress made and the challenges that remain. As deepfake technologies grow more sophisticated, the need for advanced detection methods, capable of handling diverse and evolving threats, becomes increasingly crucial.

2.3 The AASIST Architecture

AASIST, introduced by Jung et al. [5], represents a significant advancement in end-to-end audio processing models. Its primary innovation lies in the integration of sinc convolution and a RawNet2-based encoder, coupled with sophisticated graph learning techniques. This unique combination allows AASIST to excel in both feature extraction and classification tasks, setting it apart from conventional architectures. The model's approach to handling waveform inputs, particularly its advanced representation processing components, has been pivotal in enhancing its overall performance. These developments have been instrumental in AASIST's achievements in various benchmarks, as detailed in Sect. 2.2.

2.4 Whisper

Whisper, developed by OpenAI [14], is a state-of-the-art transformer-based speech recognition model. It is distinguished by its extensive pretraining on an enormous dataset comprising 680,000 h of diverse audio samples. This extensive pretraining regime enables Whisper to offer robust performance across a wide range of languages and accents, significantly reducing the necessity for task-specific fine-tuning. Its versatility and scalability make it an ideal candidate for integration into various speech-related applications, ranging from transcription to more complex tasks like speech synthesis and deepfake detection. Whisper's design embodies the cutting-edge advancements in the field of transformer-based models, harnessing the power of large-scale datasets to achieve unprecedented levels of accuracy and reliability in speech recognition.

3 Methods and Data

3.1 Methods

This study aims to enhance the AASIST architecture by incorporating elements of OpenAI's Whisper model [14] at the front end, as depicted in Fig. 1-(c). Initially, the AASIST framework employed SincNet filters on raw waveforms for feature extraction (Fig. 1 Panel a), which later evolved to utilize wav2vec 2.0 as the feature extractor (Fig. 1-(b)). Model performance will be evaluated using EER.

Whisper Model

The Whisper model, as outlined by OpenAI [14], is adept at processing raw waveform inputs $x_{1:L}$ to generate a sequence of spectro-temporal representations $o_{1:N}$, where L represents the number of samples in the waveform. As depicted in Fig. 1-(c), the Whisper-large-v2 variant, a specific configuration of the model, includes a series of carefully designed layers to optimize audio processing. Initially, a preprocessing unit transforms the raw waveform into a log-Mel spectrogram. This transformation is crucial for capturing the essential frequency and time characteristics of the audio input.

Following the preprocessing stage, the model incorporates two convolution layers. These layers are instrumental in enhancing the local features of the spectrogram, making the subsequent processing by the transformer encoder more effective. After these convolution layers, a position embedding layer is introduced to encode the temporal information of the audio sequence, a critical aspect for understanding the context in speech.

The core of the Whisper model comprises 32 transformer encoder layers. These layers are the backbone of the model, responsible for capturing complex patterns and relationships within the audio data. The transformer architecture, known for its effectiveness in handling sequential data, allows the Whisper model to process audio with remarkable accuracy and detail.

In our implementation, we omitted the decoder layers that are present in the original Whisper model. These layers are primarily used for speech recognition tasks, and since our focus is on utilizing the encoder-generated embeddings for spoofing detection, they were not required. The length of the spectro-temporal representation sequence, denoted as N, is set to 1500 for all Whisper model variants, determined by the position of the embedding layers.

Müller et al. [13] observed that the performance in spoofing detection is notably enhanced when the waveforms are not truncated to 4-s subsamples. In line with this finding, we chose to use a 30-s input sample for our experiments, which is consistent with the default setting of the Whisper model.

Given that Whisper was initially pretrained exclusively on bona fide (genuine) data [14], we hypothesized that its performance in spoofing detection could be further enhanced by fine-tuning it with a mix of bona fide and spoofed in-domain training data. Additionally, recognizing the limitations of our training dataset, which consists of samples from the ASVSpoof2019 LA subset, we implemented data augmentation techniques to account for potential deepfaking methods not present in the training data but likely encountered in the test data.

To address this, we introduced data augmentation for the training set, aiming to enhance the model's robustness and generalization capability. This strategy is in line with the findings presented in the referenced papers [5,17]. We experimented with three distinct variants of data augmentation:

No Data Augmentation (No DA): In this baseline approach, we trained the model using the original dataset without any augmentation. This setup serves as a control to gauge the effectiveness of the other augmentation techniques.

Coloured Additive Noise: Here, we introduced colored additive noise to the training data. This type of noise is known to simulate a variety of real-world acoustic environments, thereby preparing the model to handle diverse and challenging audio conditions.

Convolutive Noise + Impulsive Noise + Coloured Additive Noise: In this comprehensive approach, we combined convolutive noise, impulsive noise, and coloured additive noise. The inclusion of convolutive noise aims to replicate the effects of different transmission channels and acoustic environments, while impulsive noise mimics sudden, non-continuous disturbances. This combination of noises presents a more rigorous training scenario, aiming to significantly enhance the model's ability to generalize across various audio spoofing techniques.

To explore the potential of fine-tuning and data augmentation, we implemented two versions of the Whisper model: one using the original pretrained version (**Our Method 1**), and another that underwent additional fine-tuning with the mixed dataset (**Our Method 2**), incorporating the described data augmentation strategies. These implementations are designed to assess how each approach influences the model's proficiency in detecting audio spoofing in varied and potentially unseen scenarios.

Postprocessing

In the postprocessing stage, the spectro-temporal representations $o_{1:N}$ undergo a sophisticated transformation via a RawNet2-based encoder. This encoder is pivotal in extracting higher-level features from the input representations, which are essential for the subsequent stages of audio analysis.

The RawNet2 encoder, as described in the paper by Jung et al. [6], is an advanced deep neural network specifically designed to handle raw waveforms for robust speaker verification. It is characterized by its ability to process raw audio data directly, bypassing the need for traditional handcrafted features. This approach allows for a more nuanced extraction of speaker-specific characteristics, directly from the waveform.

As the spectro-temporal representations pass through the RawNet2-based encoder, they are transformed into a more refined feature map $\mathbf{S} \in \mathbb{R}^{C \times F \times T}$. Here, C represents the number of channels, F denotes the number of spectral bins, and T stands for the number of time frames. Each of these dimensions plays a critical role:

Channels (C): This dimension captures various aspects of the audio signal, allowing the network to analyze different features in parallel.

Spectral Bins (F): The spectral bins represent the frequency components of the audio signal. By capturing a wide range of frequencies, the network can discern subtle nuances in the audio.

Time Frames (T): The time dimension ensures that the temporal dynamics of the speech signal are adequately represented. This is crucial for understanding the context and progression of spoken words or sounds.

The RawNet2-based encoder employs several layers, including gated convolutional layers and residual blocks, to effectively capture these dimensions. The gated convolutions control the flow of information through the network, allowing it to focus on the most relevant features. The residual blocks help in preserving the integrity of the input signal while enabling deeper layers in the network to learn complex patterns.

AASIST Backend

The feature map $\mathbf{S}$ derived from the RawNet2 encoder is fed into the AASIST backend, as depicted in Fig. 1-(d). This backend is intricately designed to further analyze the high-level features obtained from $\mathbf{S}$. The initial phase in the AASIST backend involves constructing two types of graphs: spectral ($\mathcal{G}_s \in \mathbb{R}^{N_s \times d_s}$) and temporal ($\mathcal{G}_t \in \mathbb{R}^{N_t \times d_t}$). In these expressions, N_s and N_t denote the number of nodes in the spectral and temporal graphs, respectively, while d_s and d_t represent the dimensionality of each node within these graphs.

Subsequent to their creation, these spectral and temporal graphs are fused to generate a unified spectro-temporal graph, denoted as $\mathcal{G}_{st}$. This fusion is a pivotal step in integrating the frequency and time-related information of the audio signal, essential for effective spoofing detection.

The combined graph $\mathcal{G}_{st}$ then undergoes advanced processing through a heterogeneous stacking graph attention mechanism. This technique is crucial for highlighting the most relevant features in the graph by weighting the connections between nodes based on their importance. Following this, a max graph operation is applied, which serves to further refine the feature representations by aggregating information from across the graph.

The final step in the AASIST backend is the application of a readout scheme. This step is responsible for interpreting the processed graph data and categorizing the input audio as either bona fide or spoofed. The readout scheme plays a critical role in translating the complex graph-based representations into a final decision, leveraging the rich information encoded within the spectro-temporal graph.

Table 1. Results Comparison

Model	ASVspoof 2021 DF		In the Wild	
	EER%	Related Work	EER%	Related Work
GMM+LFCC	25.25%	a	37.49%	a
LCNN	25.26%	a	35.14%	a
ASSERT	21.58%	a	**24.73%**	a
Res2Net	19.47%	a	36.62%	a
RawNet2	20.55%	b	49.00%	
ASSIST	19.77%	a	34.81%	a
Wav2Vec 2.0 + ASSIST + SL + DA	**2.85%**		**10.49%**	
Our Method 1 (Base) + No DA	12.25%		36.79%	
Our Method 1 (Base) + Colored DA	12.18%		37.52%	
Our Method 1 (Base) + All DAs	12.51%		35.94%	
Our Method 1 (Large V2) + No DA	9.62%		**20.91%**	
Our Method 1 (Large V2) + Colored DA	**8.67%**		23.54%	
Our Method 1 (Large V2) + All DA	10.60%		24.81%	
Our Method 2 (Base) + Fine Tune + No DA	10.78%		25.98%	
Our Method 2 (Base) + Fine Tune + Colored DA	9.62%		25.11%	
Our Method 2 (Base) + Fine Tune + All DAs	10.68%		24.09%	

Note: a. Yi et al. [24], b. Liu et al. [11], c.Tak et al. [18], and d. Martín-Doñas and Álvarez et al. [12]. Those without related work are implemented by the authors.

3.2   Data

The model's training leveraged the ASVspoof 2019 LA subsets [19,22], which are part of the larger ASVspoof challenge, a benchmark for assessing the robustness of automatic speaker verification systems against spoofing attacks. The ASVspoof 2019 LA dataset, derived from the VCTK database [21], includes a diverse set of bona fide and spoofed speech samples. It features 2,580 bona fide and 22,800 spoofed speech samples from 20 speakers, providing a solid environment for training robust spoofing detection models.

For testing, the model was evaluated against two datasets: the ASVspoof 2021 DF dataset [23] and the In-the-Wild dataset [13]. The ASVspoof 2021 DF dataset, an extension of the ASVspoof 2019 database, includes additional challenges such as compression changes and deepfake samples, reflecting the evolving landscape of audio spoofing techniques. It comprises 22,617 bona fide and 589,212 spoofed samples, recorded by 48 speakers.

In contrast, the In-the-Wild dataset, amassed in 2022, offers a different perspective by featuring real-world audio clips sourced from various online platforms that have confused many social media users. This dataset emphasizes diversity and real-world applicability by including clips of public figures and other widely circulated audio content. It consists of numerous samples, each representing a unique instance of real-world audio, thus providing a realistic testbed for evaluating the model's performance in practical scenarios. It comprised of 19,963 boni fide and 11,816 fake samples from 58 speakers.

The combination of these datasets presents a rigorous and comprehensive testing ground. The ASVspoof sets, with their controlled yet diverse spoofing techniques, offer a structured environment to assess the model's detection capabilities. Meanwhile, the In-the-Wild data introduces the complexity and variability of real-world scenarios, testing the model's generalizability and robustness against unseen and potentially more sophisticated spoofing attacks.

3.3   Implementation Details

In our setup, audio data were standardized to approximately 30 s, equivalent to 480,000 samples, through cropping or concatenation. This uniformity is crucial for maintaining consistency in input data.

For the training process, we utilized the Adam optimizer [7] with a fixed learning rate of 0.000001 to avoid overfitting with the pre-trained Whisper front-end. Considering the substantial computational requirements of the Whisper-large-v2 model, our experiments were conducted in two computational environments: one with 4 X NVidia V100 GPUs and another with 1 X NVidia A100 GPU. This approach allowed us to balance resource availability with the model's demands.

All models underwent training for 100 epochs, ensuring comprehensive learning and adaptation. To facilitate reproducibility in the research community, all source codes used in our experiments have been made available as open-source resources.

4   Results

Table 1 reveals a comprehensive comparison between our proposed methods and several established baselines and state-of-the-art models in the field. The evaluation is conducted on two datasets: ASVspoof 2021 DF and In the Wild, each posing distinct challenges for deepfake audio detection.

In the context of the ASVspoof 2021 DF dataset, traditional methods such as GMM+LFCC and LCNN exhibit EERs of 25.25% and 25.26%, respectively, while more advanced models like ASSERT and Res2Net achieve improved performance with EERs of 21.58% and 19.47%. Notably, our baseline method, denoted as Our Method 1 (Base), without any data augmentation, demonstrates competitive performance with an EER of 12.25%. The introduction of colored data augmentation (DA) slightly improves results, yielding an EER of 12.18%, while the combination of all augmentation techniques results in an EER of 12.51%. The Whisper large V2 model with colored data augmentation stands out as particularly promising with an EER of 8.67%.

In contrast, within the In-the-Wild dataset, the performance metrics vary. The GMM+LFCC baseline achieves an EER of 37.49%, while LCNN and ASSERT exhibit EERs of 35.14% and 24.73%, respectively. Our Method 1 (Base) demonstrates an EER of 36.79%, with colored data augmentation providing a marginal improvement to 37.52%. The combination of all data augmentation techniques leads to an EER of 35.94%. The Whisper large V2 model, again without data augmentation, performs exceptionally well with an EER of 20.91%.

Further improvements are observed with Our Method 2 (Base), incorporating fine-tuning and various data augmentation strategies. This model achieves competitive results with an EER of 10.78% for ASVspoof 2021 DF and 25.98% for In the Wild. Colored data augmentation and the combination of all augmentation techniques yield EERs of 9.62% and 10.68% for ASVspoof 2021 DF, and 25.11% and 24.09% for In the Wild, respectively.

Despite achieving competitive performance, our proposed method did not surpass the initial expectations, highlighting the complexity of deepfake audio detection and the need for further exploration and refinement in future research endeavors.

5 Discussion

Despite achieving competitive results, our efforts to optimize the Whisper model through fine-tuning encountered a significant challenge due to limitations in our existing GPU infrastructure. The NVidia V100 and A100 GPUs faced constraints in allocating sufficient memory for the larger variants, namely the Whisper-Large-V2 and even the Whisper-Medium model. Faced with this constraint, we explored alternative approaches while still aiming to enhance the model's performance. In response, we conducted a fine-tuning experiment using the less memory-intensive Whisper-base variant front-end in conjunction with AASIST. This specific fine-tuning process aimed to investigate the potential viability of the Whisper+AASIST architecture, serving as a proof of concept for a more tailored and resource-efficient approach within the given constraints.

The decision to fine-tune the Whisper-base variant with AASIST was motivated by the need to overcome memory limitations and optimize model performance. The results of this fine-tuning experiment, as reflected in Our Method 2, reveal promising outcomes. The Whisper model, with fine-tuning and different data augmentation strategies, achieved competitive Equal Error Rates (EERs) such as 10.78%, 9.62%, and 10.68% for various augmentation scenarios.

Although the integration of the Whisper+AASIST architecture led to an enhancement in the performance of the original AASIST architecture, the magnitude of this improvement, as observed in the results, falls short when compared to the impact observed with the incorporation of the Wav2Vec 2.0 architecture.

Upon closer examination of the architectural variances between the Whisper and Wav2Vec 2.0 encoders, it became evident that both models utilize the transformer architecture. However, a potential factor contributing to the lackluster performance of the Whisper model could be its reliance on log-mel spectrograms, compared to the more versatile CNN filters used by Wav2Vec 2.0. This deviation in approach may influence the comparative effectiveness of the two architectures. Future research could explore whether including CNN as the first feature extractor, rather than the log-mel spectrogram used by Whisper, would lead to more competitive results.

Unfortunately, resource constraints and time limitations prevented the fine-tuning of the large-v2 variants of the Whisper model. This leaves open the possibility that a fine-tuned Whisper-largev2 model might yield substantial performance improvement. Regrettably, our attempts were hindered by a shortage of VRAM, affecting both NVidia 2 X A100 and/or 4 X V100. Despite these challenges, a more extensive exploration of the Whisper architecture could uncover its true potential.

It is noteworthy to mention that the current performance, while not reaching the desired level, is on par with the performance of the Wav2Vec 2.0 model prior to fine-tuning, as documented by [18]. This comparison highlights the nuanced nature of model performance and underscores the significance of considering various factors, such as architectural differences and fine-tuning opportunities, when evaluating and optimizing speech processing models. The ongoing evolution of the Whisper+AASIST architecture positions it as a potential avenue for further exploration and refinement in the dynamic landscape of deepfake audio detection.

6   Conclusion

While our attempts to incorporate the Whisper model into AASIST architecture did not pan out as we would like, this exercise has provided valuable insights into the capabilities and limitations of different speech processing architectures. Our research demonstrates that even with resource constraints, innovative approaches like fine-tuning less memory-intensive models can offer new avenues for performance enhancement. The comparative analysis between the Whisper and Wav2Vec 2.0 models highlights the importance of architectural choices and their impact on model efficiency and effectiveness.

The findings of our study suggest that while the Whisper model shows promise, its full potential may be unlocked only with the availability of more powerful computing resources. This limitation underscores the need for ongoing research and development in the field of speech processing, particularly in optimizing models to function efficiently within the constraints of available hardware.

In conclusion, our work contributes to the evolving narrative of speech processing technology, emphasizing the significance of architectural decisions, the balancing act between resource availability and model performance, and the continuous quest for optimization in a rapidly advancing field. Future research should focus on further exploring the capabilities of the Whisper model, particularly its large-v2 variant, and investigate alternative architectures and fine-tuning strategies that could offer a more resource-efficient path to enhanced performance in speech processing applications.

References

1. Baevski, A., Zhou, Y., Mohamed, A., Auli, M.: wav2vec 2.0: a framework for self-supervised learning of speech representations. In: Advances in Neural Information Processing Systems, vol. 33, pp. 12449–12460 (2020)
2. Brewster, T.: Fraudsters cloned company director's voice in $35 million heist, police find (2021). https://www.forbes.com/sites/thomasbrewster/2021/10/14/huge-bank-fraud-uses-deep-fake-voice-tech-to-steal-millions. Accessed 30 Sept 2023
3. De Leon, P.L., Stewart, B., Yamagishi, J.: Synthetic speech discrimination using pitch pattern statistics derived from image analysis. In: Interspeech, pp. 370–373 (2012)
4. Ge, W., Panariello, M., Patino, J., Todisco, M., Evans, N.: Partially-connected differentiable architecture search for deepfake and spoofing detection. arXiv preprint arXiv:2104.03123 (2021)
5. Jung, J., et al.: AASIST: audio anti-spoofing using integrated spectro-temporal graph attention networks. In: 2022 IEEE International Conference on Acoustics, Speech and Signal Processing (ICASSP), ICASSP 2022, pp. 6367–6371. IEEE (2022)
6. Jung, J., Kim, S., Shim, H., Kim, J., Yu, H.J.: Improved RawNet with feature map scaling for text-independent speaker verification using raw waveforms. arXiv preprint arXiv:2004.00526 (2020)
7. Kingma, D.P., Ba, J.: Adam: a method for stochastic optimization. arXiv preprint arXiv:1412.6980 (2014)
8. Klontz, J.C., Klare, B.F., Klum, S., Jain, A.K., Burge, M.J.: Open source biometric recognition. In: 2013 IEEE Sixth International Conference on Biometrics: Theory, Applications and Systems (BTAS), pp. 1–8. IEEE (2013)
9. Li, X., et al.: Replay and synthetic speech detection with Res2Net architecture. In: 2021 IEEE International Conference on Acoustics, Speech and Signal Processing (ICASSP), ICASSP 2021, pp. 6354–6358. IEEE (2021)
10. Liu, X., Liu, M., Wang, L., Lee, K.A., Zhang, H., Dang, J.: Leveraging positional-related local-global dependency for synthetic speech detection. In: 2023 IEEE International Conference on Acoustics, Speech and Signal Processing (ICASSP), ICASSP 2023, pp. 1–5. IEEE (2023)
11. Liu, X., et al.: ASVspoof 2021: towards spoofed and deepfake speech detection in the wild. IEEE/ACM Trans. Audio Speech Lang. Process. **31**, 2507–2522 (2023)
12. Martín-Doñas, J.M., Álvarez, A.: The vicomtech audio deepfake detection system based on Wav2vec2 for the 2022 add challenge. In: 2022 IEEE International Conference on Acoustics, Speech and Signal Processing (ICASSP), ICASSP 2022, pp. 9241–9245. IEEE (2022)
13. Müller, N.M., Czempin, P., Dieckmann, F., Froghyar, A., Böttinger, K.: Does audio deepfake detection generalize? arXiv preprint arXiv:2203.16263 (2022)
14. Radford, A., Kim, J.W., Xu, T., Brockman, G., McLeavey, C., Sutskever, I.: Robust speech recognition via large-scale weak supervision. In: International Conference on Machine Learning, pp. 28492–28518. PMLR (2023)
15. Stupp, C.: Fraudsters use AI to mimic CEO's voice in unusual cybercrime case. Wall Street J. (2019). https://www.wsj.com/articles/fraudsters-use-ai-to-mimic-ceos-voice-in-unusual-cybercrime-case-11567157402
16. Tak, H., Jung, J., Patino, J., Todisco, M., Evans, N.: Graph attention networks for anti-spoofing. arXiv preprint arXiv:2104.03654 (2021)

17. Tak, H., Kamble, M., Patino, J., Todisco, M., Evans, N.: RawBoost: a raw data boosting and augmentation method applied to automatic speaker verification anti-spoofing. In: 2022 IEEE International Conference on Acoustics, Speech and Signal Processing (ICASSP), ICASSP 2022, pp. 6382–6386. IEEE (2022)

18. Tak, H., Todisco, M., Wang, X., Jung, J., Yamagishi, J., Evans, N.: Automatic speaker verification spoofing and deepfake detection using Wav2vec 2.0 and data augmentation. arXiv preprint arXiv:2202.12233 (2022)

19. Todisco, M., et al.: ASVspoof 2019: future horizons in spoofed and fake audio detection. arXiv preprint arXiv:1904.05441 (2019)

20. U.S. Department of Defense, Federal Bureau of Investigation, Cybersecurity and Infrastructure Security Agency: Contextualizing Deepfake Threats to Organizations (2023). https://media.defense.gov/2023/Sep/12/2003298925/-1/-1/0/CSI-DEEPFAKE-THREATS.PDF. Accessed 30 Sept 2023

21. Veaux, C., Yamagishi, J., MacDonald, K.: CSTR VCTK Corpus: English multi-speaker corpus for CSTR voice cloning toolkit [sound] (2017). https://doi.org/10.7488/ds/1994

22. Wang, X., et al.: ASVspoof 2019: a large-scale public database of synthesized, converted and replayed speech. Comput. Speech Lang. **64**, 101114 (2020)

23. Yamagishi, J., et al.: ASVspoof 2021: accelerating progress in spoofed and deepfake speech detection. arXiv preprint arXiv:2109.00537 (2021)

24. Yi, J., Wang, C., Tao, J., Zhang, X., Zhang, C.Y., Zhao, Y.: Audio deepfake detection: a survey. arXiv preprint arXiv:2308.14970 (2023)

Paralyzed or Compromised: A Case Study of Decisions in Cyber-Physical Systems

Håvard Jakobsen Ofte(✉) ⓘ and Sokratis Katsikas ⓘ

Norwegian University of Science and Technology, Teknologiveien 22, 2815 Gjøvik, Norway
{havard.ofte,sokratis.katsikas}@ntnu.no

Abstract. Human operators of Cyber-Physical Systems (CPSs) within Critical Infrastructure (CI) need to protect their systems from cyber-attacks. When CPSs are compromised the operators might be faced with the dilemma of letting the systems be compromised to maintain the operation of CPSs or to paralyze the CPSs to mitigate the attack. How human operators resolve this dilemma was investigated through a case study of the Sunburst attack within the electrical power and manufacturing CI in Norway. Four actors were interviewed regarding the dilemma, including three actors interviewed regarding their handling of the Sunburst case. The interviews with additional incident reports from one of the actors were analyzed inductively to identify how the human operators made decisions in this context. Ten themes were identified and synthesized into a logic model of the decision process. The logic model was then compared to existing theoretical models of Situation Awareness (SA) to assess if SA theory could explain the findings. This study concludes that existing SA models are compatible with the findings. Some parts of the logic model based on the findings provide unique contributions to the understanding of the decisions. One important finding is that the design of the systems related to CPSs must allow adequate mitigation alternatives. The study highlights several implications for practice and further research. Although the findings may not be generalizable beyond the setting of the case, the study contributes to bridging the recognized research gap of empirical studies of the SA of human operators of CPSs.

Keywords: Cyber-physical systems · Security · Situation Awareness · Sunburst attack

1 Introduction

The rise of Information Technology (IT) during the last decades has been characterized by the virtualization, digital processing, and efficient transfer of information. This has made us associate technological development with systems of the logical domain. Technology before the rise of IT, was in contrast first and foremost associated with the mechanization of physical processes. The industrial revolution created technology for mass manufacturing, effective means of transport and enabled societies to rely on large scale systems of energy production and consumption. Looking back through history, we can recognize that the industrial revolution introduced technology for the physical domain and the IT revolution introduced technology for the logical domain. We are now entering a time of two parallel disruptive developments that challenge both of these historical technological paradigms. One is the introduction of technology-based judgement and subjecthood i.e., Artificial Intelligence (AI). The second development is the merging of technology for the physical domain with technology for the logical domain. This last technological amalgamation has been termed Cyber-Physical Systems (CPSs) [1].

CPSs are characterized by the interaction of cyber and physical components like sensors, processors, and actuators in order to adaptively control physical systems through logical processing, often with the ambition of creating autonomous systems [2]. CPS systems are found within several domains like automated driving, automated medical devices, and Critical Infrastructure (CI) like power plants, distribution of electrical power and smart manufacturing [3]. CIs like power plants and industrial manufacturing are by definition important for society and must therefore be ensured to work as intended. In addition, they can pose serious threats to human safety and to the environment if they malfunction [4].

With the integration of Information Technology (IT) and Operational technology (OT) these infrastructures are increasingly becoming CPSs [5]. This poses a new and complex layer of risks [6]. Within IT the risks posed to the technology is often connected to cyber security. When IT is integrated into OT, one invites the possibility of threats against reliable operation and safety as a consequence of cyber security breaches [7]. The research community has pointed out that existing guidelines for cyber security are not sufficient to meet these challenges [8]. Mitigation of cyber intrusion often includes the shutdown or at least logical isolation of IT assets. But when these assets also control critical physical processes like dams or smelters, the option of shutting them down entails something fundamentally different than unavailable IT services [7].

In the crux of this dilemma is the human operator weighing the options and making the crucial decisions. These decisions must often be made fast and without sufficient information [9]. Such situations challenge the operator's awareness of the available information and the suitability of potential actions. When the cyber security suddenly fails and there has been a breach in the CPSs, a decision must be made. Should the systems be shut down preventing further compromise but leaving the physical processes paralyzed? Or should one leave the system compromised and keep physical processes operative? This study investigates this posed dilemma.

Situation awareness (SA) has been a successful theoretical framework within human factors and decision making among human operators in several critical domains [10]. Situation awareness has also been researched within the field of cyber security [11]. Situation awareness is therefore well suited as a theoretical lens for understanding the combined challenge of human operators negotiating between cyber security and operation safety or reliability within CIs. Because little research regarding this challenge currently exists, this study will be conducted as a case-study investigating how these dilemmas are negotiated in the real world today, combined with an analysis regarding how SA can be used as an explanatory model. Based on these goals the following research questions are posed in this study:

- Research Question 1 (RQ1): How do human operators of cyber-physical systems in critical infrastructure decide between continuing to use or stop using systems that might be compromised?
- Research Question 2 (RQ2): How can these decision processes be explained by existing theory of cyber-situation awareness?

The research questions are investigated through a case study of the Sunburst attack [12] within electrical power and manufacturing CI in Norway. Several actors involved in the decisions regarding continued use of potentially compromised systems within CPSs were interviewed. The collected data from the interviews was combined with the incident reports from one of the actors. This combined data was used to describe the case and how decisions regarding the dilemma were made. The results of this investigation were then compared with existing SA models to analyze if SA is suited as an explanatory framework for the human decision making. This study thus contributes to a better understanding of the posed dilemma and how human operators resolve it. This improved understanding raises important practical implications for decision making in this context as well as important implications for further research.

2 Related Work and Background

In this section the concept of CPS is defined and presented in the context of CI. Related work regarding CPS security and safety is also presented. Then research works related to human factors of CPSs are highlighted. Lastly, in this section the theoretical foundation of SA is presented and linked to the context of this case.

2.1 CPSs

The term CPS is attributed to Helen Gill in 2006 and has since been widely adopted. A CPS can be defined as: "a system that can effectively integrate cyber and physical components using the modern sensor, computing and network technologies" [3]. CPSs are quite diverse and found in several domains [2] like industry 4.0 [5], medical CPS devices [13], automated driving [14], and smart grids [15]. It is an important challenge to merge the different fields of knowledge and practice stemming from different parts of CPSs diverse technological ancestry [1]. One central issue of this discussion is the negotiation of different principal guidelines regarding security. Some studies highlight this negotiation by distinguishing between information security for the IT domain and control security for the OT domain [2]. Others point to differences in the security focus related to the CIA triad for OT (availability) and IT (confidentiality) [5]. Yet, others highlight the need for alignment between security (meaning the protection against malicious actors) and safety (meaning protection against failure of physical systems) [16].

There is currently a need for research on how to make decisions for CPSs that involve, at the same time, criteria from different fields of expertise. The common research approach is to deal with physical systems security and cyber security separately, and there are only a few studies that attempt to reconcile the two [7].

One approach to the security of CPSs within CI is the structured approach to designing CPSs provided by the Purdue model [17]. The Purdue model consists of five zones and six levels of operations that segment the controls and networks within industrial control systems [18]. The Purdue model highlights the need to carefully plan and design the connection between IT services and industrial control systems. The Purdue model thus contributes to the reconciliation of IT and OT security with guidelines on how to design system architecture. The Purdue model is also referenced in several international standards [17].

In this case study the following perspective on CPS security of CI is used: The threats of compromise are posed to the CPS through the IT domain and adversaries can attack the systems using known mechanisms researched in the field of cyber security [2]. Such cyber threats can manifest throughout the architecture of CPSs from the physical layer to the application layer [3]. However, the cyberthreats in this context have an added dimension of potential negative consequences related to the physical operations that characterize CPSs. A cyber threat thus has the potential to make the physical operations malfunction, be unreliable or in a worst-case scenario pose a threat to human or environmental safety [15]. The decisions regarding what potential actions might be most suitable in response to the threat are further complicated by the fact that the mitigations themselves also have potential negative consequences.

Common mitigation strategies in cyber security are isolation or shutdown of IT-assets [19]. Within the context of CPSs in CI such mitigations can themselves pose threats against reliable operation or safety. This is at the heart of the posed dilemma and the topic of this study is thus one example of how CPSs pose new challenges regarding the prioritization of different security principles. In existing standards and guidelines such dilemmas between principles are mentioned, but there are only general guidelines on how to handle the processes of decision. One example is how NIST acknowledges the posed dilemma followed by a recommendation of risk assessment as the method to decide: *"For example, one possible response option is to physically isolate the system under attack. However, this may have a negative impact on the OT and may not be possible without impacting operational performance or safety. A focused risk assessment should be used to determine the response action."* [19].

2.2 Human Operators in CPSs

In this study it is assumed that human operators are the actors that make such decisions. Based on the descriptions of CPSs in the research literature, this is not a given. The definitions of CPSs are agnostic regarding the need for human operators. This issue is heatedly debated in many academic circles. Techno-optimists are excited by the utopian possibilities of completely autonomous systems, whereas alarmists proclaim the imminent end of our civilization if we give up our human control of CPSs to AI [20]. Within the research literature the discussion of the necessity of human operators is often described as keeping the human-in-the-loop [21]. When the human is in-the-loop of CPSs it entails another layer of complexity regarding how the human interacts with the system, and it introduces the risk of human errors [22]. The field of human factors research has analyzed these dynamics and identified solutions for improving human performance within such systems [23]. However, when reviewing the existing human factors research literature regarding the posed dilemma, there are only a few studies that brush the topic [9, 24, 25].

2.3 Situation Awareness

Regarding the human factors of operating critical physical systems, SA is a highly recognized theoretical framework. SA has investigated human performance of operators in several critical sectors like nuclear power plant control, aviation, military operations, and surgical practices [26]. The most recognized definition of SA within human factors is the following by Endsley: *"The perception of the elements in the environment, the comprehension of their meaning, and the projection of their status in the near future"* [27].

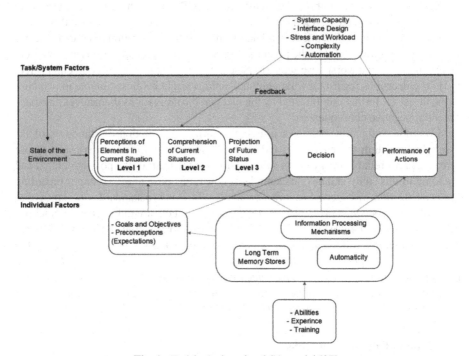

Fig. 1. Endsley's three level SA model [27]

The theoretical model of SA presented in Fig. 1 is based on cognitive psychology. At its core it understands the human operator's SA as three levels of cognition. The three levels are perception, comprehension, and projection. Human operators perceive elements of the situation which is cognitively processed to gain comprehension. Then the human operators project the situation cognitively into the future to gain awareness. The resulting awareness is used to assess the suitability of different actions. The process continues with operators making decisions and performing actions. These actions affect the environment and provide feedback loops for the operator through perception of the environment. The SA process is influenced by external factors related to the task or system as well as individual factors related to the human operator him/herself [28].

SA has also been used as a theoretical framework within the field of cyber security and is then often termed cyber-SA [29]. There is nevertheless a lack of empirical research regarding cyber-SA [11]. The existing research has dominantly been based on Endsley's theory, and this model is thus the de-facto explanatory model within cyber-SA [9].

This study aims to investigate if the existing SA theory might provide a good explanatory framework for how human operators can make well informed decisions regarding the posed dilemma of CPS security in CI. The use of SA as a theoretical lens for examining these questions is suggested in existing literature [9, 24].

2.4 The Sunburst Attack

In late 2020 it became known that the Texas-based SolarWinds network monitoring and management system had been compromised. The attack on SolarWinds dubbed Sunburst exploited a vulnerability in the update system of the module called Orion. Malicious code embedded in official Orion updates created a backdoor into the system used worldwide by public and private organizations [30]. The backdoor was used for data extraction and in some cases for inserting additional malware into affected systems. The attack seemed aimed at exfiltrating confidential and sensitive data aided by spyware inserted through the backdoor [31]. The Sunburst attack affected at least 18. 000 organizations worldwide, but the exploitation of the backdoor seems to be aimed at US entities. The attack compromised systems within governmental bodies like the Department of Defense, the Department of Commerce, and the Department of Energy, including the National Nuclear Security Administration [30]. When the news of the vulnerability was made public it soon became known that the backdoor had already been present within official update versions of Orion for several months [32].

In December 2020 organizations all over the world got notifications from Solar-Winds regarding the vulnerability of Orion. Organizations operating CPSs within CI were suddenly confronted with the possibility of having compromised systems within their operation. Research done in a digital infrastructure preparedness organization in Norway found that the Sunburst attack exposed a lack of predefined responsibilities in such situations [33]. Existing research literature on the Sunburst attack mostly focuses on the compromised high-profile US governmental bodies, and that Microsoft had some of its source code exfiltrated [30]. Yet, this attack case also provides a specific case of the dilemma presented in this paper.

3 Method

The defined research questions were examined through a case study following an established methodology [34]. The process of defining the case involved specifying the relevant criteria for the case. The case had to meet the following criteria: (a) The case had to include compromised IT systems in a setting of CPSs within CI; (b) The case had to include human operators faced with the dilemma presented in the research questions; (c) The human operators had to be in a setting where it would be reasonable to compare with the existing SA theory; (d) The case had to be of such a nature that access to data and participants was possible. Based on these criteria a preliminary interview and an in-depth interview of decision making in such cases were conducted with respondents within Norwegian CI. The preliminary interview included the posing of the criteria and the research questions and asking if the respondent knew of such a case. The in-depth interview asked about decision making processes in cases following the defined criteria. Based on these two interviews the Sunburst attack was chosen as the case for further investigation. An overview of the attack is presented in Sect. 2.4. This case was chosen because it involved the acknowledged dilemma of continued use of a potentially compromised system for monitoring networks throughout several CIs.

The case study is conducted as a single-case explanatory design, following recommended guidelines [34]. The case was investigated through three in-depth interviews with respondents from three different organizations. Three of the interviews examined this through the Sunburst case. The interviews were conducted as semi-structured interviews in Norwegian following an interview guide developed based on the research questions and the defined case. In addition, the incident reports from respondent 1 (see Table 1) related to the case were reviewed as part of the case database. A description of all participating actors as well as respondents is presented in Table 1. The actors and respondents are anonymized to preserve confidentiality.

Table 1. Respondents and provided data.

Respondent number	Actor description	Description of respondent	Provided data
1a	Security Operations Center (SOC) providing services to customers in Critical Infrastructure	SOC Director, over 10 years of relevant experience	Preliminary interview for identifying case, incident reports on Sunburst case
1b		Part of the SOC incident response team, over 10 years of relevant experience	1 in-depth case interview on decision making in the Sunburst case
2	Large actor within Norwegian critical infrastructure (manufacturing)	Security executive, over 10 years of relevant experience	1 in-depth interview on related decision making
3	National security agency within Norwegian critical infrastructure	Part of the national incident response team. Over 10 years of relevant experience	1 in-depth case interview on decision making in the Sunburst case
4	Large scale actor within Norwegian critical infrastructure (power sector)	Security executive, over 10 years of relevant experience	1 in-depth case interview on decision making in the Sunburst case

The data analysis for this case study followed a four-step process adhering to recommended guidelines [34]: (a) The data was gathered and organized into a database for the case, this included the transcription of interviews; (b) dissembling the data by coding and categorizing it into meaningful units; (c) reassembling the data, by creating a case description and an inductive explanation of the decision making process of the case; (d) interpreting the data, by comparing and contrasting the findings with the existing theoretical framework of the SA model presented in Fig. 1. The analysis process also used guidelines for the thematic analysis method when coding the meaningful units and aggregating them to themes [35]. In addition, the synthesized results from the inductive analysis of the data (a-c) were presented as a logical model of decision making [34]. The presented findings from the inductive analysis alongside the logic model, answered RQ1. The results from the inductive analysis were then used to investigate RQ2 according to guideline (d) analyzing whether existing SA models could explain the findings.

All respondents participated based on informed consent. As part of the ethical considerations the respondents were asked to approve the information presented about them and their organizations in the paper, to ensure that no sensitive information was disclosed. The quotes included in the paper were translated from Norwegian to English. The respondents were given the opportunity to revise the formulation of their own quotes. The quotes where reformulated through written correspondence with the respective respondents when they found the translated quotes misrepresented their intended meaning.

4 Findings

Based on the criteria for the case and the preliminary interviews the case of Sunburst within Norwegian CI was chosen. This case is presented from the perspective of the different actors in the following subsection. Then a thematic description of the decision-making processes will be given. The themes are then synthesized in a logical model of how the human operators decide on actions in response to compromised CPSs. The findings and the logical model are then compared with existing SA models.

4.1 The Sunburst Case from the Actors' Perspective

The SOC (Respondents 1) was responsible for SolarWinds systems in several customers. The SOC registered an advisory bulletin regarding a vulnerability in SolarWinds Orion after regular office hours on December 13, 2020. In the early morning before office hours of December 14, the SOC receives a mail from SolarWinds warning about the Sunburst attack. The SOC does not immediately recognize the severity of the attack, but this is gradually understood during the morning of December 14, while the SOC also communicates with the national security agency establishing a common understanding of the attack. Customers within CI using SolarWinds are notified throughout the morning by the SOC, by forwarding the mail from SolarWinds. In the afternoon of December 14, the SOC escalates the incident and activates its response team and procedures to the fullest extent. There were publicly available descriptions of how to verify if a system was compromised. SOC operators used these descriptions to verify if customers were compromised; meanwhile SOC specialists verified the available description of the malware. Throughout the following days the SOC conducted intense incident response activity involving security measures like isolation, patching and communication with stakeholders. This was done as a prioritized effort based on the criticality of compromised systems. On December 22 the SOC concludes its incident response and only follows up with customers regarding patching and incident evaluations.

The national security agency (Respondent 3) was made aware of the attack approximately at the same time as Respondent 1. Their first response was to verify the reality of the attack. This was done throughout December 14 in close communication with Respondent 1, among others. Warnings to CI owners within the power sector were issued, both in written form and in online briefings. The warnings and briefings were done iteratively and contained increasing levels of details regarding how to identify whether systems were compromised and how to mitigate. When patches from SolarWinds were released, Respondent 3 also distributed advisory statements regarding patching all relevant systems. In many aspects the role of Respondent 3 throughout the attack was to provide all stakeholders within the Norwegian power sector with verified and updated information during the attack. They also served as a contact point between other stakeholders.

The owner of CI within the electrical power sector (Respondent 4) received notice of the attack on the morning of December 14. They quickly confirmed that their Orion systems were affected. Based on log files they recognized that they were affected before the message from Respondent 3 arrived. The incident response routines were activated throughout the organization. The affected systems were located so that critical CPSs could be reached through them. The organization quickly segmented their networks in an effort to neutralize the attack. This was based on the information that was publicly available. After some time, it was decided to shut the compromised systems off within the most critical parts of their infrastructure. This was done after forensic material from the systems was secured. The unavailable systems resulted in reduced ability to monitor networks within these defined parts of their infrastructure, causing lowered ability to proactively operate their networks. When patches were made available, the organization decided to not patch existing systems within the most critical parts of the infrastructure, but to completely replace the affected systems.

Respondent 2 was not interviewed regarding the Sunburst case. The in-depth interview with Respondent 2 was aimed at decision making processes in related situations.

4.2 Themes Identified in the Analysis

The following is a presentation of all the themes that were identified through the analysis of the interview transcripts and the incident report. The themes are presented with a general description exemplified by respondent quotes.

Understanding Asset Topology and Functions. Several of the respondents describe how important it is that the topology and functions of the CPSs and connected systems are documented and well understood: *"You need to understand your own infrastructure. You need to comprehend what you have internally, and you need to take responsibility for it." Respondent 3.* The understanding of the functionality and topology of the assets is a prerequisite for assessing and performing mitigations: *"When we have insight into how the network is set up, how the infrastructure is, it's easier for us to evaluate quickly. For many of the customers this was the case. For some of the other customers we only* *knew that they had the system, but we didn't know much about their network. In those cases, it was essentially our responsibility just to inform and give general guidance to them because we had no insight into their environment." Respondent 1b.* We see how the SOC consider their ability to respond to attacks to be dependent on their level of insight into customers systems.

System Design. The theme of system design of CPSs was a common theme throughout the interviews. All the respondents highlighted that in order to respond adequately to threats and attacks the architecture of the CPSs had to be designed in a manner that enabled mitigation alternatives. When asked what design principles they used, the respondents pointed to the Purdue model: *"Are you familiar with the Purdue model? It involves organizing your architecture into distinct levels. You segment the system into smaller closed zones. If any issues have propagated within that closed system and haven't extended beyond it, you've effectively minimized the extent of potential damage." Respondent 1b.* It was further highlighted that this approach to system design was demanding to implement in large scale existing infrastructure and that the process is dependent upon the understanding of asset topology and functions: *"It demands a great deal of transformation technically to do it. I think it's wise to have an overall plan with annual goals. You need an overview of all your assets based on quality documentation. It is possible, but it demands a lot to get it done." Respondent 3.*

Knowledge and Skills. The respondents point to the need for a wide range of knowledge and skills to respond to attacks aimed at CPSs in CI. They highlight that the adequate response often involves a high degree of insight into the physical processes that are controlled, alongside expertise knowledge regarding the threat or attack at hand. These need to be combined to gain an understanding of the potential impact of the attack: *"We had a rather good mix of personnel. Some with security expertise, others with networking knowledge, customer insights, and SolarWinds knowledge. In our emergency response team, we had a diverse blend of individuals who understood the different technology involved in the entire system. This allowed us to engage in meaningful dialogues where experts from their respective fields could assess how the attack would impact things from their viewpoint." Respondent 1b.* The knowledge and skills available during an incident like the Sunburst attack will also influence how the response is organized regarding roles and responsibilities.

Roles and Responsibilities. The respondents highlighted the need for predefined and clear roles and responsibilities during incidents like Sunburst. The roles that need to be defined include roles connected to IT security, continued operation of industrial systems and people with defined roles regarding business impact: *"It is clear the importance of having both operational representatives and business stakeholders present in such discussions or meetings. After all, they are the ones who shoulder the risk." Respondent 4.* Several of the respondents also point out the importance of having one responsible leader for incident response with the ability and authority to make difficult decisions and maintain control over the other roles: *"If you don't have the authoritarian figure who takes responsibility, delegates, and maintains some control, it's easy for things to veer off track. Then some people end up working in parallel and have overlapping roles." Respondent 1b.* The respondents did not base the roles on any pre-defined standards; on the other hand, they highlighted that the roles were developed and optimized through training and exercises.

Training and Exercises. All respondents pointed to training and exercises as an essential preparation for mitigating attacks and handling security incidents. They also trained specifically for CPS-related scenarios: *"This is part of what we do, it's quite significant. The sites have their contingency plans or continuity plans. Naturally, we practice scenarios where we have to deactivate parts of the control system. This may be based on physical scenarios like floods or fires. And many of the sites naturally have plans to staff up, to compensate for the lack of system support."* Respondent 2. Another aspect of the training and exercises is that these are used to train on effective communication during an incident: *"When they have exercises, they practice on organizing the response and the chain of command. Because it's crucial in situations like emergencies so you don't spend a lot of time figuring out who should take responsibility or whom to contact. Knowing this is essential."* Respondent 1b. The respondents also talk about the importance of training for realistic incidents to be mentally prepared when incidents do occur.

Shared Understanding. When asked about what determines the effectiveness of incident response in CPSs the respondents highlight the importance of gaining a shared understanding of the situation. As described, the combination of different expertise and roles demands coordination. This coordination is successful when decisions are based on the best available information from several perspectives: *"If someone provides information that connects with other information, suddenly you see the bigger picture. It is important that people in a response team share information regardless if they think it is important or not. Information might prove important when received by someone with a different expertise or combined with information from others. We all sat together and worked in that way."* Respondent 1b. The sharing of different understandings was especially important when assessing the potential impact of incidents.

Assessing Impact. The first thing to assess during an attack is the nature of the attack and the potential impact it will have in the infrastructure that is attacked. The respondents explain that the quality of the information regarding an attack is key regarding effective mitigation. In the case of the Sunburst attack there was quite detailed information available when the attack was made known: *"When the news was released, it came with a full report on the vulnerability and how you could exploit it. It was a security company that had discovered the vulnerability, so you got a very comprehensive write-up. That way, you knew if the system was vulnerable and what indicators to look for."* Respondent 1b. In other attacks such information is not available and this adds to the complexity of responding.

Assessing Mitigation Alternatives. The respondents explained how the assessment of different possible mitigations was at the center of the response decisions. These assessments were reliant upon information gathered through the processes described in previously presented themes. The assessment consists of identifying the potential mitigations and then assess them regarding their effectiveness and what the mitigations will cost in terms of loss of functionality: *"One knows that if you take the system offline or make any changes to it, it creates significant challenges in terms of operations. From a security perspective, one might not fully understand this or have an overview of the* *consequences it will have. So, that is perhaps the difficult part here as well. From the security side, this threat is viewed as highly dangerous. However, the operations side may not perceive it that way."* Respondent 4. The respondents also highlight that these assessments can cause prolonged response times because of uncertainty: *"The biggest challenge lies in explaining the situation and reaching a decision. Trying to take some action based on a concrete picture, so you're not just standing there waiting. Waiting, analyzing, and discussing. That's the real challenge—to maintain progress in handling it."* Respondent 4. The respondents conclude that decisive action is necessary to avoid this issue.

Decisive Action. The respondents explain that one will never have met one's need for information before decisions must be made regarding mitigating attacks against CIs. This according to the respondents must be met with decisive actions from a leader with authority: *"What is important, is that you have someone—a leader—who takes clear charge and has both the authority and the courage to cut through. They must genuinely drive decision-making and accept that decisions made can be wrong. Because you can always gather more information, and not be able to move forward—that is maybe the worst thing you can do."* Respondent 4. The respondents also made very clear that in cases of compromised CPSs in critical infrastructure the decisions are first and foremost aimed at the safe operation of infrastructure; IT security is a secondary priority: *"The ones making the major decisions directly impacting the plant operation must be based locally, because you need to fully understand what the consequences are. It is particularly important for the safety of personnel. You cannot have anyone manipulating the systems unless those that are responsible for safe operations are fully aware of the ramifications."* Respondent 2. This also highlights the importance of communication between stakeholders during incidents.

Communication with Stakeholders. One important aspect throughout the case is the communication between different stakeholders. All respondents communicated with stakeholders throughout the Sunburst attack. The different actors had different roles regarding such communication. The SOC focused on communicating the updated information to their customers: *"We had very good and close dialogue with the customers. For some we provided information about indicators they could look for themselves. Others we assisted in looking for the indicators. The level of assistance was based on a prioritization of criticality. Still, we maintained a close dialogue with all the customers throughout the incident."* Respondent 1b. The national security agency had a different role: they gave briefings for the whole power industry regarding the situation with verified information: *"Our first priority is to uncover, what is actually true regarding the attack? Does this match? We were in early contact with the local support for the software. We tried to coordinate information from briefing to briefing. We answered questions like: when is the next opportunity for updated information, when is the briefing; What do we do in the meantime? And we tried to get in contact with the supplier, which is not always easy because they're in a tough spot."* Respondent 3.

4.3 Logic Model of Decision Making

The identified themes from the interviews represent issues that the respondents find relevant and important regarding how to make decisions between continuing to use or stop using potentially compromised systems in CIs. To better explain the process of making such decisions, the themes are synthesized into a logical model. The model has two major parts; the first is the preparations that are done before an attack (left side) and the second is the response to the attack (right side). The preparations are split in two types, namely the technical aspects (top) and the human aspects (bottom). Within each of the aspect types the respective preparations correspond to the identified themes. The different parts of the preparations within each type are dependent upon each other in a step-by-step fashion shown by arrows. The two types of preparations affect each other. Likewise, the response to an incident is split into the two stages of shared understanding (top) and making and communicating decisions (bottom). The two stages consist of respective parts of the response process that corresponds to the identified themes. The stage of shared understanding (top, right) also corresponds to an identified theme. The dependence between parts of each stage is also shown by arrows. The stages are shown to potentially repeat cyclically by the arrows going both ways between them. The model also shows with arrows (from left to right) how different parts of the response process are dependent upon different parts of the preparations.

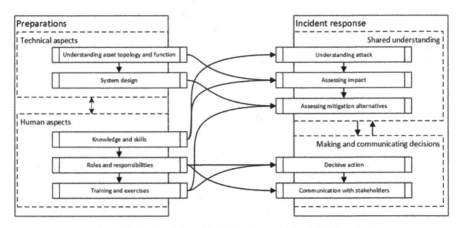

Fig. 2. Logic model of decision-making in CPSs

The model shows how decisions are made regarding to use or not to use systems that might be compromised. The decisions are based upon a shared understanding of the attack, its impact, and an assessment of the available mitigation alternatives. This shared understanding is dependent upon the technical understanding of asset topology and function, as well as on a system design that allows for adequate mitigation alternatives. The human operators use their combined knowledge to gain a shared understanding during an incident, and this process demands training and exercise to carry out effectively in collaboration. To implement the decisions, the operators need to take decisive action and communicate it effectively. The decisiveness is dependent on well-defined roles and responsibilities honed through training and exercises. The actions need to be communicated to stakeholders and this communication also provides information regarding the often-needed iteration of a shared understanding.

5 Discussion

The model presented in Fig. 2 presents the findings from the inductive analysis of the case material. When we compare this to Endsley's model of SA [27] in Fig. 1, we see some clear similarities. The identified stage of shared understanding consists of three parts: understanding the attack, assessing impact, and assessing mitigation alternatives. If we compare this to the SA model, we can recognize that the understanding is achieved in levels in both models. The three parts of shared understanding in Fig. 2 do not completely match the SA model. One could argue that both understanding the attack and assessing impact are mostly related to comprehension (level 2) in the SA model. Assessing mitigation alternatives is highly related to projection (level 3) in the SA model. Level 3 in the SA model may also be overlapping with parts of assessing impact in the Logical model. The stage of making and communicating decisions in Fig. 2 overlaps to a large degree with decision and performance of action in the SA model. The similarity is especially clear if we consider the communication with stakeholders as overlapping with the feedback loop of the SA model.

When we consider the preparations, we see a strong similarity with the factors shown to influence the SA in Endsley's model. The technical aspects of the preparations highly overlap with the task/system factors in the SA model. The human aspects in Fig. 2 overlaps with the individual factors of the SA model. We can see that knowledge and skills and training and exercises in Fig. 2 are highly similar to abilities, experience, and training in Fig. 1. One could further argue that roles and responsibilities in Fig. 2 overlaps with goals and objectives and preconceptions in Fig. 1. In total the models are highly similar; this strengthens the argument that existing SA theory can explain the decision-making processes related to the dilemma posed in this study.

There are nevertheless some differences that are important to highlight. In the Endsley's SA model there is a clear individual perspective. The model explains how individual operators gain and use SA. The logic model presented in this study does not have an individual perspective, but rather an organizational perspective on decision making. This can to some extent explain the lack of themes connected to the cognitive processes like information processing mechanisms in the individual factors of the SA model. In addition, level 1 of the SA model is only partially overlapping with the logic model. The last point can arguably be explained by how participants were asked about their decisions in the Sunburst case. This might have reduced the respondents' focus on the monitoring of elements in the situation prior to the recognition of the attack.

One possible alternative explanation from existing SA theory that might resolve these discrepancies are SA models for groups [36]. One candidate is the Team SA model synthesized by Salmon et al., [37]. This model for example includes common/shared picture as part of the SA process. Still, the Team SA model is presented at a higher abstraction level, so it only indicates many of the details present in the logic model of Fig. 2. Another alternative explanation is the Distributed SA model [38]. This model allows for a stronger connection between the technical aspects and shared understanding in Fig. 2. On the other hand, the Distributed SA model is less specific than Endsley's model regarding the process of decision making and action. Within the research literature investigating cyber-SA, Endsley's model is almost exclusively referenced regardless of the level of analysis i.e., even group and system level cyber-SA research use the individual model of Endsley as explanatory model [9]. There is thus a gap regarding theoretical SA models that are developed for explaining the type of decision-making processes investigated in this study. This leaves Endsley's model as the most fitting existing theoretical explanatory model.

The logic model in Fig. 2 is presenting specific dependencies between preparations and incident response regarding the posed dilemma that Endsley's model is too general to encompass. This is a unique contribution regarding understanding of how these dilemmas are resolved by the process of decision making. This case study shows how specific knowledge and skills are needed to understand attacks against CPSs and to assess their potential impacts. The knowledge and skills needed for these tasks are seldom found in individual operators alone. This is because the knowledge of IT-based attacks and the functionality of CPSs are two distinct expertise areas. Actors within CI should therefore organize and train on the collaboration between experts from these different fields of expertise.

Additionally, the importance of system design is something not captured by existing SA models. The respondents clearly stated that the mitigation alternatives one has during an attack on CPSs are totally dependent upon the design of one's systems. If the systems are designed in a way that allows for fast and secure segmentation in accordance with the guidelines of the Purdue model [17], the response has a far greater array of potential mitigation alternatives. The segregation or segmentation of networks are often far less invasive than shutdowns or manual control options. This is one of the most important focus areas for the respondents, because existing CI that are gradually converted to CPSs are often not adhering to these design principles. This leaves human operators with few mitigation alternatives that they know will be effective. The dilemma is in these cases very realistic where the decision is between letting the system be compromised or paralyzing the system through shutdowns or manual operation. When the CPSs are designed properly one can with confidence isolate parts of the systems and let other parts operate largely unaffected.

It is important to recognize that though the findings in this study provide unique contributions, these are only based on a quite restrictive case of operators of CPSs in CI. The study only investigated the case of the Sunburst attack. Had other attacks or cases been investigated, other findings might have resulted. Further the relative low number of respondents makes the findings less generalizable. This is made even more relevant given that the respondents all came from Norwegian CI actors, which is a specific context that may have affected the findings [39]. Despite these limitations the study presents empirically-based findings within a recognized research gap [40]. There are few studies examining incident response from the human operators' side, and even fewer studying the human SA in this setting [11]. This study provides clear recommendations for practice including the need for specific preparations regarding attacks against CPSs in CI as well as a more tailored presentation of the decision process itself in comparison with existing

SA theory. This study also implicates the need for further research regarding SA in such settings. A complete Goal-directed Task analysis of SA could complement and validate the findings of this study and provide a more generalizable model of decision making within this setting too [41].

6 Conclusion

This case study investigated the dilemma of human operators of CPSs in CI regarding continuing to use or stop using compromised systems to maintain CPS operations. This was investigated through a case study of the Sunburst attack [12] in Norwegian CI within the electrical power and the manufacturing sectors. An inductive analysis of interviews with four different actors and the incident reports from one of them answered the first research question (RQ1): How do human operators of cyber-physical systems in critical infrastructure decide between continuing to use or stop using systems that might be compromised? The inductive analysis identified ten distinct themes that explained how such decisions were made in the considered case. The findings were synthesized and presented in Fig. 2 as a logical model of the decision process. A deductive comparison of the logical model with existing theoretical SA models answered the second research question (RQ2): How can these decision processes be explained by existing theory of cyber-SA? The analysis compared Endsley's individual SA model [27] with the logical model and found many similarities and some discrepancies. Other existing models of SA were discussed as alternative explanations, but none of them explained the logical model better than Endsley's model.

The findings provide a unique contribution that explains the decision-making process of human operators of CPSs. The study thus contributes to bridging a recognized research gap regarding human operators of CPSs within CI. Although the explanations provided in this case study have limited generalizability, they provide clear indications for further research as well as implications for practice. The study shows how preparations of technical and human aspects directly affect the operators' ability to respond adequately to attacks against the CPSs. One important example is that the design of the systems provides the operator with mitigation alternatives. If the technical systems are designed in the right way, the operator may well be able to paralyze only a minor part of the CI to mitigate compromised systems. The possibility to adapt mitigation against attacks on CPSs seems like the most promising way forward. Then the potential harm of necessary mitigations against attacks will be minimized. This would arguably be even more important if we hand the control of CPSs in large scale infrastructure of critical importance over to AI in the future.

Acknowledgments. This work was supported by the Research Council of Norway (Norges Forskningsråd) under Project number 333900 *"Situation awareness in virtual security operations centers"* and Project number 310105 *"Norwegian Centre for Cyber Security in Critical Sectors (NORCICS)"*.

Disclosure of Interests. The first author was employed in a research position with Respondent 1 (See Table 1.) at the time of this study. The authors had no other known competing financial interests or personal relationships that could have appeared to influence the work reported in this paper.

References

1. Baheti, R., Gill, H.: Cyber-physical systems. Impact Control Technol. **12**, 161–166 (2011)
2. Ashibani, Y., Mahmoud, Q.H.: Cyber physical systems security: analysis, challenges and solutions. Comput. Secur. **68**, 81–97 (2017). https://doi.org/10.1016/j.cose.2017.04.005
3. Alguliyev, R., Imamverdiyev, Y., Sukhostat, L.: Cyber-physical systems and their security issues. Comput. Ind. **100**, 212–223 (2018). https://doi.org/10.1016/j.compind.2018.04.017
4. Yaacoub, J.-P.A., Salman, O., Noura, H.N., Kaaniche, N., Chehab, A., Malli, M.: Cyber-physical systems security: limitations, issues and future trends. Microprocess. Microsyst. **77** (2020). https://doi.org/10.1016/j.micpro.2020.103201
5. Kayan, H., Nunes, M., Rana, O., Burnap, P., Perera, C.: Cybersecurity of industrial cyber-physical systems: a review. ACM Comput. Surv. (CSUR) **54**, 1–35 (2022). https://doi.org/10.1145/3510410
6. Lezzi, M., Lazoi, M., Corallo, A.: Cybersecurity for industry 4.0 in the current literature: a reference framework. Comput. Ind. **103**, 97–110 (2018). https://doi.org/10.1016/j.compind.2018.09.004
7. El-Kady, A.H., Halim, S., El-Halwagi, M.M., Khan, F.: Analysis of safety and security challenges and opportunities related to cyber-physical systems. Process. Saf. Environ. Prot. **173**, 384–413 (2023). https://doi.org/10.1016/j.psep.2023.03.012
8. Akbarzadeh, A., Katsikas, S.: Unified IT&OT modeling for cybersecurity analysis of cyber-physical systems. IEEE Open J. Ind. Electron. Soc. **3**, 318–328 (2022). https://doi.org/10.1109/ojies.2022.3178834
9. Ofte, H.J., Katsikas, S.: Understanding situation awareness in SOCs, a systematic literature review. Comput. Secur., 103069 (2022). https://doi.org/10.1016/j.cose.2022.103069
10. Stanton, N.A., Salmon, P.M., Walker, G.H., Salas, E., Hancock, P.A.: State-of-science: situation awareness in individuals, teams and systems. Ergonomics **60**, 449–466 (2017). https://doi.org/10.1080/00140139.2017.1278796
11. Gutzwiller, R., Dykstra, J., Payne, B.: Gaps and opportunities in situational awareness for cybersecurity. Digit. Threats Res. Pract. **1** (2020). https://doi.org/10.1145/3384471
12. Willett, M.: Lessons of the SolarWinds hack. Survival **63**, 7–26 (2021). https://doi.org/10.1080/00396338.2021.1906001
13. Dey, N., Ashour, A.S., Shi, F., Fong, S.J., Tavares, J.M.R.: Medical cyber-physical systems: a survey. J. Med. Syst. **42**, 1–13 (2018). https://doi.org/10.1007/s10916-018-0921-x
14. Kim, K., Kim, J.S., Jeong, S., Park, J.-H., Kim, H.K.: Cybersecurity for autonomous vehicles: review of attacks and defense. Comput. Secur. **103**, 102150 (2021). https://doi.org/10.1016/j.cose.2020.102150
15. Yohanandhan, R.V., Elavarasan, R.M., Manoharan, P., Mihet-Popa, L.: Cyber-physical power system (CPPS): a review on modeling, simulation, and analysis with cyber security applications. IEEE Access **8**, 151019–151064 (2020). https://doi.org/10.1109/access.2020.3016826
16. Aven, T.: A unified framework for risk and vulnerability analysis covering both safety and security. Reliab. Eng. Syst. Saf. **92**, 745–754 (2007). https://doi.org/10.1016/j.ress.2006.03.008
17. Boyes, H., Hallaq, B., Cunningham, J., Watson, T.: The industrial internet of things (IIoT): an analysis framework. Comput. Ind. **101**, 1–12 (2018). https://doi.org/10.1016/j.compind.2018.04.015

18. Obregon, L.: Secure architecture for industrial control systems. SANS Institute, White Paper (2015)
19. Stouffer, K., et al.: Guide to operational technology (OT) security. NIST Special Publication, 800-882, Rev. 803 (2023). https://doi.org/10.6028/NIST.SP.800-82r3
20. Turchin, A., Denkenberger, D.: Classification of global catastrophic risks connected with artificial intelligence. AI Soc. **35**, 147–163 (2020). https://doi.org/10.1007/s00146-018-0845-5
21. Nunes, D.S., Zhang, P., Silva, J.S.: A survey on human-in-the-loop applications towards an internet of all. IEEE Commun. Surv. Tutorials **17**, 944–965 (2015). https://doi.org/10.1109/comst.2015.2398816
22. Jirgl, M., Bradac, Z., Fiedler, P.: Human-in-the-loop issue in context of the cyber-physical systems. IFAC-PapersOnLine **51**, 225–230 (2018). https://doi.org/10.1016/j.ifacol.2018.07.158
23. Kadir, B.A., Broberg, O., da Conceicao, C.S.: Current research and future perspectives on human factors and ergonomics in industry 4.0. Comput. Ind. Eng. **137**, 106004 (2019). https://doi.org/10.1016/j.cie.2019.106004
24. Carreras Guzman, N.H., Wied, M., Kozine, I., Lundteigen, M.A.: Conceptualizing the key features of cyber-physical systems in a multi-layered representation for safety and security analysis. Syst. Eng. **23**, 189–210 (2020). https://doi.org/10.1002/sys.21509
25. Pinto, R., Gonçalves, G., Tovar, E., Delsing, J.: Attack detection in cyber-physical production systems using the deterministic dendritic cell algorithm. In: 25th IEEE International Conference on Emerging Technologies and Factory Automation (ETFA), pp. 1552–1559. IEEE (2020). https://doi.org/10.1109/etfa46521.2020.9212021
26. Endsley, M.R., Garland, D.J.: Theoretical underpinnings of situation awareness: a critical review. Situation Awareness Anal. Meas. **1**, 3–21 (2000)
27. Endsley, M.R.: Toward a theory of situation awareness in dynamic systems. Hum. Factors **37**, 32–64 (1995). https://doi.org/10.1518/001872095779049543
28. Endsley, M.R.: Designing for Situation Awareness: An Approach to User-Centered Design. CRC Press (2016). https://doi.org/10.1201/9780203485088
29. Jajodia, S., Liu, P., Swarup, V., Wang, C.: Cyber Situational Awareness. Springer, New York (2009). https://doi.org/10.1007/978-1-4419-0140-8
30. Alkhadra, R., Abuzaid, J., AlShammari, M., Mohammad, N.: Solar winds hack: in-depth analysis and countermeasures. In: 12th International Conference on Computing Communication and Networking Technologies (ICCCNT), pp. 1–7 (2021). https://doi.org/10.1109/ICCCNT51525.2021.9579611
31. Coco, A., Dias, T., van Benthem, T.: Illegal: the SolarWinds hack under international law. Eur. J. Int. Law **33**, 1275–1286 (2022). https://doi.org/10.1093/ejil/chac063
32. Martínez, J., Durán, J.M.: Software supply chain attacks, a threat to global cybersecurity: SolarWinds' case study. Int. J. Saf. Secur. Eng. **11**, 537–545 (2021). https://doi.org/10.18280/ijsse.110505
33. Aakre, S., Aarland, M.: Når en høypålitelig organisasjon blir utsatt for en normalulykke. Praktisk økonomi finans **39**, 34–47 (2023). https://doi.org/10.18261/pof.39.1.4
34. Yin, R.K., Campbell, D.T.: Case Study Research and Applications: Design and Methods. SAGE Publications, Inc., Thousand Oaks, California (2018)
35. Braun, V., Clarke, V.: Thematic Analysis. American Psychological Association (2012)
36. Kaber, D.B., Endsley, M.R.: Team situation awareness for process control safety and performance. Process. Saf. Prog. **17**, 43–48 (1998). https://doi.org/10.1002/prs.680170110
37. Salmon, P.M., et al.: What really is going on? Review of situation awareness models for individuals and teams. Theor. Issues Ergon. Sci. **9**, 297–323 (2008). https://doi.org/10.1080/14639220701561775

38. Stanton, N.A., et al.: Distributed situation awareness in dynamic systems: theoretical development and application of an ergonomics methodology. Ergonomics **49**, 1288–1311 (2006). https://doi.org/10.1080/00140130600612762
39. Gjesvik, L.: Comparing Cyber Security. Critical Infrastructure Protection in Norway, the UK and Finland. NUPI Report (2019)
40. Gil, M., Albert, M., Fons, J., Pelechano, V.: Engineering human-in-the-loop interactions in cyber-physical systems. Inf. Softw. Technol. **126**, 106349 (2020). https://doi.org/10.1016/j.infsof.2020.106349
41. Endsley, M.R., Connors, E.S.: Foundation and challenges. In: Cyber Defense and Situational Awareness, pp. 7–27 (2014). https://doi.org/10.1007/978-3-319-11391-3_2

Cognitive Digital Twins for Improving Security in IT-OT Enabled Healthcare Applications

Sandeep Pirbhulal[1]($\boxtimes$), Sabarathinam Chockalingam[2], Habtamu Abie[1], and Nathan Lau[3]

[1] Norwegian Computing Center, Oslo, Norway
{Sandeep,Habtamu.Abie}@nr.no
[2] Department of Risk and Security, Institute for Energy Technology, Halden, Norway
Sabarathinam.Chockalingam@ife.no
[3] Grado Department of Industrial and Systems Engineering, Virginia Tech, Blacksburg, VA, USA
nkclau@vt.edu

Abstract. Digital Twins (DTs), serving as virtual replicas of physical systems, facilitate novel pathways for real-time monitoring, and informed decision making in different healthcare applications such as remote surgery, hospital management, and telemedicine. In the rapidly evolving landscape of cyber security, the emergence of DTs has provided unparalleled capabilities of preempting cyber threats, testing incident response strategies, and compliance testing. Moreover, Cognitive Digital Twins (CDTs) not only replicate physical systems but also have the ability to learn and make decisions. However, such a human-in-the-loop decision making approach is lacking for improving security in Information Technology (IT) and Operational Technology (OT) infrastructures while IT-OT integration in healthcare introduces new cyber security concerns and an increasing threat landscape. In this study, we developed a conceptual CDT-based adaptive cyber security framework for IT-OT enabled healthcare applications which has the potential to address cyber threats in varying situations. This framework integrates physical and virtual healthcare twin for healthcare service providers in addition to a knowledge base of security/privacy events and cognitive cycle for facilitating the human-in-the-loop approach. This framework could enhance cyber security in IT-OT healthcare by incorporating interdisciplinary fields such as adaptive security, health information exchange, human factors, IT-OT integration, risk management, among others. This study also presents some prominent use cases for IT-OT healthcare systems.

Keywords: Cognitive digital twins · IT-OT integration · Cyber security · Healthcare · Operational Technology · Privacy

1 Introduction

1.1 Overview

The recent development in cutting edge technologies like Internet of Things (IoTs), Digital Twins (DTs), augmented reality, and advanced data analytics present invaluable applications in many critical domains such as air traffic monitoring, e-health, smart cities,

A. Moallem (Ed.): HCII 2024, LNCS 14729, pp. 153–163, 2024.
https://doi.org/10.1007/978-3-031-61382-1_10

and smart grids, among others. For these critical domains, Information Technology (IT) and Operational Technology (OT) are significant for optimization and customization of their respective functions. The convergence of IT and OT introduces specific cyber security challenges, like the combination of legacy OT systems with modern IT networks that expose difficult-to-patch vulnerabilities, lack standardization, increase attack surface due to integration complexity, thereby creating potential pathways for cyber threats to move between the two types of technology. The security challenges raised by IT-OT integration require real-time and secured communication between different stakeholders. Meanwhile, attackers are using advanced technology, such as Artificial Intelligence (AI)/Machine Learning (ML) and behavioral biometrics, to disrupt the regular operations of healthcare sectors. Therefore, there is a need to develop an approach to effectively monitor, predict, respond to and recover from security threats against different healthcare applications in a timely manner that confines any negative consequences [1].

To achieve a high-level of cyber security, closed-feedback loop AI can be developed to provide a deep, interconnected understanding of the IT-OT enabled healthcare systems, and to autonomously monitor, analyze and adapt to threats and contexts in Critical Infrastructures (CIs). A closed-feedback loop AI typically refers to a system where the output or actions of an AI model influence and potentially modify the input data for future iterations [2]. This feedback loop allows the AI system to learn and improve over time based on the outcomes of its own actions, which is powerful for self-learning to adapt to dynamic environments and improve their performance based on real-world outcomes. Cognitive Digital Twins (CDTs) presents a promising approach to develop the closed feedback loop AI for monitoring, predicting, responding to and recovering from cyber threats based on virtual simulation, data-driven capability, and behavioral and impact analysis.

We have conducted preliminary research on CDT that is self-learning and proactive, combining Digital Twins (DTs) and cognitive capabilities to interpret and predict unforeseen security issues of the physical system [3]. In [4], we proposed a three-stage framework for enhancing cyber security in healthcare using DT technology consisting of three key modules: (a) physical-twin, (b) cyber-twin, and (c) cyber security automation. In [5], we highlighted the importance of cognitive architecture for simulating human cognitive behavior in cyber security for monitoring, analyzing, and responding to changing security threats to Cyber Physical Systems (CPS). Later, we applied the developed cognitive architecture for developing a CDT for healthcare applications [3]. The past experience in [5] led to the realization that human cognitive capabilities have a huge potential to understand the behavior of digital and physical twins and can be embedded into support decision-making in real systems. Addressing the diverse cyber security threats in the changing environment through a dynamic CDT solution can also be useful for training professionals and improving system performance in IT-OT healthcare.

1.2 Our Contributions

In this paper, we proposed a conceptual CDT approach that mainly includes developing physical and virtual twins, real-time synchronization between them, knowledge base for security and privacy events from IT and OT healthcare systems, and cognitive healthcare decision-making loops. The cognitive cycle in the proposed conceptual framework can be primarily used for simulating human cognitive behavior to automate deployment of cyber security measures against evolving cyber threats. Our approach involves closed-feedback loop techniques between the physical healthcare twin and virtual healthcare twin for investigating complex behaviors of different healthcare stakeholders and systems involved and adapting to security variations in the cognitive process of IT and OT healthcare systems.

1.3 Structure of the Paper

The rest of this paper is structured as follows: Section 2 describes the related work, followed by the proposed framework in Sect. 3. Section 4 presents different use cases and scenarios that could utilize the proposed framework. Finally, Sect. 5 presents conclusions and future work directions.

2 Related Work

This section reviews key studies and developments within (cognitive) DTs in cyber security, highlighting how our work addresses some of the open challenges and extends existing knowledge.

A well-known issue is the slow and reactive nature of current cyber defense mechanisms. Nguyen proposed the Cybonto conceptual framework and ontology to address this issue [6]. This framework aims to utilize DTs and Human Digital Twins (HDTs) to simulate and understand adversaries' behaviors and tactics for proactive cyber defense. The Cybonto ontology, built on psychological theories and network centrality algorithms, documents constructs and cognitive paths to enhance digital cognitive architectures. Nguyen's use of DTs and HDTs represents a new approach to proactive defense strategies and extends the current digital cognitive architectures; however, the demonstration of the framework is lacking.

Pirbhulal et al. discusses a novel way to improve security in healthcare systems by employing DTs with IoTs [4]. This approach could help predict and identify potential cyber-attacks/threats, thereby enhancing the protection of patient safety and healthcare services seamlessly in real-time. Moreover, Pirbhulal et al. suggests that DTs can play a crucial role in cyber security by offering insights into potential attacks, identifying system weaknesses, and helping develop better defense mechanisms. They also point out that while the use of DTs has many benefits for cyber security, more applied research with experiments and simulations are necessary for reliable applications in healthcare. In addition, Pirbhulal et al. presents a novel CDT architecture aimed at enhancing cyber security in IoT-based smart homes for telemedicine [3]. The approach focuses on dynamic threat detection and mitigation through continuous monitoring, analytics, and simulation within a cyber twin. Their work also emphasizes the use of AI and ML for analyzing complex behaviors and adapting to evolving security threats and the environment.

Other studies examine DT applications in different domains including smart cities and maritime. Sabeur et al. detailed the S4AllCities project's development of three distinct DTs for enhancing cyber and physical security of smart urban spaces [7]. This project utilizes distributed edge computing IoT, malicious actions information detection system, and augmented context management system under a system of systems architecture. It focuses on real-time observations and data processing for intelligent monitoring and threat detection, incorporating advanced AI techniques and data fusion frameworks for improved situational awareness in urban environments. Xu et al. introduces a novel framework named LATTICE, which incorporates curriculum learning into the DT-based anomaly detection method ATTAIN to optimize its learning paradigm [8]. This approach is designed to improve anomaly detection in CPS by assigning difficulty scores to data samples, thus enabling the model to learn from easy to difficult samples. LATTICE has been evaluated using publicly available datasets from CPS testbeds, demonstrating its superiority over ATTAIN and other state-of-the-art anomaly detectors in terms of F1 score on model performance and training efficiency, while maintaining competitive detection delay times. Epiphaniou et al. integrated cyber modeling and simulation with DTs and threat characterization for security assessments in IoT and CPS [9]. They presented a comprehensive study on cyber resilience testing, detailing methodologies for integrating cyber standards and simulation standards to address IoT/CPS vulnerabilities. Their work also includes a case study on the Port of Southampton, demonstrating how DTs can simulate cyber-attack scenarios and improve resilience. Epiphaniou et al. contributed to cyber resilience in CIs with a novel approach that combines DTs with AI-enabled threat characterization and cyber modeling and simulation standards.

Finally, Eman Shaikh et al. investigated the security of DTs, which is also essential in applications for safety-critical domains like healthcare [10]. Eman Shaikh et al. presents a comprehensive framework for assessing the security of DTs in various domains, such as healthcare, using probabilistic model checking [10]. Their framework incorporates multi-layered security analysis, including both attack and defense mechanisms across physical, communication, virtual, and application layers of DT systems. Their study also emphasizes the use of Markov Decision Processes and Discrete-Time Markov Chains to model and analyze the security properties and attack probabilities within these systems. One of the key contributions of their work includes a detailed case study on in-patient monitoring systems in the healthcare sector, demonstrating the framework's application to evaluate the likelihood of successful attacks and the effectiveness of defense strategies. Due to the several advantages of DT technology in healthcare sectors, it has been used in different medical applications such as remote healthcare [11], thoracic healthcare monitoring and diagnosis [12], digitalization in healthcare [13], early mental illness detection [14], personalized therapeutics and pharmaceutical manufacturing [15], inpatients' falls risk management [16], resilient patient-centered healthcare services [17].

In summary, the literature contains studies that address both the use of DTs in cyber security for different domains in addition to dealing with cyber security of DTs. The main applications of DTs for cyber security included anomaly detection, cyber resilience testing. However, there are several open issues, which we aim to address in this work: the aspect of IT-OT convergence, which is becoming more prominent in CPS, and the essential feature of human-in-the-loop for informed and improved decision-making based on the outputs from DTs. Finally, other essential use cases are missing, like ensuring data privacy and compliance while using robots to assist patients, through DTs in safety-critical application domains like healthcare.

3 Proposed Framework

In this study, we develop a CDT-enabled approach for securing healthcare systems. This can provide secure communication between patients and healthcare providers, which in turn ensures end-end security of critical health applications in addition to data privacy and compliance, as shown in Fig. 1. A CDT represents a sophisticated blend of DT with AI and ML capabilities including human-in-the-loop approach, creating dynamic virtual replicas that can learn, adapt and make informed decisions. Unlike traditional DTs, CDTs incorporate cognitive functions that enable learning, adaptation, and improved decision making. The developed framework consists of mainly three parts: (i) physical healthcare twin, (ii) virtual healthcare twin, and (iii) cognitive healthcare decision making cycle as shown in Fig. 1.

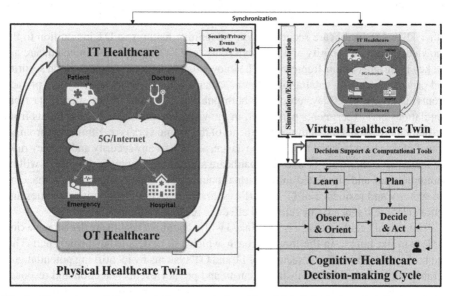

Fig. 1. Illustration of Proposed Conceptual Cognitive Digital Twin-based Adaptive Cyber Security Framework for IT-OT enabled Healthcare.

Physical Healthcare Twin. The first part is an IT-OT based physical healthcare system, in which different stakeholders such as patients, doctors, emergency services, hospitals share sensitive medical information via 5G and the internet. For instance, in remote healthcare infrastructures, both IT and OT systems are used to facilitate remote services. Efficient patient data management through Electronic Health Records (EHRs) [18] represent an example of IT systems. On the other hand, the OT part of this infrastructure could be wearable sensors used to monitor patient's health, acquire, and transmit data to the hospital in addition to actuators like an airbag in a fall detector [19]. However, integrating IT and OT enables healthcare providers to offer services like telehealthcare more effectively. Since IT and OT systems in healthcare have different predefined capabilities, features and priorities, integrating these two creates new vulnerabilities, making healthcare systems susceptible to cyber-attacks and evolving threat landscape. In healthcare and other safety-critical domains, it is almost impossible to perform cyber security testing on real infrastructures as sensitive healthcare services such as patient monitoring, telemedicine, remote surgery needs to be constantly available and cannot be halted. Thus, cyber twins of physical healthcare systems can be useful in such situations. For instance, analyzing massive volumes of data from IT and OT systems of healthcare systems to identify patterns and anomalies, which may indicate potential ongoing cyber-attacks and also to some extent automate certain cyber security tasks.

Virtual Healthcare Twin. The second part of this framework is the dynamic virtual representation of the physical healthcare components, systems, and processes. This is mainly in the digital world with real mapping to their entire lifecycle by utilizing physical information, virtual information, and interaction between both sources. Existing studies have developed DTs for cyber security, mainly anomaly detection, in addition to healthcare applications [20, 21]. They are primarily focused on how to use DT for either IT or OT healthcare security, adding cognitive features to DT in addition to the knowledge base on security and privacy events for IT-OT integration in healthcare are the key highlights of our framework. The knowledge base in our framework on security and privacy events is a catalog of different scenarios. It comprises security and privacy events involving IT-OT systems from both publicly available information, data from simulations and experiments performed in the virtual healthcare twin, and inputs from the human involved. One of the key elements of this framework is real-time synchronization of physical and virtual twins. For instance, as soon as any security and privacy risks are identified either from IT and OT healthcare systems in the physical world, it will be communicated and simulated in the virtual counterpart. This is mainly for enhancing the security and resilience of IT and OT systems by providing predictive analytics and actionable intelligence on targeted and effective response actions.

The virtual healthcare twin is also linked with a cognitive healthcare decision making cycle to utilize human-in-the-loop approach, which will be detailed in the next part. This can be useful to improve the security of IT and OT systems by identifying potential vulnerabilities and providing real-time security and privacy events detection and response by receiving inputs and/or validating the diagnosis performed by the decision support via human-in-the-loop, which is essential.

Cognitive Healthcare Decision-Making Cycle. The third part is the cognitive healthcare decision making cycle, which includes the cognitive model based on Observe, Orient, Decision, Act (OODA) loop concept [22], decision support and computational tools using AI/ML, and feedback loops for continuous learning. This allows dynamically perceiving the IT-OT healthcare circumstances, individuals and social environment behaviors considering the human-in-the-loop approach. This cognitive model has four main stages: learn, plan, observe & orient, and decide & act [5, 25] for continuously collecting, analyzing, and predicting security-related information and medical information to anticipate potential cyber incidents/data breaches and provision appropriate mitigation and/or response measures. The proposed framework applies the feedback loop of decision-making cycle with the physical healthcare twin and virtual healthcare twin to efficiently improve security. This feature will allow the physical healthcare twin to have human-in-the-loop inputs, and also offer human insights while simulating and experimenting with security events in the virtual world.

4 Use Cases and Scenarios

In this section, the different use cases and scenarios on the use of our proposed framework in the healthcare domain are discussed from smart healthcare to remote monitoring and use of social robots for patient support to enable resilient societies.

4.1 Personalized Patient Care and Treatment

In general, the developed framework can be useful for helping patients in understanding different care options, assisting with personal data ownership, secure personalized treatment, and informed decision-making on specific treatments. Current healthcare systems lack efficient ways for testing treatments in advance, but our proposed framework also has the potential to safely enable doctors for testing different treatment options on virtual twins of patient's before using it. This will allow healthcare service providers to acquire an overview of how the individual will respond to the specific treatment. The use of CDT can allow all these capabilities. For example, with our framework, it is possible to develop secure virtual twins of patients, doctors can simulate the impact of various chemotherapy regimens for a cancer patient, allowing them to select the best possible option for the patients.

Moreover, the existing approaches also lack surgery planning, personalized medicine, disease modeling, and epidemic management since privacy is one of the major concerns. For instance, this is impeding the growth of personalized medicine as the treatment plan is developed through their personal health information, which in this context requires data privacy of patient's to be handled in a better way. Through our developed framework, this issue can be addressed to some extent with the help of knowledge base on security and privacy events. To that end, we can utilize the privacy scenarios in the knowledge base in addition to the inputs from the human-in-the-loop for identifying potential privacy risks and their impact in personalized patient care through virtual healthcare twins in advance. This can be done through virtual simulation and experimentation to identify best possible actions before deployment.

4.2 Remote Patient Monitoring

Another important use case for our developed framework is secure real-time monitoring of patients. In healthcare, remote monitoring is essential in some situations, where patients need continuous care and support. Some examples of remote monitoring applications for patients that have chronical illness, mental health issues, diabetes, sleep apnea in addition to accidents. One of the main challenges with remote healthcare monitoring is security, because attackers might eavesdrop on real-time communication using potential vulnerabilities in the system. Thus, our developed framework can be used to identify and respond to the cyber security risks. The virtual accessibility of healthcare can provide better understanding of IT-OT cyber-attacks and risks and facilitates the detection and prediction of intentional and unintentional risks.

For example, a flooding attack is one of the potential attacks in remote patient monitoring. This can make it hard for the healthcare providers to identify the potential cause that has compromised the availability of a specific medical device in the infrastructure. In such scenarios, our proposed framework can support identifying the potential cause in real-time, corresponding vulnerabilities (example: vulnerable ports of the devices by performing simulation and experiments in the virtual twin), and how to mitigate it. Human-in-the-loop in our framework can also be used to train and test operators on the remote diagnostic process to identify the extent of the compromise, level of availability and integrity of the control and safety systems and take appropriate actions to respond to a loss of control.

As a part of Adaptive Security for Smart Internet of Things in eHealth (ASSET) project [23], we developed a testbed for monitoring the health data remotely. In [24], we developed the DT infrastructure based on the ASSET testbed [23]. Based on these developments, we intend to apply our proposed framework for improving security of daily activities, end-end monitoring of patients in smart homes. Also, the developed framework will serve as an input for other related activities such as autonomous adaptive security for 5G-enabled IoT systems in Norwegian Centre for Cybersecurity in Critical Sectors (NORCICS) project [25], and dynamic safety and security risk assessment for different critical applications in European Lighthouse to Manifest Trustworthy and Green AI (ENFIELD) project [26].

4.3 Assistive and Social Robots in Care

The third use case is about the applicability of our developed framework in assistive and social robots to offer secure and reliable smart care services. The use of assistive and social robots to support healthcare services are becoming popular, especially for elderly, individuals requiring rehabilitation, and those with disabilities [27, 28]. Social robots in healthcare are designed to interact with people in a personal and engaging manner, providing support, companionship, and assistance in various health-related contexts [29]. As a hospital where robots are used for care services, it is important to ensure the data privacy and compliance of data gathered from different stakeholders for providing personalized support, companionship, and assistance in various health-related contexts. This is to ensure that it complies with laws and regulations like GDPR. Our proposed framework has potential to address these issues since it includes a human-in-the-loop approach for receiving inputs on user willingness to share data and corresponding privacy risks.

Likewise, as a part of the User-centered Security Framework for Social Robots in Public Space (SecuRoPS) project, we use social robots to offer personalized services to citizens/passengers [31, 32]. To that end, it is important to understand users' willingness to share personal information and which type of personal information they are willing to share with social robots in public space for receiving personalized services. For this purpose, we conducted pilot studies involving potential users', which is time consuming and cumbersome. However, our developed CDT based framework can play an important role in addressing this issue in the healthcare sector by modeling how social robots collect, store and process data, social robot developers can identify potential data breaches. On the other hand, healthcare workers and managers can use humanoid robots as an assistant in their daily routines [30]. Security is one of the important concerns in such applications as they are dealing with patients in some cases. Moreover, there is no comprehensive overview of different security risks corresponding to it. Therefore, our framework can support in identifying different potential security risks corresponding to such application through simulations and experiments in virtual twins in addition to inputs from humans that can validate the diagnostic.

4.4 Enhancing Resilience in Healthcare Technologies

The developed framework can be useful for critical healthcare applications such as in cancer diagnosis to recognize potential vulnerable functions for increasing cyber resilience. Considering the software complexity of healthcare systems, there is a need for a completely automated solution to support cyber resilience assessments in real-world situations. In [33], it was addressed how to achieve cyber resilience for diagnosing lung cancer using DTs. However, it does not include inputs from both IT and OT systems, also the human-in-the-loop approach was not considered. These factors are important for ensuring resilience in healthcare. Therefore, our proposed conceptual framework includes a catalog based on security and privacy events with inputs from IT-OT systems that can be helpful in enhancing the resilience of healthcare systems by preventing cyber threats and reducing the negative effects or possible recovery to some extent using training and previously acquired knowledge. CDT may improve cyber resilience and build on security, policy, and risk management to provide the trustworthy required for healthcare employees, partners and patients to work with a hospital for embracing digitization efforts.

5 Conclusions and Future Work Directions

As IT and OT become more integrated in healthcare applications, this has increased the potential of adversaries to gain access and even disrupt legacy OT systems due to the emergence of new attack surfaces. Some well-known attacks, including malware, ransomware, can cause operational disruptions and even physical damage in healthcare infrastructures. Therefore, in this study, we developed a conceptual framework for improving security for IT-OT enabled healthcare systems. Important components of this framework include the twin technology, cognitive science, decision support and computational tools, and human-in-the-loop approach. DTs have already been proposed for cyber security and healthcare applications, which lack integrating IT-OT along with knowledge base on security and privacy events and cognitive capabilities. In line with this, the proposed conceptual CDT-based adaptive cyber security framework addresses unique security challenges of IT-OT integration in healthcare. We also presented four different use cases and scenarios on healthcare for potential application of our conceptual framework. Some future work directions of this study are evaluating the applicability and feasibility of the proposed conceptual framework using the suggested use cases and scenarios, identifying opportunities up to which extent proposed framework can be used for improving cyber security training, knowledge transfer and awareness.

Acknowledgments. This research is funded from the Research Council of Norway through, the SFI Norwegian Centre for Cybersecurity in Critical Sectors (NORCICS), with the project number #310105 and User-centred Security Framework for Social Robots in Public Space (SecuRoPS), with the project number #321324 in addition to INTPART projects, Reinforcing Competence in Cybersecurity of Critical Infrastructures: A Norway-US Partnership (RECYCIN), with the project number #309911 and International Alliance for Strengthening Cybersecurity and Privacy in Healthcare (CybAlliance), with the project number #337316.

Disclosure of Interests. The authors declare that they do not have competing interests.

References

1. Nguyen, T.N.: Toward human digital twins for cybersecurity simulations on the metaverse: ontological and network science approach. JMIRx Med. **3**(2) (2022)
2. Pagan, N., Baumann, J., Elokda, E., De Pasquale, G., Bolognani, S., Hannák, A.: A classification of feedback loops and their relation to biases in automated decision-making systems. arXiv preprint arXiv:2305.06055 (2023)
3. Pirbhulal, S., Abie, H., Shukla, A., Katt, B.: A cognitive digital twin architecture for cybersecurity in IoT-based smart homes. In: Suryadevara, N.K., George, B., Jayasundera, K.P., Mukhopadhyay, S.C. (eds.) ICST 2022. LNEE, vol. 1035, pp. 63–70. Springer, Cham (2022). https://doi.org/10.1007/978-3-031-29871-4_8
4. Pirbhulal, S., Abie, H., Shukla, A.: Towards a novel framework for reinforcing cybersecurity using digital twins in IoT-based healthcare applications. In: 2022 IEEE 95th Vehicular Technology Conference (VTC2022-Spring), pp. 1–5. IEEE (2022)
5. Abie, H.: Cognitive cybersecurity for CPS-IoT enabled healthcare ecosystems. In: 2019 13th International Symposium on Medical Information and Communication Technology (ISMICT), pp. 1–6. IEEE (2019)
6. Nguyen, T.N.: Cybonto: towards human cognitive digital twins for cybersecurity. arXiv preprint arXiv:2108.00551 (2021)
7. Sabeur, Z., et al.: Digital twins for the intelligent detection of malicious activities in urban spaces (2022)
8. Xu, Q., Ali, S., Yue, T.: Digital twin-based anomaly detection with curriculum learning in cyber-physical systems. ACM Trans. Softw. Eng. Methodol. (2023)
9. Epiphaniou, G., Hammoudeh, M., Yuan, H., Maple, C., Ani, U.: Digital twins in cyber effects modelling of IoT/CPS points of low resilience. Simul. Model. Pract. Theory **125**, 102744 (2023)
10. Shaikh, E., Al-Ali, A.R., Muhammad, S., Mohammad, N., Aloul, F.: Security analysis of a digital twin framework using probabilistic model checking. IEEE Access **11**, 26358–26374 (2023)
11. Chen, J., Shi, Y., Yi, C., Du, H., Kang, J., Niyato, D.: Generative AI-driven human digital twin in IoT-healthcare: a comprehensive survey (2024). arXiv preprint arXiv:2401.13699
12. Avanzato, R., Beritelli, F., Lombardo, A., Ricci, C.: Lung-DT: an AI-powered digital twin framework for thoracic health monitoring and diagnosis. Sensors **24**(3), 958 (2024)
13. Patil, Y.M., Chintalapati, P.V., Kandasamy, B., Balasubramanian, S.: Exploring digital twin technologies to examine transformation in healthcare systems. In: Digital Twin Technology and AI Implementations in Future-Focused Businesses, pp. 140–161. IGI Global (2024)
14. Abilkaiyrkyzy, A., Laamarti, F., Hamdi, M., El Saddik, A.: Dialogue system for early mental illness detection: towards a digital twin solution. IEEE Access (2024)

15. Fischer, R.P., Volpert, A., Antonino, P., Ahrens, T.D.: Digital patient twins for personalized therapeutics and pharmaceutical manufacturing. Front. Digit. Health **5**, 1302338 (2024)
16. Wickramasinghe, N.: Establishing a digital twin architecture for superior falls risk prediction using a Bayesian network model. In: Dimensions of Intelligent Analytics for Smart Digital Health Solutions, pp. 376–394. Chapman and Hall/CRC (2024)
17. Capriulo, M., Pizzolla, I., Briganti, G.: On the use of patient-reported measures in digital medicine to increase healthcare resilience. In: Artificial Intelligence, Big Data, Blockchain and 5G for the Digital Transformation of the Healthcare Industry, pp. 41–66. Academic Press (2024)
18. Ahmad, R.W., Salah, K., Jayaraman, R., Yaqoob, I., Ellahham, S., Omar, M.: The role of blockchain technology in telehealth and telemedicine. Int. J. Med. Informatics **148**, 104399 (2021)
19. Wang, C., Lu, W., Narayanan, M.R., Redmond, S.J., Lovell, N.H.: Low-power technologies for wearable telecare and telehealth systems: a review. Biomed. Eng. Lett. **5**, 1–9 (2015)
20. Xu, Q., Ali, S., Yue, T., Nedim, Z., Singh, I.: KDDT: knowledge distillation-empowered digital twin for anomaly detection. In: Proceedings of the 31st ACM Joint European Software Engineering Conference and Symposium on the Foundations of Software Engineering, pp. 1867–1878 (2023)
21. Lu, C., Xu, Q., Yue, T., Ali, S., Schwitalla, T., Nygård, J.: EvoCLINICAL: evolving cyber–cyber–digital twin with active transfer learning for automated cancer registry system. In: Proceedings of the 31st ACM Joint European Software Engineering Conference and Symposium on the Foundations of Software Engineering, pp. 1973–1984 (2023)
22. Richards, C.: Boyd's OODA Loop (2020)
23. Khan, A., Anwar, Y.: Robots in healthcare: a survey. In: Arai, K., Kapoor, S. (eds.) Advances in Computer Vision. AISC, vol. 944, pp. 280–292. Springer, Cham (2020). https://doi.org/10.1007/978-3-030-17798-0_24
24. Berhanu, Y., Abie, H., Hamdi, M.: A testbed for adaptive security for IoT in eHealth. In: Proceedings of the International Workshop on Adaptive Security, pp. 1–8 (2013)
25. Orlauskis, V., Pirbhulal, S.: Real-time implementation of digital twin for IoT based smart homes. NR-Notat, DART/14/22 (2022)
26. https://www.ntnu.edu/norcics
27. https://www.enfield-project.eu/
28. Kyrarini, M., et al.: A survey of robots in healthcare. Technologies **9**, 8 (2021)
29. González-González, C.S., Violant-Holz, V., Gil-Iranzo, R.M.: Social robots in hospitals: a systematic review. Appl. Sci. **11**, 5976 (2021)
30. Fernandes, A., Reegård, K., Kaarstad, M., Eitrheim, M., Bloch, M.: Humanoid robots in healthcare: lessons learned from an innovation project. In: 2023 32nd IEEE International Conference on Robot and Human Interactive Communication (RO-MAN), pp. 429–434. IEEE (2023)
31. Oruma, S.O.: Towards a user-centred security framework for social robots in public spaces. In: Proceedings of the 27th International Conference on Evaluation and Assessment in Software Engineering, pp. 292–297 (2023)
32. Oruma, S.O., Ayele, Y.Z., Sechi, F., Rødsethol, H.: Security aspects of social robots in public spaces: a systematic mapping study. Sensors **23**(19), 8056 (2023)
33. Zhang, J., Li, L., Lin, G., Fang, D., Tai, Y., Huang, J.: Cyber resilience in healthcare digital twin on lung cancer. IEEE Access **8**, 201900–201913 (2020)

Viz⁴NetSec: Visualizing Dynamic Network Security Configurations of Everyday Interconnected Objects in Home Networks

Noëlle Rakotondravony[1], Henrich C. Pöhls[2]([✉]), Jan Pfeifer[2],
and Lane Harrison[1]

[1] Worcester Polytechnic Institute, Worcester, MA, USA
[2] Passau Institute of Digital Security, University of Passau, Passau, Germany
`hp@sec.uni-passau.de`

Abstract. Controlling the communication of devices within a network by compartmentalization or segmentation is one of many techniques to protect and improve the overall security of networked systems. Meaningful instrumentation of network segmentation requires having an overview of the devices that participate in the network; only then users can seize control of what devices are allowed to do in terms of communication. In this work, we consider a minimized set of network security controls (i.e. allow connections, allow in-bound-only, allow out-bound-only) that can be implemented using modern routers with built-in firewall or even Software Defined Networking (SDN) capabilities. We present Viz⁴NetSec, a node-link diagram for visualizing typical home user network scenarios. The visualization is integrated in an existing smart home control software and provides an interactive interface through which a smart home user can find, dynamically interact with, and isolate devices by setting SDN flow rules. The aspect of *dynamicity* in this paper is important as we envision that everyday users would reasonably need interactions to trigger configuration changes that directly change the network's or the device's behavior because this enabled users to configure network rules in a trial and error or 'gamified' fashion. Thus, dynamicity empowers adapting security decisions (mostly in the sense of privacy) to their ever-changing everyday digital lives. We conclude this work with an evaluation of the proposed network visualization, discussing how home network users can use the available functionalities in Viz⁴NetSec to perform the isolation of devices within the network as the most simple security related task.

Keywords: Network Security · Smart Home · Dynamic Interaction · SDN

Supplementary Information The online version contains supplementary material available at https://doi.org/10.1007/978-3-031-61382-1_11.

1   Introduction

Predictions estimate the number of Smart Home Devices (SHDs) is rising and the IoT market is set to reach 483 billion US$ between 2022 and 2027 [15]. The connectivity of those SHD is between the home's Internet router to reach cloud services and to other devices within the same home. However, research shows that security deficiencies [21] and privacy problems of numerous such SHDs cause "digital harms" [6]. According to Sagar Joshi [21], an average smart home could face over 12,000 hacker attacks every week, underscoring the need for security measures in smart homes. While "privacy was not a primary consideration in users' adoption decisions [for smart speakers] but did serve as a deterrent for some non-users" [26], we assume that the inhabitants of smart homes —when educated on privacy-related topics and empowered by usable tools— would decide that at least some network communication capabilities of their devices are neither deemed really necessary nor always favored.

Empowering users is crucial. In the case of smart speakers, Lau et al. argued that "current smart speaker privacy controls are rarely used, as they are not well-aligned with users' needs" [26]. Examples of how this can be facilitated by physical interaction, like a physically closable lid on a webcam working as a "physical kill switch" [49], have been proposed. In this paper, we work from the following hypothesis:

> Smart home users, once enabled with usable controls,
> will use such controls to increase their privacy
> and the security-posture of their networks.

We emphasize two goals for such a usable control interface:

- First, the visualization shall be suitable for novice users that will have to cope with the ever-growing number of interconnected devices in modern households; globally the average was already at 17.1 devices per home in 2022 [48].
- Second, the interaction shall allow a dynamic control of the communication of the devices. In the prototype we simply control the devices' network connectivity, but filtering traffic can be done more granularly [57,67].

1.1   First Goal: Visualization for Simple Smart Home Tasks

This work's focus is put on visualizations of typical home user scenarios. The network's hierarchy in home deployments is usually flat, e.g. devices have a direct wireless connection to the router, and there are usually only few layers in the technical network infrastructure. To limit the possibilities of what to visualize, Viz^{4}NetSec starts simply: it shows the connections between the device and the router. We also simplify the control of these connections and only make rules based on the endpoint and the direction of the communication. As a result, we have incoming and/or outgoing traffic or no communication with the smart home device. The control and visualization can be further fine-grained by adding additional network segmentation, like microsegmentation [44], and then disabling communication links between the segment and the router. This will result in some SHDs being able to talk to others within their segment.

For Viz^{4}NetSec, we leverage tree-based visualizations and node-link layouts for displaying relationships, and group entities with simple hierarchies [20,54]. In more detail, we use a force-directed graph implemented within the open-source application for smart home control, Home Assistant [16]. The representation of Viz^{4}NetSec depicted in Fig. 5 shows the visual representation of all communication links of the home network. While this study primarily aims to simplify network visualization for smart home users, it recognizes the vastness of the IoT landscape. The focus for the prototype was on widely-used Wi-Fi devices, as Wi-Fi is a comfortable and widely adopted protocol [9].

1.2   Second Goal: Dynamicity of the Exercised Control

We consider the aspect of *dynamicity* to be of paramount importance as we hypothesize

- firstly, that everyday users would reasonably need interactions that trigger configuration changes immediately;
- secondly, that everyday users would be enabled to dynamically adjust the allowed actions of a device according to what communications they feel are tolerable due to changes in their situations;
- finally, that everyday users might want to explore what communication they minimally need to allow in order to achieve the required functionality.

On the one hand, *dynamicity* allows users to configure network rules in a trial and error fashion, *e.g.*, "What happens to the functionality if I disable the Internet for this smart light bulb?". On the other hand, it can empower users to adapt their security decisions (mostly in the sense of privacy) to the dynamically changing environment of their digital life, *e.g.*, "Enable the security camera to stream images to the Internet when I leave my home, not when I am at home". They also might want to adapt to situations, *e.g.* "Allow communication of a SHD with the Internet when performing a software update, while in normal daily operation the device stays unconnected to the internet." We integrated the capabilities of SDN [33] to monitor the network's connections for the Viz^{4}NetSec visualization and to directly control the network's flow. Our prototype offers the functionality to isolate a device on the network using SDN flow rules when clicking on the device in the visual representation.

Isolating and controlling the communication of devices within a network is not a new technology. Among the strategies to achieve this are compartmentalization [60] or segmentation [34]. Both strategies have been successfully used in small and large networks [39]. However, configuration possibilities grow with an increased number of devices in the network, and in most situations, the task to configure them in an optimal way is in the hand of network administrators [64]. Professional system administrators could therefore benefit from tools to support such simple tasks, and home users that are not professionally trained even more so. From this basic interaction, the tool can be enhanced with more commands, offering an extended version for more sophisticated smart home users. In this work, we start from a minimized set of network security controls (*i.e.* allow connections, allow in-bound-only, allow out-bound-only) that can be implemented using modern routers with built-in firewall or SDN capabilities.

2 Related Work

2.1 Network Security Configuration

Software-Defined Networking (SDN) is the technical basis of our (and others' e.g. [18,44]) solution to heighten the network security in smart homes, and to enforce segmentation and isolation in detail [44]. At the center of the SDN architecture lies a network controller, which comes in various forms, from open-source implementations to proprietary ones [40]. The concept of programmable networks isn't new (see Nunes *et al.* [40] for an overview) and predates today's well-known protocols like OpenFlow [41]. We opted for SDN because its flexibility also supports more complex network configurations [40] still offering reasonable speed [37] for enough dynamicity.

SDN controllers, such as OpenDaylight (ODL), ONOS, Cisco APIC, and Juniper's Contrail, often feature Graphical User Interfaces (GUI) that present a topological view of the network (see Fig. 1a). Node-link layouts are commonly used for security and privacy related network visualizations, e.g. the tool Ether-Ape [61] (see Fig. 4a) showing the communicating devices, or the browser extension Lightbeam[1] (see Fig. 1b) visualizing externally loaded web content.

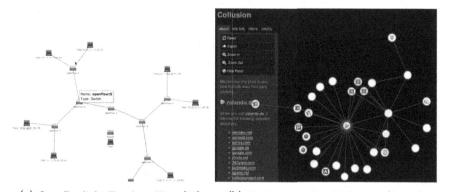

(a) OpenDaylight Topology View [42].   (b) Firefox extension Lightbeam [27, 23].

Fig. 1. Visualizations of networks using graphs and node-link layouts.

---

[1] formerly known as Collusion.

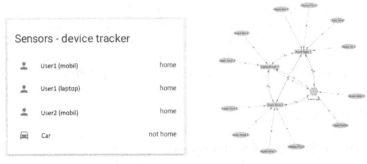

(a) Nmap Tracker example [25].   (b) ZHA Map example [46].

Fig. 2. Visualizations within Home Assistant.

Especially for Home Assistant [16], natively integrated visualizations like the NMAP Tracker [17] (Fig. 2a) or ZHA Map [68] (Fig. 2b) have been developed. The NMAP Tracker's visualization serves more to detect if mobile IoT devices are "reachable" within the network to trigger actions, e.g. when the car is at home. ZHA Map maps devices utilizing the Zigbee Protocol [68]. However, it does not provide any dynamic interaction with the visualized network topology and is mainly used for troubleshooting.

In this work, we implement a graphical tool to simplify interacting with the many capabilities offered by an SDN. Our visualization Viz^{4}NetSec aims at representing the underlying network logically segmented and structured based on SDN configurations, in order to facilitate the dynamic configuration of the network itself by the user.

2.2 Network Security Visualization

Traditional home network systems come with interactive router dashboards [53] (*e.g.* Fig. 3-top). User studies showed that dashboards can help users implement

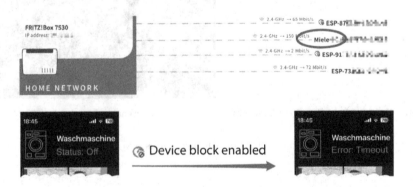

Fig. 3. Blocking Internet connectivity per device on a commercial router's UI for a connected washing machine (top) and the result in the user's app (bottom).

fundamental network configurations [59], scheduling [4], and security measures for their devices and smart appliances [11,66].

Network visualization is widely researched [38,55]. Graph-based views like the one from the open-source project EtherApe in Fig. 4a address shortcomings of tabular representations in built-in commercial interfaces [19]. Shiravi *et al.* [56] and Guimarães *et al.* [13] surveyed the state of the art visualization techniques for network security and management. They identified node-link and topological views as being prevalent representation techniques [29,30].

Additionally, modern approaches to network visualizations underline the importance of interactivity and controls. The ability to fine-tune devices' configurations through an interactive interface can help users protect their resources from misuse in a timely and responsive manner [22,45]. In both small and large networks, the ability to control or customize the visual attributes and representations of the network visualization itself can help a user make sense of the underlying network in a faster and more personalized way [35,38].

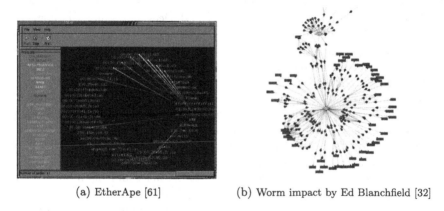

(a) EtherApe [61]   (b) Worm impact by Ed Blanchfield [32]

Fig. 4. Visualizations for computer networks using node-link diagrams.

While market and off-the-shelf tools are often geared at advanced users [19], extending the table-like representations they offer can also help novice home-users benefit from a visual monitoring of their network infrastructure and configurations. Ball *et al.* show that the graphical approach to security can increase users' awareness and confidence when the visualizations maintain simplicity, usability, and enable controls [3]. Poole *et al.* argue that the graphical representation of a home network should mimic the way households conceptualize their home networks, for example, in a simple entity-link fashion [50], also suggesting the adequacy of node-link diagram proposed in other research. Other researchers propose that the design and usability of home network visualization sould fit into both the users' technical skills but also the daily routines of the households [7,62]. Thus, masking complexities to users while providing interactions to low-level details for more advanced administrators is essential to home users' experience. For instance, network segmentation is a challenging security concept to visualize. It requires a clear overview of the network structure [14]. To address that, tree-like visualizations can be leveraged to simplify the modeling of network layouts and its hierarchy [36,54]. Using a tree diagram, the layout of an SDN-based IoT structure is simplified as a connection between all things at home and the Internet [1].

In this paper, we build on node-link diagram based approaches to implement Viz[4]NetSec, a visualization of dynamic network security configurations for home networks. We visualize the software-defined layout of the network in simple and customizable tree-like representations. We implement interactivity that translates complex security concepts (such as segmentation) to actionable tasks that allow (non-expert) home users to dynamically update their devices' network connectivity (e.g., to the Internet) and receive instant real network feedback upon every interaction with the visualization.

2.3   Home User Scenarios

Numerous studies have delved into the security challenges and privacy implications associated with Internet of Things (IoT) devices, particularly in home user scenarios. In their study of the privacy perception of smart speaker users, Lau *et al.* posit that users shall take "more agency" but that it is "difficult to effectively manage one's privacy", and that users are lacking the tools to empower them in light of "the current choice [of] architectures of technology in general" [26]. In line with this, Kumar *et al.* show that from the technological and social perspectives on the growing ubiquity of connected IoT devices, security and privacy are major directions of studies for smart home systems [24].

Yan *et al.* [65] suggest that security and privacy measures must be implemented at every layer of the IoT infrastructure. In particular, home users of different technical skill levels could benefit from visually understanding the communication not only between end-point devices, but also between the home network and the Internet, which Ul Rehman *et al.* [63] highlight as an important element of security threats to home network.

The works by Waseem *et al.* [18] and Osman *et al.* [44] demonstrate the added value of SDN-enabling a smart home network to reinforce security. Osman *et al.* show that *microsegmentation, i.e.* putting a device into one of potentially many small and isolated network segments based on the device's functional description, can help to prevent that an attacked device can spread the attack to other devices using the case of the famous Mirai botnet [2]. Mirai, found first in 2016, targeted "a wide range of networked embedded devices such as IP cameras, home routers (many vendors involved), and other IoT devices" [47]. While both approaches are based on automatically grouping devices and configuring the SDN, the authors also acknowledge the necessity of a human intervention for when a microsegmentation interferes and blocks any desired connectivity[2].

In this work, we aim at enabling everyday users to dynamically adjust the allowed communication of devices in their smart homes' SND-enabled network to

---

[2] "[...] when it "breaks the Internet" and stalls the vital functions of the smart home." [2].

what they judge are tolerable in their use cases. To achieve that, the implemented visualization is interactive and has dynamicity: it is based on information from the SDN and it translates interactions into changed SDN flow rules to directly influence devices' connectivity within the network.

3   Viz⁴NetSec: A Network Visualization for Improving Home Network Security Through Dynamic Interaction

Figure 5 shows our approach Viz⁴NetSec where each connected device is represented as a node in a force-directed graph which represents its logical position within the SDN. When a node is selected in the visualization, the corresponding entry in a tabular view (displayed next to it) is highlighted and the selected node increases in size slightly. Additionally other devices for which the SDN has logged recent network communication get highlighted as well (see yellow nodes in Fig. 5). A demo video[3] as well as the source code[4] are available online.

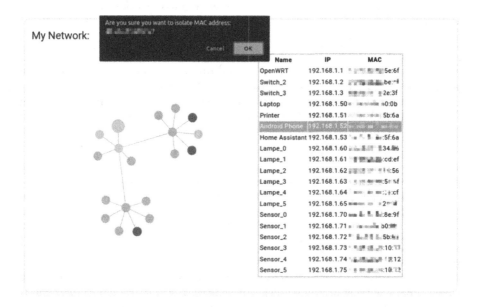

Fig. 5. Viz⁴NetSec integrated as a card in the Home Assistant interface. Selected node appears slightly larger, and the corresponding table row is highlighted. Yellow are nodes that previously communicated with the one selected; green = online; red = offline. Pressing *DELETE* opens a pop-up and asks for user's permission to isolate selected node. Shown network has six smart lamps, six smart sensor devices and laptop, printer and mobile phone; devices are grouped logically into network segments using two SDN switches (See also Fig. 7b). (Color figure online)

---

[3] Video of Viz⁴NetSec: https://youtu.be/Q57DYiuhmBY or https://henrich.poehls. com/papers/video_viz4netsec_interactions.mp4.

[4] Home Assistant integrated Viz⁴NetSec: https://github.com/pfeifer-j/visualization.

Additionally, the user is asked whether there should be a change in the device's connectivity, *i.e.* if the device selected shall become isolated.

We tried the visualization within a real world setup with smart devices like smart lights (e.g., Shelly LED DUO E27, tapo LED L530E), smart plugs (e.g., tapo Smart Plug Mini Smart Wi-Fi Socket) and other smart devices (e.g., GW1100 weather station). Figure 6 shows the general setup for our prototypical implementation. All used smart devices were chosen just as examples of devices that are commercially available[5] and supported by the commonly used Home Assistant [16].

3.1 Technical Prototype Using Open-Source Components

The Viz^{4}NetSec visualization (Fig. 5) is implemented as a card in the user interface of the open-source home automation platform Home Assistant [16]. Home Assistant markets itself by emphasizing its support for local control and increased privacy. Due to its vast array of community-driven extensions and robust customizability, Home Assistant has emerged as a go-to solution for smart home beginners and enthusiasts [16]. We choose to implement Viz^{4}NetSec in Home Assistant because like Home Assistant consolidates various smart home devices under a single interface regardless of their manufacturers, Viz^{4}NetSec is also vendor-agnostic when it comes to the visualization and control of network communication of various devices. Our prototypical setup is depicted in Fig. 6.

The visual interface of Viz^{4}NetSec is rendered using the d3.js library [8] based on data acquired from the SDN. It is displayed using a web browser on a standard tablet with a touchscreen for user interaction with Home Assistant. Viz^{4}NetSec is realized as a module within Home Assistant. All software necessary to generate the visualization and send the users' isolation commands runs alongside with Home Assistant on the first Raspberry Pi 4 Model B[6] [31].

To receive an overview of the local network and to take control of the devices' communications, the prototype uses an SDN-capable router running open-source OpenWRT [43], and Open vSwitch (OVS) [28]. OpenWRT is an alternative firmware adding SDN-related functions among other customization capabilities for many commercially available standard routers. In tandem, (OVS) is a multilayer, open-source virtual switch, optimized for network automation through programmatic extensions, all while accommodating standard management interfaces and protocols. Together, they offer a powerful suite for precise network traffic management and control [28,43]. The LuCi API of the OpenWRT router facilitates the extraction of information about connected devices [5]. We ran a second Raspberry Pi [31] as router using OpenWRT and Open vSwitch (OVS) and USB 3.0 Ethernet adapters for wired connectivity.

---

[5] The authors declare that they have no known competing financial interests or personal relationships that could have appeared to influence the work reported in this paper.

[6] Raspberry Pi 4 Model B running Raspbian OS v.11 with quad-core Cortex-A72 at 1.5GHz with 8GB LPDDR4-3200 SDRAM memory.

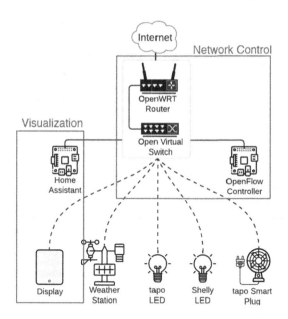

Fig. 6. An overview of the physical components in the prototype; wired connections are blue lines, dotted blue lines represent connections via Wi-Fi. (Color figure online)

In an SDN, a controller is responsible for managing network functions. On the third Raspberry Pi [31] the open-source, python-based software Ryu [52]. It receives instructions from the Viz^{4}NetSec interface and controls SDN network devices, like switches and routers using the OpenFlow protocol [52] accordingly.

3.2 Features of Viz^{4}NetSec

In the following, we provide the background on Viz^{4}NetSec's main features.

3.2.1 Feature 1: Network and Communication Flow Visualization

The main visualization in Viz^{4}NetSec consists of circle objects built using d3.js library. The relationships between the circles or nodes are sourced from the JSON data obtained from API calls to the SDN controller. Each circle object represents one node or device in the network. Each entry in the JSON data contains details such as name, IP address, MAC address, host, and information on whether the device is currently reachable[7]. These details are added as attributes to the nodes. Based on the host information, a link connects the nodes to a central circle, which symbolizes the OpenWRT router by default. This first of two visualization modes, called the *Physical Visualization*, is shown in Fig. 7a

---

[7] Note: The "reachable" flag is not accurately set in latest LuCi.rpc release due to a bug [51].

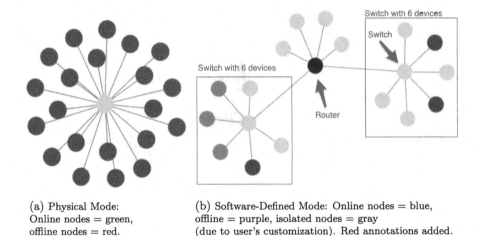

(a) Physical Mode:
Online nodes = green,
offline nodes = red.

(b) Software-Defined Mode: Online nodes = blue,
offline = purple, isolated nodes = gray
(due to user's customization). Red annotations added.

Fig. 7. Viz^{4}NetSec: Different modes auto generated from SDN information.

The second mode, *Software-Defined Visualization*, is shown in Fig. 7b. It portrays device interconnections based on OVS switch statistics. The API call to OVS results in a specific JSON format for each flow rule. The information gained from the flow rule can be utilized to visualize the communications between devices. When a switch receives a packet, a flow rule is generated, signaling active communication between the source and destination devices[8] specified in the rule. Flow rules can be retained for a variable duration and would enable our visualization to depict either only very recent communication between devices or communication over extended periods.

Upon clicking a node, flow rules with the device's IP address as the source highlight the respective communication endpoints, the destination address. Additionally, flow rules can influence network structure, by grouping devices in the same software-defined subnet together[9]. Figure 7b visualizes a smart home's network split into three segments facilitating SDN functionality: Six smart lights and six sensors are each attached to a separate OVS virtual switch.

In both physical and in the software-defined mode, the user can select each node (see Fig. 5). Further information like name, IP, and MAC address are displayed in a table and the user can initiate a dialog to isolate the device, *i.e.* instructing the SDN controller to disable its network communication by setting restrictive SDN flow rules.

3.2.2 Feature 2 - Dynamic Updates
While the concept behind this feature seems straightforward, its practical application poses challenges. Simply reloading the graph after a specified time inter-

---

[8] We currently hide broadcast communications and filter out flows with broadcast addresses.

[9] In order to make this distinction, a VLAN must be set up.

val is the obvious solution, but such an approach leads to the undesirable consequence of resetting the graph's structure on every update. Utilizing d3.js's physics engine allows nodes can be dragged around and automatically arrange themselves using the force-directed graph[10]. In future, we add a solution to preserve the positioning of the nodes during updates. For now, the basic update feature provides the user with the option to set a time interval, after which the visualization is reloaded. During an update, new API calls are made in the background and the SVG created by d3.js is re-rendered.

3.2.3   Feature 3 - Dynamic Network Flow Control

In the prototype the initial steps into network flow control can be directly influenced, giving dynamic control to the user by allowing them to interact with the SDN for completely isolating devices or re-joining them to the network. To do this, a device must first be selected in the visualization, as shown in Fig. 5. Following this, the user can press the *DELETE* key to trigger isolation. It is worth noting that switches, routers, and Home Assistant itself cannot be isolated due to potential unforeseen consequences for the network[11]. Before a device is isolated, a popup notifies the user about the upcoming action, ensuring they fully comprehend its implications. Once confirmed, the node changes to a gray color (by default), signifying that a flow rule has been dispatched to the OVS in the background. After a brief period, the rule is applied, restricting the isolated device's to solely communicate with the router.

To revoke this flow rule and reintegrate the device back into the network, the user needs to select the isolated device and press the *ENTER* key. Subsequently, the node resumes its original color, indicating its reactivated status. Isolated devices are consistently stored in the blacklist, located under /data/ within the project's directory structure. This feature harbors significant potential for future work: It is conceivable to introduce subnetting features, more nuanced isolation options including port-blocking, and direct control of smart devices, such as activating lights, directly from the graph.

3.2.4   Feature 4 - Customization

Users' preferences for visualizations can often be subjective, making customization options crucial. Table 1 shows the various elements, including size, shape, color, and movement, to adjust the visualization using the interface shown in Fig. 8.

To elevate the user experience and streamline customization, color wheels and sliders have been integrated for certain parameters within the editor. These additions enhance the intuitive nature of the interface, making the customization process more user-friendly.

---

[10] Video of Viz^{4}NetSec: https://youtu.be/Q57DYiuhmBY or https://henrich.poehls. com/papers/video_viz4netsec_interactions.mp4.

[11] The list of such protected devices can be configured.

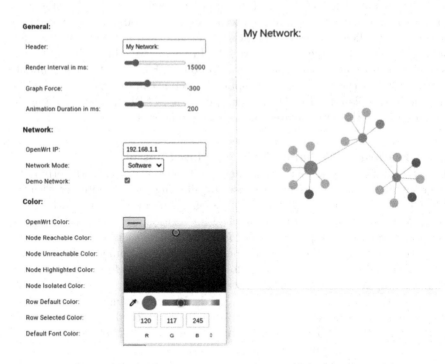

Fig. 8. Editor to change the visual appearance of the nodes in Viz⁴NetSec.

Table 1. Description of various parameters to customize Viz⁴NetSec.

General	
Header	Name of the network
Render Interval	Time until an update happens
Graph Force	Strength of the physics engine
Animation Duration	Animation time for events
Network	
OpenWrt IP	IP address of the source router
Network Mode	Network visualization mode
Demo Network	Demo network for development
Color	
Colors	Colors for fonts, nodes, and links in each state
Shape	
Shape	Size for nodes and links in each state

4   Discussion and Future Work

In this section, we discuss the different features of Viz^{4}NetSec and its integration within Home Assistant for smart home network use cases. We use the methodologies described by Staheli *et al.* when evaluating visualization tools designed for cyber security [58]. Their work provides a model for the different elements of a security visualization, so called *dimensions*, that can be evaluated. Using *critique* as the technique for evaluating Viz^{4}NetSec, we categorize our discussion within the following dimensions. For each evaluated dimension we briefly describe the scope but refer the reader to [58] for more details:

- *Algorithmic efficiency*: We provide empirical system performance measures, and an evaluation of scalability.
- *Usability and learnability*: How easily a user can use and learn the visual interface?
- *Component interoperability*: How well does Viz^{4}NetSec fit with already existing system?
- *Cognitive workload*: From a cognitive science perspective, how hard does the person have to think to accomplish their tasks while using the system?
- *Task performance*: How well does the user perform a predefined task using Viz^{4}NetSec?
- *Feature set utility*: How useful are the set of features available?

For each selected dimension, we describe how our approach to the design of Viz^{4}NetSec features (see Sect. 3) helps users to achieve the set goals: visualization for simple smart home tasks (see Sect. 1.1), and dynamicity of the exercised control (see Sect. 1.2). Moreover, we discuss limitations of Viz^{4}NetSec as well as potential future directions that current features could enable.

4.1   Algorithmic Efficiency

4.1.1   Time to Visualize the Force Directed Graph

In the relatively small network illustrated in Fig. 6 with eight active participants plus a computer used for performance measurement the average time to run the visualization is below 500 ms for page load and graph rendering without waiting for the arrangement of the graph. Specifically without waiting for the arrangement of all nodes in the graph to stabilize, the average is around 350 ms, the duration fluctuated between 250 ms and 475 ms across 50 measurements[12]. However, Viz^{4}NetSec editor features a force-directed graph whose time to stabilize varies based on the specified strength. To ensure graph readability, users can customize the strength that determines nodes proximity (see Fig. 8); a value

---

[12] Time measured over 50 runs in Google Chrome Version 116.0.5845.142 on Windows 10, Intel Core i7-4790k at 4.0 GHz and 16 GB of DDR3 RAM. One Raspberry Pi Model 4B ran Viz^{4}NetSec and sent the API calls, another one received them and ran SDN controller. Stabilization measured by event times logged to Chrome's Development Console.

of -300, which we chose as default, spaces the nodes further apart. On average, for this small-scale setup and using default settings, the graph requires between 600 ms and 825 ms to fully load and stabilize (see footnote 12).

To assess visualization time on a larger scale, demo networks with 20, 100, and 250 devices were constructed. To only measure the time to show the graph the API calls to the SDN controller are replaced with static data. With the default physics strength of -300, the stabilization times were slightly longer than the small-scale setup: around 0.653 s, 1.320 s, and 3.664 s, respectively (see footnote 12). However, it is worth noting that in larger networks, API calls might introduce additional delays, although graph rendering remains fairly consistent as long as the rendering hardware is not saturated.

4.1.2   Time to Isolate a Device from the Network

The time for an API call to the SDN controller that updates the ruleset governing the flow is almost immediate. However, for dynamicity the more important metric is the duration until the new rule effectively takes action. The interval until a device looses network connectivity, *i.e.*, is isolated due to the flow rule in effect[13], ranges from 3 s to 7 s. Reintegrating an isolated device back into the network takes slightly less time, with a duration between 2 s to 5 s.[14]

4.1.3   Network Delay

Upon measuring the performance of the network, no noticeable difference was observed between an OpenWRT router using its default configuration and the same router using OVS. Further testing, especially in larger-scale networks, is necessary to draw more comprehensive conclusions.

4.2   Usability and Learnability

Viz^{4}NetSec offers a visualization-based approach to facilitate the understanding of a complex concept that is the segmentation of a SDN architecture. The force-directed node-link diagram maps the logical layout of the system. Furthermore, Viz^{4}NetSec follows a network visualization approach that is well-studied in literature, broadly used in modern tools, and has been demonstrated to help user understand the underlying technical construct of a network. Learnability is supported as the dynamicity would allow a user to 'see' the effect on the networked device when interacting with the visualized node representing it, *e.g.* it is unreachable in the app once isolated and going gray in the visualization.

Future Work: It remains as future work to study the effects that logically separating networks from their physical reality of wired or wireless communication links using Software Defined Networking would have on the learnability. If users would have a mental model that wireless devices communicate directly with

---

[13] measured using a ping to Google from a laptop as the device to become isolated.

[14] Note: We assume the application of flow rules to become even faster if a dedicated OpenWRT router is used as hardware instead of a Raspberry Pi running OpenWRT.

one central wireless router in their network they would need to learn that an SDN-enabled router could logically group them into different networks.

4.3   Component Interoperability

We briefly explain that Viz^{4}NetSec was added into the existing smart home control software Home Assistant [16]. Not only does Viz^{4}NetSec integrate into the Home Assistant workflow, as a data visualization component, it also acts as an interface to the network flow controller (see Fig. 6). The software code, as well as step-by-step setup instructions are made available on the following repository https://github.com/pfeifer-j/visualization.

In general we observe benefits for interoperability if the management of smart home devices for home automation is grouped alongside the network communication management of the same networked devices. For example, with the current interoperability of Viz^{4}NetSec, the user could open the Viz^{4}NetSec card for troubleshooting and checking if the device is still online in the network, or if there would be a problem in switching a smart lamp on within the related task modeled elsewhere within Home Assistant.

Future Work: A more closely link of the node in the network visualization with the device's identification within Home Assistant would increase interoperability even further: on first instance, users could more easily re-identify known networked devices in the visual representation of the networks, e.g. by the same name, by a link to the device's configuration within Home Assistant's interface. Further, integration of the SDN data on which Viz^{4}NetSec works could allow to take SDN events (like node online or offline or a predefined inter-node communication) as triggers for Home Assistant's so called automations. Also vice versa, one could make an automation trigger certain flow rules, e.g. have a "privacy please" scene within Home Assistant that not only lowers the window shades but also isolates microphone based assistants from the Internet facilitating the SDN functionality.

4.4   Cognitive Workload and Task Performance

In its current prototype, Viz^{4}NetSec integrates within Home Assistant as an extension of the community-maintained tool. It complements the dashboard-like representation offered by the open-source integration for smart home. Viz^{4}NetSec configuration does not incur additional burden on the user beyond regular setup of add-on components to Home Assistant.

Future Work: To further understand the cognitive effort from using Viz^{4}NetSec, controlled user studies are required to measure task performance, success rate, satisfaction, and frustration.

4.5 Feature Set Utility

The visualization offered by Viz^{4}NetSec harmonizes the network configuration of the devices, regardless of their brands. The node-link diagram masks the complex configurations and segmentations offered by the SDN structure, and simplifies the representation of the network layout as flattened connections between switches, routers, and end-point devices. While in a traditional router interface, disconnecting devices might be a few clicks away, Viz^{4}NetSec users manipulate the interactive graphical representation to isolate or disconnect the device instantly.

Through the interactivity, controls, and visualizations offered by Viz^{4}NetSec, users no longer need to monitor what each smart home device is internally doing. Instead of having to disable communications to the outside from within vendor specific device interfaces and trust the device to adhere to that, the trust is shifted towards the network management system that gathers the data for the visual feedback and executes the user's commands given within the visualization. By that design, the visualization reflects information from the network interface. This goes as far as assisting the user in identifying devices that the user was not yet or no longer aware[15] of, detecting changed communication behavior[16] or that do not need a steady connectivity to the Internet.

Future Work: User studies are needed to identify new features, fine-grained controls that users deemed necessary to enhance their privacy and their control thereof, and to redefine the scope of potential future directions such that they align with real-life user (attack) scenarios.

Moreover, the aspect of dynamicity is generally applicable in both directions, *i.e.* on the one hand the visualization is directly influenced by the underlying network's activity and reflects its configuration. On the other hand, the interactions with the visualization get directly reflected in the network's configuration. While our prototype exposes initial work for both directions, future work is planned: We want to add a feature to visualize most current communications, alike the interface of EtherApe (see Fig. 4a). Furthermore, users should visually be able to replay past communication behavior, and review previous network communications. The latter may enable users to familiarize what the devices' communication behavior is[17] when they are not watching them. From a security point of view such a screen shot could be triggered if an additionally deployed intrusion detection system (IDS) would signal an alerting behavior.

---

[15] Ethnographic studies called it "lovingly neglected infrastructures" (in the German original its "liebevoll vernachlässigte Infrastrukturen" [12]).

[16] Just on 9th Jan. 2024 a user wondered "Why is my LG Washing Machine using 3.6 GB of data/day?" https://twitter.com/Johnie/status/1744556503183585471 (accessed 31.01.2024).

[17] This could enable them to find devices scanning the network using broadcasts or washing machines sending data to the Internet like discussed in footnote 16.

5   Conclusion

We present Viz^{4}NetSec, a network visualization for helping home users to dynamically configure their network and thus increase security and privacy in a smart home system context. As the number of connected smart home devices (SHD) continues to grow, techniques such as Software Defined Networking (SDN) have emerged as an effective way to help user reinforce or adjust their network policies. Viz^{4}NetSec implements node-link diagram to reflect complex concepts such as network microsegmentation [44] that a modern SDN offers — all within software so, without requiring the user to buy additional hardware switches or re-cable a network. It is integrated as a card to Home Assistant, a well-maintained open-source integration tool for smart homes. We choose Home Assistant because it nicely consolidates various smart home devices under a single interface regardless of their manufacturers [16], and Viz^{4}NetSec does the same offering a vendor-agnostic visualization and control of network communication of various devices without the need to understand vendor specific user interfaces.

Viz^{4}NetSec features a simple, customizable tree-like representation of the underlying logical network. Its interactivity enables home users to dynamically adjust their network policies (such as connectivity to the Internet) and receive instant visual feedback upon every update. All in all, our approach to Viz^{4}NetSec combines a visualization for simple smart home tasks with a support for dynamicity of the visually exercised controls.

The software code of the current prototype, as well as step-by-step setup instructions are made available online (https://github.com/pfeifer-j/visualization). In its current prototype version, Viz^{4}NetSec visualizes the network layout configured using an underlying SDN and empowers the user to control each device's connectivity within such a network. Already the current prototype stage's initial features helped us identify future research directions towards novel visualizations and dynamic interactions techniques to, on one hand, visualize the variety of information gathered from an SDN-based architecture, and on the other, hand ease the facilitation of its rules for fine-grained control.

Finally, one could add metrics based on an automated assessment of the security-posture or a privacy-increase. Hence, a given network configuration for a specific device or set of devices would get a score. This could lead to users sharing such "best" configurations leading to a gamification [10] of increasing the privacy and security of smart home networks.

Acknowledgments. The work of Pöhls and Pfeifer was funded by the Bavarian Ministry of Science and Arts (Germany) under the `ForDaySec.de` project.

References

1. Albany, M., Alsahafi, E., Alruwili, I., Elkhediri, S.: A review: secure internet of thing system for smart houses. Procedia Comput. Sci. **201**, 437–444 (2022)
2. Antonakakis, M., et al.: Understanding the Mirai Botnet. In: 26th USENIX Security Symposium, pp. 1093–1110. USENIX Association (2017)

3. Ball, R., Fink, G.A., North, C.: Home-centric visualization of network traffic for security administration. In: IEEE Symposium on Visualization for Cyber Security, pp. 55–64. ACM (2004)
4. Blue, R., Dunne, C., Fuchs, A., King, K., Schulman, A.: Visualizing real-time network resource usage. In: Goodall, J.R., Conti, G., Ma, K.-L. (eds.) VizSec 2008. LNCS, vol. 5210, pp. 119–135. Springer, Heidelberg (2008). https://doi.org/10.1007/978-3-540-85933-8_12
5. Brady, F.: openwrt-luci-rpc documentation rel.1.1.16 (2023). https://readthedocs.org/projects/openwrt-luci-rpc/downloads/pdf/stable/. Accessed 25 Oct 2023
6. Buil-Gil, D., et al.: The digital harms of smart home devices: a systematic literature review. Comput. Hum. Behav. **145**, 107770 (2023)
7. Crabtree, A., Rodden, T., Hemmings, T., Benford, S.: Finding a place for UbiComp in the home. In: Dey, A.K., Schmidt, A., McCarthy, J.F. (eds.) UbiComp 2003. LNCS, vol. 2864, pp. 208–226. Springer, Heidelberg (2003). https://doi.org/10.1007/978-3-540-39653-6_17
8. D3.js. D3.js - Data-Driven Documents v.7.8.5 (2023). https://d3js.org/. Accessed 01 Jan 2024
9. Danbatta, S., Varol, A.: Comparison of Zigbee, Z-wave, Wi-Fi, and bluetooth wireless technologies used in home automation (2019). Accessed 15 June 2023
10. Dicheva, D., Dichev, C., Agre, G., Angelova, G.: Gamification in education: a systematic mapping study. J. Educ. Technol. Soc. **18**(3), 75–88 (2015)
11. Dini, M.T., Sokolov, V.: Internet of Things security problems. arXiv preprint arXiv:1902.08597 (2019)
12. Eckhardt, D., Freiling, F., Herrmann, D., Katzenbeisser, S., Pöhls, H.C.: Sicherheit in der Digitalisierung des Alltags: Definition eines ethnografisch-informatischen Forschungsfeldes für die Lösung alltäglicher Sicherheitsprobleme. In: 13. Jahrestagung des Fachbereichs Sicherheit der Gesellschaft für Informatik e.V. (GI Sicherheit 2024). LNI (2024)
13. Guimaraes, V.T., Freitas, C.M.D.S., Sadre, R., Tarouco, L.M.R., Granville, L.Z.: A survey on information visualization for network and service management. IEEE Commun. Surv. Tutor. **18**(1), 285–323 (2015)
14. Gupta, K., Pandey, A., Chan, L., Yadav, A., Staats, B., Borkin, M.A.: Portola: a hybrid tree and network visualization technique for network segmentation. In: IEEE Symposium on Visualization for Cyber Security, pp. 1–5 (2022)
15. Hnatyuk, K.: Internet of things (IoT) statistics: 2022/2023 (2023). https://marketsplash.com/internet-of-things-statistics. Accessed 30 Nov 2023
16. Home Assistant Developers. Home Assistant (ver. 2023.8) (2023). https://www.home-assistant.io/. Accessed 25 Oct 2023
17. Home Assistant Developers. Nmap tracker (2023). https://www.home-assistant.io/integrations/nmap_tracker/. Accessed 25 Oct 2023
18. Iqbal, W., et al.: ALAM: anonymous lightweight authentication mechanism for SDN-enabled smart homes. IEEE Internet Things J. **8**(12), 9622–9633 (2021)
19. Jeong, C.Y., Chang, B.H., Na, J.C.: A survey on visualization for wireless security. In: 4th International Conference on Networked Computing and Advanced Information Management, pp. 129–132 (2008)
20. Jianu, R., Rusu, A., Hu, Y., Taggart, D.: How to display group information on node-link diagrams: an evaluation. IEEE Trans. Visual Comput. Graphics **20**(11), 1530–1541 (2014)
21. Joshi, S.: 70 IoT statistics to unveil the past, present, and future of IoT (2023). https://learn.g2.com/IoT-statistics. Accessed 15 June 2023

22. Kan, Z., Hu, C., Wang, Z., Wang, G., Huang, X.: NetVis: a network security management visualization tool based on treemap. In: 2nd International Conference on Advanced Computer Control, pp. 18–21 (2010)

23. Klassen, C.: Lightbeam (2023). lightbeam.chikl.de. Accessed 11 Jan 2024

24. Kumar, S., Tiwari, P., Zymbler, M.: Internet of Things is a revolutionary approach for future technology enhancement: a review. J. Big data **6**(1), 1–21 (2019)

25. Ladefoged, J.: Device tracker - first home/last home (2017). https://community.home-assistant.io/t/device-tracker-first-home-last-home/30036. Accessed 30 Nov 2023

26. Lau, J., Zimmerman, B., Schaub, F.: Alexa, are you listening? Privacy perceptions, concerns and privacy-seeking behaviors with smart speakers. Proc. ACM Hum.-Comput. Interact. **2**(CSCW) (2018)

27. Lechtenbörger, J.: Das verworrene web (2019). www.informationelle-selbstbestimmung-im-internet.de/Collusion.html. Accessed 01 Jan 2024

28. Linux Foundation. Open vSwitch (v. 2.14.3) (2023). https://www.openvswitch.org/

29. Livnat, Y., Agutter, J., Moon, S., Erbacher, R.F., Foresti, S.: A visualization paradigm for network intrusion detection. In: 6thIEEE SMC Information Assurance Workshop, pp. 92–99. IEEE (2005)

30. Livnat, Y., Agutter, J., Moon, S., Foresti, S.: Visual correlation for situational awareness. In: 2005 IEEE Symposium on Information Visualization, INFOVIS 2005, pp. 95–102. IEEE (2005)

31. Raspberry Pi Ltd. Raspberry pi 4 model b (2023). https://www.raspberrypi.com/products/raspberry-pi-4-model-b/. Accessed 13 Oct 2023

32. Lima, M.: Visual complexity website (2024). http://www.visualcomplexity.com/vc/project.cfm?id=268. Accessed 14 Jan 2024

33. Masoudi, R., Ghaffari, A.: Software defined networks: a survey. J. Netw. Comput. Appl. **67**, 1–25 (2016). Accessed 25 Oct 2023

34. May, C.J., Hammerstein, J., Mattson, J., Rush, K.: Defense in depth: foundations for secure and resilient it enterprises. The Software Engineering Institute (2006)

35. McPherson, J., Ma, K.-L., Krystosk, P., Bartoletti, T., Christensen, M.: PortVis: a tool for port-based detection of security events. In: ACM Workshop on Visualization and Data Mining for Computer Security, pp. 73–81 (2004)

36. Neumann, P., Schlechtweg, S., Carpendale, S.: ArcTrees: visualizing relations in hierarchical data. In: EuroVis, pp. 53–60 (2005)

37. Nguyen-Ngoc, A., Lange, S., Geissler, S., Zinner, T., Tran-Gia, P.: Estimating the flow rule installation time of SDN switches when facing control plane delay. In: German, R., Hielscher, K.-S., Krieger, U.R. (eds.) MMB 2018. LNCS, vol. 10740, pp. 113–126. Springer, Cham (2018). https://doi.org/10.1007/978-3-319-74947-1_8

38. Nobre, C., Meyer, M., Streit, M., Lex, A.: The state of the art in visualizing multivariate networks (2019). https://osf.io/upbm2

39. NSA. Manageable network plan (2015). https://nsarchive.gwu.edu/sites/default/files/documents/2725523/Document-2-11.pdf

40. Nunes, B.A.A., Mendonca, M., Nguyen, X.-N., et al.: A survey of software-defined networking: past, present, and future of programmable networks. IEEE Commun. Surv. Tutor. **16**(3), 1617–1634 (2014)

41. Open Networking Foundation. OpenFlow Switch Specification (ver. 1.5.1). https://www.opennetworking.org/wp-content/uploads/2014/10/openflow-switch-v1.5.1.pdf

42. OpenDaylight Project. Viewing network topology (2023). https://nexus. opendaylight.org/content/sites/site/org.opendaylight.docs/master/userguide/ manuals/userguide/bk-user-guide/content/_viewing_network_topology.html. Accessed 30 Nov 2023
43. OpenWRT. OpenWRT Project (v. 21.02.3). https://openwrt.org/
44. Osman, A., Wasicek, A., Köpsell, S., Strufe, T.: Transparent microsegmentation in smart home IoT networks. In: 3rd USENIX Workshop on Hot Topics in Edge Computing (HotEdge). USENIX Association (2020)
45. Parulkar, G., Schmidt, D., Kraemer, E., Turner, J., Kantawala, A.: An architecture for monitoring, visualization, and control of gigabit networks. IEEE Netw. **11**(5), 34–43 (1997)
46. Pires, A.: Zigbee network map - red dashed lines (2020). https://community. home-assistant.io/t/zigbee-network-map-red-dashed-lines/216670. Accessed 30 Nov 2023
47. Plohmann, D., Enders, S.: Malpedia by Fraunhofer FKIE (2019). https://malpedia. caad.fkie.fraunhofer.de/details/elf.mirai. Accessed 20 Jan 2024
48. Plume. Plume IQ 1H 2022 smart home market report (2022)
49. Pöhls, H.C., Rakotondravony, N.: Dynamic consent: physical switches and feedback to adjust consent to IoT data collection. In: Streitz, N., Konomi, S. (eds.) HCII 2020. LNCS, vol. 12203, pp. 322–335. Springer, Cham (2020). https://doi.org/10. 1007/978-3-030-50344-4_23
50. Poole, E.S., Chetty, M., Grinter, R.E., Edwards,W.K.: More than meets the eye: transforming the user experience of home network management. In: 7th ACM Conference on Designing Interactive Systems, pp. 455–464 (2008)
51. Read the Docs. OpenWRT LuCI RPC Documentation (2023). https:// readthedocs.org/projects/openwrt-luci-rpc/downloads/pdf/stable/. Accessed 13 Oct 2023
52. Ryu SDN Framework Community. Ryu SDN Framework v.4.34 (2023). https:// ryu.readthedocs.io/en/latest/. Accessed 13 Oct 2023
53. Sarikaya, A., Correll, M., Bartram, L., Tory, M., Fisher, D.: What do we talk about when we talk about dashboards? IEEE Trans. Visual Comput. Graphics **25**(1), 682–692 (2018)
54. Schulz, H.-J.: Treevis.net: a tree visualization reference. IEEE Comput. Graphics Appl. **31**(6), 11–15 (2011)
55. Scott-Brown, J., Bach, B.: NetPanorama: a declarative grammar for network construction, transformation, and visualization (2023)
56. Shiravi, H., Shiravi, A., Ghorbani, A.A.: A survey of visualization systems for network security. IEEE Trans. Visual Comput. Graphics **18**(8), 1313–1329 (2011)
57. Spielvogel, K., Pöhls, H.C., Posegga, J.: TLS beyond the broker: enforcing fine-grained security and trust in publish/subscribe environments for IoT. In: Roman, R., Zhou, J. (eds.) STM 2021. LNCS, vol. 13075, pp. 145–162. Springer, Cham (2021). https://doi.org/10.1007/978-3-030-91859-0_8
58. Staheli, D., et al.: Visualization evaluation for cyber security: trends and future directions. In: 11th Workshop on Visualization for Cyber Security, pp. 49–56 (2014)
59. Starks, J., Song, L., Allen, J.K., Mistree, F.: Integrating user preference into improved home appliance scheduling. In: International Design Engineering Technical Conferences and Computers and Information in Engineering Conference, vol. 85390, p. V03BT03A048. ASME (2021)
60. Stawowski, M.: Network security architecture. ISSA J. **7**, 34–38 (2009)
61. Toledo, J.: EtherApe: a live graphical network monitor tool (2000). http:// etherape.sourceforge.net. Accessed 01 Jan 2024

62. Tolmie, P., Pycock, J., Diggins, T., MacLean, A., Karsenty, A.: Unremarkable computing. In: SIGCHI Conference on Human Factors in Computing Systems, pp. 399–406 (2002)
63. UlRehman, S., Manickam, S.: A study of smart home environment and its security threats. Int. J. Reliab. Qual. Saf. Eng. **23**(03), 1640005 (2016)
64. Wagner, N., et al.: Towards automated cyber decision support: a case study on network segmentation for security. In: IEEE Symposium Series on Computational Intelligence, pp. 1–10 (2016)
65. Yan, Z., Zhang, P., Vasilakos, A.V.: A survey on trust management for Internet of things. J. Netw. Comput. Appl. **42**, 120–134 (2014)
66. Yermalovich, P.: Dashboard visualization techniques in information security. In: International Symposium on Networks, Computers and Communications (ISNCC), pp. 1–6. IEEE (2020)
67. Zavalyshyn, I., Duarte, N.O., Santos, N.: HomePad: a privacy-aware smart hub for home environments. In: IEEE/ACM Symposium on Edge Computing (SEC), pp. 58–73 (2018)
68. zha ng. zha-map: a visualization tool for Zigbee Home Automation (2023). https://github.com/zha-ng/zha-map. Accessed 25 Oct 2023

Authentication Method Using Opening Gestures

Shogo Sekiguchi[✉], Shingo Kato, Yoshiki Nishikawa, and Buntarou Shizuki

University of Tsukuba, 1-1-1 Tennodai, Tsukuba, Ibaraki 305-8573, Japan
{sekiguchi,skato,nishikawa,shizuki}@iplab.cs.tsukuba.ac.jp

Abstract. Smart locks can be used to improve door security. However, code- (e.g., PIN and passwords) and biometric-based (e.g., fingerprints and faces) authentication methods in smart locks can be spotted, limiting their usability in real life. In this study, we present an authentication method that uses a gesture to open a door (opening gesture). In this method, the user performs their own opening gesture to open a door, then authentication is performed based on the unique behavioral characteristics of their opening gesture. This design may have the following merits. First, the user can design their opening gesture in a way that reflects their preferences, making the gesture easily memorable. Second, it is difficult to imitate the movements since they inherently contain individuality. Finally, an opening gesture, unlike a biometric features such as a face or fingerprints, can be changed if it is duplicated by an attacker. To examine the idea of our authentication method, we asked participants to design their own opening gestures and perform them for data collection. Capacitive sensors, pressure sensors, and an IMU were used to measure the movements of the gestures. The results showed that a Random Forest with 11 gestures could reach an average precision rate of 0.816 and an average FAR of 0.015. Our shoulder hacking experiment with 8 participants showed that our system archived a FAR of 0.000 for the imitated gestures by *nonusers*. These showed resistance to imitation by attackers.

Keywords: motion-based authentication · door · behavioral biometric · inertial measurement unit · touch pressure · capacitive sensing · personal characteristic

1 Introduction

Smart locks can be used to improve door security. However, code- (e.g., PIN and passwords) and biometric-based (e.g., fingerprints and faces) authentication methods in smart locks can be spotted, limiting their usability in real life [30]. Knowledge-based methods are vulnerable to shoulder hacking [10]. While biometric-based methods are the potential to be duplicated for abuse. For these reasons, users might hesitate to use these authentication methods [10,13].

A. Moallem (Ed.): HCII 2024, LNCS 14729, pp. 186–203, 2024.
https://doi.org/10.1007/978-3-031-61382-1_12

In this study, we present an authentication method that uses a gesture to open a door (opening gesture). In this method, the user performs their own opening gesture to open a door, then authentication is performed based on the unique behavioral characteristics of their opening gesture. This design may have the following merits. First, the user can design their opening gesture in a way that reflects their preferences, making the gesture easily memorable. Second, it is difficult to imitate the movements since they inherently contain individuality. Finally, an opening gesture, unlike a biometric features such as a face or fingerprints, can be changed if it is duplicated by an attacker.

To examine the idea of our authentication method, we asked participants to design their own opening gestures and perform them for data collection. With these data, we examined the performance of our authentication method. The results showed resistance to imitation by attackers. The contributions of our work can be summarized as follows:

- We analyzed user-defined opening gestures to elicit common features, finding Code-Length, Number-of-Fingers, and Finger-Identity to be the most preferred.
- The user and nonuser performance showed that there may be a trade-off between imitation resistance and overall authentication accuracy.
- Opening gestures were found to be feasible for interaction, and were an efficient, accurate, and private authentication technique for the doorknob.

2   Related Research

Currently, widely commercialized products adopt two major authentication methods: code- and biometric-based, which are simple to use and can achieve high authentication performance. To improve the performance of authentication, researchers have proposed leveraging a wider range of features [10,13,22]. For example, capacitance can identify users based on their hand shapes on touch screens [9], while bioimpedance differences across users' forearms have been explored [7]. Pressure sensors have been utilized to recognize users based on their touch force on an object [15,16]. Another approach recognizes users by extracting their motion characteristics with an inertial measurement unit (IMU) [5,12,17]. Since these sensors are inexpensive compared to sensors used for fingerprint, face, or iris recognition [3,4,6], we combine these sensors to achieve more robust and inexpensive authentication. In this section, we mainly reviewed authentication methods leveraging capacitive sensing, pressure sensing, and IMU sensing.

There are challenges with code- and biometric-based methods. Code-based authentication is prone to shoulder hacking when used in public. Memorable passwords are often easy to break, while it is difficult to remember secure passwords [20]. Biometric-based authentication relies on the user's unique physical characteristics, thereby ensuring high security. However, users may hesitate to use such technology due to privacy concerns, since immutable biometric features carry significant risks when duplicated [22]. To meet to these challenges, researchers have proposed a motion-based authentication method (e.g., [2, 28]). It leverages dynamic biometric features of gestures to improve code memorability. In this section, we compare our work with research on authentication that utilizes biometrics features.

2.1   Authentication Methods Leveraging Capacitive Sensing

The capacitive touch screen is the most common interaction interface on today's mobile devices. Due to its sensitivity to the human body, many researchers have tried to leverage it for authentication. CapAuth [9] authenticates user based on the contact area on which they place their fingers on the screen. Bodyprint [14] uses the capacitive touch screen of smartphones as an image scanner to authenticate the users based on the contact features of different body parts (e.g., ear, palm, and finger). These methods rely on static biometric features for authentication, which may be insecure if they were duplicated [22].

Dynamic biometric features have been tried to solve this concern. Rilvan et al. [26] used the frames of capacitance data while swiping on a capacitive touch screen for authentication. Feng et al. [8] extracted features from gestures on a capacitive touch screen to perform authentication by combining these data with additional IMU sensor glove information. Similar to Bodyprint, BioTouch [31] utilizes a capacitive touch screen on a smartphone for image scanning, authenticating users based on the touch motion feature of the finger. These methods using capacitive sensing illustrate the feasibility of motion-based authentication. Similarly, we employ opening gestures that were private and potentially efficient, given their execution feasibility.

2.2   Authentication Methods Leveraging Pressure Sensing

Pressure sensing is widely used for authentication because it can be unique to users, and thus difficult to imitate. Abbas et al. [1] proposed a user authentication method based on behavioral biometrics during the interaction of tapping on simple shapes (circle, square, rectangular, triangle, cross, and check-mark), utilizing 25 features, including coordinates, duration, distance, and velocity and employing supervised learning. Use the Force [15] explicitly combines touch pressure with pin code, significantly expanding the code space and achieving higher security. Pelto et al. [24] created more intricate and personalized touch dynamics for authentication by enabling users to simultaneously touch the screen of mobile devices with multiple fingers.

These methods improve the accuracy of traditional authentication technologies by utilizing touch pressure, while also limited hacking resistance. Notably, no methods reviewed shoulder hacking. In contrast, we assess the resistance of our method to shoulder hacking through experiments.

2.3   Authentication Methods Leveraging IMU Sensing

Other methods authenticate users by extracting their motion characteristics with IMU sensors. Liu et al. [18] leveraged built-in IMU sensors on smartphones to gather biometric features from the vibrations of the user's lower jaw and attempt authentication. Feng et al. [8] performed authentication by extracting features from IMU sensor glove information when touching the screen. Similar to capacitive sensing, these methods using IMU sensing have demonstrated the feasibility of motion-based authentication.

2.4   Authentication Methods Leveraging Opening Gesture

Code- and biometric-based methods can be spotted, limiting their usability in real life [30]. Researchers have proposed dynamic authentication methods, which track features continuously to avoid static authentication behavior. SmartHandle [11] attempts authentication by attaching an IMU to a doorknob and collecting the trajectory and speed of hand movements when opening a door. SenseHandle [27] uses swept frequency capacitive sensing and an acoustic sensor in addition to a IMU to capture interactions when opening a door for authentication. In contrast to these systems, we attempt to use pressure, capacitive, and inertial sensing for opening gesture authentication.

3   Exploring the Design Space of Opening Gestures

In this section, we ask participants to design opening gestures for authentication in real-life scenarios, exploring the design space of practical opening gestures. Additionally, we evaluate the authentication performance of data collected from the participants.

3.1   Participants

We recruited 10 participants from the same laboratory as the authors (all male, M = 23.3 y.o., SD = 2.06 y.o.) as volunteers. Of the participants, nine were right-handed, and one was ambidextrous. Regarding the direction in which their door opens at home, six answered that it opens to the left, while four answered that it opens to the right.

3.2   Hardware

The door that was used had a doorknob with a width of 135 mm, a diameter of 15 mm, and a shaft diameter of 20 mm. The height from the floor to the center of the shaft was 1000 mm, and the door opened it opens to the left (Fig. 1a). We wapped the doorknob with copper tape as electrodes to measure its capacitance. A capacitor was charged through a digital output pin of a microcomputer with a 1 MΩ resistor in series. On the discharge (measurement) side, the copper tape was connected in parallel with the charging side, featuring a 1 kΩ resistor in series, and linked to a digital input pin of the microcomputer for capacitance measurement. The capacitance was determined by measuring the time required for charging. The door was conductive and magnetic. The doorknob part was

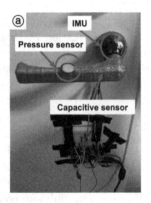

Fig. 1. Hardware installation on the door handle. (a) Front view and sensor placement. (b) Example of gesture demonstration.

nonconductive and nonmagnetic, but considering the influence of the door itself, we wrapped it with insulating tape before wrapping it with copper tape. A pressure sensor (Alpha's MF01A-N-221-A04) was installed at the center of the top of the doorknob handle. An IMU (Akizuki Tsusho's AE-LSM9DS1-I2C) was installed at the center of the top of the doorknob shaft. Arduino Uno R3 was used as a microcomputer to receive data from each sensor and to measure capacitance.

3.3 Procedure

Similar to code-based authentication, opening gestures are designed by individual users. Therefore, similar to existing research [29, 30], we asked the participants to freely design their preferred opening gestures for authentication and analyzed the features they exploited in the design of their own opening gestures.

After explaining our idea to the participants, they were asked to design opening gestures. The instruction was, "Please design opening gestures for authentication in this scenario that you would like to use in real life." To inspire participants to design their own opening gestures, we introduced them to seven features frequently used in other gestures and pressure-based interaction methods [19, 21, 25], such as Code-Length (number of times to turn the doorknob), Touch-Pressure, Number-of-Fingers (for grasping the doorknob), Touch-Duration, Finger-Identity (order of the fingers used to touch the doorknob), Gripping-Hand (e.g., both hands or right hand) and Touch-Location. During the design, the participants were encouraged to include any other features they liked and were free to test their gestures until they were satisfied. After this, the participants were asked to reveal their gestures by demonstrating them to the experimenter and noting them in the questionnaire. They were also asked to describe the features they had used in their designs in the questionnaire. Then, each participant performed the gestures they designed 20 times (Fig. 1b), which involved performing them 10 times, taking a 60-seconds break, and then performing them another 10 times.

3.4   Results

In total, we collected 11 opening gestures (9 participants × 1 gesture +1 participant × 2 gestures). Table 1 and Fig. 2 show the gestures that were noted in the questionnaire. Although the participants were allowed to use any features they liked, almost half of the gestures (designed by P1, P3, P4, P6, and P10) were based on opening motions without many distinctive features.

Table 1. Opening gestures designed by the participants. Note that P2 designed two gestures.

Participant	Opening Gesture
P1	Placing the thumb on the shaft and turning normally
P2	Grasping the doorknob with the left hand and turning it once. Grasping the doorknob firmly with the left hand and turning it downward
P3	Turning the doorknob using the little finger, ring finger, and middle finger
P4	Turning the doorknob for roughly 0.5 s with enough grip strength for turning it, with the fingers other than the thumb of the right hand, placing each finger between its second and third joints on the handle
P5	Touching the inside of the lever, then touching the outside and turning it once
P6	Grasping the doorknob by the left hand, with the thumb under the doorknob, and then turning it quickly
P7	Grasping the doorknob from the little finger to the index finger and then turning it
P8	Without thinking, turning the doorknob with the right hand in the shape of a thumb-up
P9	Grasping the doorknob, turning it once, returning it to its original position, and turning the doorknob again
P10	Holding the knob with the base of the fingers other than the thumb and turning it with the thumb in a neutral position in the air

There was an average of 4.00 features (SD = 1.10) used in the design of eash gesture. Figure 3a shows the number of gestures that were leveraged each feature. In total, Code-Length was the most frequently used feature (used by all participants). Meanwhile, roughly half of the gestures leveraged Touch-Pressure, Number-of-Fingers, Finger-Identity, Gripping-Hand, and Touch-Location. In comparison, Touch-Duration was only used in a few gestures.

We analyzed the distribution of the features in the gestures, as shown in Fig. 3b. Because Finger-Identity and Touch-Location were dependent on other features, we did not analyze these two features. As shown in Fig. 3b, the Code-Length of 90% of gestures was only 1, implying that the participants favored short gestures. Of the Touch-Pressure 75% included a neutral grip, suggesting

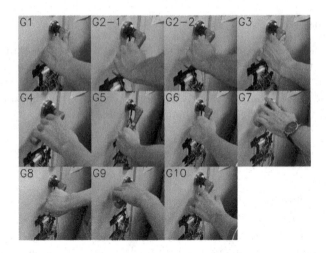

Fig. 2. Gestures designed by the participants.

that participants were not very concerned with pressure. Similarly, 100% of the Touch-Duration was 0.5 s, suggesting that participants were not very concerned about the duration. Regarding Number-of-Fingers, 86% of gestures leveraged four or more fingers, while 14% leveraged three fingers suggesting that the participants preferred opening gestures with a stable grip. Half of the Gripping-Hand gestures were performed with either hand, suggesting that both the left and right hands could be used to turn the doorknob. However, the participant who did not mention the hand for gestures opened the door with their left hand in this experiment, since the doorknob used was a left-opening type.

3.5   Feature Visualization

Eleven sensors (a capacitive sensor, a pressure sensor, three axis acceleration sensors, three axis gyro sensors, and three axis magnetic sensors) were used to measure the motion of the opening gestures (Fig. 1a). Similar to Ohmura et al. [23], we obtained a feature vector of 56 dimensions (11 sensors × 5 features + 1 duration feature), with fatures being the mean, variance, standard deviation, kurtosis, and skewness of 11 sensors, and the duration of the gestures. The principal component analysis (PCA) showed that the cumulative contribution rate exceeded 50% after the fourth principal component (Fig. 4). Among the 56 features, we extracted 31 by selecting those with an absolute value of main component scores of 0.2 or higher (Fig. 5). Another PCA was performed on the 31 extracted features. Figure 6 shows the results of dimension reduction down to the second principal component to examine how the participant data were distributed. As this figure shows, the data were spread out for each participant, suggesting the possibility that these 31 features could discriminate between participants.

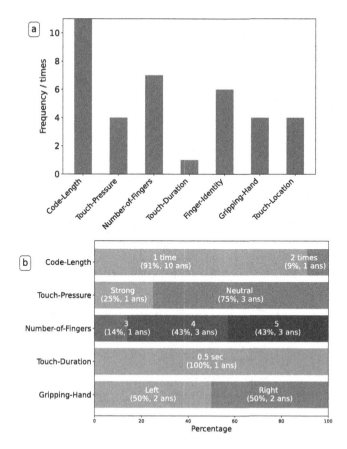

Fig. 3. Analysis of the features used in the gestures in Table 1. (a) The number of gestures with different features. (b) Distribution of the features.

3.6 Machine Learning

The results of 10-fold cross-validation using Random Forest with 31 features are summarized in Table 2. G1 denotes the gesture designed by P1. Since P2 designed two gestures, G2-1 and G2-2 are shown. This table shows that even similar gestures (G3, G4, G6, G10) can be classified with a precision rate of 0.94 or higher. This also shows that complex gestures (G1, G2-2, G5) can be classified with a precision rate of 0.87 or higher. However, some gestures (G2-1, G7, G8) were shown to be inaccurate, with a precision rate of 0.48 or lower. In the future, these inaccurate gestures should be analyzed.

4 Experiment: Shoulder Hacking

To explore whether it is possible to reject gestures made by *nonusers*, we conducted another experiment to examine the vulnerability of opening gestures to shoulder hacking.

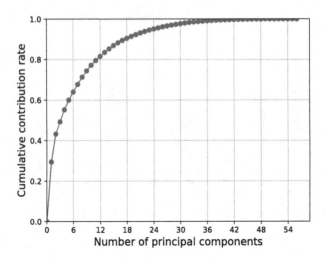

Fig. 4. Cumulative contribution rate changes.

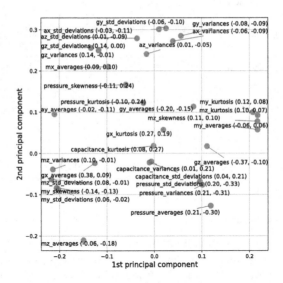

Fig. 5. PCA performed on 56 features. We plotted 31 features whose absolute value of principal component score was 0.2 or more. The numbers in parentheses are the scores of the third and fourth principal components.

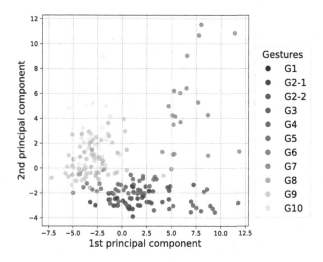

Fig. 6. PCA performed on 31 extracted features. G1 denotes the gesture designed by P1. Since P2 designed two gestures, G2-1 and G2-2 are shown.

Table 2. Authentication performance. Gesture G1 denotes the gesture designed by P1. Since P2 designed 2 gestures, G2-1 and G2-2 are shown.

Gesture	G1	G2-1	G2-2	G3	G4	G5	G6	G7	G8	G9	G10	Average
Precision rate	0.875	0.483	1.000	1.000	1.000	1.000	0.941	0.250	0.700	0.727	1.000	0.816
F-measure	0.778	0.571	0.963	0.974	0.919	1.000	0.865	0.187	0.467	0.516	0.750	0.726
FAR	0.010	0.077	0.000	0.000	0.000	0.000	0.005	0.046	0.015	0.015	0.000	0.015

4.1 Participants

We recruited eight participants from the same laboratory as the authors (all male, M = 22.8 y.o., SD = 0.66 y.o.) as volunteers. Six were right-handed, one was left-handed, and one was ambidextrous.

4.2 Procedure

The same door used in Sect. 3 was used to collect the data. The experiment consisted of the following two phases.

Data Collection. Three out of the eight participants (*users*) participated in the data collection. As in Sect. 3.3, we asked the participants to freely design their desired opening gestures for authentication.

After we had explained our idea to the participants, they were asked to design opening gestures. The instruction was, "Please design opening gestures for authentication in this scenario that you would like to use in real life." To inspire the participants to design their own opening gestures, we introduced them to the seven features mentioned earlier. In their designs, the participants were encouraged to include any other features they liked and were free to test their gestures until they were satisfied. After this, they were asked to reveal the gestures by noting them in the questionnaire. They were also asked to enumerate the features they had used in their design among the seven features in the questionnaire. Then, each participant performed their designed gesture 20 times (Fig. 1b), by performing it 10 times, taking a 60-s break, and then performing it another 10 times. The participants' hand movements were video recorded (Fig. 7).

Hacking. After the data collection, we conducted a hacking experiment. Five participants (*nonusers*) who had not participated in the data collection took part in this experiment, which was divided into two sessions.

In the first session, the participants were asked to watch a video (Fig. 7) recorded during the data collection and imitate the three gestures designed by the *users*. While imitating the gestures, they were asked seven features used in the gestures by filling in the questionnaire used in Sect. 4.2. Then, each participant performed each of the three gestures 20 times.

In the second session, the participants were asked to imitate the gestures by watching the video and the seven features answered by the *users* in the data collection. Then, the participants performed each of the three gestures 20 times.

Fig. 7. Example of a gesture video.

4.3   Results

In total, we collected three opening gestures (3 *users* × 1 gesture). Table 3 shows the gestures designed by the *users*, that had been noted in the questionnaires.

We counted the features in these gestures (Fig. 8). Because Finger-Identity and Touch-Location were dependent on other features, we did not count them. As shown in Fig. 8b, *nonusers* could roughly estimate the *users*' gestures. There is no difference in the distribution of Code-Length, Number-of-Fingers, and

Table 3. Opening gestures designed by the *users* in the data collection.

User	Opening Gesture
U1	Quickly moving the doorknob down, standing for roughly 0.5 s, and then attempting to open it by turning
U2	Holding the tip of the doorknob, touching it with the thumb in the shape of a thumbs-up, turning it twice, and releasing
U3	Turning the doorknob with the thumb applying force to the thumb

Gripping-Hand, suggesting that these were easy to estimate by *nonusers*. The Touch-Pressure was 3 (neutral) or higher by *users*, whereas 20% of Touch-Pressure was 2 (slightly weak) by *nonusers*, suggesting that nonusers estimated the pressure to be weaker. The Touch-Duration ranged from 1.0 to 2.0 s by the *users*, while it ranged from 0.5 to 1.5 s by *nonusers*, suggesting that *nonusers* estimated gestures to be shorter. However, Touch-Pressure and Touch-Duration are subjective, with a possibility that the participant's subjective and actual pressure differed.

4.4 Feature Visualization

As in Sect. 3, we performed a PCA to examine how the participant data were distributed. Figure 9 shows the results of dimension reduction down to the second principal component. In this figure, U1 denotes the gestures designed by the *users* #1. NU1 denotes the gesture imitated by the *non-user*. 'only-video' denotes the first session, in which non-users watched only the gesture video. 'video&info' denotes the second session, in which *nonusers* watched the gesture video and the features mentioned by the *users*. As Fig. 9 shows, the data were spread out for each participant, suggesting the possibility that these features could classify participants. In particular, U3 is scattered with the 1st principal component = 5.0 or higher, while *nonusers* gestures that imitate *users* (NU1-NU5 in Fig. 9c) are classified with the first principal component = 5.0 or less. This indicates that it may be difficult to imitate even if videos and features are open.

4.5 Machine Learning

We performed authentication by classifying between *users* and *nonusers* using Random Forest. The results are summarized in Table 4. Due to an imbalance in *users* and *nonusers* data, we used a Balanced Random Forest. The ratio of test data to training data was 0.5, indicating that the results show the performance of our system when a user registered their own gesture 10 times on the doorknob of the user's private room.

In this analysis, we conducted two simulations. The first is to test if *nonusers* could open the door by imitating *users'* gestures. To this end, we trained a model with 10 *users* gestures and 200 *non-users'* gestures imitating the *users'* gestures and the model with the rest of the data (U1 vs. NU1, U2 vs. NU2, and U3

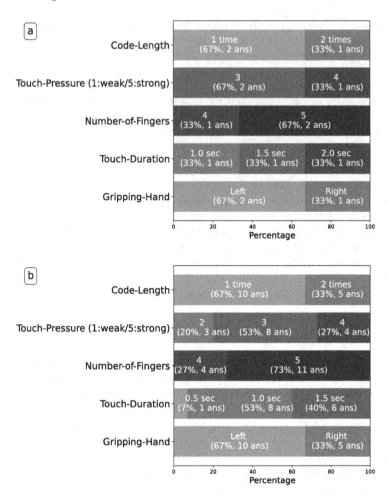

Fig. 8. Analysis of the features used in the designed gestures. (a) Distribution of the features by the *users* in the first session. (b) Distribution of the features estimated by the *nonusers* in the second session.

vs. NU3). The second simulation was to test if *nonusers* could open the door by performing random gestures, including the ones where *nonusers* imitated *users'* gestures. To this end, we trained a model with 10 *users'* gestures and 300 *nonusers'* gestures and tested it with the rest of the data (U1 vs. all-NU, U2 vs. all-NU, and U3 vs. all-NU).

The average accuracy and TAR by *users* and *nonusers* (U vs. NU) was 0.988. All FARs were 0.000, showing that *users* were not misclassified as *nonusers*. The average accuracy for *nonusers* authentication (U vs. all-NU) was 0.975. The average FAR was 0.025, meaning that other *users'* gestures imitated by *nonusers* were misclassified as *users'* gestures.

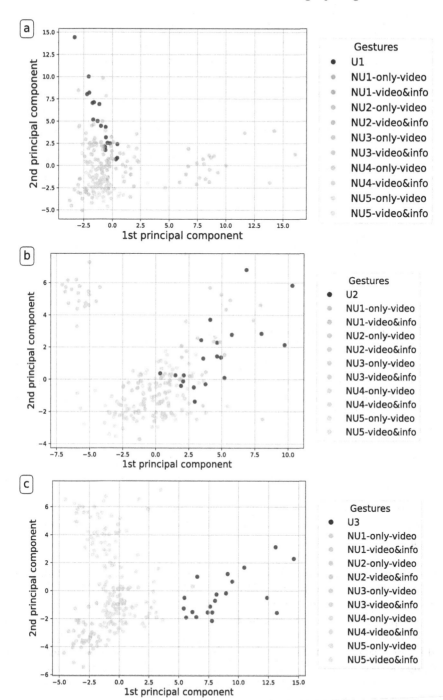

Fig. 9. PCA performed on the extracted features. Dimensions were compressed to the second principal component and displayed. (a) PCA on the data obtained when *nonusers* imitated U1. (b) PCA when *nonusers* imitated U2. (c) PCA when *nonusers* imitated U3.

U1 vs. all-NU had the highest accuracy among all *users*. However, the U1 vs NU1 accuracy was lower than that of U3 vs. NU3. U3 vs. NU3 had the highest accuracy among other *users*, while U3 vs. all-NU had the lowest accuracy among all *users*. This result shows a trade-off between imitation resistance and overall authentication accuracy.

Table 4. Classification between *users* and *nonusers*.

Performance	U1 vs. NU1	U2 vs. NU2	U3 vs. NU3	U1 vs. all-NU	U2 vs all-NU	U3 vs all-NU
Accuracy rate	0.982	0.982	1.000	1.000	0.980	0.946
Precision rate	1.000	1.000	1.000	–	–	–
Recall rate	0.800	0.800	1.000	–	–	–
F-measure	0.889	0.889	1.000	–	–	–
TAR	0.982	0.982	1.000	–	–	–
FAR	0.000	0.000	0.000	0.000	0.020	0.054

5   Discussion and Future Work

Opening Gestures in Authentication. In Sect. 3, we analyzed the opening gestures based on *users'* preferred features. In Sect. 4, we showed that our system has a FAR of 0.000 for *nonusers* imitated gestures and an average FAR of 0.025 for all *nonusers* gestures. Therefore, the opening gestures have the potential to be used for authentication.

User-Designed Gesture Implications. In Sect. 3, Code-Length, Number-of-Fingers, and Finger-Identity were the most preferred features when designing opening gestures. This result not only supports the design of our system but could also direct interaction techniques based on opening gestures (e.g., recognizing persons entering/leaving and operating IoT devices to control lights or to play music when a door is opened/closed).

Future Work. We showed Code-Length, Number-of-Fingers, and Finger-Identity to be the most preferred features. However, there is a possibility that other features (e.g., Touch-Pressure, Touch-Duration) might not align well with our system. We plan to improve the system to sense other features during opening and explore the feasibility of using these features. In addition, our participants were highly homogeneous in terms of age. Validating the performance with added participants is also needed. Furthermore, since opening gestures could change over time, even if users intentionally intend to maintain them, a long-term evaluation of our system is necessary.

6   Conclusion

We presented an authentication method using opening gestures.

Analyzing the participants' defined gestures showed that Code-Length, Number-of-Fingers, and Finger-Identity were the features they preferred the most. Our system was implemented on a door, testing its authentication performance on data from 10 participants. Capacitive sensors, pressure sensors, and an IMU were used to measure the movements of the gestures. The results showed that a Random Forest with 11 gestures could reach an average precision rate of 0.816 and an average FAR of 0.015.

Our shoulder hacking experiment with 8 participants showed that our system archived a FAR of 0.000 for the imitated gestures by *nonusers*. An average FAR of 0.025 for all gestures was shown. For these reasons, the *users* and *nonusers* performance also showed that there might be a trade-off between imitation resistance and overall authentication accuracy.

In the future, we will use a system that senses more features to verify the actual performance. Additionally, we will examine the system's performance by long-term evaluation, since opening gestures might change over time.

References

1. Abbas, G., Humayoun, S.R., AlTarawneh, R., Ebert, A.: Simple shape-based touch behavioral biometrics authentication for smart mobiles. In: Proceedings of the 2018 International Conference on Advanced Visual Interfaces, AVI 2018, pp. 50:1–50:3. Association for Computing Machinery (2018)
2. Ali, A.B.A., Ponnusamy, V., Sangodiah, A.: User behaviour-based mobile authentication system. In: AC3S 2019, Advances in Computer Communication and Computational Sciences, pp. 333–343 (2019)
3. Andriotis, P., Tryfonas, T., Oikonomou, G.: Complexity metrics and user strength perceptions of the pattern-lock graphical authentication method. In: Tryfonas, T., Askoxylakis, I. (eds.) HAS 2014. LNCS, vol. 8533, pp. 115–126. Springer, Heidelberg (2014). https://doi.org/10.1007/978-3-319-07620-1_11
4. Azimpourkivi, M., Topkara, U., Carbunar, B.: Camera based two factor authentication through mobile and wearable devices. Proc. ACM Interact. Mob. Wearable Ubiq. Technol. **1**(3), 35:1–35:37 (2017)
5. Buriro, A., Crispo, B., Delfrari, F., Wrona, K.: Hold and sign: a novel behavioral biometrics for smartphone user authentication. In: 2016 IEEE Security and Privacy Workshops (SPW), pp. 276–285 (2016)
6. no Centeno, M.P., Guan, Y., van Moorsel, A.: Mobile based continuous authentication using deep features. In: Proceedings of the 2nd International Workshop on Embedded and Mobile Deep Learning, EMDL 2018, pp. 19–24. Association for Computing Machinery (2018)
7. Cornelius, C., Peterson, R., Skinner, J., Halter, R., Kotz, D.: A wearable system that knows who wears it. In: Proceedings of the 12th Annual International Conference on Mobile Systems, Applications, and Services, MobiSys 2014, pp. 55–67. Association for Computing Machinery (2014)

8. Feng, T., et al.: Continuous mobile authentication using touchscreen gestures. In: 2012 IEEE Conference on Technologies for Homeland Security (HST), HST 2012, pp. 193–198. Institute of Electrical and Electronics Engineers (2012)

9. Guo, A., Xiao, R., Harrison, C.: CapAuth: identifying and differentiating user handprints on commodity capacitive touchscreens. In: Proceedings of the 2015 International Conference on Interactive Tabletops & Surfaces, ITS 2015, pp. 277–280. Association for Computing Machinery (2015)

10. Gupta, S., Buriro, A., Crispo, B.: Demystifying authentication concepts in smartphones: ways and types to secure access. Mob. Inf. Syst. **2018**, 2649598:1–2649598:16 (2018)

11. Gupta, S., Buriro, A., Crispo, B.: SmartHandle: a novel behavioral biometric-based authentication scheme for smart lock systems. In: Proceedings of the 2019 3rd International Conference on Biometric Engineering and Applications, ICBEA 2019, pp. 15–22. Association for Computing Machinery (2019)

12. Ehatisham-ul Haq, M., et al.: Authentication of smartphone users based on activity recognition and mobile sensing. Sensors (Basel, Switzerland) **17** (2017)

13. Ho, G., Leung, D., Mishra, P., Hosseini, A., Song, D., Wagner, D.: Smart Locks: lessons for securing commodity internet of things devices. In: ASIA CCS 2016, pp. 461–472. Association for Computing Machinery (2016)

14. Holz, C., Buthpitiya, S., Knaust, M.: Bodyprint: biometric user identification on mobile devices using the capacitive touchscreen to scan body parts. In: Proceedings of the 33rd Annual ACM Conference on Human Factors in Computing Systems, CHI 2015, pp. 1419–1428. Association for Computing Machinery (2015)

15. Krombholz, K., Hupperich, T., Holz, T.: Use the Force: evaluating force-sensitive authentication for mobile devices. In: Proceedings of the Twelfth USENIX Conference on Usable Privacy and Security, SOUPS 2016, pp. 355–366. USENIX Association (2016)

16. Kudo, M., Yamana, H.: Active authentication on smartphone using touch pressure. In: Adjunct Proceedings of the 31st Annual ACM Symposium on User Interface Software and Technology, UIST 2018, pp. 55–57. Association for Computing Machinery (2018)

17. Lee, W.H., Lee, R.B.: Implicit smartphone user authentication with sensors and contextual machine learning. In: 2017 47th Annual IEEE/IFIP International Conference on Dependable Systems and Networks (DSN), pp. 297–308. IEEE Computer Society (2017)

18. Liu, J., Song, W., Shen, L., Han, J., Ren, K.: Secure user verification and continuous authentication via earphone IMU. IEEE Trans. Mob. Comput. **21**(9), 2017–2030 (2022)

19. Luca, A.D., Hang, A., Brudy, F., Lindner, C., Hussmann, H.: Touch me once and i know it's you! implicit authentication based on touch screen patterns. In: Proceedings of the SIGCHI Conference on Human Factors in Computing Systems, CHI 2012, pp. 987–996. Association for Computing Machinery (2012)

20. Masuno, R.: Passwords and cognitive psychology. IPSJ SIG Techn. Rep. **2010-CSEC-49**(1), 1–6 (2010)

21. Murao, K., Tobise, H., Terada, T., Iso, T., Tsukamoto, M., Horikoshi, T.: Mobile phone user authentication with grip gestures using pressure sensors. In: Proceedings of the 12th International Conference on Advances in Mobile Computing and Multimedia, MoMM 2014, pp. 143–146. Association for Computing Machinery (2014)

22. Nakanishi, I.: Biometric modality challenges and future prospects. IEICE ESS Fund. Rev. **16**, 185–195 (2023)

23. Ohmura, R., Naya, F., Noma, H., Kogure, K.: Architectural overview of a sensor network for supporting nursing activities. IPSJ SIG Tech. Rep. **2009**(8), 1–8 (2009)

24. Pelto, B., Vanamala, M., Dave, R.: Your identity is your behavior - continuous user authentication based on machine learning and touch dynamics. In: 2023 3rd International Conference on Electrical, Computer, Communications and Mechatronics Engineering (ICECCME), pp. 1–6 (2023)

25. Quinn, P., Lee, S.C., Barnhart, M., Zhai, S.: Active edge: designing squeeze gestures for the Google Pixel 2. In: Proceedings of the 2019 CHI Conference on Human Factors in Computing Systems, CHI 2019, pp. 1–13. Association for Computing Machinery (2019)

26. Rilvan, M.A., Chao, J., Hossain, M.S.: Capacitive swipe gesture based smartphone user authentication and identification. In: 2020 IEEE Conference on Cognitive and Computational Aspects of Situation Management (CogSIMA), CogSIMA 2020, pp. 1–6. Institute of Electrical and Electronics Engineers (2020)

27. Rodriguez, S.D., Mecke, L., Alt, F.: SenseHandle: investigating human-door interaction behaviour for authentication in the physical world. In: SOUPS 2022, USENIX Symposium on Usable Privacy and Security (2022)

28. Saini, B.S., et al.: A three-step authentication model for mobile phone user using keystroke dynamics. IEEE Access **8**, 125909–125922 (2020)

29. Vatavu, R.D., Wobbrock, J.O.: Clarifying agreement calculations and analysis for end-user elicitation studies. ACM Trans. Comput.-Hum. Interact. **29**(1), 5:1–5:70 (2022)

30. Yi, X., et al.: Squeez'In: private authentication on smartphones based on squeezing gestures. In: Proceedings of the 2023 CHI Conference on Human Factors in Computing Systems, CHI 2023, pp. 532:1–532:15. Association for Computing Machinery (2023)

31. Zhang, C., Li, S., Song, Y., Meng, Q., Lu, L., Hou, M.: BioTouch: reliable reauthentication via finger bio-capacitance and touching behavior. Sensors **22**(3), 655:1–655:16 (2022)

Investigating University QR Code Interactions

Jeremiah D. Still$^{(\boxtimes)}$, Thomas Morris, and Morgan Edwards

Old Dominion University, Norfolk, VA 23508, USA
{jstill,tmorr001,mthom122}@odu.edu

Abstract. Although engaging with Quick Response (QR) codes presents a security risk, little observational data exists exploring the impact of informational cues on engagement. While naturalistic observations of on and off-campus QR code engagement by Vidas et al. (2013) demonstrated that curiosity instead of informational-driven needs motivate engagement, it seems informational cues should play a role in security-based decisions. Over a decade later, our study investigates naturalistic engagement with QR codes on campus with a focus on flyer informational cues. The flyers were placed in busy campus areas and regularly checked for visibility by research assistants. We captured the number of users engaging with the QR code by flyer type (i.e., blank, university logo only, phishing job ad). Study participants were asked to complete a brief survey sharing their security experience, motivations, and predicted future behavior. Our flyer engagement was low, similar to Vidas et al. (2013), particularly considering the size of our campus student population. We showed that the engagement across the flyer types increased as informational cues increased. It is encouraging to see low engagement, given these suspicious flyers. This shift towards information seeking over simple curiosity most likely reflects users' greater awareness of QRishing attacks.

Keywords: Cybersecurity · Human Factors · Phishing

1 QR Codes: Human-Centered Cybersecurity

End-users often overestimate their cybersecurity expertise and capabilities [1]. Users often lack the cybersecurity knowledge and means to protect themselves. As technological systems from work and home computing environments merge [2], impacted assets from a security breach can be both personal and organizational. A lack of situational awareness can carry significant costs for our economy. Maintaining an appropriate amount of knowledge is difficult as technology quickly evolves. We recently saw a societal increase in Quick Response (QR) code usage - especially in marketing. It even made for a memorable Super Bowl ad in 2022 [3]. Coinbase had a sixty-second ad showing only a colorful QR code moving across the television screen. Coinbase engaged their audience by drawing on their curiosity [4, 5]. QR codes hide their target in a visual code. Those square matrix barcodes allow us to access websites, offers, and coupons. Historically, they are used to allow easy website access, but barriers initially slowed widespread adoption. Now, most cellular phones have cameras, the code is easy to manufacture, and, as a result, QR codes have been adopted in numerous industries [6, 7]. Global QR code usage has quadrupled from 2022 to 2023 [8]. The most popular usage includes URLs (46%), files (31%), vCards (7%), and social media links (4%). The pandemic brought QR codes back to the forefront through the use of contactless payments, menus, and check-ins [8]. This growth has increased phishing attacks [9].

Phishing is defined as an act of deception intended to steal a person's private information. Conventionally, we think of phishing attacks as when someone sends you an e-mail posing as a legitimate source (e.g., their bank) to gain access to your personal data (e.g., bank account information). These attacks can lead to monetary and privacy losses for unsuspecting users. Phishing attacks are social engineering attacks [10, 11], because they focus on exploiting the human element instead of a technical hack. Cyber defenders introduced security indicators meant to help prevent end-users from falling victim to browser phishing, but the indicators still failed to offer significant protection [12, 13]. For example, Alsharnoby, Alaca, and Chiasson (2015) showed only 53% of phishing websites were detected even when participants were primed to identify them. Along similar lines, it was found that users spent very little time looking at the security indicators. Historically, phishing attacks have taken the form of webpages or emails; however, in recent years, new forms of this attack are gaining in popularity [14]. For instance, QR codes can be deployed by attackers in public areas. For example, malicious QR codes have been planted near or onto parking meters, which drivers typically scan during the parking payment process. If the wrong QR code is scanned, their payment information and login credentials are stolen through a counterfeit website [9]. It is challenging to prevent hijacking attacks as QR codes are used on a massive scale and they are scanned in uncontrolled environments [15]. Therefore, we must depend on users' ability to identify a QRishing attack. For example, in the parking payment process, users should check for stickers placed over existing QR codes. Similarly, users should pause and search for trustworthy informational cues (e.g., branding and the appropriateness of content given the surroundings) before scanning a QR code.

2   End User Vulnerability and Risk Mitigation

QR codes give users an efficient way to access URLs and files on mobile devices by preventing the need to type long addresses. They are familiar to the public and employed in contexts that are high stakes (e.g., providing personal information during a hotel check-in). Unfortunately, hackers are using the platform maliciously [16]. Whether the attackers are covering a legitimate QR code or planting a QR code, users are becoming victims of cyber-attacks. According to ReliaQuest's report (2023), QR code attacks increased 51% between January and August. They claim this increase in attacks is due to the prevalence of phones with QR code scanners and due to users interacting with those codes without consideration of authenticity.

To mitigate risk, users must understand how a QR code can be malicious. It can send users to compromised websites to install malware, present them with a fake login page, or exploit a software bug to infect their phone. Next, they need to know what to do before scanning a QR code to help mitigate risk. Users need to determine whether the

QR code in the sticker or flyer form is trustworthy. For example, does the flyer contain enough informational cues to judge trustworthiness? Making a good decision requires you to check the surface for modifications (i.e., sticker covering the original QR code), consider the creator (i.e., do you know them), and the genuineness of the flyer. Similar to e-mail and website phishing attacks, end-users should look for red flags.

Kumar et al. (2022) surveyed end-users of QR codes and found that more than half had safety concerns when using a QR code. They reported looking for informational cues like brand logos or QR codes with higher pixel density and larger sizes. Unfortunately, over one-third of those surveyed reported no concern for their safety during QR code usage. It appears many users are aware of threats associated with QR code usage and are looking for cues to determine trustworthiness.

Over a decade ago, Vidas et al. (2013) examined some aspects of how user engagement is impacted by informational cues. They posted over one hundred QR flyers in public locations in Pittsburgh, Pennsylvania. Three types of flyers were employed: 1. QR code only (with and without usage instructions) 2. QR code with research study recruitment information 3. Rip-off tabs only without QR code for the same research recruitment information. Across four weeks, 61% of the flyers had been scanned by at least one person. Notably, most of the users (i.e., 75%) stated they scanned the QR code out of curiosity. They found that few wanted to learn more about the flyers' content. To further support this perspective, they found that as informational cues increased, engagement decreased. That is, viewers were more likely to visit the URL associated with the QR code only than the QR code surrounded by research study recruitment information. Vidas et al. (2013) also performed a follow-up surveillance study on their university campus to examine how many viewers subsequently scanned the QR code and continued to the target URL. They provided evidence that most users scanning a QR code (i.e., 85%) continue to the URL.

We investigated the usage of QR codes in a naturalistic setting similar to Vidas et al. (2013) but focused on the impact of informational cues on engagement. We examined: 1) How often university students scan QR codes on flyers and 2) Whether engagement would be impacted by informational cues on QR code flyers. We used three flyer designs: blank, university logo, and fake job ad. The blank flyer only showed the QR code. Given the lack of any informational cues, this QR code should not be scanned. The QR code with the university logo was expected to create some trustworthiness by association with a trusted brand (c.f., Kumar et al., 2022). Finally, the fake job ad was intended to create the most trust; it aligned the message with the surrounding context, and the flyer showed the name of the supposed creator. Because it was a fake ad, the name on the ad, Dr. Amy Miller, was not an employee of the university, but the content of the ad - seeking student help and offering flexible scheduling - seems to be a conventional message for a university campus. We predicted that engagement would increase as informational cues on the paper flyers increased.

3 Studying University QR Interactions

3.1 Addressing Ethical Concerns

To accomplish the research aims of this study, data had to be collected in the real world. Collecting naturalistic QR code usage behavior in a traditional laboratory environment is impossible. According to the university IRB, we had two ethical concerns to address with this study. First, the design is not a conventional naturalistic observation; it is a contrived observation because the flyers were placed in the environment for the express purpose of this study, and we manipulated the flyer design. Although the aim of the study was to examine factors that contribute to risky QR code use, it was important to provide standard protections for participants as well as to provide more immediate positive outcomes for participants. To this end, participants' data remained anonymous. No unique identifying visitor information was recorded for those who used the QR code and technical data that was collected from the encounter (e.g., browser, OS, screen resolution, geographic region) was described to the participant. The PI's contact information was provided for those who had further questions. In addition to this, participants were provided with guidance for safe QR code practices. This is the first paragraph they encountered:

QR codes direct you to a link you may not be able to see. Due to this, it is important that you only scan QR codes when it is necessary and when you have taken the time to decide if the QR code should be trusted. This is because sometimes people will use QR codes to redirect you to websites that aim to steal your information. If it is possible, try to preview the link the QR code sends you to before deciding to go to the link. Also, if possible, try searching online for the information or manually typing the website link instead of scanning the QR code. It is important that you slow down and consider not all QR codes will direct you to legitimate websites, even if the QR code appears in a legitimate location or expected location. For detailed information on QR code risks and remedies, please read the announcement created by ODU IT security and planning.

Following this introduction, they learned about the risks of using QR codes and how they can be used maliciously (e.g., cyber attackers can direct them to a fake login; attempt to collect personal information). They learned to protect themselves against malicious QR codes (e.g., never scan a QR Code from an untrusted source; check for stickers). At the end of the risks and remedies educational piece, they were provided a URL to more cyber security and information security tips [18]. Finally, participants were asked to complete a follow-up five-question survey as part of the study or, if they were finished, to close the page. The IRB committee approved all stimuli and procedures.

3.2 Procedure

Three flyer designs varied the amount of informational cues available to the viewer and were distributed across campus. The flyers were posted on bulletin boards in the student library, university student center, and engineering building for a duration of one week. After the week, the codes were moved to a new location. The order was counterbalanced, so after three weeks, all three QR codes were displayed once in each of the buildings. The QR code availability was reviewed every two to three days to ensure it was still visible on the bulletin board. The QR code would direct participants to Qualtrics when scanned. Participants were informed the QR code was part of a research study, and then a description of the associated risks of interacting with QR codes and recommendations for ways to limit risk were provided. Anonymous user data were collected, including viewing time, browser type, OS version, operating system, and screen resolution. Participants then had the option to respond to five survey questions:

1. Have you been trained in cybersecurity in the past?
2. Do you consider yourself a cybersecurity expert?
3. How concerned are you with cybersecurity?
4. How frequently do you plan to scan QR codes in the future?
5. What motivated you to scan this QR code?

3.3 Apparatus and Stimuli

Three flyer designs were created and printed: blank, with a university logo, and a fake job ad (taken from an e-mail Phishing example). The blank flyer had no additional information cues; it only showed the QR code (see Fig. 1). The QR code with the university logo was intended to have more credibility via association with a trusted brand (see Fig. 2). Finally, the phishing flyer for the fake job was created with the intent of aligning the QR code message with the surrounding university research context; to further increase credibility, it included the name of the supposed creator (see Fig. 3). Those who scanned a QR code flyer were directed to the Qualtrics platform where they had access to information about the study and had the option to complete the five-item survey.

3.4 Participants

Our possible participants included anyone within our large university population located in the southeastern region of the United States of America (55% females: 18,678 under-graduate and 4,816 graduate enrollment) as well as visitors to campus. Twenty-two participants scanned the QR code flyers. The following anonymous user data were collected: browser type (Chrome: 8, Safari: 14), Phone Platform (Android: 8, iPhone: 14), Operating System (Android: 10–13; iPhone: 15–16), and screen resolution (360×760: 4, 385×854: 2, 390×844: 1, 412×869: 2, 414×896: 7, 428×926: 6).

Fig. 1. Blank QR Code Flyer

4   Results

4.1   Viewing Time

Only two participants viewed the QR code Qualtrics information page for more than four seconds (i.e., 57 s and 110 s). These participants were associated with the university logo flyer (see Fig. 2). Those two participants were also the only ones who completed the

Fig. 2. QR Code with ODU Logo Flyer

five-question survey. The majority of the viewers bounced on page arrival ($n = 17$) in less than 2 s. The remaining participants only skimmed the landing page ($n = 3$) for less than 5 s.

Students,

We understand the needs and demands of a student's schedule, so we offer flexible schedules that enable you to earn money weekly and keep up with your coursework and extracurricular activities. Scan this QR code and give me your Telephone number, major/minor and email address for more details:

Thank you so much!

Dr. Amy Miller

Fig. 3. QR Code Phishing (Fake Job Ad) Flyer. The flyer addresses students and is signed by Dr. Amy Miller. The body of the message says, "We understand the needs and demands of a student's schedule, so we offer flexible schedules that enable you to earn money weekly and keep up with your coursework and extracurricular activities. Scan this QR code and give me your Telephone number, major/minor and email address for more details".

4.2 Engagement by Flyer Type

The descriptive data clearly suggest that flyer informational cues increase engagement. Of the 22 user engagements, the blank flyer only got 18% engagement. Adding the university logo to the flyer captured 32%. While the phishing flyer for the fake job was the most effective, with 50% of the overall engagement (Fig. 4).

※ Blank

ᴴ Logo

⌀ Phishing

Fig. 4. This pie chart displays the number of interactions per flyer type. The dotted pattern represents the blank, the square pattern represents the flyer with the university logo, and the diagonal line pattern represents the phishing flyer.

4.3 University Logo Survey Responses

Unfortunately, most users did not complete the survey. The only two responses were associated with the university logo flyer. Neither user reported having cybersecurity training and neither consider themselves to be experts. They were moderately and slightly concerned with cybersecurity. They were neutral about their planned future QR code scanning behavior. When prompted about their motivations for scanning the QR code, both of their responses centered around curiosity (e.g., why is the QR code blank?).

5 Discussion

In this study, we obtained a measure of QR code engagement on a large university campus in the southeastern region of the United States of America. Given the size of our campus student population, we discovered that engagement with our QR codes was low. While this level of engagement was similar to a previous on-campus study [5], the total number of engagements (22 users) was unexpectedly low. Because engagement was indexed only by participants who followed the QR code link, it is possible that other methods of engagement were missed. For instance, overall engagement rates might be higher if engagement included QR code use along with the total number of views of the flyers themselves. Without knowing precise viewing rates, it is difficult to gauge the exact impact of each flyer design. Even so, we find it unlikely that the flyers went unviewed. High-traffic locations and sustained visibility were key aspects of this procedure. Specifically, the flyers were placed in high-traffic campus areas, like the library and student center, for a week. Second, a research assistant ensured the flyers' visibility every two or three days.

Another consideration tied to engagement is viewer motivation. Due to the naturalistic aspects of the study, it was not possible to know in advance the proportion of individuals who would encounter each QR code design or predict their individual motivations. For instance, it is possible that more engagement with the phishing flyer was observed because a high proportion of participants also happened to be looking for a job. Similar types of motivated searching are less likely to drive interactions with the other two QR code flyer designs.

Using the QR code out of curiosity, as reported by these two participants, supports the findings of other QR code studies [4, 5]. Similarly, curiosity and alignment with the situational context (i.e., needing a job) are reported reasons for falling victim to phishing scams [19, 20].

Even with the overt report that they used the QR code out of curiosity, data from two participants must be considered with caution. The majority of the data collected suggest that informational cues were related to QR code engagement. Specifically, as we predicted, as informational cues increased, engagement with the flyers increased. The most scanned flyer was the phishing fake job ad, followed by the university logo and the blank flyer. Greater engagement with the university logo QR code compared to the non-branded QR code replicates previous findings [17] that QR code users are more likely to trust flyers with band logos. The fact that the phishing fake job ad had more engagement than the simple branded logo, suggests that providing relevant content as an informational cue can further increase trust. While these results are not consistent with Vidas et al. (2013) (i.e., QR code-only flyers had the most engagement), we believe this difference reflects users' growing awareness of threats associated with QR coding usage [17]. Although QR code use presents personal and, potentially, professional risk, we are encouraged to see low engagement with suspect QR codes. This technology, like others, has advanced to a point that it is easy to use and has wide-ranging appeal. As usage has increased, agents who create malicious QR codes have become more skillful at disguising QRishing attacks making it difficult for users to determine risk. Because of this, users may have to become overly dependent on QR code reader security features.

References

1. Cain, A.A., Edwards, M.E., Still, J.D.: An exploratory study of cyber hygiene behaviors and knowledge. J. Inf. Secur. Appl. **42**, 36–45 (2018)
2. Morris, T.W., Still, J.D.: Cybersecurity hygiene: blending home and work computing. In: Patterson, W. (ed.) New Perspectives in Behavioral Cybersecurity. CRC Press, Boca Raton, FL (2023)
3. Gabe, L.: What was that? Coinbase's QR code Super Bowl commercial confuses viewers (2022). https://www.usatoday.com/story/sports/Ad-Meter/2022/02/13/coinbase-qr-code-super-bowl-ad-crypto-commercial-confuses-viewers/6778949001/
4. Seeburger. J.: No cure for curiosity: linking physical and digital urban layers. In: Proceedings of the 7th Nordic Conference on Human-Computer Interaction: Making Sense Through Design, pp. 247–256. ACM (2012)
5. Vidas, T., Owusu, E., Wang, S., Zeng, C., Cranor, L.F., Christin, N.: QRishing: the susceptibility of smartphone users to QR code phishing attacks. In: Proceedings of the 2013 Workshop on Usable Security (USEC 2013) (2013)

6. Ozkaya, E., Ozkaya, H.E., Roxas, J., Bryant, F., Whitson, D.: Factors affecting consumer usage of QR codes. J. Direct Data Digit. Mark. Pract. **16**, 209–224 (2015)
7. Dreyer, K.: 20 million Americans scanned a QR Code in October. https://www.comscore.com/Insights/Infographics/20-Million-Americans-Scanned-a-QR-Code-in-October. Assessed 18 Jan 2024
8. Ricson, E.: QR code usage statistics 2022–2023: 433% scan increase and 438% generation boost. https://www.qrcode-tiger.com/qr-code-statistics-2022-q1. Assessed 18 Jan 2024
9. Sharevski, F., Devine, A., Pieroni, E., Jachim, P.: Phishing with malicious QR codes. In: 2022 European Symposium on Usable Security (2022)
10. Mitnick, K.D., Simon, W.L.: The Art of Deception: Controlling the Human Element of Security. Wiley (2003)
11. Yeboah-Boateng, E.O., Amanor, P.M.: Phishing, SMiShing & vishing: an assessment of threats against mobile devices. J. Emerg. Trends Comput. Inf. Sci. **5**, 297–307 (2014)
12. Dhamija, R., Tygar, J.D., Hearst, M.: Why phishing works. In: Proceedings of the SIGCHI Conference on Human Factors in Computing Systems (CHI). ACM Press, Montreal, Canada (2006)
13. Krombholz, K., Frühwirt, P., Kieseberg, P., Kapsalis, I., Huber, M., Weippl, E.: QR code security: a survey of attacks and challenges for usable security. In: Tryfonas, T., Askoxylakis, I. (eds.) Human Aspects of Information Security, Privacy, and Trust. LNCS, vol. 8533, pp. 79–90. Springer, Cham (2014). https://doi.org/10.1007/978-3-319-07620-1_8
14. Desolda, G., Ferro, L.S., Marrella, A., Catarci, T., Costabile, M.F.: Human factors in phishing attacks: a systematic literature review. ACM Comput. Surv. (CSUR) **54**, 1–35 (2021)
15. Picard, J., Landry, P., Bolay, M.: Counterfeit detection with QR codes. In: Proceedings of the 21st ACM Symposium on Document Engineering (2021)
16. Barr, L.: FBI warns criminals are using fake QR codes to scam users (2022). https://abcnews.go.com/Politics/fbi-warns-criminals-fake-qr-codes-scam-users/story?id=82371866
17. Kumar, N., Jain, S., Shukla, M., Lodha, S.: Investigating users' perception, security awareness and cyber-hygiene behaviour concerning QR code as an attack vector. In: Stephanidis, C., Antona, M., Ntoa, S. (eds.) HCI International 2022 Posters. HCII 2022. CCIS, vol. 1583, pp. 506–513. Springer, Cham (2022). https://doi.org/10.1007/978-3-031-06394-7_64
18. Old Dominion University: Safe Computing. https://www.odu.edu/information-technology-services/security/safe-computing. Accessed 18 Jan 24
19. Vishwanath, A., Herath, T., Chen, R., Wang, J., Rao, H.R.: Why do people get phished? Testing individual differences in phishing vulnerability within an integrated, information processing model. Decis. Support. Syst. **51**, 576–586 (2011)
20. Moody, G.D., Galletta, D.F., Dunn, B.K.: Which phish get caught? An exploratory study of individuals' susceptibility to phishing. Eur. J. Inf. Syst. **26**, 564–584 (2017)

Exploring ICS/SCADA Network Vulnerabilities

Hala Strohmier$^{(\boxtimes)}$ [ID], Aaryan R. Londhe[ID], Chris A. Clark[ID], Ronit Pawar[ID],
and Brian Kram[ID]

University of South Carolina Aiken, Aiken, SC, USA
`hala.strohmier@usca.edu`

Abstract. This paper investigates vulnerabilities in the University of South Carolina Aiken (USCA) Centre's IP infrastructure, focusing on ICS/SCADA network security. The study follows a systematic approach, incorporating the CIS (Center for Internet Security) security controls methodology throughout the project phases, including asset identification, vulnerability assessment, risk assessment, and flexibility study. The asset identification phase utilized tools such as Nmap, Maltego and Lansweeper to comprehensively identify and catalog assets within the network. Subsequently, the vulnerability assessment phase employed tools like OpenVAS, Nexpose, Nessus and manual penetration testing to uncover potential weaknesses. The research team then conducted a risk assessment using the FAIR (Factor Analysis of Information Risk) Methodology to quantitatively analyze and prioritize identified risks. In parallel, a flexibility study was undertaken to assess the system's adaptability to potential threats. Collaborating with the technology service department(TSD), the research team addressed the identified vulnerabilities. This research paper provides a thorough exploration of ICS/SCADA network vulnerabilities, offering insights into the effectiveness of the CIS security controls methodology in enhancing cybersecurity measures.

Keywords: ICS/SCADA · Cybersecurity · Vulnerablity Assessment · Operations Center · CIS Security Controls · Factor Analysis of Information Risk (FAIR) · Network Security · Risk Assessment

1 Introduction

Industrial Control Systems (ICS) and Supervisory Control and Data Acquisition (SCADA) networks constitute the backbone of critical infrastructures, playing a pivotal role in the seamless operation of essential services. As these systems become increasingly interconnected and reliant on digital technologies, they also become susceptible to a growing array of cyber threats. The security of ICS/SCADA networks is paramount to safeguarding industries such as energy, water supply, and manufacturing [1].

© The Author(s), under exclusive license to Springer Nature Switzerland AG 2024
A. Moallem (Ed.): HCII 2024, LNCS 14729, pp. 215–233, 2024.
https://doi.org/10.1007/978-3-031-61382-1_14

This research delves into the intricate landscape of ICS/SCADA network vulnerabilities, with a specific focus on the operation center's IP infrastructure at the University of South Carolina Aiken (USCA). The escalating complexity of these networks, coupled with the ever-evolving threat landscape, necessitates a comprehensive exploration of potential weaknesses. Addressing these vulnerabilities is crucial not only for protecting critical assets but also for maintaining the reliability and resilience of the interconnected systems that underpin modern society.

2   Literature Review

The security of Industrial Control Systems (ICS) and Supervisory Control and Data Acquisition (SCADA) networks has garnered significant attention in the realm of cybersecurity due to their pivotal role in critical infrastructure. The literature on ICS/SCADA security underscores the growing complexity of these systems and the corresponding increase in vulnerabilities.

Numerous studies have highlighted the evolving threat landscape surrounding ICS/SCADA networks. Researchers have demonstrated the feasibility of cyber-attacks targeting critical infrastructure, emphasizing the need for robust security measures. Incidents such as Stuxnet have underscored the potential real-world impact of cyber threats on industrial processes, amplifying the urgency for proactive security strategies [2,3].

The adoption of comprehensive security frameworks has become imperative in addressing the multifaceted challenges of ICS/SCADA security. The Center for Internet Security (CIS) security controls framework has emerged as a prominent guideline for enhancing cybersecurity defenses in critical infrastructure settings. Studies evaluating the effectiveness of the CIS controls have shown promising results in fortifying ICS/SCADA networks against a spectrum of cyber threats.

Risk assessment methodologies play a crucial role in identifying and prioritizing vulnerabilities in ICS/SCADA environments. The Factor Analysis of Information Risk (FAIR) methodology has gained recognition for its ability to provide a quantitative analysis of risks associated with identified vulnerabilities. Research has demonstrated the applicability of FAIR in diverse contexts, contributing to the understanding of risk in ICS/SCADA systems [4,5].

Asset identification and vulnerability assessment tools are integral components of a robust cybersecurity strategy. Studies have utilized tools like Nmap, Nessus, and OpenVAS for identifying assets and assessing vulnerabilities in ICS/SCADA networks. These tools contribute to a comprehensive understanding of the network landscape and potential points of weakness.

Collaboration between cybersecurity researchers and industry practitioners is crucial for addressing identified vulnerabilities. Literature has highlighted successful cases where collaboration with technology departments and industry experts has led to the effective mitigation of cybersecurity risks in ICS/SCADA environments [6].

In summary, the literature review reveals a growing awareness of the challenges posed by cyber threats to ICS/SCADA networks. The adoption of frameworks like CIS security controls, methodologies such as FAIR, and the use of advanced tools for asset identification and vulnerability assessment collectively contribute to the evolving landscape of cybersecurity in critical infrastructure settings.

3   Methodology

This research integrates a comprehensive methodology, incorporating the Center for Internet Security (CIS) Critical Security Controls (CIS Controls) for asset identification, vulnerability assessment, and risk analysis. The research methodology integrates the Center for Internet Security (CIS) security controls, a recognized framework designed to fortify cybersecurity defenses. The study follows a structured approach, encompassing the following:

- Asset identification
- Vulnerability assessment
- Risk analysis
- Feasibility Study and Effectiveness Evaluation
- Factor Analysis of Information Risk (FAIR)
- Quantifiable risks associated with these vulnerabilities.
  - Identify Assets
  - Identify Threat Scenarios
  - Identify Vulnerability Severity
  - Determine Threat Capability
  - Calculate Risk
  - Prioritize Risks
  - Implement Mitigation Measures

3.1   CIS Critical Security Controls (CIS Controls)

Phase 1: Asset Identification: We used sophisticated tools such as Maltego, Nmap, and Lansweeper to systematically enumerate and categorize assets within the USCA network. Maltego played a pivotal role in visually representing and linking information, while Nmap and Lansweeper were instrumental in conducting comprehensive network discovery, security auditing, and detailed asset profiling. This approach is necessary to gain a clear understanding of the devices being scanned, providing valuable insights for subsequent phases of the process.

Phase 2: Vulnerability Assessment: A thorough examination of identified assets using tools such as Nexpose, Nessus, and OpenVAS was conducted to proactively identify and address vulnerabilities within the system. This proactive approach aimed to enhance the overall security posture of the system by uncovering potential weaknesses and ensuring that appropriate measures could be taken to mitigate any security risks. Manual penetration testing was employed to validate and supplement automated assessments, providing a more comprehensive understanding of the system's security landscape and ensuring robust protection against potential threat.

Phase 3: Risk Assessment: Leveraging findings from the vulnerability assessment, we systematically assessed the risks associated with each vulnerability. To further enhance the depth of our risk assessment, we employed the Factor Analysis of Information Risk (FAIR) methodology. This comprehensive approach not only facilitates a detailed understanding of potential risks but also enables effective risk prioritization. By prioritizing risks, organizations can focus resources on addressing the most critical vulnerabilities, thereby enhancing overall security posture and mitigating potential threats more efficiently.

Phase 4: Feasibility Study and Effectiveness Evaluation: Conducting a feasibility study to evaluate the practicality of implementing proposed security measures, encompassing a thorough assessment of viability and effectiveness, was the initial step. In collaboration with the Technology Services Department (TSD), we ensured alignment with organizational goals and addressed technical feasibility considerations. Once the security suggestions were implemented, a meticulous testing phase was initiated to reevaluate vulnerabilities, ensuring their proper resolution and assessing the overall effectiveness of the measures. This comprehensive approach, from feasibility study to post-implementation testing, is necessary for informed decision-making, optimal security enhancement, and ongoing risk management.

3.2   Factor Analysis of Information Risk (FAIR)

Phase 1: Identify Assets: Enumerating and identifying assets affected by vulnerabilities involved a comprehensive assessment that encompassed servers, printers, applications, and critical systems within the USCA network. This process aimed to provide a thorough understanding of the diverse assets scanned and yielded valuable insights into their information. In addition, we meticulously sorted the IP addresses, concentrating specifically on USCA's Operations Centre. This focused approach has contributed to a thorough understanding of connected devices, ensuring a comprehensive grasp of the network's infrastructure.

Phase 2: Identify Threat Scenarios: Identifying potential threat scenarios for each vulnerability, delving into various methods attackers might employ to exploit vulnerabilities and compromise the identified assets. Developing 3 to 4 instances for each vulnerability, outlining specific threat scenarios. This comprehensive exploration is essential to understanding the diverse ways in which vulnerabilities can be exploited, providing insights that aid in crafting robust security measures. By anticipating potential threats, organizations can proactively strengthen their defenses and mitigate risks effectively.

Phase 3: Identify Vulnerability Severity: Evaluating the severity of each vulnerability by leveraging findings from Nexpose, Nessus, and OpenVAS. This assessment considered factors such as Ease of Exploitation, Scope of Impact, Ease of Detection, Availability Impact, Mitigation Difficulty, and Existence of Public Exploits. Employing a scoring scale from 1 to 10 for each factor, we calculated averages to derive a final rating. This systematic approach is necessary to quantitatively measure the potential risk posed by vulnerabilities, providing a comprehensive and objective basis for prioritizing remediation efforts. It ensures that resources are allocated effectively, addressing the most critical vulnerabilities that pose significant threats to the security of the system or network [7,8].

Phase 4: Determine Threat Capability: Assessing the capabilities of potential threat actors who could exploit vulnerabilities, taking into account factors such as skill level, resources, and motivations. Assigned a score out of 10 to gauge their proficiency and intent. This evaluation is crucial to understanding the potential threat landscape and tailoring security measures accordingly. By comprehensively assessing threat actors' capabilities, organizations can better anticipate and prepare for potential attacks, ensuring that defense strategies are aligned with the likely tactics, techniques, and procedures of adversaries [8].

Phase 5: Calculate Risk: Applying the formula: Risk = (Vulnerability Severity × Threat Capability) to quantify the risk associated with each vulnerability, utilizing the values obtained in the previous phase. This calculation is essential for prioritizing vulnerabilities based on their potential impact and the capabilities of potential threat actors. By assigning a numerical value to the risk, organizations can systematically prioritize remediation efforts, focusing on addressing vulnerabilities that pose the highest risk to the security of the system or network. This approach ensures a strategic and efficient allocation of resources to enhance the overall cybersecurity posture [7].

Phase 6: Prioritize Risks: Ranking the calculated risks to prioritize mitigation efforts, giving precedence to vulnerabilities with higher calculated risks.

Phase 7: Implement Mitigation Measures: Developing and implementing mitigation measures based on prioritized risks, which involved actions such as patching vulnerabilities, implementing security controls, or modifying system architecture. Collaborating closely with the Technology Services Department (TSD) to comprehensively explain the vulnerabilities and conduct a thorough study, facilitating the implementation of the most effective security measures. This collaborative approach is necessary to ensure that mitigation efforts align with organizational goals, technical feasibility, and the severity of identified risks.

This dual-methodology approach, coupled with collaboration with the Technology Services Department (TSD), ensures a holistic and effective strategy for addressing vulnerabilities and enhancing the cybersecurity posture of the USCA network.

4 Conducting the Research

Our research for the ICS/SCADA network vulnerabilities at USCA's Operation Centre followed a meticulous process, incorporating a series of well-defined steps to ensure accuracy and depth in our findings.

4.1 Asset Identification and Vulnerability Assessment

In our initial phase, termed the asset identification phase, the project owner provided us with specific subnets to focus on, including xxx.xxx.178.0/24, xxx.xxx.179.0/24, xxx.xxx.182.0/24, xxx.xxx.185.0/24, xxx.xxx.186.0/24, xxx.xxx.188.0/24, xxx.xxx.190.0/24, xxx.xxx.198.0/24, and xxx.xxx.199.0/24. Our task was to gather as much information as possible about the devices within these subnets, including details such as the operating system, device names, and other relevant information.

To accomplish this, we researched and identified three powerful tools for asset identification: Nmap, Maltego, and Lansweeper. These tools are known for their effectiveness in providing comprehensive insights into the characteristics of networked devices. Subsequently, we initiated scans on the specified subnets using the most aggressive and powerful scanning capabilities offered by these tools.

The gathered information encompassed critical details such as the operating systems employed, device names, MAC addresses, and running services on each device. Once the data was documented, we meticulously sorted and filtered the IPs to focus exclusively on those related to the USCA Operation Centre, following the specific instructions provided by our project owner. This refined inventory ensured that our subsequent phases would be targeted and aligned with the assets directly relevant to the operations center, facilitating a more focused and efficient security assessment.

In the vulnerability assessment phase, following the finalization of the IP list associated with the USCA Operation Centre, we conducted research to identify the most effective vulnerability scanning tools. Opting for a comprehensive approach, we selected three tools: OpenVAS, Nexpose, and Nexus. It's noteworthy that we utilized the professional version of Nexus, provided by our university specifically for this research.

Proceeding with the chosen tools, we initiated the vulnerability scanning process by inputting the identified IPs. The scanning approach adopted was the most aggressive setting available in these tools to ensure a thorough examination. Upon completion of the scans, our next step involved meticulously documenting the vulnerabilities detected by these tools. This documentation served as a foundational step in understanding and addressing the identified vulnerabilities in the USCA Operation Centre's network. Also using our expertise, we did manual testing to uncover vulnerabilities that were not discovered by the vulnerability scanner.

4.2   Risk Assessment

After concluding the vulnerability assessment, the subsequent phase involved a comprehensive risk assessment utilizing the Factor Analysis of Information Risk (FAIR) methodology. The FAIR process unfolds in the following step.

Assets Identification and Threat Scenarios: We listed and identified assets affected by vulnerabilities, such as servers, databases, applications, or critical systems. For each vulnerability, determine potential threat scenarios by exploring various ways attackers could exploit vulnerabilities and compromise identified assets.

Vulnerability Severity: We assessed the severity of each vulnerability based on findings from Nexpose, Nessus, and OpenVAS. Consider factors like Ease of Exploitation, Scope of Impact, Ease of Detection, Availability Impact, Mitigation Difficulty, and Existence of Public Exploits. Assign a score out of 10 for each factor and calculate an overall score.

Examples of Factors

– Ease of Exploitation: Refers to how straightforward it is for an attacker to exploit a vulnerability.
– Scope of Impact: Assesses the potential reach or extent of consequences resulting from vulnerability exploitation.
– Ease of Detection: Evaluates how easily security professionals can identify vulnerability exploitation.
– Availability Impact: Assesses potential harm to system or service availability if a vulnerability is exploited.
– Mitigation Difficulty: Evaluate how challenging it is to apply effective countermeasures to address vulnerability.
– Existence of Public Exploits: Considers whether attackers can readily access tools or techniques to exploit the vulnerability.

Threat Capability and Calculating Risk: Again assigning a score out of 10, we evaluated the capabilities of potential threat actors who might exploit vulnerabilities, considering skill level, resources, and motivations. Utilize the formula Risk=(Vulnerability Severity×Threat Capability) to calculate the risk score for each vulnerability. This quantitative measure provides insights into the potential impact and likelihood of exploitation.

Prioritize Risks: We rank the calculated risks from the previous phase to prioritize mitigation efforts. Focus on addressing vulnerabilities with higher calculated risks first, ensuring a strategic allocation of resources to address the most critical security concerns.

This systematic FAIR methodology allows for a comprehensive understanding of the risk landscape associated with vulnerabilities. By factoring in asset identification, potential threat scenarios, vulnerability severity, and threat capability, organizations gain actionable insights to prioritize and implement effective risk mitigation strategies.

4.3 Feasibility Study and Effectiveness Evaluation

In the Feasibility Study and Effectiveness Evaluation phase, collaboration with the Technology Services Department (TSD) was paramount. We engaged in a detailed explanation of identified vulnerabilities, providing insights into the best mitigation strategies. Once a consensus was reached and we were confident in the chosen mitigation strategy, TSD took charge of the implementation. After the security measures were successfully implemented, we conducted thorough testing to ascertain their effectiveness. This involved a comprehensive vulnerability assessment utilizing both automated tools and manual testing methodologies used earlier. The objective was to ensure that the identified issues were not only addressed but also effectively resolved, validating the robustness of the implemented security measures. This collaborative and iterative approach aimed to enhance the overall cybersecurity posture of the USCA network.

5   Findings and Results

5.1   Asset Identification

Upon scanning with Nmap, Lansweeper, and Maltego, we obtained details of the assets. We then sorted out the IPs related to the operation centre as specified by the Project Owner. The IPs related to the operation center are: xxx.xxx.185.10, xxx.xxx.188.11, xxx.xxx.186.9, xxx.xxx.185.3, xxx.xxx.185.26, xxx.xxx.186.109, xxx.xxx.198.4, xxx.xxx.186.205, xxx.xxx.178.126, xxx.xxx.179.252, xxx.xxx. 185.7, xxx.xxx.185.157, xxx.xxx.185.160, xxx.xxx.185.163, xxx.xxx.185.17, xxx.xxx.185.179, xxx.xxx.185.18, xxx.xxx.185.182, xxx.xxx.185.198, xxx.xxx. 185.5, xxx.xxx.185.78, xxx.xxx.185.82, xxx.xxx.185.87, and xxx.xxx.185.9. These IPs are associated with the operation centre, and we gathered details such as device names, MAC addresses, device types, and running OS for each. This targeted approach enhances our understanding of the assets within the operation centre, ensuring a more effective vulnerability assessment and mitigation strategy (Table 1 and Fig. 1).

5.2   Vulnerability Assessment

Commencing the vulnerability assessment, we utilized tools like Nexpose, Nessus, and OpenVAS, complemented by manual penetration testing to uncover vulnerabilities potentially missed by automated scans. Post-assessment, the focus shifted to vulnerabilities of high and medium severity. The identified vulnerabilities and their impacted assets include:

Table 1. USCA's Operation Centre IPs

IP Address	Vendor	OS	Open Ports
xxx.xxx.185.10	Linux	Linux 3.2–4.9	22, 80, 443, 4444
xxx.xxx.188.11	Linux	Linux 3.2–4.9	22, 80, 443, 4444
xxx.xxx.186.9	Linux	Linux 3.2–4.9	80, 1935, 5959
xxx.xxx.185.3	–	Brother DCP-8065D printer	80
xxx.xxx.185.26	–	–	NA
xxx.xxx.186.109	Linux	Linux 3.2–4.9	22, 80, 443, 4444
xxx.xxx.198.4	Linux	Linux 3.2–4.9	22, 80, 443, 4444
xxx.xxx.186.205	Linux	Linux 3.2–4.9	22, 80, 443, 4444
xxx.xxx.178.126	-	Brother MFC-8460N	80
xxx.xxx.179.252	–	–	NA
xxx.xxx.185.7	–	Brother HL-2270DW	80
xxx.xxx.185.157	Linux	Linux 3.10–4.11	443
xxx.xxx.185.160	Microsoft	Microsoft Windows Server 2019	135, 139, 445, 3389
xxx.xxx.185.163	Linux	Linux 3.10–4.11	443
xxx.xxx.185.17	Linux	Linux 2.6 13–2.6 32	80, 443
xxx.xxx.185.179	Microsoft	Microsoft Windows Server 2019	135, 139, 445, 3389
xxx.xxx.185.18	Linux	Linux 2.6 13–2.6 32	80, 443
xxx.xxx.185.182	Microsoft	Microsoft Windows 10 1909	135, 139, 445, 3389
xxx.xxx.185.198	Microsoft	Microsoft Windows Server 2019	135, 139, 445, 3389
xxx.xxx.185.5	–	Apple AirPort Extreme WAP	80, 3011
xxx.xxx.185.78	Linux	Linux 2.6.32	22, 80, 443, 10001
xxx.xxx.185.82	Linux	Linux 2.6.32	22, 80, 443, 10001
xxx.xxx.185.87	Microsoft	Microsoft Windows 10 1909	135, 139, 445, 3389
xxx.xxx.185.9	Linux	Linux 2.6 13–2.6 32	80, 443

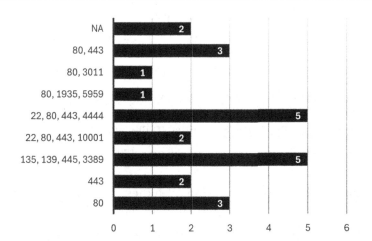

Fig. 1. Count of IP Addresses by Open Ports

1. HTTP Brute Force Logins with Default Credentials. This vulnerability involves attackers attempting to gain unauthorized access to the system by repeatedly trying different usernames and passwords.

- **Impacted Assets:** xxx.xxx.178.126, xxx.xxx.185.17, xxx.xxx.185.18, xxx.xxx.185.9

2. Lack of HTTPS Implementation. The absence of HTTPS implementation poses a security risk as it leaves communications between users and the website unencrypted.

- **Impacted Assets:** xxx.xxx.185.10, xxx.xxx.188.11, xxx.xxx.186.9, xxx.xxx.186.109,   xxx.xxx.198.4,   xxx.xxx.186.205,   xxx.xxx.178.126, xxx.xxx.185.17, xxx.xxx.185.18, xxx.xxx.185.5, xxx.xxx.185.9

3. SSL/TLS: Renegotiation Dos Vulnerability/deprecated TLS V1.0 and TLS V1.1 Protocol Detection. This vulnerability pertains to weaknesses in SSL/TLS protocols, potentially leading to Denial of Service (DoS) attacks.

- **Impacted Assets:** xxx.xxx.185.10, xxx.xxx.188.11, xxx.xxx.186.9, xxx.xxx.186.109,   xxx.xxx.198.4,   xxx.xxx.186.205,   xxx.xxx.185.160, xxx.xxx.185.179,   xxx.xxx.185.182,   xxx.xxx.185.198,   xxx.xxx.185.78, xxx.xxx.185.82, xxx.xxx.185.87

4. Default or Guessable SNMP Community Names: Public (SNMP-read-0001). This vulnerability involves using default or easily guessable SNMP community names, potentially exposing sensitive information.

- **Impacted Assets:** xxx.xxx.185.26, xxx.xxx.178.126, xxx.xxx.179.252, xxx.xxx.185.3, xxx.xxx.185.7

5. SNMP Credentials Transmitted in Clear Text (SNMP-Clear Text-Credential). This vulnerability highlights the risk of transmitting SNMP credentials in plaintext, making it susceptible to interception.

- **Impacted Assets:** xxx.xxx.185.26, xxx.xxx.178.126, xxx.xxx.179.252

6. SSH Terrapin Prefix Truncation Weakness. This vulnerability involves a weakness in SSH (Secure Shell) related to Terrapin prefix truncation.

- **Impacted Assets:** xxx.xxx.185.10, xxx.xxx.186.205, xxx.xxx.188.11, xxx.xxx.198.4

This meticulous approach to addressing vulnerabilities enhances the precision of mitigation strategies, fortifying the USCA network's overall security.

5.3   Risk Assessment

Our risk assessment relies on the FAIR methodology, a structured approach comprising multiple phases to assign a risk score. This score plays a crucial role in prioritizing vulnerabilities, giving heightened attention to those with higher risk scores. Additionally, we must conduct thorough research on each vulnerability, exploring its description, potential impact, and the associated consequences. This comprehensive analysis ensures that we gain a deep understanding of vulnerabilities, facilitating effective prioritization. By grasping the risks thoroughly, we can plan and implement more effective strategies to safeguard against potential threats and vulnerabilities.

1. SSL/TLS: Renegotiation DoS Vulnerability/Deprecated TLS V1.0 and TLS V1.1 Protocol Detection

– **Threat Scenarios**: During Service Disruption, an attacker exploits the Renegotiation DoS Vulnerability, causing downtime. Coordinated Resource Exhaustion attacks lead to degraded server performance. In Man-in-the-Middle Attacks, outdated TLS/SSL protocols risk unauthorized access. SSL Stripping involves forcing a downgrade, and exposing data in plaintext.

– **Vulnerability Severity:**

– *Ease of Exploitation:* 8/10
– *Scope of Impact:* 7/10
– *Ease of Detection:* 5/10
– *Availability Impact:* 8/10
– *Mitigation Difficulty:* 6/10
– *Existence of Public Exploits:* 3/10
– *Overall Severity Rating:* 6/10

– **Threat Capability:**

– *Score:* 6/10

– **Risk Score:**
  • *Risk = Vulnerability Severity × Threat Capability*
  • *Score:* 36

2, Lack of HTTPS

– **Threat Scenarios:** In Man-in-the-Middle Attacks, intercepting unencrypted communication risks unauthorized access to sensitive data. Data Tampering involves maliciously modifying unencrypted data, risking misinformation. Session Hijacking captures unencrypted session tokens, allowing unauthorized access. Eavesdropping on Confidential Information exposes sensitive data. Phishing Attacks use deceptive websites to capture user information, leading to potential identity theft or credential compromise.

- **Vulnerability Severity:**

- *Ease of Exploitation:* 5/10
- *Scope of Impact:* 8/10
- *Ease of Detection:* 6/10
- *Availability Impact:* 4/10
- *Mitigation Difficulty:* 3/10
- *Existence of Public Exploits:* 5/10
- *Overall Severity Rating:* 5/10

- **Threat Capability:**

- *Score:* 3/10

- **Risk Score:**

- *Risk = Vulnerability Severity × Threat Capability*
- *Score:* 15

Default or Guessable SNMP Community Names: Public

- **Threat Scenarios:** In Unauthorized Access to SNMP Devices, attackers use default or commonly guessed SNMP community names, resulting in unrestricted access, potential retrieval of sensitive information, and device configuration modification. Device Configuration Tampering involves exploiting default community strings to alter SNMP-enabled device configurations, leading to service disruptions, unauthorized access, or compromised device integrity. Information Disclosure occurs when attackers leverage default SNMP community names to extract sensitive information, leading to the unauthorized disclosure of device details or network topology.

- **Vulnerability Severity:**
  - *Ease of Exploitation:* 8/10
  - *Scope of Impact:* 9/10
  - *Ease of Detection:* 5/10
  - *Availability Impact:* 7/10
  - *Mitigation Difficulty:* 6/10
  - *Existence of Public Exploits:* 8/10
  - *Overall Severity Rating:* 7.2/10

- **Threat Capability:**

- *Score:* 6/10

- **Risk Score:**

- *Risk = Vulnerability Severity × Threat Capability*
- *Score:* 43.2

SNMP Credentials Transmitted in Cleartext

- **Threat Scenarios:** During Network Sniffing, attackers eavesdrop on network traffic to capture SNMP credentials transmitted in cleartext, resulting in unauthorized access to SNMP-enabled devices and potential unauthorized configuration changes or information disclosure. Credential Interception involves malicious actors intercepting SNMP traffic containing cleartext credentials, compromising network security. In Man-in-the-Middle Attacks, attackers position themselves between the SNMP manager and agent to intercept cleartext credentials, leading to unauthorized access, device manipulation, or unauthorized information retrieval from SNMP-enabled devices. The use of Credential Sniffing Tools by attackers allows them to capture SNMP credentials transmitted in cleartext, potentially leading to unauthorized access, service disruptions, unauthorized configuration changes, or information disclosure.

Vulnerability Severity:

- *Ease of Exploitation:* 6/10
- *Scope of Impact:* 8/10
- *Ease of Detection:* 4/10
- *Availability Impact:* 5/10
- *Mitigation Difficulty:* 7/10
- *Existence of Public Exploits:* 6/10
- *Overall Severity Rating:* 6/10

- **Threat Capability:**
  - *Score:* 5/10

- **Risk Score:**

- *Risk = Vulnerability Severity × Threat Capability*
- *Score:* 30

HTTP Brute Force Logins with Default Credentials

- **Threat Scenarios:**In Unauthorized Actions by Attackers, successful brute force login allows attackers to perform unauthorized actions within the web application, compromising data integrity and introducing malicious content. Credential Guessing Attacks involve attackers launching brute force attacks against HTTP login pages using default credentials, leading to unauthorized access to web applications or services and potentially resulting in data breaches or unauthorized action.

- **Vulnerability Severity:**

- *Ease of Exploitation:* 7/10

- *Scope of Impact:* 8/10
- *Ease of Detection:* 5/10
- *Availability Impact:* 3/10
- *Mitigation Difficulty:* 6/10
- *Existence of Public Exploits:* 8/10
- *Overall Severity Rating:* 6/10

- **Threat Capability:**

- *Score:* 8/10

- **Risk Score:**

- *Risk = Vulnerability Severity × Threat Capability*
- *Score:* 48

SSH Terrapin Prefix Truncation Weakness

- **Threat Scenarios:** In a Man-in-the-Middle Attack, the attacker exploits the Terrapin Prefix Truncation Weakness to manipulate SSH connections, leading to the interception and potential alteration of transmitted data between the client and server. Unauthorized Access occurs when an adversary takes advantage of the vulnerability to truncate prefixes in SSH traffic, attempting unauthorized access to a system by exploiting weakened cryptographic protections. Additionally, Data Manipulation ensues as the vulnerability is exploited to modify the content of SSH traffic, allowing attackers to manipulate commands or data transmitted between the client and server.

- **Vulnerability Severity:**

- *Ease of Exploitation:* 7/10
- *Scope of Impact:* 8/10
- *Ease of Detection:* 5/10
- *Availability Impact:* 7/10
- *Mitigation Difficulty:* 6/10
- *Existence of Public Exploits:* 6/10
- *Overall Severity Rating:* 6.5/10

  Threat Capability:

- *Score:* 7/10

- **Risk Score:**

- *Risk = Vulnerability Severity × Threat Capability*
- *Score:* 45.5

5.4   Mitigation Measures

SSL/TLS: Renegotiation Dos Vulnerability/Deprecated TLS V1.0 and TLS V1.1 Protocol

– Firstly, we prioritize updating our software regularly, focusing on the SSL/TLS library and server software to address any known vulnerabilities, such as the renegotiation DoS vulnerability. Additionally, we optimize our SSL/TLS configuration settings to minimize the impact of renegotiation. This involves considering options to limit its frequency or even disabling renegotiation based on the specific server software in use. In cases where uncertainty or assistance is needed, we recommend reaching out to the vendor or support community associated with the server software for guidance on configurations and updates.

Lack of HTTPS

– We've installed a valid SSL/TLS certificate for robust HTTPS encryption, ensuring the confidentiality and integrity of transmitted data. All resource references, both internal and external, have been updated to exclusively use HTTPS. Additionally, we've configured automatic redirection of HTTP traffic to the secure HTTPS version, activated HSTS for enhanced security, and established a well-protected environment for secure user-system communication.

Default or Guessable SNMP Community Names: Public

– Firstly, we've strengthened security by changing the SNMP community string from the default "public" to a resilient, non-guessable value, heightening protection against unauthorized access. Additionally, to fortify security, we've embraced strong authentication mechanisms, particularly SNMPv3, which supports secure authentication and encryption, providing an advanced layer of protection for SNMP communications. To exercise greater control, we've configured access control lists (ACLs) to restrict SNMP access solely to authorized IP addresses or specific network ranges. As a proactive step, we conduct regular audits of SNMP configurations, enabling the detection and rectification of any instances of default or weak community strings.

HTTP Brute Force Logins with Default Credentials

– Firstly, we've proactively replaced default credentials for all systems and applications with strong, unique passwords. This foundational step significantly reduces the risk associated with default login information, fortifying our security stance. Additionally, to mitigate the impact of brute force attacks, we've enforced account lockout policies, limiting the number of failed login attempts and enhancing security by temporarily locking out accounts displaying suspicious activity. Furthermore, we've introduced Multi-Factor Authentication (MFA) to add an extra layer of security, requiring users to provide multiple forms of verification for authentication.

SNMP Credentials Transmitted in Cleartext

– To enhance the security of our SNMP (Simple Network Management Protocol) implementation, we've adopted SNMPv3, which offers secure transmission through encryption and authentication mechanisms. Specifically, we've configured SNMPv3 with robust authentication protocols to ensure the confidentiality and integrity of transmitted credentials. In addition, access control lists (ACLs) have been employed to restrict SNMP access solely to authorized devices, minimizing the risk of unauthorized interception.

SSH Terrapin Prefix Truncation Weakness

– To enhance SSH server security, we've upgraded our software to patch against the Terrapin vulnerability. Additionally, we've temporarily disabled vulnerable key exchange algorithms, like ChaCha20-Poly1305, and reached out to the vendor for guidance on specific configurations and updates. These proactive steps ensure a more secure SSH server environment. Additionally, to address any uncertainties or seek assistance in this process, we've proactively reached out to the vendor or support community associated with our server software (Fig. 2).

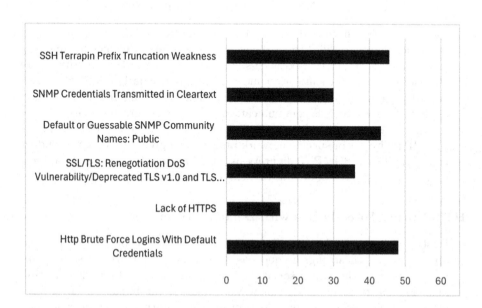

Fig. 2. Risk Score of Vulnerabilities

6   Conclusion

6.1   Summary of Findings

This research has meticulously identified and examined significant security vulnerabilities within various network protocols, providing insights into the potential threats and risks associated with these weaknesses. Notably, the SSL/TLS renegotiation vulnerability presents a substantial risk of service disruption and resource exhaustion, while the absence of HTTPS implementation exposes users to diverse attacks like man-in-the-middle and session hijacking. Additionally, vulnerabilities stemming from default or easily guessed SNMP community names and the cleartext transmission of SNMP credentials may result in unauthorized access and information disclosure. The study also delves into the risks linked to HTTP brute force logins and the SSH Terrapin Prefix Truncation Weakness, emphasizing the possibilities of unauthorized actions and data manipulation.

It is crucial to highlight the significance of manual penetration testing, as demonstrated in the discovery of the default password vulnerability, which was identified through manual testing rather than automated vulnerability scanners. This underscores the importance of human intervention in uncovering nuanced vulnerabilities that automated tools might overlook. This emphasizes the significance of having a responsible disclosure program because penetration testers worldwide, each possessing diverse expertise and perspectives, can identify vulnerabilities within the system.

Furthermore, regular assessments using scanners such as Nexpose, Nessus, and OpenVAS are imperative. This approach ensures continuous monitoring and vulnerability identification, especially in educational institutions like USCA, where maintaining a secure environment is of utmost importance.

Also the incorporation of both CIS (Center for Internet Security) and FAIR (Factor Analysis of Information Risk) methodologies greatly benefited this project's risk assessment. CIS provided a structured approach for implementing security controls, ensuring comprehensive vulnerability management. Meanwhile, FAIR's systematic risk scoring process offered a quantitative way to assess and prioritize risks, leading to a nuanced understanding of potential impacts. The synergy between these methodologies resulted in a robust risk assessment framework, identifying critical vulnerabilities and facilitating the development of effective mitigation strategies. This integrated approach enhanced the overall resilience and security of the network environment.

6.2   Limitations

1. **Scope of Manual Human Pen-testing:** Another limitation stems from the reliance on manual human penetration testing. The effectiveness of manual testing is subject to the expertise of the researcher conducting the assessments. The research acknowledges the variability in the skill levels of different researchers, with some being advanced penetration testers and others having

varying levels of expertise. This introduces a potential limitation in the thoroughness and accuracy of manually identified vulnerabilities. The diversity in skill levels among researchers may impact the comprehensiveness of the vulnerability assessment [9,10].

2. **Limited Vulnerability Scanners:** One notable limitation of this research lies in the use of only three automated vulnerability scanners-Nexpose, Nessus, and OpenVAS. While these scanners are reputable and widely used, there are several other prominent tools in the market, such as Qualys and Acunetix, which were not included in this study. The exclusion of these alternative scanners may result in a potential oversight of vulnerabilities that they might have been more adept at identifying. The findings may not represent the full spectrum of vulnerabilities present in the systems under investigation [9,10].

3. **Dynamic Nature of Cybersecurity:** The rapidly evolving landscape of cybersecurity poses an inherent limitation to any research in this domain. The vulnerabilities identified and discussed in this study are based on the state of technology up to the knowledge cutoff date. New vulnerabilities may emerge after this date, rendering the research susceptible to being outdated. The dynamic nature of cyber threats emphasizes the need for continuous monitoring and updates to stay abreast of the latest vulnerabilities [11,12],

References

1. Samtani, S., Yu, S., Zhu, H., Patton, M., Chen, H.: Identifying SCADA vulnerabilities using passive and active vulnerability assessment techniques. In: 2016 IEEE Conference on Intelligence and Security Informatics (ISI), pp. 25–30. IEEE (2016)
2. Nankya, M., Chataut, R., Akl, R.: Securing industrial control systems: components, cyber threats, and machine learning-driven defense strategies. Sensors **23**(21), 8840 (2023)
3. Kaura, C., Sindhwani, N., Chaudhary, A.: Analysing the impact of cyber-threat to ICS and SCADA systems. In: 2022 International Mobile and Embedded Technology Conference (MECON), pp. 466–470. IEEE (2022)
4. Francia III, G. A., Thornton, D., Dawson, J.: Security best practices and risk assessment of SCADA and industrial control systems. In: Proceedings of the international conference on security and management (SAM), p. 1. The Steering Committee of The World Congress in Computer Science, Computer Engineering and Applied Computing (WorldComp) (2012)
5. Shypovskyi, V.: Enhancing the factor analysis of information risk methodology for assessing cyberresilience in critical infrastructure information systems. Polit. Sci. Secur. Stud. J. **4**(1), 25–33 (2023)
6. Christensen, K.K., Petersen, K.L.: Public-private partnerships on cyber security: a practice of loyalty. Int. Aff. **93**(6), 1435–1452 (2017)
7. Tunggal, A.T.: How to Perform a Cybersecurity Risk Assessment. UpGuard (2018). Accessed 19 Oct 2023. https://www.upguard.com/blog/how-to-perform-a-cybersecurity-risk-assessment
8. Cybersecurity risk assessments. SailPoint (2023). Accessed 19 Oct 2023. https://www.sailpoint.com/identity-library/cybersecurity-risk-assessments/

9. Stefinko, Y., Piskozub, A., Banakh, R.: Manual and automated penetration testing. Benefits and drawbacks: modern tendency. In: 2016 13th International Conference on Modern Problems of Radio Engineering, Telecommunications and Computer Science (TCSET), pp. 488–491. IEEE (2016)

10. Alavi, S., Bessler, N., Massoth, M.: A comparative evaluation of automated vulnerability scans versus manual penetration tests on false-negative errors. In: Proceedings of the Third International Conference on Cyber-Technologies and Cyber-Systems, IARIA, Athens, Greece, pp. 18–22 (2018)

11. Cremer, F., et al.: Cyber risk and cybersecurity: a systematic review of data availability. Geneva Papers Risk Insur.-Issues Pract. **47**(3), 698–736 (2022)

12. Johnston, A.C.: A closer look at organizational cybersecurity research trending topics and limitations. Organ. Cybersecur. J. Pract. Process People **2**(2), 124–133 (2022)

Electrical Muscle Stimulation System for Automatic Reproduction of Secret Information Without Exposing Biometric Data

Takumi Takaiwa, Shinnosuke Nozaki, Kota Numada, Tsubasa Shibata, Sana Okumura, Soichi Takigawa, Tetsushi Ohki[ID], and Masakatsu Nishigaki[(✉)][ID]

Shizuoka University, Hamamatsu, Shizuoka, Japan
nisigaki@inf.shizuoka.ac.jp

Abstract. Biometric data is personal information, which leads to the psychological resistance of the user. Using biometric-based FIDO authentication eliminates the risk of biometric data leakage outside the local device. However, the risk of biometric data leakage remains because presenting biometric data to the device is necessary at the time of authentication. As a solution to this problem, we propose Human Parameterized Locality Sensitive Hash (HPLSH), which enables user authentication without revealing biometric data by using biometric data not as data but as a "medium for transforming data." This concept aims to generate authentication information by transforming a seed through the human body so that the user can be identified without revealing biometric data. As a concrete design of HPLSH, we used the keyboard and the user's response to EMS. The user wears an EMS-generating device on the forearm, and when electrical stimulation is administered to the forearm from the EMS-generating device, the user's fingers involuntarily move to interact with the keyboard and generate authentication information. In this paper, we discuss the concept of HPLSH and its implementation. We examine the feasibility of the proposed method through a preliminary user experiment.

Keywords: Biometric Recognition · HPLSH (Human Parameterized Locality Sensitive Hash) · EMS (Electrical Muscle Stimulation) · FIDO

1 Introduction

An effective method for password-less authentication involves combining FIDO authentication [1] with biometrics, (termed "FIDO biometrics" in this study). This method uses the local device's private key activated by biometrics to authenticate the device against the server through public-key cryptography. In the case of FIDO biometrics, biometric information is exclusively stored on the device, minimizing the risk of leakage from the communication path between the device (client) and the server or from the authentication server. Encrypting and storing biometric information on the local device (or storing the raw biometric information in a secure area on the local device) further reduces the risk of biometric theft. However, it is important to note that as biometric recognition requires users to present information to a biometric sensor, there remains a potential risk

A. Moallem (Ed.): HCII 2024, LNCS 14729, pp. 234–249, 2024.
https://doi.org/10.1007/978-3-031-61382-1_15

of biometric information theft during the recognition process. Many types of biometric data are exposed on the body and can be observed by an attacker. Even under-the-skin biometric information can be compromised by an attacker who illegally installs biometric sensors around the user. Therefore, the use of observable/measurable biometric information induces psychological resistance among users.

To address this issue, encrypting and storing biometric information locally on the device is not sufficient. In addition to this, there is a need for an authentication method that eliminates the necessity of presenting biometric information on the device. The requirements for such a method are as follows:

- (Non-exposure requirement) Biometric recognition can be performed without ever exposing the biometric data.

In this study, we propose a method to meet the non-exposure requirement by using biometric information as a "data-transforming medium" rather than treating it as data. Specifically, we formulate human parameterized locality sensitive hash (HPLSH) with an input-output relationship changes that varies depending on the biometric information "b." We generate registration information, denotes as v^T, by inputting a seed "s" into the HPLSH. During authentication, the same seed is used in the HPLSH to generate the authentication information "v," and authentication succeeds if "v^T" $=$ "v."

The HPLSH transforms the seed "s" into a specific value through the human body, enabling the verification of identity based on its similarity while concealing biometric data (though mathematical one-way-ness, or irreversibility, as in encryption cannot be guaranteed). The seed "s" corresponding to the input of HPLSH is essentially a random number, and the data observed is the result of transmitting the seed (random number) through the human body.

Since the input-output relationship of HPLSH is contingent on the human body, obtaining the same hash value is not possible even when providing the same seed to different users. Due to body condition, environmental condition and measurement errors, there may be slight variations in biometric data within users. However, the hash values will align if the change in biometric data falls within a threshold value.

In this case, we used the keyboard and the user's response to electrical muscle stimulation (EMS) to implement HPLSH. The user wears an EMS-generating device on the forearm, and when electrical stimulation is administered to the forearm from the EMS-generating device, the user's fingers involuntarily move to interact with the keyboard. The user's forearm muscle (muscle composition) corresponds to "b," the electrical stimulus corresponds to "s," and the keyboard keystroke information corresponds to "v." The characteristics of the EMS-type HPLSH are as follows:

- Reverse engineer the forearm muscle "b" or the electrical stimulus "s" from the keystroke information "v" poses a significant challenge. (However, the guarantee of cryptographic one-way-ness remains uncertain.)
- Even for the same user, a slight alteration in the state of forearm muscle "b" will result in a slight adjustment in finger movement. Similarly, depending on the wearing condition of the EMS device, the position of the electrical stimulation "s" may undergo slight variations, affecting hand movements even for the same user. However,

the keystroke information "v" remains consistent as long as these changes in finger movements fall within the range where the keys to be typed remain unchanged.

- Different users possess different forearm muscle compositions "b," leading to different keystroke information "v," even when the electrical stimulus "s" is identical.
- Increasing the number of pulses in the electrical stimulus "s" corresponds to an augmentation in the string length of the keystroke information "v." Theoretically, this enables the generation of a keystroke "v" with more entropy than humans can store.

Section 2 introduces related research, and Sect. 3 presents the approach to solving the problems of current biometric systems, describing the proposed method. Section 4 details an implementation of the proposal method with FIDO biometric authentication. In Sect. 5, we demonstrate that finger movements under electrical stimulation vary from person to person and evaluate the feasibility of generating keystroke information. Section 6 is some further discussions of the proposed method, and Sect. 7 summarizes the study.

2   Related Work

2.1   Password-Less Authentication

Remote logins are required for users to access the Internet services. Because password authentication, the prevailing method until now, possess numerous issues in terms of both security and convenience, the momentum for password-less authentication is rapidly increasing [2].

Remote Biometric Recognition. Biometric recognition stands as an alternative method to password authentication, offering the advantages of not requiring keyboard operations and being immune to the risk of being forgotten, lost, or stolen. It is widely used in various situations. However, the biometric data used in biometric recognition is traceable [3] due to its "lifelong immutability and irreplaceability," and faces challenges related to spoofing [4]. Therefore, it is not enough to simply shift from the conventional client-server password authentication to biometric recognition (remote biometric recognition).

Template protection technology [5] offers a partial solution to this problem. Template-protected biometrics, used together with techniques for biometric matching in the encrypted form, can safeguard the biometric information stored on the server through encryption. However, the management of encryption keys for biometric encryption remains a challenging issue.

FIDO Authentication. Fast identity online (FIDO) authentication [1] and its combinational use of biometrics (FIDO biometrics) are gaining attention as methods to address the problems associated with remote biometrics. FIDO authentication is a framework for device authentication against servers based on public-key cryptography, wherein a public key is stored on the server, and a private key is kept on the user's local device. FIDO biometrics uses biometrics to activate the private key within the device (see Fig. 1). Biometric information (and secret keys) stored in secure areas within the device, such as the TEE [6], cannot be extracted from the device. Since biometric recognition is not involved in device authentication, there is no need to register biometric information on the server, and biometric information is not leaked from the server or from the communication path between the device (client) and server.

TEE(Trusted Execution Environment)

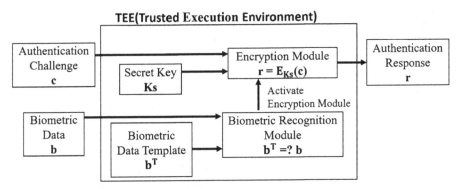

Fig. 1. Overview of activation of private keys in FIDO biometrics

However, the user must present his/her biometric data to the device when activating the secret key. Because presenting biometric data to a biometric sensor is required, there is still a risk of biometric data being stolen. In general, biometric data exposed on the user's body are used for the conventional biometric recognition and can, therefore, be observed by an attacker. With the advancement of sophisticated cameras, capturing high-resolution images of the iris and fingerprints from a distance has become possible. There have been reported instances where attackers duplicated artificial fingers from such photographs, successfully impersonating the target [7]. Even for under the skin biometric data, attackers can phish for biometric data by illegally placing biometric sensors around the user or by setting up a dummy website posing as a cloud service, tricking users into logging in based on biometric recognition. This induces psychological resistance to the use of observable biometric data.

PBI. Takahashi et al. developed a Fuzzy Signature [8], which can directly use biometric information as a secret key for public-key cryptography. They constructed a public biometric infrastructure (PBI) using a Fuzzy Signature, serving as a realization of public key infrastructure (PKI) based on biometric information. Also, PBI can be viewed as a scheme in which the secret key of FIDO biometrics is substituted with biometric information.

In PBI, biometric information (private key) and public keys are directly linked, and public-key cryptography ensures that the risk of biometric information leakage from the public key registered on the server and the communication path between the device and server is sufficiently minimized. However, presenting one's biometric data to the device during authentication remains an issue, as long as biometric data used in PBI are observable.

2.2 EMS

Electrical muscle stimulation (EMS) [9] is a technique primarily used in medical rehabilitation to induce involuntary muscle movements in response to electrical stimuli.

Electric Auth. Chen et al. exploited the variations in involuntary movements induced by EMS, attributed to differences in muscle composition between users, to develop a biometric recognition method called "ElectricAuth" [10]. During registration, the user's forearm was subjected to n types of electrical stimuli, and the motion of the fingertips (acceleration and twisting) in response to each electrical stimulus was recorded. During authentication, an electrical stimulus is randomly selected from the n types of stimuli and applied to the user, and authentication is based on whether the fingertip movements match those recorded during registration.

ElectricAuth is a biometric recognition method that takes advantage of the fact that different users respond differently to the same electrical stimulus. Since the response to electrical stimulation is involuntary, imitating the biometric response to electrical stimulation is challenging, even if someone else attempts to impersonate the user. ElectricAuth uses biometric data as "authentication data", in which the similarity of the biometric data is checked directly. It is different from using biometric data as a "medium that transforming seeds into specific values", in which the similarity in how the seeds were transformed is checked.

BioSync. Nishida et al. developed "BioSync" [11], facilitating the synchronization of muscle activity with others to support the mutual sharing of kinesthetic experiences. The sender's muscle activity measured by an electromyography (EMG) meter attached to the sender's forearm was conveyed to the receiver by applying electrical stimulation through an EMS device attached to the receiver's forearm. Because the body's muscle composition differs among users, calibration between the sender and receiver is necessary for accurate synchronization of muscle activity.

Mutual sharing of body motion sensations is also effective in medical rehabilitation. Takigawa et al. applied a similar system to neurorehabilitation therapy, inducing the paralyzed hand of a hemiplegic patient to hold a grasping posture symmetrical to that of the non-paralyzed hand [12]. Here, the non-paralyzed hand of the same user acts as the sender, and the paralyzed hand serves as the receiver.

Possessed Hand. Tamaki et al. developed the "Possessed Hand" [13], which uses electrical stimulation to externally control the user's hand and finger movements. Attaching an EMS device to the user's forearm and controlling the applied electrical stimulation allow the user's fingers to be forced into the desired postures. By applying this mechanism, it will be possible to install the body manipulations of others onto one's own body [14]. Since the body's muscle composition differs among users, accurate body manipulation requires calibration for each user.

3 Human Parameterized Locality Sensitive Hash

3.1 Issues with the Current Biometric System

As described in Sect. 2.1, to realize password-less authentication that is both convenient and secure, it necessitates an authentication method eliminating the need to present biometric information on a local device. Again, the requirements are as follows:

(Non-exposure requirement): Biometric recognition can be performed without ever exposing the biometric data.

3.2 Approach to Solving the Problem: HPLSH

This study proposes a method to fulfill the non-exposure requirement by using biometric information as a "data-transforming medium" rather than treating it as data. Specifically, we expand on the concept of locality sensitive hash (LSH) [15] to create a human parameterized locality sensitive hash (HPLSH), where the input-output relationship varies depending on biometric information.

The structure of HPLSH is outlined below:

- b: Biometric data; a parameter determining the input-output relationship of HPLSH. The biometric data for the same person may vary slightly each time it is acquired due to body condition, environmental condition, and measurement error. Let "b^T" represent the biometric data at registration (template) and "b" denote biometric information at authentication. If the person is the correct match, we expect $|b^T - b| \leq \theta_b$, where "θ_b" serves as the threshold for biometric information, representing the upper limit of fluctuation within the same person.
- s: Seed; the input of HPLSH.
- v: Hash value; the output of HPLSH.
- HPLSH: Human Parameterized Locality Sensitive Hash; Given a biometric data "b" and a seed "s," it produces the output "v." $v = \text{HPLSH}_b(s)$. $\text{HPLSH}_{b^T}(s) = \text{HPLSH}_b(s)$ if and only if $|b^T - b| \leq \theta_b$. Otherwise, $\text{HPLSH}_{b^T}(s) \neq \text{HPLSH}_b(s)$.

HPLSH converts the seed "s" into a hash value "v" through the human body (using biometric data "b") and observes it, allowing for identity verification through the similarity of the hash value "v" while concealing the biometric data "b" (although mathematical one-way-ness as in encryption cannot be guaranteed). Let $v^T = \text{HPLSH}_{b^T}(s)$ represent the hash value for biometric "b^T" and seed "s" during registration, and $v = \text{HPLSH}_b(s)$ for biometric "b" and seed "s" during authentication. $v^T = v$ holds only when $|b^T - b| \leq \theta_b$.

The information observed and used for authentication is "v," signifying the outcome of passing the seed (random number) "s" through the human body (biometric data "b"). Thus, HPLSH achieves authentication without exposing biometric data "b" to biometric sensor.

The input-output relationship of HPLSH is based on biometric data "b". Thus, HPLSH cannot generate the same hash value "v" even when the same seed "s" is provided to different users, as biometric data "b" is contingent on the individual. Meanwhile, due to body condition, environmental condition, and measurement error, slight variations in biometric "b" each time it is acquired, even for the same user. However, if the change in biometric "b" falls within the threshold value θ_b, the hash value "v" will match. This satisfies the non-exposure requirement.

3.3 EMS-Type HPLSH

In this specific implementation of HPLSH, we propose a method to observe the involuntary muscles response to EMS as keyboard input. The user wears an EMS device on his/her forearm and positions his/her fingers on the keyboard. It is deemed challenging to reverse engineer the forearm muscle state "b" or the electrical stimulus "s" from the keystroke information "v" (however, it is unknown whether cryptographic one-wayness or irreversibility can be guaranteed). The configuration of the EMS-type HPLSH is shown in Fig. 2.

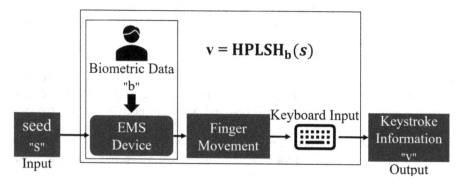

Fig. 2. Configuration of EMS-type HPLSH

Even for the same user, there can be a slight difference between the state of the forearm muscles at registration "b^T" and that during authentication "b." Therefore, the hand movements can vary slightly even when the same electrical stimulus "s" is applied. However, if the change in finger motion is within the range where the key to be pressed remains unchanged, the keystroke information at registration "v^T" and that during authentication "v" will match. The change in biometric "b" may result from variations in the forearm muscles themselves or differences in the measurement environment. In the former case, slight discrepancies in the state of the forearm muscles between registration and authentication, such as, muscle fatigue, can lead to differences in hand movements. In the latter case, slight variations in the wearing state of the EMS device between registration and authentication may cause a slight shift in the location where electrical stimulation is applied, resulting in difference in hand movement.

As different users possess different forearm muscle compositions "b," we anticipate larger changes in hand movements for the same electrical stimulus "s" applied to different persons. In other words, the alteration in finger movements may lead to striking different keys and obtaining distinct keystroke information "v."

Increasing the number of pulses in the electrical stimulus "s" enables an increase in the number of fingers strikes on the keyboard. Essentially, this extends the length of the keystroke "v." Theoretically, this enables the generation of a "v" with more entropy than humans can store.

In this implementation of the EMS-type HPLSH, only the flexion and extension movements of the fingers are controlled by an EMS device attached to the forearm. Therefore, the EMS device cannot move the upper arm, and each finger can always press the same key. In the future, attaching an EMS device to the upper arm and enabling control of forearm motion will allow pressing different keys for each finger. Theoretically, this enables the generation of a "v" with more entropy.

4   Password-Less Authentication Using HPLSH

In this Section, let us consider enhancing FIDO biometrics by combining HPLSH, as a concrete example of HPLSH implementations. The activation mechanism of the secret key in the local device of FIDO biometrics (Fig. 1) is implemented using HPLSH. We describe the registration and authentication flow of the upgraded remote password-less authentication system (Fig. 3) with the proposed method.

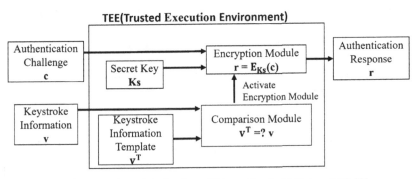

Fig. 3. Overview of Activation of Private Key in EMS-type HPLSH

4.1   Registration Procedure

The registration procedure is as follows:

1. The user wears the EMS device on his/her forearm and places his/her fingers on the keyboard.
2. Seed "s" are randomly selected.
3. Apply electrical stimuli to the forearm via the EMS device based on the seed "s."
4. Involuntary movements of the user's fingers are generated, and the keyboard is keyed.
5. Keystroke information "v^T" is registered in the user's local device. Additionally, the seed "s," the position of the EMS device attached on the forearm, and the position of fingers placed on the keyboard are registered.

4.2 Authentication Procedure

The authentication procedure is as follows:

1. The user wears the EMS device on his/her forearm and places his/her fingers on the keyboard, as registered in Step 5 of registration procedure.
2. The EMS device applies electrical stimuli to the user's forearm based on the seed "s."
3. Involuntary movements of the user's fingers are generated, and the keyboard is pressed.
4. The keystroke information "v" is compared with "v^T," and the secret key is activated if there is a match.

4.3 Management of Secret Information

The keystroke information "v," the seed "s," the position of the EMS device attached on the forearm, and the position of fingers placed on the keyboard are observable to the attacker. However, it would be challenging to reverse engineer the biometric information (forearm muscle status "b") from this information (though it is unknown whether cryptographic one-way-ness can be guaranteed or not). The keystroke "v" is the secret information used to activate the private key in the local device, and an attacker can use the observed keystroke "v" to perform a replay attack.

In FIDO authentication, however, user authentication to activate the private key in the local device can only be conducted when physically face-to-face with the device. Therefore, for an attacker to observe the keystroke information "v," they must be physically close to the legitimate user during authentication. The attacker cannot execute a remote attack to steal the keystroke template "v^T" in the local device, either, as "v^T" is stored in a secure area within the device (TEE). Furthermore, even if the keystroke "v" is exposed to the attacker, any information corresponding to biometric information is not contained in "v", and the legitimate user can freely update it by changing the seed "s." For the above reasons, compared to the conventional FIDO biometrics, which involves the risk of biometric leakage, the privacy concern of the enhanced FIDO biometrics with the proposed method is significantly reduced.

However, the proposed method, which requires an EMS device and keyboard, has a disadvantage in terms of convenience compared to the conventional FIDO biometrics. In this regard, we hope that the advancement of EMS-based human body control technologies will mature enough to use EMS devices without inconvenience and become sufficiently user-friendly.

5 Preliminary User Experiments

In this section, a preliminary experiment is conducted to verify the feasibility of the proposed method. The following three objectives are to be verified in this experiment:

1. Identify electrical stimuli "s" (pairs of electrodes) to move participants' fingers.
2. Verify the degree to which participants' fingers can be moved using the identified electrical stimuli "s." (Evaluation of the True Acceptance Rate)

3. Verify the degree to which participants' fingers will be moved using other participants' identified electrical stimuli "s." (Evaluation of the False Acceptance Rate with zero-effort)

The participants are three male university students (user 1 ~ user 3) in their twenties. This study was performed by the Declaration of Helsinki and was approved by the Research Ethics Committee of Shizuoka University in compliance with the Regulations on Research Involving Human Subjects at Shizuoka University. The methods, hazards, and benefits of the experiment were explained to the subjects and their consent was obtained before the experiment.

5.1   Identification of Electrical Stimulation "s"

Generally, when controlling the movement of the fingers, multiple electrodes are attached to the forearm, and two of them are used as the active electrode and the return electrode, respectively, to apply electrical stimulation to the forearm. The pair of the active electrode and the return electrode for moving each participant's finger is identified. There is a previous study [12] on the identification of the pair of electrodes, and the experiment was conducted in the same way.

We identified the pair of electrodes that moved the fingers enough to type on the keyboard when electrical stimulation "s" was applied. In this experiment, 24 electrodes were attached to the left arm (Fig. 4). Each electrode was 20 mm wide, 30 mm long, and 24 mm pitch. Six gel electrodes per row were fixed with a belt. The experiment employed four belts, which resulted in a total of 24 electrodes placed on the inner side of the forearm.

The electrical stimulation used was a biphasic pulse with a pulse width of 200 μs, a period of 30 ms, and a voltage of 18 V. Figure 4 shows that electrode 1 was set as the active electrode (red), and electrode 2 was set as return electrode (blue), and electrical stimulation is applied. Then, electrodes 3 to 24 were set as the return electrode, respectively, and electrical stimulation was applied. Subsequently, electrode 2 was set as the active electrode, and the same procedure with each electrode other than electrode 2 set as the return electrode, respectively, was repeated. In this way, electrical stimulation is applied to all combinations of active electrode and return electrode.

In this experiment, fingers were placed on the keyboard so that the little finger, ring finger, middle finger, index finger, and thumb came on the keys q/w/e/r/v, respectively. For example, if the index finger typed on the keyboard (key r was typed) when the active electrode was electrode 1 and the return electrode was electrode 5, the electrical stimulation "s" to move the index finger would be identified as "active electrode number: return electrode number" is "1:5."

The participants carried out the above identification of the electrode pair twice each. After the first identification experiment, the electrodes were not removed, and the second identification experiment was conducted 10 min later.

Table 1 shows the results of the experiment, showing the combinations of electrodes identified to move each of the five fingers, by participant and by finger, in the form of "active electrode number: return electrode number." If more than one pair of electrodes was found to move a particular finger, up to fifteen pairs are listed in Table 1 for reasons

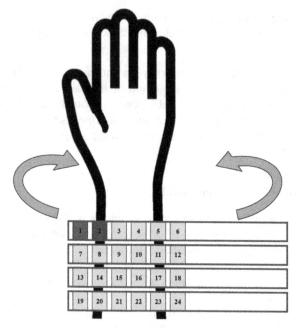

Fig. 4. Belt-shaped 24-pad electrodes on left forearm (Color figure online)

of space limitation, and the number of pairs that could not be listed is indicated in parentheses. (User 1 was able to identify the electrical stimulation "s" (pair of electrodes) to move all fingers, but User 2 could not identify the pair of electrodes to move the little finger, middle finger, and thumb, and User 3 could not identify the pair of electrodes to move the thumb.).

5.2 User Authentication

In Sect. 5.1, we identified the electrical stimulus "s" (pairs of electrodes) to move each finger. In this section, we discuss the true acceptance rate between same participants and the false acceptance rate between different participants (zero-effort impostors), using the first experimental result of each user as the template and the second result as the query. In the preliminary stage of the study, we did not apply the electric stimulus "s" registered in the template to the participants but simulated the user authentication experiment by comparing the information in Table 1, which was obtained in Sect. 5.1.

True Acceptance Rate. The electrode pair of each finger in the first identification experiment of each participant (user 1 to user 3) was the template, and the electrode pair of each finger in the second identification experiment of the same participant was the query. We checked to what extent the pairs of electrodes in the template of each participant (user i, $i = 1, 2, 3$) matched the pairs of electrodes in the template of the participant (user j, $j = 1, 2, 3$, $j = i$).

For example, for the index finger (key r) in Table 1, user 3's template contained 15 pairs of patterns (pairs of electrodes) for pressing key r, and the query contained 12 pairs

Table 1. Result of the electric stimulation "s" (pair of electrodes) identification experiment

Finger	User					
	User1_template	User1_query	User2_template	User2_query	User3_template	User3_query
Little finger (Key q)	5:19 5:21 5:22 11:6	5:6 5:11 6:12 11:5 11:18	N/A	N/A	1:11, 2:11, 4:11, 6:11, 7:11, 10:11, 11:1,12:18, 17:1, 17:02, 17:03, 17:04, 17:05, 17:07, 17:08, (+ 2)	3:11, 4:11, 6:17, 7:11, 8:11, 10:11, 13:11, 14:11, 18:10
Ring finger (Key w)	1:17, 1:22, 1:24, 2:17, 2:23, 2:24, 5:01, 5:08, 7:23, 7:24, 8:23, 10:23, 12:02, 12:03, 12:04, (+ 7)	1:17, 1:24, 2:23, 3:23, 4:17, 5:01, 5:02, 5:03, 5:08, 5:20, 5:21, 6:05, 6:08, 6:20, 10:23, (+ 11)	2:17, 2:23, 3:23, 4:17, 4:23, 5:23, 6:17, 6:23, 7:23, 8:17, 8:23, 9:17, 9:18, 9:23, 10:23, (+ 27)	1:18, 1:23, 2:17, 2:18, 2:23, 3:23, 4:17, 5:23, 6:17, 6:23, 7:17, 7:18, 7:23, 8:17, 8:18, (+ 41)	2:16, 5:06, 9:07, 11:04, 11:08, 11:10, 11:14, 11:16, 11:19, 11:20, 11:21, 13:16, 16:02, 16:06, 16:08, (+ 22)	3:16, 5:06, 6:16, 11:03, 11:04, 11:14, 11:16, 11:19, 11:20, 11:21, 20:16
Middle finger (Key e)	7:17, 8:16, 9:16, 11:16, 12:18, 13:16, 14:16, 15:16, 18:08, 18:10, 19:17, 21:16, 22:09, 23:11, 24:18	8:16, 10:16, 12:06, 14:16, 16:06, 16:23, 18:08, 18:11, 18:17, 18:19, 18:20, 18:21, 21:18, 21:24, 22:08, (+ 5)	2:06, 2:19, 3:06, 4:06, 6:10, 12:02, 13:06, 14:06, 18:02, 18:06, **21:06**	13:6	1:15, 2:15, 3:09, 3:15, 4:09, 5:03, 5:04, 5:08, 5:09, 5:12, 5:14, 5:15, 5:19, 5:20, 6:15, (+ 29)	1:05, 1:09, 2:09, 2:15, 3:15, 4:15, 5:02, 5:03, 5:07, 5:08, 5:14, 5:15, 6:09, 6:15, **21:06**, (+ 30)
Index finger (Key r)	6:7 10:24	18:4	N/A	N/A	**1:10**, **2:05**, **2:10**, **3:10**, 4:10, **6:10**, 7:10, 10:02, 10:03, **10:05**, 10:06, **12:10**, 18:10, 18:11, 24:18	**1:10**, **2:05**, **2:10**, **3:10**, **6:10**, 6:24, 8:05, **10:05**, 12:05, **12:10**, 24:03, 24:07,
Thumb (Key v)	4:17 6:10 14:22	2:22	N/A	N/A	N/A	N/A

of patterns for pressing key r, of which 7 pairs were common patterns. When the results are interpreted from the perspective of "the pattern of the template of user 3 registered in the registration phase was applied to user 3 in the authentication phase," pattern matches (i.e., the application of electrical stimulation that caused user 3 to press the key r in the registration phase resulted in the same key presses for user 3 in the authentication phase) occurred at a rate of 7/15. That is, the true acceptance rate of the user 3 was 7/15. The true acceptance rates for all participants are shown in the diagonal components of Table 2.

The results show that the true acceptance rate was not satisfactory in this experiment. Factors such as fatigue of the participants' forearms and the fact that the participants' hand positions inevitably move slightly during the experiment may have affected to this. Measures are needed to improve the accuracy of authentication (true acceptance rate).

Table 2. True Acceptance Rate and False Acceptance Rate

Little finger (Key q)	User1_query	User2_query	User3_query
User1_template	0/4	0/4	0/4
User2_template	N/A	N/A	N/A
User3_template	0/18	0/18	3/18
Ring finger (Key w)	User1_query	User2_query	User3_query
User1_template	8/22	6/22	0/22
User2_template	6/42	31/42	0/42
User3_template	0/37	10/37	7/37
Middle finger (Key e)	User1_query	User2_query	User3_query
User1_template	4/15	0/15	1/15
User2_template	0/11	1/11	1/11
User3_template	1/45	1/45	13/44
Index finger (Key r)	User1_query	User2_query	User3_query
User1_template	0/2	0/2	0/2
User2_template	N/A	N/A	N/A
User3_template	0/15	0/15	7/15
Thumb (Key v)	User1_query	User2_query	User3_query
User1_template	0/3	N/A	N/A
User2_template	N/A	N/A	N/A
User3_template	N/A	N/A	N/A

False Acceptance Rate. The electrode pair of each finger in the first identification experiment of each participant (user 1 to user 3) was the template, and the electrode pair of each finger in the second identification experiment of the different participant was the query. We checked to what extent the pairs of electrodes in the template of each participant (user i, i = 1, 2, 3) matched the pairs of electrodes in the template of the participant (user j, j = 1, 2, 3, j ≠ i).

For example, for the middle finger (key e) in Table 1, user 2's template contained 11 pairs of patterns (pairs of electrodes) for pressing key e, and user 3's query contained 45 pairs of patterns for pressing key e, of which only one pair was common pattern. When the results are interpreted from the perspective of "the pattern of the template of user 2 registered in the registration phase was applied to user 3 in the authentication phase," pattern matches (i.e., the application of electrical stimulation that caused user 2 to press the key e in the registration phase resulted in the same key presses for user 3 in the authentication phase) occurred at a rate of 1/11. That is, the false acceptance rate of the zero-effort attack for user 3 impersonating user 2 was 1/11. The false acceptance rates for all participants are shown in the non-diagonal components of Table 2.

The results show that impersonation is relatively difficult in the proposed method. However, the experiment carried out here was a simulated experiment and a zero-effort impersonation. Actual experiments on impersonation with effort should also be conducted.

6 Discussion

6.1 Challenges of the Proposed Method

As mentioned in Sect. 3.3, in our current implementation of the EMS-type HPLSH, only the flexion and extension movements of the fingers are controlled by an EMS device attached to the forearm. In the future, we hope to expand the method so that the EMS system can allow unrestricted input of all keys to a keyboard. This involves combining the control of finger movements, achieved by attaching an EMS device to the forearm, with the control of the forearm, facilitated by attaching an EMS device to the upper arm. In addition, it is crucial to verify through user experiments to what extent the body condition "b", environmental condition, and measurement condition change, the keystroke information "v" remains the same.

As mentioned mainly in Sect. 4.3, the one-way-ness or irreversibility nature of HPLSH is not confirmed yet. It is necessary to cryptographically verify whether it is impossible to reverse engineer biometric information "b" or seed "s" from the keystroke information "v," or reverse engineer biometric information "b" from the keystroke information "v" and seed "s."

6.2 Application of the Proposed Method

One potential method of information transmission involves direct communication with a microchip implanted in the brain [16]. With brain-machine interface (BMI), the brain can send/receive a large amount of data to/from computers via the implanted microchip rapidly. This means that, however, if malicious data are included, a large amount of malicious data may flow into the brain via the microchip all at once.

To secure BMI communication via the implanted microchip in the brain, it is necessary to incorporate a "fuse (overcurrent protection)" function into the input device connected to the implanted microchip. Keyboard inputs using biometric responses via an EMS can serve as a fused input device.

The data transmission to a receiver with an implanted microchip in the brain and wearing an EMS device in the arm proceeds as follows:

1. The sender sends the data "d" intended for transmission to the EMS device of the receiver.
2. The EMS device of the receiver converts the data "d" into an electrical stimulus "s."
3. The receiver connects a keyboard to the input port of the implanted microchip in his/her brain.
4. The receiver places his/her hand on the keyboard.
5. The EMS device of the receiver applies the electrical stimulus "s" to the receiver's arm.

6. The receiver types on the keyboard according to the electrical stimulus "s."

The receiver can semi-automatically type a large amount of data with the assistance of the EMS device. If the receiver notices himself/herself typing anything suspicious or unusual while the receiver is typing, he/she can immediately remove his/her hand from the keyboard to physically stop the keystrokes.

7 Conclusion

Using FIDO and PBI eliminates the need to register biometric information on the server, thus solving the device (client)-server problem in remote biometric recognition. However, the problem of presenting biometric data to biometric sensors must be a remaining issue to be resolved. In this study, we proposed HPLSH in which biometric data is no used as an input value but as a "data-transforming medium." HPLSH can test the identity of a person based on the similarity of their biometric data while hiding it (although it cannot guarantee mathematical one-way-ness, such as encryption) by converting the seed into a specific value through the human body and observing it, making it possible to verify authentication information without ever revealing biometric data. As a concreate example of our proposal, we implemented EMS-type HPLSH and conducted a basic experiment.

Acknowledgments. This study was supported in part by the JST Moonshot-type R&D project JPMJMS2215. We would like to thank Mr. Masakatsu Takayanagi, for his assistance in developing the experiment device.

References

1. FIDO Alliance. https://fidoalliance.org/. Accessed 1 Feb 2024
2. The New York Times. https://www.nytimes.com/wirecutter/blog/what-are-passkeys-and-how-they-can-replace-passwords/. Accessed 1 Feb 2024
3. Ratha, N.K., Connell, J.H., Bolle, R.M.: Enhancing security and privacy in biometrics-based authentication systems. IBM Syst. J. **40**(3), 614–634 (2001)
4. Rui, Z., Yan, Z.: A survey on biometric authentication: toward secure and privacy-preserving identification. IEEE Access **7**, 5994–6009 (2018)
5. Rathgeb, C., Uhl, A.: A survey on biometric cryptosystems and cancelable biometrics. EURASIP J. Inf. Secur. **2011**(1), 1–25 (2011)
6. Sabt, M., Achemlal, M., Bouabdallah, A.: Trusted execution environment: what it is, and what it is not. In: IEEE Trustcom/BigDataSE/Ispa 2015, vol. 1, pp. 57–64. IEEE, Helsinki (2015)
7. BBC. https://www.bbc.com/news/technology-30623611. Accessed 1 Feb 2024
8. Takahashi, K., Matsuda, T., Murakami, T., Hanaoka, G., Nishigaki, M.: Signature schemes with a fuzzy private key. Int. J. Inf. Secur. **18**, 581–617 (2019)
9. Knibbe, J., Alsmith, A., Hornbæk, K.: Experiencing electrical muscle stimulation. Proc. ACM Interact. Mob. Wearable Ubiquit. Technol. **2**(3), 1–14 (2018)
10. Chen, Y., Yang, Z., Abbou, R., Lopes, P., Zhao, B.Y., Zheng, H.: User authentication via electrical muscle stimulation. In: Proceedings of the 2021 CHI Conference on Human Factors in Computing Systems, pp. 1–15 (2021)

11. Nishida, J., Suzuki, K.: BioSync: a paired wearable device for blending kinesthetic experience. In: Proceedings of the 2017 CHI Conference on Human Factors in Computing Systems, pp. 3316–3327 (2017)
12. Takigawa, S., Mimura, H.: Development of contralaterally controlled functional electrical stimulation to realize multiple grasping postures with data glove. Sens. Mater. **33**, 3645–3656 (2021)
13. Tamaki, E., Miyaki, T., Rekimoto, J.: PossessedHand: techniques for controlling human hands using electrical muscles stimuli. In: Proceedings of the SIGCHI Conference on Human Factors in Computing Systems, pp. 543–552 (2011)
14. NTT DOCOMO. https://www.docomo.ne.jp/english/corporate/technology/rd/technical_journal/bn/vol25_3/004.html. Accessed 2 Feb 2024
15. Andoni, A., Indyk, P., Laarhoven, T., Razenshteyn, I., Schmidt, L.: Practical and optimal LSH for angular distance. In: Advances in Neural Information Processing Systems, vol. 28 (2015)
16. BBC. https://www.bbc.com/news/technology-68137046. Accessed 1 Feb 2024

Author Index

A

Abie, Habtamu II-153
Akbarzadeh, Aida II-3
Alashwali, Eman I-3
Alghamdi, Samiah I-170
Aly, Yomna I-188
Amirullah, Muhammad Nur Rifqi I-161
Arik, Marko II-20
Asif, Rameez I-97
Aung, Hane I-97
Azab, Mohamed II-56
Azevedo, Daniela I-212

B

Bagley, Steven I-170
Barik, Kousik I-281
Binsedeeq, Arwa I-30

C

Canite, Malaya Jordan I-296
Carpent, Xavier I-30
Chockalingam, Sabarathinam I-281, II-153
Clark, Chris A. II-215
Colomo-Palacios, Ricardo II-84
Conner, David Brookshire I-232
Cranor, Lorrie I-3

D

Darmawaskita, Nicole II-40

E

Edwards, Morgan II-204
Erdodi, Laszlo II-3

F

Fernandes, Clarissa I-64
Fu, Fang I-265
Furnell, Steven I-30, I-43, I-116, I-170

G

Geng, Hanxiao I-265
Gervassis, Nicholas I-30
Gkioulos, Vasileios II-84
Gračanin, Denis II-56
Gray, Cameron I-43
Gray, Kathleen I-138

H

Hansen, Derek I-296
Harrison, Lane II-164
Hasegawa, Ayako A. I-245
Hof, Tineke I-126
Houmb, Siv Hilde II-3
Huaira Reyna, Nimrod Max I-296

I

Ikeda, Miho I-245
Ismail Nawang, Nazli I-161

J

Jacobs, Danielle Renee II-40

K

Kameishi, Kumiko I-245
Kanamori, Sachiko I-245
Kato, Shingo II-186
Katsarakes, Alex I-53
Katsikas, Sokratis II-134
Kieffer, Suzanne I-212
King, Kenneth II-56
Kram, Brian II-215
Kraus, Lydia I-64

L

Lau, Nathan II-153
Lee, Anthony II-56
Legay, Axel I-212
Lo Iacono, Luigi II-98
Londhe, Aaryan R. II-215

Loupasakis, Michail   II-70
Lugo, Ricardo Gregorio   II-20
Luo, Jing   I-265
Luo, Qian   II-121

M

Marmorato, Paola   I-64
McDaniel, Troy   II-40
Melvin, Clare   I-97
Mendoza, Antonette   I-138
Misra, Sanjay   I-281
Morris, Thomas   I-53, II-204
Munteanu, Cosmin   I-188

N

Nishigaki, Masakatsu   II-234
Nishikawa, Yoshiki   II-186
Nozaki, Shinnosuke   II-234
Numada, Kota   II-234

O

Ofte, Håvard Jakobsen   II-134
Ohki, Tetsushi   II-234
Okumura, Sana   II-234
Ottis, Rain   II-20

P

Pawar, Ronit   II-215
Pfeifer, Jan   II-164
Pirbhulal, Sandeep   II-153
Pöhls, Henrich C.   II-164
Potamos, Georgios   II-70
Prasetyoningsih, Nanik   I-161
Prior, Suzanne   I-77
Putri, Windy Virdinia   I-161

R

Rakotondravony, Noëlle   II-164
Ramaj, Xhesika   II-84
Ramelot, Justine   I-212
Renaud, Karen   I-77
Richmond, Ethan James   I-296

S

Sánchez-Gordón, Mary   II-84
Schooley, Benjamin   I-296
Sekiguchi, Shogo   II-186
Shibata, Tsubasa   II-234
Shizuki, Buntarou   II-186
Soltvedt, Tore Geir   II-3
Stavrou, Eliana   II-70
Still, Jeremiah D.   I-53, II-204
Stobert, Elizabeth   I-64
Strohmier, Hala   II-215

T

Takaiwa, Takumi   II-234
Takigawa, Soichi   II-234
Taylor, Deborah   I-97
Thunem, Harald P.-J.   I-281
Tolsdorf, Jan   II-98
Tugcu, Ezgi   I-116

V

van der Kleij, Rick   I-126
Venables, Adrian Nicholas   II-20
Vinayagam Sivasundari, Kalyani   II-121

W

Wani, Tafheem Ahmad   I-138

Z

Zhang, Xin   I-265